A COMMON GRAVE

A COMMON GRAVE

Being Catholic
in English America

Susan Juster

Published by
THE OMOHUNDRO INSTITUTE OF
EARLY AMERICAN HISTORY AND CULTURE,
WILLIAMSBURG, VIRGINIA,
and the
UNIVERSITY OF NORTH CAROLINA PRESS,
CHAPEL HILL

The Omohundro Institute of Early American History & Culture (OI)
is an independent research organization sponsored by William & Mary and
the Colonial Williamsburg Foundation. On November 15, 1996, the OI
adopted the present name in honor of a bequest from Malvern H.
Omohundro, Jr., and Elizabeth Omohundro.

Cover art: Rosary found in St. John's site. Ca. 1638.
Courtesy Historic St. Mary's City

Library of Congress Cataloging-in-Publication Data
Names: Juster, Susan, author.
Title: A common grave : being Catholic in English America / Susan Juster.
Description: Williamsburg, Virginia : The University of North Carolina
Press, [2025] | Includes bibliographical references and index.
Identifiers: LCCN 2024062241 | ISBN 9781469686226 (cloth) |
ISBN 9781469686233 (epub) | ISBN 9781469687803 (pdf)
Subjects: LCSH: Catholic Church—North America—History. |
Catholics—North America—History. | BISAC: RELIGION /
Christianity / Catholic | RELIGION / History
Classification: LCC BX1402 .J87 2025 | DDC 282/.7—dc23/eng/20250216
LC record available at https://lccn.loc.gov/2024062241

For product safety concerns under the European Union's General
Product Safety Regulation (EU GPSR), please contact gpsr@mare-nostrum.co.uk
or write to the University of North Carolina Press and Mare Nostrum Group B.V.,
Mauritskade 21D, 1091 GC Amsterdam, The Netherlands.

ACKNOWLEDGMENTS

HALFWAY THROUGH MY YEAR as the Robert C. Ritchie Distinguished Fellow in Early American History at the Huntington in 2014–2015, while awaiting readers' reports for the manuscript that became *Sacred Violence in Early America* (2016), I started thinking about my next project. A hallway conversation with my fellow Fellow Ann Little sparked a new line of inquiry that culminated in *A Common Grave*. "Did you ever notice how many Jesuits there are running around the English colonies in the seventeenth century?" Ann asked. "Even in Boston!" By the time I left California to return to Ann Arbor, I had spent several happy months digging through what the Huntington Library had to offer on Catholics in post-Reformation England and the early English Atlantic. In many respects, *Sacred Violence* and *Common Grave* are bookends to the same project: unearthing the deep, tangled historical roots of the religious cultures that met in English America and exploring how these cultures were shaped by their colonial environment.

Many institutions, archives, and colleagues contributed their time, money, and expertise to this project. A fellowship in 2022 from the John Simon Guggenheim Memorial Foundation funded a full year of writing. The staff of the Joseph Mark Lauinger Memorial Library at Georgetown University, Lambeth Palace Library in London, the British Library, the William L. Clements Library at the University of Michigan, the National Archives of the United Kingdom, the Huntington Library, the Massachusetts Historical Society, the Maryland Historical Society, and the Maryland State Archives provided invaluable support in identifying and tracking down sources. A special thanks to Silas Hurry and the archaeological team at Historic St. Mary's City in 2017 for the guided tour of the site, including the reconstructed 1667 brick chapel and its churchyard. Although I had already spent two years at that point combing through documents looking for stray references to Jesuits, "papists," and the "popishly affected" in written sources, the material reality of the chapel and its unnamed and unmarked graves was the real origin point for *A Common Grave*.

My academic home for the past thirty years, the Department of History at the University of Michigan, has always represented for me the best of what a public research university can offer: institutional support in the forms of sabbaticals and funding for travel and conferences on the one hand, and brilliant colleagues and students on the other hand. My bread-and-butter undergraduate course, a one-semester introduction to "Religion in America," which I subtitled "From the Reformation to the Rapture," gave me the opportunity to think broadly about what religion is and does with smart and inquisitive students whose own beliefs spanned the full spectrum from principled unbelief to fervent fundamentalisms of every stripe. They were my first, and most honest, audience for the ideas tested out in *Common Grave*. The Graduate Student Instructors I was privileged to work with (Alyssa Penick, Jennifer Playstead, Andy Rafael Aguilera, Sophie Wunderlich, and Brian Ho) and my co-Instructor during the difficult COVID semester of Winter 2022 (the dynamic Melissa Borja) each brought their own expertise to the course, allowing me to tackle new topics and historiographies with greater confidence. When I announced that I had accepted the position of Director of Research at the Huntington in Fall 2022, the students gave me a card signed by all of them and, joined by my history department colleagues, a rousing ovation after the last lecture of the semester. Thank you all.

Members of my writing group (Valerie Kivelson, Hussein Fancy, Helmut Puff, Paolo Squatriti, and Sueann Caulfield) workshopped Chapter 2 at a crucial point when I wasn't sure the fragments I had collected would cohere into a meaningful story. Graduate students in my seminar in Early American History bravely read the first draft of the book: thanks to Jessie Bakitunda, Erin Johnson, Emma Olson, Jennifer Playstead, Leopoldo Solis Martinez, and Hannah Tweet. Good friends at Michigan also deserve a shout-out for lending a sympathetic ear and a warm heart: Netta Berlin, Angela Dillard, Lisa Disch, Andreas Gallus, Arnold Juster, Mika Lavaque-Manty, Danielle Lavaque-Manty, Anne Manuel, Curt Mark, Tim McKay, Scott Spector, and Abby Stewart, many of whom happen to belong to the book club that Mika and I founded in 2005 (nicknamed "the Trollopistes" for our shared love of Anthony Trollope and nineteenth-century literature in general) after we had spent a wonderful year as Faculty Fellows at Michigan's Institute for the Humanities. Valerie Kivelson always deserves special mention in my Acknowledgments as my most incisive reader and best friend (sorry, Ron Suny!). Our weekly lunches, which began twenty years ago when we co-taught an undergraduate seminar in religion, magic, and witchcraft in the early modern world, have continued even after my relocation to Southern California—only now it's breakfast for me, and it's on Zoom. Thank you, Val.

As those of us in the humanities know all too well, institutional support for advanced research has been atrophying for years. I am keenly aware that the kind of support I enjoyed at Michigan—including salary support to top off external research grants, funding for a graduate student research assistant while chairing a department, and, last but certainly not least, a collegiate professorship—is not available to everyone. I am profoundly grateful that I can now help provide this crucial support in my new role at the Huntington, a place that has been near and dear to my heart since my first short-term fellowship there in 2012. Old and new friends and colleagues have welcomed me to Southern California, providing moral support as I navigated the challenges of finishing a book manuscript while starting a new job. On top of offering a collective thanks to the Huntington community of Fellows and Curators, I'd like to single out several people who volunteered to read portions of the manuscript or shared their extensive knowledge of early modern history with me: David Hall, Matt Kadane, Ann Little, Peter Mancall, Andrés Reséndez, Roy and Louise Ritchie, Brett Rushforth, Sharon Salinger, Terri Snyder, Abby Swingen, and Vanessa Wilkie.

Portions of Chapter 3 appeared in the April 2017 issue of the *William and Mary Quarterly* as "Planting the 'Great Cross': The Life, and Death, of Crosses in English America." This essay was first delivered at the University of Southern California in 2015 as part of a *WMQ*–EMSI Workshop on "World and Ground: New Early American Histories" and was subsequently the subject of a colloquium at the Omohundro Institute of Early American History and Culture in 2016, where I benefited from the astute criticism of Christopher Grasso, Brett Rushforth, Karin Wulf, and Joshua Piker, among others. I thank the *WMQ* for permission to reprint parts of the article here.

Three friends read the entire manuscript, in addition to the two superb outside readers for the Omohundro Institute. Sharon Salinger was the first to read a full draft of the book and kept asking, "But what is it about?" until I came up with a satisfactory answer. Val Kivelson and Matt Kadane pushed me to clarify and extend arguments that existed in shadow form and helped me find the right tone. Eric Seeman and Alison Games were the ideal external readers: their remarkably detailed reports offered generosity and rigor in equal measure, and suggestions both big and small for improving the argument. They each asked more of the manuscript than I could provide, but I hope the final product meets with their approval. Nick Popper and Emily Suth of the Omohundro Institute provided multiple rounds of editing before handing the manuscript over to Kathy Burdette and the OI's team of fact checkers, an extraordinary service that few, if any, other presses provide to authors. Nick and I may have wrangled over my fondness for contractions and the first person, but he allowed me to write the book I wanted to write in the end. I own all its failings.

CONTENTS

LIST OF ILLUSTRATIONS

LIST OF ABBREVIATIONS

Archives of Maryland   *Archives of Maryland Online,* msa.maryland.gov

Fulham Papers   The Fulham Papers at Lambeth Palace Library, London

Maryland Wills   *Maryland Wills,* Ancestry.com, Maryland, U.S., Wills and Probate Records, 1635–1777 [database online], Provo, Utah, Ancestry.com Operations, Inc., 2015

MPA   Archives of the Maryland Province of the Society of Jesus, Lauinger Library, Georgetown University, Washington, D.C.

SPG   Society for the Propagation of the Gospel

TNA   The National Archives, Kew, U.K.
CO (Colonial Office)
PRO (Public Record Office)

WMQ   *William and Mary Quarterly*

A COMMON GRAVE

Overview

EARLY IN THE 1600S, on the windswept shores of Acadia, the French explorer Samuel de Champlain observed a Catholic priest and a Protestant minister "fall to with their fists on questions of faith." But when the two men died of scurvy within days of one another, Champlain's men "put them into the same grave, to see whether dead they would live in peace, since living they had never been able to agree." At roughly the same time in Jamestown, Virginia, an English settler was buried inside the first Anglican church in North America with a silver Catholic reliquary in his coffin, to the surprise of the archaeologists who discovered the silver box four hundred years later. Two graves, twelve hundred miles and an empire apart, dating from the earliest days of European colonization of North America. In each a Catholic body resides next to the material remains of those they would have viewed as adversaries in principle, if not always in practice. Transgressing imperial and religious boundaries, these two graves are a synecdoche of the vexed place of Catholics in early American religious history—a people seemingly "out of place" who nevertheless lie in disturbing proximity to their Protestant neighbors.[1]

The common grave is an apt metaphor for the messy reality of religious heterogeneity in colonial English America. People of different faiths who often fought bitterly with one another in post-Reformation Europe found themselves living, and dying, in improvised communities that were multilingual, multiracial, and religiously diverse. All of North America was a shared grave in the sense that Champlain evoked: full of bodies that were forced by circumstance to coexist whether they wanted to or not. The earliest English

---

1. Samuel de Champlain, *Les voyages de la Nouvelle France occidentale, dicte Canada, faits par le Sr. de Champlain Xainctongeois* (Paris, 1632), quoted in Francis Parkman, *France and England in North America*, I (New York, 1983), 186; Gabriel Sagard and Edwin Tross, *Histoire du Canada et voyages que les frères mineurs récollets y ont faits pour la conversion des infidèles depuis l'an 1615*, I (Paris, 1866), 26; John Mack Faragher, *A Great and Noble Scheme: The Tragic Story of the Expulsion of the French Acadians from Their American Homeland* (New York, 2005), 19–20 (quotation on 20); William M. Kelso, *Jamestown: The Buried Truth* (Charlottesville, Va., 2006), 187–188.

colonies were common graves in a more literal sense as well, as disease, star-
vation, and Indian wars devastated many of the settlements in a few short
years. An entire colony vanished in Roanoke in the 1580s, and fewer than
half of the men and women who stepped ashore in Jamestown and Plymouth
in 1607 and 1620 survived the first harsh winter. The English outposts in the
Caribbean were, justifiably, known as death traps for most of the colonial
period. Compared to its powerful rival to the south, New Spain, the English imperial project was notoriously uncoordinated and chaotic for most of
the seventeenth century, leaving the first generation of migrants to fend for
themselves in an alien landscape among peoples they did not understand.
Their failures are well known.[2] But amid the violence and disorder of early
colonial conquest and settlement was a concurrent process of coexistence and
adaptation. This process has been mapped with great sophistication for Native
America through the lens of "encounter," and scholars of Atlantic slavery
have developed powerful models of cultural syncretism and creolization to
explain how Africans survived the brutality of capture and enslavement in the
Americas.[3] But the almost universal assumption that English America was
a Protestant place has meant that historians have paid less attention to how
people of rival religious faiths—Protestant, Catholic, Muslim, Jewish—also
experienced their own forms of colonial encounter and creolization in the
seventeenth and early eighteenth centuries.

This is a book about the practice of religious coexistence in a colonial environment. I choose "coexistence" over the more common term, "pluralism," for
a reason: pluralism is widely, if implicitly, understood to be the waystation on
the road to tolerance and freedom. Living in a more religiously plural society
than the one they left behind, early Euro-Americans learned (often begrudgingly) to tolerate, then to respect, different faiths. This has been the standard
narrative of American religious history, which sees a direct line between the
colonial experience of diversity and the constitutional protection of religious

2. James Horn, *A Kingdom Strange: The Brief and Tragic History of the Lost Colony of Roanoke* (New York, 2010); Bernard Bailyn, *The Barbarous Years: The Peopling of British North
America; The Conflict of Civilizations, 1600–1675* (New York, 2012); Kathleen Donegan, *Seasons of Misery: Catastrophe and Colonial Settlement* (Philadelphia, 2014); Alison Games, *The
Web of Empire: English Cosmopolitans in an Age of Expansion, 1560–1660* (New York, 2008).

3. To cite only two influential examples: Daniel K. Richter, *Before the Revolution: America's Ancient Pasts* (Cambridge, Mass., 2011); Ira Berlin, *Many Thousands Gone: The First Two
Centuries of Slavery in North America* (Cambridge, Mass., 1998).

freedom enshrined in the First Amendment.[4] The concept of coexistence is less teleological; it captures a moment in time rather than a predestined historical process. Much in the way that Richard White's foundational concept of the "middle ground" helped reorient Native American history away from predetermined narratives of loss and displacement toward a reckoning with the give-and-take of Native-European interactions in a fluid forcefield of political uncertainty, the notion of coexistence opens up a more contingent approach to the study of colonial religious identity.[5]

Thinking of religious identity as contingent may be a counterintuitive proposition in the post-Reformation era. Of all the inherited identities English settlers brought to their colonial ventures, none was arguably more overdetermined than religion: unlike race, ethnicity, status, or even gender—all of which were in a considerable state of flux in the sixteenth and seventeenth centuries, and some of which were still in a pupal form of development—religious identity had been forged by centuries of political and military intervention that presumably fixed the boundaries of who was a Protestant, a Catholic, a Jew, a Muslim, in law and blood. In England, the theological and ecclesiastical boundaries separating Protestant from Catholic were supposed to have been settled by the time the first explorers set foot on North American soil. To be sure, there were individuals who eluded easy categorization—"hermaphrodite Christians," in the language of the day, people who said one thing and did another. But a complex legal and political machinery was in place to make sure that conformity to the Church of England was the glue that held the nation together. As overseas expansion added new territories to

---

4. See, for example, Richard W. Pointer, *Protestant Pluralism and the New York Experience: A Study of Eighteenth-Century Religious Diversity* (Bloomington, Ind., 1988); Carla Gardina Pestana, *Liberty of Conscience and the Growth of Religious Diversity in Early America, 1636–1786* (Providence, R.I., 1986); Thomas J. Curry, *The First Freedoms: Church and State in America to the Passage of the First Amendment* (New York, 1986); Chris Beneke, *Beyond Toleration: The Religious Origins of American Pluralism* (New York, 2006); Sally Schwartz, *"A Mixed Multitude": The Struggle for Religious Toleration in Colonial Pennsylvania* (New York, 1987). Evan Haefeli effectively critiques this approach in his sweeping overview of colonial religious politics, *Accidental Pluralism: America and the Religious Politics of English Expansion, 1497–1662* (Chicago, 2021), introduction, 1–13.

5. Richard White, *The Middle Ground: Indians, Empires, and Republics in the Great Lakes Region, 1650–1815* (New York, 1991). I am invoking White's paradigm, not as a historical model to apply to different colonial arenas of encounter, but as a heuristic insight into the way that the lived experience of encounter is always ad hoc and provisional.

the fledgling empire, and three nations became one after the Act of Union of 1707, religious and political identity were supposedly fused into one powerful hegemon: Protestant Britain. Dissenters had been absorbed progressively into the body politic through landmark legislation like the 1689 Act of Toleration, which, although not relieving them of all the legal disabilities of Nonconformity, had allowed non-Anglicans to worship in peace. At the heart of this monolith was the Anglican parish, numbering nearly ten thousand on the eve of colonization, a vast infrastructure of churches and churchyards that knit the spiritual topography into a nearly unbroken fabric. Scholars of English religion like to point out that every inhabitant of the British Isles was in ear's range of the sound of church bells during the seventeenth and eighteenth centuries.[6]

For some time, this historiographical consensus—a powerful pillar of the scholarly construction of the first British empire—has been fraying. Beneath the facade of ecclesiastical conformity and Protestant patriotism, there was a more fluid understanding of faith that allowed for improvisation, accommodation, dissimulation, and, when circumstances permitted, resistance. This is not a new insight for historians of English Nonconformity who have plumbed the fissures of the Anglican establishment to recover all the ways that a host of radical Protestants (Puritans, Baptists, Quakers, Familists) lived unorthodox religious lives after the foundational 1559 Act of Uniformity. Anglicans themselves hardly presented a united front, especially after the death of Elizabeth I, riven as they were between High and Low Church factions that threatened to blur the boundary between orthodoxy and heterodoxy on both the puritan and popish ends of the spectrum. Waves of penal legislation and ecclesiastical visitations launched by the Tudors and the Stuarts did not succeed in rooting out Nonconformity or smoothing out internal divisions within the Church of England. Even under the harsh Clarendon Code of

6. Geraldine Heng, *The Invention of Race in the European Middle Ages* (New York, 2018); David Nirenberg, *Neighboring Faiths: Christianity, Judaism, and Islam in the Middle Ages and Today* (Chicago, 2014); Linda Colley, *Britons: Forging the Nation, 1707–1837* (New Haven, Conn., 1994); Carla Gardina Pestana, *Protestant Empire: Religion and the Making of the British Atlantic World* (Philadelphia, 2010). Isaac Bagrave's 1642 sermon to Parliament complained of "equivocators" and "hermaphrodite Christians" (quoted in Alexandra Walsham, *Church Papists: Catholicism, Conformity, and Confessional Polemic in Early Modern England* [Woodbridge, U.K., 1993], 9). On the relationship between the Church of England and dissenters, see Ralph Stevens, *The Reception of the Toleration Act, 1689 to 1720* (Woodbridge, U.K., 2018); Andrew C. Thompson, ed., *The Oxford History of Protestant Dissenting Traditions*, II, *The Long Eighteenth Century, c. 1689–1828* (Oxford, 2018).

the 1660s, which criminalized Nonconformist worship in private homes, enforcement always lagged considerably behind prescription—a pattern that would be repeated in North America when colonial authorities got around to re-creating the legal framework of religious establishment.[7]

The study of English Catholicism, in particular, has made a forceful case for the continued vitality of traditional ways of worshipping God among those who rejected the Reformed liturgy.[8] The revisionist interpretation that burst onto the scholarly scene in the 1990s overturned conventional readings of a sickly medieval Church routed by a robust and disciplined program of reform by insisting that traditional Christianity was thriving before and after the seismic events of 1517 and 1534. There is broad agreement that Catholics were still the silent majority of professing Christians well into the Elizabethan era, despite their legal status as heretics. Even if "quietly conformist Protestants" outnumbered traditionalists by the end of the Tudor era, the death

7. Peter Marshall, *Heretics and Believers: A History of the English Reformation* (New Haven, Conn., 2017); Peter Lake, *The Boxmaker's Revenge: "Orthodoxy," "Heterodoxy," and the Politics of the Parish in Early Stuart London* (Stanford, Calif., 2001); Steven Pincus, *1688: The First Modern Revolution* (New Haven, Conn., 2009); Andrew R. Murphy, *Conscience and Community: Revisiting Toleration and Religious Dissent in Early Modern England and America* (University Park, Pa., 2001); Ethan H. Shagan, *Popular Politics and the English Reformation* (Cambridge, 2003); George Southcombe and Grant Tapsell, *Restoration Politics, Religion, and Culture: Britain and Ireland, 1660–1714* (Basingstoke, U.K., 2010); Peter Lake and Michael Questier, eds., *Conformity and Orthodoxy in the Early Stuart Church, c. 1560–1660* (Rochester, N.Y., 2000); Christopher Haigh, *English Reformations: Religion, Politics, and Society under the Tudors* (Oxford, 1993); David D. Hall, *The Puritans: A Transatlantic History* (Princeton, N.J., 2021); Rosemary Moore, *A Light in Their Consciences: Early Quakers in Britain, 1646–1666* (University Park, Pa., 2000); Barry Reay, *The Quakers and the English Revolution* (New York, 1985). On internal Anglican divisions under the early Stuarts, see Questier, "Arminianism, Catholicism, and Puritanism in England during the 1630s," *Historical Journal,* XLIX (2006), 53–78; Alexandra Walsham, "The Parochial Roots of Laudianism Revisited: Catholics, Anti-Calvinists, and 'Parish Anglicans' in Early Stuart England," *Journal of Ecclesiastical History,* XLIX (1998), 620–651.

8. J. C. H. Aveling, *The Handle and the Axe: The Catholic Recusants in England from Reformation to Emancipation* (London, 1976); John Bossy, *The English Catholic Community, 1570–1850* (London, 1975); Lisa McClain, *Lest We Be Damned: Practical Innovation and Lived Experience among Catholics in Protestant England, 1559–1642* (New York, 2004); Alexandra Walsham, *Catholic Reformation in Protestant Britain* (Farnham, U.K., 2014); James E. Kelly and Susan Royal, eds., *Early Modern English Catholicism: Identity, Memory, and Counter-Reformation* (Leiden, 2017); Walsham, *Church Papists*; Lucy E. C. Wooding, *Rethinking Catholicism in Reformation England* (New York, 2000); Ronald Corthell et al., eds., *Catholic Culture in Early Modern England* (Notre Dame, Ind., 2007).

of a sovereign and the crowning of a new monarch always created openings, however temporary, when latent beliefs could surface, when rituals performed in secret could take place in consecrated space again, when the sacred objects targeted by iconoclasts could emerge from their hiding places and once again adorn chapels and private chambers. We know that the open practice of Catholicism flourished in the years surrounding James I's accession in 1603, Charles I's in 1625, and (most dramatically) James II's in 1685.[9]

But trying to sort England's Christians into opposing camps misses the larger truth that, as Michael Questier puts it, "It is virtually impossible to talk coherently of single phenomena called 'Catholicism' and 'Protestantism'" after the Reformation. Rather than two stable formations from which variants split off, Protestantism and Catholicism were shifting constellations of practice, belief, emotion, memory, and political calculation. Scholars in recent years have been more interested in finding moments where the practice of Protestantism and Catholicism converged on the ground, where civil and ecclesiastical authorities tolerated rather than punished difference, where connivance and dissimulation provided cover for heterodoxy to flourish despite the emergence of powerful state churches. In this new scholarly paradigm, the Reformation did not cleave Europe's Christians into mutually exclusive camps so much as force them to find new ways to coexist.[10]

In colonial British American historiography, the story of religion has likewise been overwhelmingly a Protestant one. Two narratives dominate the literature: the proliferation and triumph of dissenting sects in the seventeenth

9. Marshall concludes in his survey of the English Reformation that Protestants were "certainly the minority" in the early Elizabethan era outside of London, though by 1590 "quietly conformist Protestants" were probably in the majority; see *Heretics and Believers*, 464, 543. The revisionist interpretation is widely attributed to Eamon Duffy's landmark book, *The Stripping of the Altars: Traditional Religion in England, 1400–1580* (New Haven, Conn., 1992), followed by Haigh's pluralistic account, *English Reformations*. See Marshall's even-handed assessment of this historiographical turn in "(Re)defining the English Reformation," *Journal of British Studies*, XLVIII (2009), 564–586.

10. Michael C. Questier, *Catholicism and Community in Early Modern England: Politics, Aristocratic Patronage, and Religion, ca. 1550–1640* (New York, 2006), 66. For three excellent studies of convergence and connivance drawn from different parts of the Atlantic world, see Laura M. Chmielewski, *The Spice of Popery: Converging Christianities on the Early American Frontier* (Notre Dame, Ind., 2012); Benjamin J. Kaplan, *Divided by Faith: Religious Conflict and the Practice of Toleration in Early Modern Europe* (Cambridge, Mass., 2007); Stuart B. Schwartz, *All Can Be Saved: Religious Toleration and Salvation in the Iberian Atlantic World* (New Haven, Conn., 2008). This is not to deny the brutality of religious war in the sixteenth and seventeenth centuries, a topic explored at length in the scholarly

century and the fitful emergence of an Anglican establishment everywhere south of New England in the eighteenth century. But this focus on the particular varieties of reform that clashed in the colonies has left the larger category of "Protestantism" (and, by extension, of its counterpart, "Catholicism") unexamined.[11] It is tempting to assume we know what the larger family is when examining the offshoots that sprouted, grew, split again, and became entangled in the spiritual wilds of North America. The history of non-Protestant communities, in turn, has been relegated to studies of small communities: enslaved African Muslims in the Lowcountry, Sephardic Jews operating in port towns, Jesuit-run manors in Maryland. These microcommunities appear as dots in an otherwise vast Protestant expanse, not connected into a larger pattern nor bleeding out into the surrounding map to create zones of religious indeterminacy. Where historians of colonial religion see syncretism or hybridity, it is almost always in the context of European encounters with Native or African peoples, not with one another.[12]

A Common Grave is an exploration of Catholic life and faith across the earliest English colonies—an exercise in connecting the dots. In Protestant England, Catholics were "everywhere and nowhere." Ever since the seesaw politics of reform had reached an uneasy accommodation in England under Elizabeth I, English Catholics (now branded "recusants" for their self-recusal from the established church) had lived a twilight existence dimly visible in

---

literature. Anti-Catholicism was, after all, one of the bedrock principles on which the English empire / nation was founded, and thousands of Catholics were imprisoned, dispossessed, or executed during Britain's penal age. But behind these ugly episodes of sectarian violence lies an equally potent reality of religious commingling, which is the focus of this book. For a useful sampling of the secondary literature on the religious violence of the Reformation era, see Mark Konnert, *Early Modern Europe: The Age of Religious War, 1559–1715* (Toronto, 2006); Susan Juster, *Sacred Violence in Early America* (Philadelphia, 2016); Barbara B. Diefendorf, *Beneath the Cross: Catholics and Huguenots in Sixteenth-Century Paris* (New York, 1991); Charles W. A. Prior and Glenn Burgess, eds., *England's Wars of Religion Revisited* (Farnham, U.K., 2011).

11. Mark Valeri explores this homogenizing tendency in *The Opening of the Protestant Mind: How Anglo-American Protestants Embraced Religious Liberty* (New York, 2023).

12. See, for example, Richard W. Pointer, *Encounters of the Spirit: Native Americans and European Colonial Religion* (Bloomington, Ind., 2007). Notable exceptions include John Smolenski, *Friends and Strangers: The Making of a Creole Culture in Pennsylvania* (Philadelphia, 2010); Chmielewski, *Spice of Popery;* Kristen Block and Jenny Shaw, "Subjects without an Empire: The Irish in the Early Modern Caribbean," *Past and Present,* no. 210 (February 2011), 33–60. It is not a coincidence that many of these works explore religious identity in regions where the English, Spanish, and French empires abutted one another.

the archives. Their faith driven underground, their priests hunted down and executed, their children taken away from them, and their dead denied Christian burial, recusants learned to live in the shadows. In English America, Catholics have largely vanished from view outside of a handful of denominational histories and provincial studies of Maryland—the one colony founded by a Catholic proprietor. Long dismissed as fanciful bugbears haunting the orthodox imagination, Anglo-Irish Catholics are in fact everywhere in the annals of colonial history. Some of the earliest colonizing projects, now long forgotten, were proposed by Catholic courtiers: Thomas Gerard and George Peckham envisioned a Catholic enclave in southern New England during the 1580s, whereas Thomas Arundell and Tristram Winslade plotted separate expeditions to "North Virginia" in 1604–1605. These projects didn't come to fruition, but from north to south, Catholics and their priests pop up with surprising frequency in town, colonial, and church records—in Lord Baltimore's colony of Maryland, of course, but also in the fishing ports of Newfoundland, the cities and farms of the Middle Atlantic, and the tiny islands of the Caribbean archipelago, where thousands of Irish rebels, convicts, and servants were sent in the seventeenth century. All this is to say nothing of the thousands of enslaved Africans and Natives laboring in the English colonies who might also be labeled "Catholic" by virtue of baptism in the home countries (the kingdom of Kongo and Angola were officially Christian nations during the era of the Atlantic slave trade) or at the hands of French, Spanish, and Portuguese missionaries in North America. Yet Catholics were routinely undercounted in colonial censuses and ignored in official correspondence.[13]

In addition to this blindness toward the presence of non-Protestants in English America, the study of colonial Catholicism has been hampered by the same reluctance to subject the larger category to interrogation, to pull apart the phenomenon of post-Reformation "Catholicism" and ask what, if anything, connected all the varieties of peoples who have been labeled "Catholic" in post-Reformation Anglo-America. We have broad studies of the Catholic American diaspora written from a Catholic perspective, but the diasporic framework is itself a symptom of the tendency to think in categorical terms about religious identity.[14] A diaspora is usually defined by the bond between some authentic identity (Jewishness, Blackness) and the homeland

13. Frances Dolan, "Gender and the 'Lost' Spaces of Catholicism," *Journal of Interdisciplinary History*, XXXII (2002), 641–665 (quotation on 642); Haefeli, *Accidental Pluralism*, 83–95 (quotation on 93).

14. For example, see Robert Emmett Curran, *Papist Devils: Catholics in British America, 1574–1783* (Washington, D.C., 2014).

from which the community sharing that identity has been exiled, making it an unwieldy framework for considering a community that was as racially, ethnically, and linguistically diverse as colonial Catholicism. The alternative paradigm of an "Atlantic" community (the Black Atlantic, the Red Atlantic, the Green Atlantic, the Puritan Atlantic, to name just several recent iterations) is less tethered to essentialist notions of group identity than "diaspora" and more focused on the space in between the original homeland and the final destinations of wandering peoples. Even within this capacious rubric, however, it is difficult to avoid assigning fixed identities to people who might inhabit multiple or partial, debased or overdetermined, versions of the core category.[15]

One reason why colonial Catholics are so elusive to identify and fix in time and space is because early modern Catholicism was a global community—but global in a distinctively early modern way. In contrast to what would later be termed "ultramontane" Catholicism, early modern traditional Christians did not have strong ties to Rome or to the papacy as an institution. The locus of their religious identity remained rooted in local structures: the parish, the local saint to whom the parish might be dedicated, personal networks of kith and kin among whom they performed the rituals of faith. Rather than being an ecclesiastical monolith, the late medieval Church was—in Peter Marshall's words—"alarmingly unregulated," spawning "an exponential growth of pious lay initiatives, a dazzling array of devotional choices, and some occasional shameless hucksterism" that fanned the flames of reform by the sixteenth century. The unruly localism of late medieval Catholicism remained strong after the Reformation, but, under the driving force of the missionary orders founded to combat the spread of Protestantism (notably the Jesuits), this localized faith began to disperse around the globe with stunning speed. Starting in the 1540s, Jesuits took the Counter-Reformation on the road, traveling and proselytizing from Central Europe to Iberia, India, China, Japan,

---

15. A useful introduction to the history of the term "diaspora" and its deployment in contemporary scholarship is Khachig Tölölyan, "Rethinking Diaspora(s): Stateless Power in the Transnational Moment," *Diaspora*, V (1996), 3–36. "Atlantic" community: Allan Greer and Kenneth Mills, "A Catholic Atlantic," in Jorge Cañizares-Esguerra and Erik R. Seeman, eds., *The Atlantic in Global History: 1500–1800* (Upper Saddle River, N.J., 2007), 3–19; Paul Gilroy, *The Black Atlantic: Modernity and Double Consciousness* (Cambridge, Mass., 1993); Jace Weaver, *The Red Atlantic: American Indigenes and the Making of the Modern World, 1000–1927* (Chapel Hill, N.C., 2014); Peter D. O'Neill and David Lloyd, eds., *The Black and Green Atlantic: Cross-Currents of African and Irish Diasporas* (Hampshire, N.Y., 2009); Heather Miyano Kopelson, *Faithful Bodies: Performing Religion and Race in the Puritan Atlantic* (New York, 2014).

Ethiopia, the Congo, Mexico, Brazil, and the many islands of the East and West Indies. Global Catholicism in the age of Atlantic empires was the creation of missionaries and their converts and, in time, of the creole communities who sprang up throughout the Americas. Like the Atlantic empires that provided them shelter, these colonial Catholic enclaves were simultaneously local and global in ways that are difficult to grasp from a modern perspective. We are accustomed to thinking of the global as overwhelming the local—homogenizing vernacular cultures; disrupting, if not decimating, familial and neighborhood-based ties; operating through megalithic corporate forms. This was not how global Catholicism, or any early modern global formation, worked. And when Jesuit missionaries made their way to English America starting in the 1630s, they encountered the same dilemma of adapting a universal liturgy to conditions on the ground.[16]

Part One—"Finding Catholics in the Early English Atlantic"—explores these questions of identity and indeterminacy from both a hemispheric and a local perspective. Surveying the entire sweep of England's North American colonies, from Newfoundland to Nevis, over the first century of colonial settlement, my aim in these chapters is to pull colonial Catholics into a single frame of analysis while not flattening the category beyond all recognition or losing sight of the regional and racial particularities that shaped the lives of Catholics in English America. Doing so requires stipulating a baseline

16. Marshall, *Heretics and Believers*, 22. Peter Brown's classic study of the cult of saints suggested that from its founding era, the universal Catholic Church was in fact made up of local "micro-Christendoms" that had a local and regional flavor; see Brown, *The Cult of Saints: Its Rise and Function in Late Christianity* (Chicago, 1981). On the emergence of the missionary orders and their role in creating global Catholicism in the early modern world, see Luke Clossey, *Salvation and Globalization in the Early Jesuit Missions* (New York, 2008); Thomas Banchoff and José Casanova, eds., *The Jesuits and Globalization: Historical Legacies and Contemporary Challenges* (Washington, D.C., 2016); Ronnie Po-chia Hsia, "Jesuit Foreign Missions: A Historiographical Essay," *Journal of Jesuit Studies*, I (2014), 47–65; Dauril Alden, *The Making of an Enterprise: The Society of Jesus in Portugal, Its Empire, and Beyond, 1540–1750* (Stanford, Calif., 1996); John O'Malley et al., eds., *The Jesuits: Cultures, Sciences, and the Arts, 1540–1773* (Toronto, 2019), particularly part 3, "Mobility: Overseas Missions, and the Circulation of Culture." On global Catholicism in the Americas, see Megan Armstrong, "Transatlantic Catholicism: Rethinking the Nature of the Catholic Tradition in the Early Modern Period," *History Compass*, V (2007), 1942–1966; Erin Kathleen Rowe, *Black Saints in Early Modern Global Catholicism* (New York, 2019); Kenneth Mills, "The Naturalisation of Andean Christianities," in Hsia, ed., *The Cambridge History of Christianity*, VI, *Re-formation and Expansion, c. 1500–c. 1660* (Cambridge, 2007), 504–535; Osvaldo F. Pardo, *The Origins of Mexican Catholicism: Nahua Rituals and Christian Sacraments in Sixteenth-Century Mexico* (Ann Arbor, Mich., 2004).

definition of "Catholicism," a risky endeavor in light of the blurry nature of confessional boundaries in early modern Anglo-America. The starting point for most studies of Catholicism is simple: baptism at the hands of a priest or missionary. There are good reasons for making baptism the sine qua non of Catholic identity. Baptism was the sacramental gateway into the family of God for medieval and early modern Christians. This didn't change with the Reformation (though the meaning of the sacrament did), but unlike Protestants, Catholics believed that baptism was the *first* step on the road to Christianization, a journey that could take many detours but that (in the eyes of the Church) could never be entirely abandoned. Baptism was a seal of religious belonging that could not be effaced. From this common sacramental origin, Europe's lay Catholics could and did go in startlingly different directions in terms of how they practiced their faith, and the Catholic Church fought a rearguard battle against local heterodoxy for its entire premodern history. The proliferation of local saints and rituals was reined in somewhat by the reforming 1563 Council of Trent, but lived religion in Catholic countries continued to be marked by a wide range of folk belief and practice even as its missionaries created a global Church.[17]

Recognizing this local variation within global Catholicism allows us to place enslaved Africans, Native converts, Irish servants, and English recusants in the same confessional basket by virtue of baptism despite the vast disparities in their situations.[18] White, Black, and Native colonial Catholics lived very different religious lives, and it's legitimate to ask whether someone

17. Shona Helen Johnston's superb Ph.D. dissertation, "Papists in a Protestant World: The Catholic Anglo-Atlantic in the Seventeenth Century" (Georgetown University, 2011), is a model for this kind of "broad canvas" study of Catholicism in colonial North America. See also R. Scott Spurlock, "Catholics in a Puritan Atlantic: The Liminality of Empire's Edge," which surveys the evidence for Catholic presence throughout English America (in Crawford Gribben and Spurlock, eds., *Puritans and Catholics in the Trans-Atlantic World, 1600–1800* [London, 2015], 21–46). Contrary to popular usage, the area we call British North America encompassed more than the continental colonies along the eastern seaboard; it also included the Caribbean colonies. Throughout the book, I use the term "North America" in this broader geographical sense. According to the Catholic Church, baptism "seals the Christian with the indelible spiritual mark (*character*) of his belonging to Christ" (*Catechism of the Catholic Church*, 2d ed. [Vatican, 1997], part 2, 324, https://www.usccb .org/sites/default/files/flipbooks/catechism/326/). William A. Christian, Jr., *Local Religion in Sixteenth-Century Spain* (Princeton, N.J., 1981), is a brilliant introduction to Catholic localism in the Reformation era.

18. Scholars of the Catholic Atlantic are more comfortable including baptized Africans within the rubric of Catholicism; as Greer and Mills put it, "In the colonies of Spain, Portugal, and France, millions of Africans and peoples of African descent, both enslaved

who was baptized against their will or under conditions of extreme stress should be considered in the same breath with a white planter who emigrated to Maryland in order to practice his faith freely.[19] But we can just as legitimately ask whether a Lancashire gentlewoman who received communion daily in her family's private chapel has anything in common with a Spanish peasant who prayed to a local saint of pagan origin and rarely went to church. *A Common Grave* is written in acknowledgment, not ignorance, of these differences and with the conviction that we can learn something valuable about how religious identity was navigated in English America if we suspend the question of authenticity and treat all baptized men and women as nominal Catholics (as indeed the law and Protestant polemic did), at least in specific contexts and for specific heuristic purposes.

Writing a history of colonial Catholicism means confronting the Protestant bias endemic in colonial historiography. By "Protestant bias," I mean not only

---

and free, were exposed to Catholicism and made it their own" ("A Catholic Atlantic," in Cañizares-Esguerra and Seeman, eds., *Atlantic in Global History*, 12). Kristen Block points out that enslaved African Catholics in New Spain—unlike Native peoples—were held to the same standards of orthodoxy as Jewish *conversos* by the Spanish Inquisition, in recognition of the validity of their baptisms (*Ordinary Lives in the Early Caribbean: Religion, Colonial Competition, and the Politics of Profit* [Athens, Ga., 2012], 35). Historians of Africa disagree, often vehemently, with this assessment; James Sweet, for example, discounts most baptisms of Africans as coerced and invalid, whereas John Thornton sees a vibrant Afro-Catholic culture emerging in the Kongo. See Sweet, *Recreating Africa: Culture, Kinship, and Religion in the African-Portuguese World, 1441–1770* (Chapel Hill, N.C., 2003); Thornton, "The Development of an African Catholic Church in the Kingdom of Kongo, 1491–1750," *Journal of African History*, XXV (1984), 147–167.

19. On the question of the "authenticity" of Native converts to Christianity, see Joel W. Martin, "Introduction," in Martin and Mark Nicholas, eds., *Native Americans, Christianity, and the Reshaping of the American Religious Landscape* (Chapel Hill, N.C., 2010), 1–20; Kenneth M. Morrison, "The Solidarity of Kin: The Intersection of Eastern Algonkian and French-Catholic Cosmologies," in Morrison, *The Solidarity of Kin: Ethnohistory, Religious Studies, and the Algonkian-French Religious Encounter* (Albany, N.Y., 2002), 147–172; Linford D. Fisher, *The Indian Great Awakening: Religion and the Shaping of Native Cultures in Early America* (New York, 2012), chap. 4, "Affiliating," 84–106; Emma Anderson, *The Betrayal of Faith: The Tragic Journal of a Colonial Native Convert* (Cambridge, Mass., 2007); James Axtell, "Were Indian Conversions Bona Fide?" in Axtell, *After Columbus: Essays in the Ethnohistory of Colonial North America* (New York, 1988), 100–121. Daniel K. Richter estimates that 20 percent of the Iroquois were "sincere Christians" by the late 1670s ("Iroquois versus Iroquois: Jesuit Missionaries and Christianity in Village Politics, 1642–1686," *Ethnohistory*, XXXII [1985], 1–16 [quotation on 8]).

an exclusive focus on Protestant communities as constituting the entirety of lived religion in the colonies but also a disposition to privilege texts over ritual, belief over behavior, the individual over the collective, and the ideological over the material. Since its inception as a field, American religious history has treated Catholics as rhetorical constructions of antipapist polemic or as interlopers, "intestine enemies." At the most basic level, this has meant a reluctance to acknowledge the existence of those Catholics (English, Irish, French, Spanish, Native, African) living amid the majority Anglo-Protestant inhabitants of early America. But finding Catholics is more than a question of numbers. It is also a matter of looking at different types of sources and asking different questions. Foregrounding Catholic life and religious practice means paying as much attention to the material world (rosary beads, crucifixes, baptismal fonts, gravestones, relics, devotional objects, psalters, embroidered altar cloths, shrines) as to the textual world (sermons, holy books, spiritual journals, catechisms). It means paying as much attention to what people do—fast, feast, process, kneel, pray, observe the Sabbath, attend mass, receive communion, perform penance, receive last rites—as to what they write. And it means embedding believers in a dense matrix of social relationships and institutional networks rather than considering them as individual souls seeking a personal relationship with the divine. To study colonial Catholic life is to study women as the primary ritual participants in a cycle of feasting and fasting, to study the confluence of European, African, and Native spiritual traditions as missionaries brought enslaved peoples and servants into the Church (often against their will), to follow the faithful into their homes and private chapels as they married, christened infants, buried their loved ones, and prayed for their souls.[20]

20. Jon Butler, "Historiographical Heresy: Catholicism as a Model for American Religious History," in Thomas Kselman, ed., *Belief in History: Innovative Approaches to European and American Religion* (South Bend, Ind., 1991), 286–309; Robert Emmett Curran, ed., *Intestine Enemies: Catholics in Protestant America, 1605–1791; A Documentary History* (Washington, D.C., 2017). More recent scholarship has begun to dismantle this entrenched but artificial distinction between a doctrinal Protestantism and a material Catholicism; see, for example, Erik R. Seeman, *Speaking with the Dead in Early America* (Philadelphia, 2020); David Morgan and Sally M. Promey, eds., *The Visual Culture of American Religions* (Berkeley, Calif., 2001); Ruben Suykerbuyk, *The Matter of Piety: Zoutleeuw's Church of Saint Leonard and Religious Material Culture in the Low Countries (c. 1450–1620)* (Leiden, 2020); Bridget Heal, "Visual and Material Culture," in Ulinka Rublack, ed., *The Oxford Handbook of the Protestant Reformations* (Oxford, 2015), 601–620.

The image of a common grave also speaks to the importance of Christian ritual (baptism, communion, marriage, burial) as the central meeting ground of rival religious cultures in early Anglo-America. Part Two takes up the question of ritual and how it was exported, modified, and creolized in English America. As scholars of English religion have long observed, Catholics who were otherwise quite successful in keeping their beliefs and their devotional practices (observing fast days, offering prayers for the dead) secret from prying neighbors and episcopal visitations could not escape public exposure during the sacramental moments of their faith: communion could not be administered without a priest, and the dead needed to be buried in consecrated ground. Part Two explores, in as much depth as the sources allow, the rituals of life (baptism, godparentage, communion, feasting and fasting, marriage) and death (last rites, burial, prayers for the dead) around which colonial Catholics organized their religious lives.

More than an account of Catholic sacramental practice in English America, however, these chapters provide a broader framework for understanding "sacramental politics" in a colonial environment. The sacraments were not just the occasions when Catholics were most visible; they were also the site of encounter between the diverse ethnic/racial/religious communities that comprised the entire spectrum of colonial faith, from Native and African animist traditions to radical Protestantism and missionary Catholicism. There were many "contact zones" in English America, borderlands both geographic and imagined where contrasting modes of being and doing came face to face—sometimes to shatter, sometimes to fuse. The sacraments were one such contact zone. The disorder of religious institutions, endemic in every region outside New England in the seventeenth century, meant that Euro-Americans found it difficult, if not impossible, to re-create the normal liturgical rhythms of life in the New World. Beyond the Puritan commonwealths, believers of all persuasions were too often left to improvise colonial versions of the rituals that marked important life passages without clergy to assist or churches in which to gather, and the result was a hodgepodge of ritual practices among all sects. The sacramental inadequacies of white settlers were highlighted when they encountered Indigenous and, later, African peoples who had ritual complexes of their own and who (mostly) scorned the missionaries' invitations to convert or at least outwardly conform to European patterns of belief and practice. We have sophisticated ethnographic descriptions of how Native peoples and people of African descent incorporated and then turned Christian baptism and burial to their own cultural and political ends, but few comparable discussions of the politics of sacramental exchange among Euro-Americans.[21]

The chronological boundaries of *A Common Grave* are, roughly, from 1600 to 1750. The mid-eighteenth century marks a watershed in the history of Protestant-Catholic relations in British North America with the annexation of two predominantly Catholic colonies from Spain and France, respectively, after the Seven Years' War: Florida and Quebec. In both cases, the Catholic population of English America surged (though the population boom was fleeting in Florida, as many Spanish residents fled to Cuba after the British seized control), bringing the problem of Catholic subjects in a Protestant empire into sharp relief. Anti-Catholicism surged as well in the original English colonies as the predominantly Protestant inhabitants faced the specter of a numerous and powerful Catholic community operating within their borders for the first time. Britain's accommodation of its new Catholic subjects, allowing them to practice their faith freely, only added fuel to the fire of Protestant bigotry. There are good reasons, therefore, for ending before these seismic shifts in the political, religious, and demographic landscape of English America occurred. Before 1750, the vast majority of Catholics in the English colonies were Irish servants, enslaved Natives and Africans, and white recusants well-practiced in the arts of concealment and deception; after 1763, most were men and women who had lived the entirety of their lives as Catholics in Catholic nations, free to worship openly and legally. How these two distinct Catholic communities coexisted with one another and with the British empire and its American successor is the subject for another book.[22]

---

21. Robbie Ethridge and Sherie M. Shuck-Hall, *Mapping the Mississippi Shatter Zone: The Colonial Indian Slave Trade and Regional Instability in the American South* (Lincoln, Neb., 2009), esp. the introduction, 1–62. To name just two such discussions: Jason R. Young, *Rituals of Resistance: African Atlantic Religion in Kongo and the Lowcountry South in the Era of Slavery* (Baton Rouge, 2007); Erik R. Seeman, *Death in the New World: Cross-Cultural Encounters, 1492–1800* (Philadelphia, 2011).

22. See Leslie Woodcock Tentler, *American Catholics: A History* (New Haven, Conn., 2020); Maura Jane Farrelly, *Papist Patriots: The Making of an American Catholic Identity* (New York, 2012); Catherine O'Donnell, "John Carroll and the Origins of the American Catholic Church, 1783–1815," *WMQ*, 3d Ser., LXVIII (2011), 101–126; Jay P. Dolan, *In Search of an American Catholicism: A History of Religion and Culture in Tension* (New York, 2002). As Valeri argues, the nature of anti-Catholicism also changed in significant ways after midcentury; see *Opening of the Protestant Mind*, chap. 5, "Power, Ceremony, and Roman Catholicism," 132–167.

In keeping with the historiographical and methodological aims of finding Catholics in the English Atlantic, *A Common Grave* explores a wide array of sources: court records, assembly minutes, governors' correspondence, letters and diaries, missionary reports, account books, parish and episcopal records, marriage and burial registers, wills and probate inventories, newspapers, travel narratives, archaeological findings, material culture, antiquarian local histories. The sources tilt heavily toward the demographic and the institutional rather than the personal and reflective, and I lean on studies of Catholic ritual and domestic life in England during this period to suggest possible forms of accommodation and adaptation for recusants living in remote outposts. The historiography on Catholicism in non-English colonies is useful here as well; the reports of Franciscan, Dominican, and Jesuit missionaries operating in Spanish, French, and Portuguese territories are a particularly rich source of insight into the *colonial* nature of Catholic practice in the Americas. Catholic missionaries in the Iberian and French Caribbean operated under the same conditions of scarcity, endemic racial violence, and stunted institutions as their coreligionists in Protestant colonies despite their favorable political and legal position. Missionaries everywhere in the Atlantic world faced the miseries of death and disease and the affronts of unruly and religiously indifferent parishioners whether they served Catholic or Protestant monarchs.

The paucity of archival sources for the earliest decades also means that I turn to accounts of later-eighteenth- and even (on occasion) early-nineteenth-century religious encounters to capture as fully as possible Catholic sacramental life in the English colonies. Sacramental records exist only for the Jesuit missions in Maryland starting in the 1760s, for example, so we have no reliable numbers for baptisms, marriages, or burials before this time. The extreme demographic and political instability of the sugar islands in the seventeenth century—the heyday of Irish Catholic emigration to the British West Indies—left few archival traces, and not until the establishment of the missionary arm of the Anglican Church (the SPG, or Society for the Propagation of the Gospel in Foreign Parts) in 1701 do we begin to have regular on-the-ground descriptions of religious life in Barbados, Jamaica, and the Leeward Islands. Accounts of enslaved Africans' religious life are almost nonexistent before the emergence in the late eighteen and nineteenth centuries of a transatlantic abolitionist movement that invested heavily in slave narratives as a recruitment tool. There are significant methodological problems with using these sources to illuminate earlier practices, especially in the case of abolitionist-sponsored slave narratives and SPG reports, both of which were deeply mediated by Protestant voices and interests. To study a fugitive faith on the margins of empire, however, one must sometimes venture far afield to entertain as many voices as possible, situated across time and space.

Inevitably, much of the particular geopolitical context that shaped Catholic life in Anglo-America after the Reformation disappears from view in such a broad-brush approach. I have tried to provide some of this context where it seems especially relevant; it is impossible to understand the shifting fortunes of English Catholics in Maryland without reference to the winds of civil war that blew through the colony in the 1640s and 1650s, for example. It is no surprise that the religiopolitical upheavals of the long seventeenth century, from the Civil Wars to the Restoration, the Glorious Revolution of 1688, and the Jacobite uprisings of 1715 and 1745, generated so many of the documents that serve as the spine of the book. Political crises brought colonial Catholics into view and hence have filtered much of our knowledge of this clandestine community. But readers interested in learning how the treacherous political and legal landscape of post-Reformation Britain affected the private and public lives of Anglo-American Catholics in more detail would benefit from looking elsewhere.[23]

At the end of the day, *A Common Grave* is not so much a confessional study of a particular religious community as it is an exploration of the paradigmatic colonial experience of coexistence and reinvention on the ground. Like so many colonial histories, it is a story with no center but many peripheries. In Anglo-American scholarship, the colony of Maryland has long served as the undisputed center of colonial Catholicism, exerting a gravitational pull that has obscured the true geographic, linguistic, and racial complexity of the many Catholic communities of English America. What would a history of Catholicism look like if we decentered Maryland, acknowledged the presence

---

23. Fortunately, there are fine studies of the political history of British and North American Catholicism: see Antoinette Sutto, *Loyal Protestants and Dangerous Papists: Maryland and the Politics of Religion in the English Atlantic, 1630–1690* (Charlottesville, Va., 2015); Pestana, *Protestant Empire;* Helen Kilburn, "Catholics in the Colonies: Nation, Religion, and Race in Seventeenth-Century Maryland" (Ph.D. diss., University of Manchester, 2018); Alan Dures and Francis Young, eds., *English Catholicism, 1558–1642*, 2d ed. (New York, 2022); Peter Lake, "Antipopery: The Structure of a Prejudice," in Richard Cust and Anne Hughes, eds., *Conflict in Early Stuart England: Studies in Religion and Politics, 1603–1642* (London, 1989), 72–106; Walsham, *Church Papists;* John D. Krugler, *English and Catholic: The Lords Baltimore in the Seventeenth Century* (Baltimore, 2004); Curran, *Papist Devils.*

of African, Irish, and Indigenous Catholics alongside white English recusants in the colonies, and—most radically—destabilized the very category of
denominational identity itself and asked how colonial Christians navigated
the porous boundaries of Protestantism and Catholicism as they struggled to
make new lives for themselves in a new land? This book is my attempt to tell
that story.

PART ONE

Finding Catholics in the Early English Atlantic

Introduction

NO ONE KNOWS HOW MANY Catholics lived in the English colonies nor how many traveled through on their way to somewhere else—as missionaries, exiles, sailors, soldiers, servants, or transported felons. Not for lack of trying: colonial census takers made periodic attempts to count the Catholics in their provinces, usually when another "popish plot" was discovered (or maliciously invented), and scholars have followed their paper trail assiduously, peering into the shadows of colonial life to identify those fugitives who might have escaped the bureaucratic gaze. The conclusion of one frustrated census taker, who could find only "a Catholic here and there," has been the refrain of scholars ever since. But locating Catholics was never just a numbers game, then or now. To count Catholics, one has to first figure out how to define them and name them. To go in search of early modern Catholics in the interstices of a Protestant empire is to confront fundamental questions about the nature of faith, of identity, of community. These are questions that the rupturing of Western Christianity by the Reformation forced every individual in the British Isles to confront for themselves and their neighbors. Religious identity—specifically, Protestant identity—became the lodestone around which other identities orbited in early modern England: civic, legal, political, economic, and, in time, imperial and racial. To be a Protestant was to be a loyal subject of the crown, a rights-bearing member of civil society, a free commercial agent, a proud member of an Atlantic empire, and eventually a white person who enjoyed racial privileges denied to enslaved Indigenous and African people. To be a Catholic was to be none of these things or, at best, to be these things only partially and always ambiguously.[1]

Part One explores the shifting demographic, political, cultural, and material terrain of "Catholicness" in post-Reformation England and its overseas dominions. Once the 1559 Act of Uniformity finally established the Church of England on a stable footing after decades of confessional confusion and violence, Catholicism was a proscribed faith whose practice incurred harsh penalties. In keeping with Elizabeth I's determination not to "make windows into men's souls," however, *being* a Catholic was never illegal in England—only *practicing* Catholicism. Conformity in behavior, not orthodoxy in belief, was the goal of the Elizabethan penal code. As long as Christians attended their parish church semiregularly, took communion three times a year, paid their levies, and refrained from attending Catholic services or harboring priests or missionaries, they were by and large left alone by the pursuivants—those who rooted out Nonconformity and heresy on behalf of the courts. The experience of being a proscribed and persecuted minority nonetheless left "lasting scars" on the Catholic community no matter how mild the actual enforcement of the penal laws.[2]

Conformity was not a bright line separating the godly from the reprobate, however, but an ambiguous terrain composed of multiple shades of gray. Contemporaries lined up Catholics on a sliding scale of subversion, ranging from those who publicly renounced the Church of England and its ceremonies (excommunicates) to those who "recused" themselves from attending services at their local church and paid the fines assessed (recusants), to those who did attend their parish church but continued to adhere to the old religion in private (church papists). Only church papists were exempt from the penal laws, though not from informal censure and low-level harassment. Of these three categories, church papists are the most elusive: the term itself, like that of the more generic "papist," was a term of abuse, an insult (rather than an official designation) that circulated largely outside of formal governmental and ecclesiastical circles. Church papists occupied "a kind of confessional limbo," in

1. From the 1763 census commissioned by Bishop Richard Challoner, rpt. in "Ragguaglio dello stato della religione cattolica nelle colonies inglesi d'America [An Account of the Condition of the Catholic Religion in the English Colonies of America]," *Catholic Historical Review*, VI (1921), 517–524 (quotation on 521).

2. Kenneth L. Campbell, *Windows into Men's Souls: Religious Nonconformity in Tudor and Early Stuart England* (New York, 2012), 4; Alexandra Walsham, *Catholic Reformation in Protestant Britain* (Farnham, U.K., 2014), 3.

Alexandra Walsham's words, neither in nor out, though by the early 1600s the phrase was being used (pejoratively) in bureaucratic reports and canon law in belated recognition that the legal term "recusant" was not sufficient to account for all forms of Nonconformity.[3]

Even these categories were not fixed: how, for example, should we label a woman who attended her parish church regularly but also attended the occasional secret mass held by itinerant Jesuits passing through her village? Or the man who baptized his child first in his local church using the rites of the Church of England and again at his home using the Roman form of the liturgy? Individuals might move in and out of these categories of resistance and accommodation over their lifetime, and families often divided up the risks of recusancy by having one member (usually the husband) attend the parish church while the others maintained Catholic devotions at home. What about the "serial converts," those who switched allegiances multiple times within one lifetime—as many as eight times, in the case of Anthony Tyrrell? Or those who denied *any* allegiance to the old Church but were nonetheless suspected of furtive attachment, such as crypto-Catholics, those with the "face of a Protestant and the heart of a papist?" It is not surprising that contemporaries deployed a host of hybrid terms to describe the papists and "suspected papists" in their midst. Thomas Wright's 1596 taxonomy listed *"church Papists, schismatics, half-Catholics, Catholic-like Protestants, external Protestants,* and *external Catholics,"* whereas Isaac Bagrave's 1642 sermon to Parliament warned of the *"equivocators"* and *"hermaphrodite Christians"* lurking in the heart of the capital. Almost every law passed against Catholics in the English colonies was directed at "Papists *and Suspected* Papists," in explicit acknowledgment of the inability to firmly affix religious identity. As hard as it may be for those of us who were trained to see the Reformation as a watershed event to appreciate, it remains the case that most English men and women were probably neither exclusively Protestant nor exclusively Catholic in the first century following Henry VIII's break with Rome but lived an "ambidextrous religious life," in Christopher Haigh's useful phrase.[4]

3. Alexandra Walsham, *Church Papists: Catholicism, Conformity, and Confessional Polemic in Early Modern England* (Woodbridge, U.K., 1999), 3 (quotation), 10, 88.

4. "Serial converts": Holly Crawford Pickett, "Motion Rhetoric in Serial Conversion Narratives: Religion and Change in Early Modern England," in Lowell Gallagher, ed., *Redrawing the Map of Early Modern English Catholicism* (Toronto, 2012), 84–112. As she points out, "One could not easily check both Catholic and Protestant on the imaginary census form of seventeenth-century England" (89). See also Katy Gibbons, "'When He

Thwarted by any easy classification scheme to identify "true" Catholics, historians have taken various approaches to the problem of counting traditional Christians in post-Reformation England. Most accept as a starting point John Bossy's estimate that approximately forty thousand Catholics lived in England in 1603, a figure rising dramatically to sixty thousand by the early 1640s. It is worth noting that English Catholicism was never as robust, both in numbers and public presence, as it was in the very decades that the first colonial enterprises were launched. These are numbers, however, derived from a fairly narrow definition of Catholicism: recusants, or those who demonstrated by their observable behavior their preference for the old faith by refusing to attend the Church of England. More recent efforts have broadened the scope of inquiry to include those who conformed occasionally or who preserved certain elements of Catholic devotional life in private (observing feast and fast days, for example, or burying their loved ones at home using the old rites). A more sympathetic view of accommodation is the starting point for revisionist scholars: as Walsham advises, rather than condemn conformity as "a form of spineless apathy or ethical surrender," we need to view it as "a positive option" for a persecuted people. This more expansive definition of Catholicism captures the woman in the pew who mouthed the words (in English) of the Common Prayer Book while silently fingering her rosary beads in her skirt pocket and reciting (in Latin) the Paternosters and Ave Marias; the man who subscribed to the Oaths of Allegiance and Supremacy while performing an act of "mental reservation" that nullified the obligations of the oath taker to denounce the pope; the householder who paid his tithe regularly and rented a pew in the local parish while allowing his wife and children to stay home

---

Was in France He Was a Papist and When He Was in England . . . He Was a Protestant': Negotiating Religious Identities in the Later Sixteenth Century," in Nadine Lewycky and Adam Morton, eds., *Getting Along? Religious Identities and Confessional Relations in Early Modern England: Essays in Honour of Professor W. J. Sheils* (Farnham, U.K., 2012), 176–177. John D. Krugler, *English and Catholic: The Lords Baltimore in the Seventeenth Century* (Baltimore, 2004), 16–17, is quoting Arthur Wilson's description of George Calvert, the first Lord Baltimore, as a schismatic with "the face of a Protestant and the heart of a Papist" (75). The vagueness of "Papists *and Suspected* Papists" made such acts difficult to enforce and, on at least one occasion, was the ground for annulment by the crown; the 1701 Nevis Act was disallowed because "it is not ascertained by the sd Act who shall be deemed a *reputed Papist*." See Report of Mr. Attorney General on the Acts Passed at Nevis in May and June 1701, CO 152/4, no. 53, TNA. For Christopher Haigh, see his "Church of England, the Catholics, and the People," in Haigh, ed., *The Reign of Elizabeth I* (London, 1984), 195–219 (quotation on 200).

and read from a Catholic missal instead. "Going along to get along" was a time-honored strategy of England's Catholics.[5]

At the risk of gross oversimplification, the most important differences separating Protestants from Catholics after 1559 had to do with the role of the sacraments in soteriology and the incarnational figure of the divine. The fundamental debate over sacraments was not about how many there were (seven for Catholics, two for Protestants) but what they were understood to *mean* and *do:* for Catholics, sacraments offered a direct conduit between the individual and God that was essential for personal salvation. For Protestants, the sacraments of baptism and communion—which they retained from the medieval Church while redefining them in crucial ways—were less instruments of salvation than occasions for prayer and community. The sacraments were essential for salvation to Catholics precisely because the God they worshipped had assumed material form in the world and left material traces of his saving grace behind. These material traces could take many forms—from the relics of bone left by dead saints to the healing power of a holy well or even the mere sight of the consecrated host as it was elevated above the congregation—and it was through seeing, touching, and ingesting these atoms of divinity that humans overcame their own sinful nature. Protestants, on the other hand, while accepting Christ's human nature as the original sacrifice through which the elect were saved, rejected any material vestiges of his incarnation after his death and resurrection as superstition and idolatry. And they rejected, as well, a scheme of salvation that required the faithful to form a ritual and material bond with the incarnated God, insisting that salvation was the unmerited gift of a merciful savior.

At the center of Catholic soteriology stood the figure of the priest: only he had the power to perform the sacraments, to exorcise demons in baptism, to

---

5. John Bossy, *The English Catholic Community, 1570–1850* (London, 1975); Alexandra Walsham, "'Yielding to the Extremity of the Time': Conformity, Orthodoxy, and the Post-Reformation Catholic Community," in Peter Lake and Michael Questier, eds., *Conformity and Orthodoxy in the English Church, c. 1550–1650* (Woodbridge, U.K., 2000), 213; William Sheils, "'Getting On' and 'Getting Along' in Parish and Town: Catholics and Their Neighbours in England," in Benjamin Kaplan et al., *Catholic Communities in Protestant States: Britain and the Netherlands, 1570–1720* (Manchester, U.K., 2009), 67–83. Caroline Hibbard labels the early seventeenth century the "high point of the English Counter-Reformation," a stature that the English Catholic community would not reach again until the mid-nineteenth century. See Hibbard, "Early Stuart Catholicism: Revisions and Re-revisions," *Journal of Modern History*, LII (1980), 2–34 (quotation on 9).

turn the bread and wine into the body and blood of Christ at communion, to forgive sin in penance, to unite men and women in holy matrimony, to bless the dying, and to pray for the souls of the dead. The mass was the central liturgy of Catholic worship, the occasion for the most powerful of all the sacraments (the eucharist), and the place where Catholics came together in the physical presence of the divine to see, touch, and taste him. As Lisa McClain succinctly puts it, "Without a priest, there can be no Mass. Without the Mass, Christ's body is not present. Without Christ's body, there is no saving grace."[6]

This is a far too abbreviated account of the key theological and epistemological differences that divided Protestants and Catholics, but the point is that the crux of what it meant (and means) to be Catholic after the Reformation sits at the intersection of belief and practice. A Catholic is someone who believes God is incarnate in the world, who believes that without access to the sacraments (and hence to a priest) at the pivotal moments of existence—birth, marriage, illness, death—there can be no salvation or reunion with loved ones in the afterlife. After decades of restricted access to priests and the withering of Catholic public sacramental life, these beliefs may have become habitual and residual rather than active and activating among a large segment of "old believers." But they were no less real and consequential for being buried beneath layers of fear and pragmatism. How to access latent beliefs was a dilemma for Catholic writers and missionaries at the time, and it remains a central question of this book.

Recognizing the simple axiom that those who considered themselves Catholics *were* Catholics, however they behaved in public (or in private, for that matter), we are still left with the enormous task of finding such people in the kinds of records generated by early modern metropolitan and imperial bureaucracies: censuses, shipping manifests, local and county court records, parliamentary acts and royal edicts, official correspondence between the metropole and the provinces. The itinerant lifestyle forced upon Catholic priests and the unrootedness of many lay Catholics made it difficult for officials to locate them in time and space. One such unfortunate who was snared in the official net gives us a glimpse into the transient world of Anglo Catholicism: John Russell, arrested for theft and extortion in 1730, "owned himself to be an Irish Roman Catholick, [and] was look'd upon as a Stroller." The peripatetic Russell had moved from town to town in England after a stint in France and

6. Lisa McClain, *Lest We Be Damned: Practical Innovation and Lived Experience among Catholics in Protestant England, 1559–1642* (New York, 2004), 113.

was now in London following the trail of a "Romish Priest" rumored to be in the environs of Chelsea.[7] Ecclesiastical institutional structures are more helpful. Parish registers can tell us who was baptized, married, or buried in the church; churchwardens' accounts and vestry minutes can reveal sacramental practices and identify those who failed to attend or who disrupted services out of a (perhaps latent) preference for the traditional rites; missionary reports yield a wealth of fascinating detail about everyday encounters between the laity and their often testy pastors. But even these records do not exceed the reach of the Church itself or the missionary circuit; they do not penetrate the private recesses of the household, let alone the human heart. The paucity of personal documents for the vast majority of lay Catholics, especially for women and servants, who performed the crucial task of maintaining domestic devotional habits, makes the job of tracking belief nearly impossible.

To add another layer of complexity, post-Reformation Catholicism was a faith well versed in the arts of disguise. This was a practical and legal necessity. Any priest found within the British Isles after 1585 could be arrested and executed as a traitor, and some 130 men of the cloth faced this fate between 1585 and 1646.[8] Those who harbored priests or attended their secret conventicles faced stiff penalties ranging from forfeiture of all possessions to lifetime imprisonment to death. As fears of invasion by the international Catholic powerhouses of Spain and the Holy Roman Empire rose in the late sixteenth and seventeenth centuries, the penal laws became more stifling. In 1571, mere possession of a Catholic sacramental object—a rosary, crucifix, or small medallion such as the Agnus Dei—was prohibited by the penal laws. By 1593, Catholics could not travel more than five miles from their home, a measure enacted in order to restrict their access to itinerant priests, and the fines for nonattendance at one's parish church had reached truly punitive heights—twenty pounds per month, a fortune for most households. Catholic parents could lose custody of their children if they tried to send their sons abroad for education at one of the English Jesuit colleges on the continent (Douai, St. Omer's) or if they remarried outside the faith when widowed. Under these perilous circumstances, it was better to hide one's faith under layers of obfuscation and misdirection than to face penury, prison, or the gallows.

7. "Trial of John Russel," Dec. 4, 1730 (t17301204–25), *Old Bailey Proceedings Online*, www.oldbaileyonline.org.

8. At least 371 seminary priests sent to England in the Tudor era were imprisoned, and 133 were executed (Arnold Pritchard, *Catholic Loyalism in Elizabethan England* [Chapel Hill, N.C., 1979], 8).

Still, for all these challenges, there are ways to get at—obliquely, partially—
the substratum of overt and residual Catholic belief in early modern England
and America. Knowing the arts of deception used by fugitive priests and their
abetting congregations can help us "unmask" Catholics, to use the parlance of
early modern religious controversialists. I'll explore some of the more fruitful
avenues for unmasking below. But a focus on finding individual Catholics can
stunt our understanding of how Catholicism was woven into the material and
cultural fabric of early modern life and—more important—how Catholicism
and Protestantism were fused together in new hybrid forms during the first
two centuries of reform.

This commingling took both ritual and material form, and one of the key
arguments of this book is that material culture offers a vital window into
the hidden world of Anglo-American Catholics. Not only were Catholics
strongly identified with particular objects in popular memory and in law—the
crucifix, saints' relics—but the material edifice of traditional Christianity did
not disappear overnight after the 1534 Act of Supremacy or the 1559 Act of
Uniformity. Even the stunning destruction of England's architectural religious patrimony begun by the iconoclastic boy-king Edward VI and continued at a more measured pace by his sister Elizabeth did not entirely denude
the religious landscape of Catholic material symbols. The towering market
crosses and stained glass windows of England's grand cathedrals might have
been gone by the end of the sixteenth century, but the rosaries, pocket crucifixes, Agnus Dei, psalters, and catechisms that generations of Catholics had
relied on to sustain their faith could be safely squirreled away when a nosy
neighbor showed up or another episcopal visitation was announced. And they
could be packed into trunks and hidden in pockets when recusants migrated
to new lands and set up new homes. How did Catholic sacramentals change
in meaning or power from one place to another, one generation to the next,
as they became objects of sentiment and nostalgia as well as salvific agents?
Did sacred objects lose their efficacy in the process of overseas migration and
colonial adaptation, or did they form new spiritual articulations when they
came face to face with Indigenous and African ritual complexes? What is the
role of memory in the transition from one material regime to another? These
are only some of the questions that a focus on material culture raises for the
study of post-Reform Catholicism.

Starting with basic questions about the number and location of Catholics
in the English colonies, Part One proceeds to explore more complex questions about religious identity, from the arts of deception practiced by colonial recusants to the role of material culture in providing visible markers of

suppressed or hybridized beliefs. My goal is not to make a case for restoring colonial Catholics (white, Indigenous, and Black) to their rightful place as cocreators of English America, though it may seem that way at times; my real aim is to comprehend how religious identity was understood and negotiated on the edges of empire. It's hard not to lapse into a restorationist stance when confronting the numerous ways in which Catholics have been ignored or slighted in accounts of colonial religion, but that is a denominational, not a historical, project. (And one that has been well served by generations of Catholic scholars.) Nor am I in search of an "authentic" Catholic identity that can be revealed only by peeling away the layers of cultural, political, and racial camouflage imposed by a society built on Protestant hegemony and coerced labor. Like any other belief system, Catholicism is what its practitioners make of it. They, not us, decide whether they are really Catholic or not. Putting aside the question of authenticity allows us to see Catholics where they are, not where we expect them to be.

CHAPTER ONE

"A Catholic Here and There"

Accounting for Catholics

W HATEVER uncertainty surrounds the number of professing or practicing Catholics in post-Reformation England is magnified when we turn our attention to the seventeenth-century North American colonies, where censuses were rare, opportunities for concealment abundant in a mobile and widely dispersed population, and governing structures (both of church and state) weak. By the eighteenth century, migration from Europe was more predictable and more regulated, and colonial administrators had a better set of tools at their disposal to count and manage their populations. The first semireliable censuses of colonial Catholics date from the 1690s and early 1700s. But even these censuses are woefully inadequate for estimating the population of Catholics with any degree of confidence. Counting Catholics was not just about finding individuals who preferred not to be found but also about who counted as a Catholic—and who didn't. The two largest groups of colonial Catholics didn't count for most officials, whether they be colonial governors or Anglican commissaries: Irish servants and enslaved Africans. And these two groups don't seem to have counted much for many modern historians either, who systematically underestimate their presence in English America.[1]

European Sojourners

The first Catholics to appear in English colonial accounts were travelers rather than residents: visiting Jesuit missionaries from New France, sailors from rival empires who arrived daily in the bustling port towns or who washed ashore after shipwrecks, transient laborers imported for a season, or dignitaries and

---

1. Scholars of the early English Caribbean are the exception to the rule, and much of what we know about the presence of Irish and African Catholics in colonial communities we owe to the pioneering work of Jenny Shaw, Kristin Block, Natalie A. Zacek, Donald Harmen Atkenson, and Hilary McD. Beckles. See Shaw, *Everyday Life in the Early English*

courtiers passing through on their way to and from New Spain. John Win-throp's friend Edmund Howes reported as early as 1632, "I heare the french have this summer transported a company of priests and Jesuits and such ver-mine to Canada; but how longe they will staye there, it is a question. I con-ceive the land to[o] cold for theire hott natures." These French Jesuits soon traveled south; the future martyr Isaac Jogues recounted a visit he made to the fort in Manhattan in 1647, where, to his surprise, he "saw two images on the mantelpiece,—one, of the blessed Virgin; the other, of our Blessed Louys de Gonzage." The "master of the house told him that his wife was a catholic. She was a Portuguese, brought into that country by I know not what chance; she appeared very modest and bashful." A Huguenot visitor to Boston in the 1680s reported encountering "eight or ten" papists, "three of whom are French and come to our Church, and the others are Irish; with the Exception of the Surgeon who has a Family, the others are here only in Passage."[2]

A variety of continental Catholics were imported into the colonies in a series of impractical schemes to reproduce European microeconomies. Early accounts of Catholics in Virginia note the presence of "Polanders" in 1619 who "were engaged in making tar, pitch, potash, and soap ashes," alongside German glassmakers, Italian wine cultivators, and French silk growers. In the Jerseys, Irish masons and French saltmakers worked alongside English farmers in the early years of settlement. These small microcolonies of Catholic

---

Caribbean: Irish, Africans, and the Construction of Difference (Athens, Ga., 2013); Block, *Or-dinary Lives in the Early Caribbean: Religion, Colonial Competition, and the Politics of Profit* (Athens, Ga., 2012); Zacek, *Settler Society in the English Leeward Islands, 1670–1776* (New York, 2010); Atkenson, *If the Irish Ran the World: Montserrat, 1630–1750* (Montreal, 1997); Beckles, *White Servitude and Black Slavery in Barbados, 1627–1715* (Knoxville, Tenn., 1989). The foundational work for studying the Irish in the West Indies was laid by Aubrey Gwynn nearly a century ago: see Gwynn, "Early Irish Emigration to the West Indies (1612–1643)," *Studies*, XVIII (1929), 377–393; "Early Irish Emigration to the West Indies: Part II," ibid., 648–663; "Cromwell's Policy of Transportation," ibid., XIX (1930), 602–623; "The First Irish Priests in the New World," ibid., XXI (1932), 213–228. For a rare treatment of en-slaved Catholics outside the West Indies, see Helen Kilburn, "Catholics in the Colonies: Nation, Religion, and Race in Seventeenth-Century Maryland" (Ph.D. diss., University of Manchester, 2019).

2. Edward Howes to John Winthrop, Jr., November 1632, in Massachusetts Historical Society, *The Winthrop Papers*, III, *1631–1637* (Boston, 1943), 94; Sebastien Cramoisy and Ga-briel Cramoisy, "Relation of 1647," in Reuben Gold Thwaites, ed., *The Jesuit Relations and Allied Documents: Travels and Explorations of the Jesuit Missionaries in New France, 1610–1791* . . . (Cleveland, Ohio, 1896–1901), XXXI, 99; E. T. Fisher, *Report of a French Protestant Refugee, in Boston, 1687,* trans. Edward Thornton (Brooklyn, N.Y., 1868), 30.

artisans might have caused unease among the English indentured servants and small planters among whom they lived, but if so, we have no record of it. They rarely stayed long enough to leave an imprint. The vines and silkworms planted in North America simply didn't thrive, nor did their cultivators.[3]

However much of a spectacle these visiting Catholics created in the small villages of colonial America, they did not create any lasting threat to Protestant hegemony for the simple reason that they weren't English. Some were even accommodated by their Protestant hosts: when the Jesuit Gabrielle Druillettes visited Plymouth in 1650, he dined at the home of Governor William Bradford on fish, a dish chosen in deference to the dietary restrictions of abstaining Catholics. In Boston, his host "gave me the key of a room in his house where I might in all liberty pray and perform the other exercises of my religion." His fellow Jesuit Jean Pierron opted to visit Boston in 1674 in disguise, fearing persecution in this most Puritan of colonies, but found to his relief that he was greeted hospitably and entertained at the homes of leading ministers. (The General Court was not so welcoming and issued a warrant for Pierron's arrest, at which point he chose caution over valor and fled the province.) Jesuits show up with surprising frequency in the northern colonies during the seventeenth century, a consequence of the thriving Jesuit missions in New France. And even when imperial rivalry flared into outright hostilities, priests were sometimes treated with remarkable leniency. One such example comes from 1613, when a crew of English pirates ransacked the Port Royal settlement in Acadia (now the Maritime Provinces) and carried two Jesuit prisoners back to Virginia. During their voyage, the English captain, Samuel Argall, "extended various courtesies" to the Jesuits, "allowing them to bury their dead, offering the services of an English Catholic doctor, and inviting the captive priests to dine at his table." As Laura Chmielewski explains in her account of this episode of interconfessional exchange, Atlantic travel provided Protestant warriors such as Samuel Argall the opportunity to "encounter their enemies face-to-face." Flesh-and-blood Jesuits were (sometimes) more palatable than the damning stereotypes that circulated widely in popular culture.[4]

3. Martin I. J. Griffin, "Catholics in Colonial Virginia," *Records of the American Catholic Historical Society of Philadelphia*, XXII (1911), 84–100 (quotation on 93) (hereafter cited as *Records*); Robert Emmett Curran, *Papist Devils: Catholics in British America, 1574–1783* (Washington, D.C., 2014), 123.

4. Gabrielle Druillettes, "A Narrative of a Journey to New England, 1650–1651," transcribed and translated by John Gilmary Shea, MS. S–571, Dec. 7/8, 1650, fols. 7–8, Massachusetts Historical Society, Boston; "Account of Jean Pierron," in Thwaites, ed., *Jesuit Relations*, LIX, 73; Laura M. Chmielewski, "Pierre Biard: Priest and Pirate of Mount Desert

Most of the non-English Catholics who passed through English America in the first decades of the seventeenth century did not attract the same attention, and we have only fleeting glimpses of them in the archives. Soldiers and sailors were an especially anonymous lot, their time in port short and their doings of little concern to the residents except when drunk or disorderly. Although the Navigation Acts of the 1650s and 1660s supposedly closed colonial ports to ships from the continent, Spanish, Portuguese, and French ships discharged their motley crews in Boston, New York, and later Philadelphia while awaiting lading for the return trip. John Winthrop noted in his journal that a "French shallop with some 14 men" stayed in Boston for a week in October 1642 and were "kindly entertained" even though they were "papists." The visiting crew "came to our church meeting; and the lieutenant seemed to be much affected to find things as he did, and professed he never saw so good order in any place. One of the elders gave him a French testament with Marlorat's notes [a biblical commentary written by a Huguenot theologian], which he kindly accepted and promised to read it." Two years later, a group of Portuguese sailors was a more disruptive presence in the city, joining a melee between the locals and some French visitors. A night of "pandemonium" broke out in New York City in 1701 when a troop ship of "red-coated soldiery" landed. The ship was filled with Irish recruits, a "parcel of the vilest fellows that ever wore the King's livery, the very scum of the Army in Ireland and several Irish papists among 'em," complained the governor, Lord Bellomont. In every imperial war, the ports swelled with Catholic soldiers and prisoners of war. In New York alone, Governor Clinton freed three hundred to four hundred French prisoners of war in 1748, and some forty-five Spanish prisoners continued to be imprisoned in the city in 1752—this despite the fact that in 1746, seven sloops had been commissioned to carry French and Spanish prisoners from New York to West Indian ports for exchange.[5]

Island," in Mark Meuwese and Jeffrey A. Fortin, eds., *Atlantic Biographies: Individuals and People in the Atlantic World* (Leiden, 2013), 3–29 (quotations on 25, 26). Despite Bradford's view that "Popish fasts" were "wicked and damnable," the governor served fish so his guest would not have to eat meat on Friday (quoted in Thomas H. O'Connor, *Boston Catholics: A History of the Church and Its People* [Boston, 1998], 8).

5. Richard S. Dunn and Laetitia Yeandle, eds., *The Journal of John Winthrop 1630–1649, Abridged Edition* (Cambridge, Mass., 1996), 216, 217; Shona Helen Johnston, "Papists in a Protestant World: The Catholic Anglo-Atlantic in the Seventeenth Century" (Ph.D. diss., Georgetown University, 2011), 60; William Harper Bennett, *Catholic Footsteps in Old New York: A Chronicle of Catholicity in the City of New York from 1524 to 1808* (New York,

Privateering brought foreign crews into port for longer stays, as captured sailors awaited ransom or exchange. On board prize ships were not only Catholic sailors but the clerics who ministered to them: a "big Spanish ship bound from Cadiz to Havana" was brought to New York in the early 1700s, and amid her "rich cargo of wine, oil and fruit" were some sixty passengers, including two "Fryers." A French West India Company ship captured outside Havana and unloaded in New York in 1719 included a Spanish priest and a Dominican chaplain. These prisoners represented a captive audience in more ways than one: the enterprising Anglican commissary in Charleston, Gideon Johnson, distributed copies of a Spanish-language New Testament to sailors taken by privateers in hopes of converting them. "Upon my delivering the Books to them, I asked them, by an Interpreter, what they thought of the doctrine of Transubstantiation." If the sailors responded, Johnson did not record their answer.[6]

Irish Servants

Beginning in the mid-seventeenth century, Irish servants along with political exiles from the Irish Rebellion of 1641 began to be imported into English America, swelling the number of Catholics in the colonies. Unlike transient soldiers, sailors, and visiting missionaries, servants and transported felons came to stay—at least for the seven to fourteen years it took on average to complete their indentures, provided they lived long enough to gain their freedom. There are wildly varying estimates of the number of Irish who came to the colonies before the migration tide of the mid-eighteenth century, but there is consensus that most of them were Catholics rather than Protestants. (This would change after 1740, when scholars estimate that at least two-thirds, possibly four-fifths, of all Irish migrants to the colonies were Protestants.) Contemporaries were in the habit of exaggerating the number of Irish

---

1909), 211 (Bellomont quotation), 306–311. Despite the fact that Catholics were legally barred from serving in the British army and navy, Catholic soldiers were "employed quite widely," including Irish Catholics who tended to serve in garrisons overseas. As early as 1684, Charles II decided to employ "deserving Catholics," and his successors followed suit. See John Miller, "Catholic Officers in the Late Stuart Army," *English Historical Review*, LXXXVIII (1973), 35–53 (quotations on 44–45).

6. Bennett, *Catholic Footsteps in Old New York*, 216–217, 244; Gideon Johnston to SPG Secretary, Jan. 27, 1710/11, in Frank J. Klingberg, ed., *Carolina Chronicle: The Papers of Commissary Gideon Johnston, 1707–1716* (Berkeley, Calif., 1946), 82.

wherever they appeared in the British Isles, fearing hordes of displaced papists (poor, violent, and speaking Gaelic) would swamp their cities and villages. "I understand that you have at this time but very few of your Irish papists of note in Dublin," a Londoner joked with Bishop Henry Jones in 1680, since "they flock over hither in great numbers, and are now about this Citty." A slightly breathless report from the capital announced, "Yesterday morning a private mass-house was suppressed in Black Lion court, St. Giles's, where a number of poor Irish people had assembled for their devotions. . . . It is said, in St. Giles's parish only, there are upwards of 20,000 Papists."[7]

This habit of exaggeration would carry over to the colonies. John Mould testified before the Maryland Provincial Assembly in 1681 that he overheard Henry Johnson report the arrival of "ffourty ffamilys" of Irish papists on the Susquehanna River, a number he feared would soon become "ffourty thousand," all determined "to cutt the Protestants throats." Catholic missionaries to the West Indies routinely described islands populated with tens of thousands of Irish destitute of spiritual solace—three thousand or twenty thousand on St. Christopher in the late 1630s (depending on whether one credits the archbishop of Tuam or Father Matthew O'Hartegan); fifty thousand new migrants *a year* in Barbados, Jamaica, and adjacent islands during Cromwell's Protectorate, according to the papal nuncio to Ireland. The best modern study of Catholic migration places the total number of Irish transported to North America and the Caribbean in the seventeenth century, the "vast majority of whom were Roman Catholic," at thirty thousand to fifty thousand. At either the upper or lower end, this is a substantial number. To put this in perspective,

---

7. Timothy Meagher, "Irish Immigration to Colonial America," in Meagher, *The Columbia Guide to Irish American History* (New York, 2005), 19–41; Roderick Mansell to Henry Jones, Sept. 26, 1680, Bodleian, Carte MSS 39, June 15, 1680, quoted in Gabriel Glickman, "A British Catholic Community? Ethnicity, Identity, and Recusant Politics, 1660–1750," in James E. Kelly and Susan Royal, eds., *Early Modern English Catholicism: Identity, Memory, and Counter-Reformation* (Leiden, 2017), 60–80 (quotation on 72); "Extract of a Letter from Paris, April 10," *Virginia Gazette*, July 9, 1767, 2. After the 1680s, ships from Ulster carrying hundreds of Irish servants began to arrive in the Chesapeake region, a "trickle" that became "a flood" in the eighteenth century when some 70,000–150,000 Irish Presbyterians came to North America (24). Estimates of the total eighteenth-century immigration range from 100,000–250,000, and Meagher concludes, "No more than one-third, and possibly closer to one-fifth, of all Irish immigrants" in the 1700s were Catholics (28). Of course, this still leaves a sizable population of some 20,000–50,000 Irish Catholics migrating to English America in the eighteenth century, at a conservative estimate.

the iconic Puritan migration of 1620–1640—from which all of American history supposedly flowed—numbered at most twenty-five thousand.[8]

Most of these Irish servants went to Barbados and the Leeward Islands (Nevis, Antigua, Montserrat, and St. Christopher, which were known collectively as the Lesser Antilles and grouped administratively until 1671), and together they were home to more Catholics than anywhere else in English America. Montserrat carries the distinction of being the only majority Catholic English province outside of Ireland. Nearly 70 percent of its population hailed from Ireland in the seventeenth century, earning it the nickname "The Emerald Isle of the Caribbean." Because these islands were so close together and—more important—in proximity to French and Spanish islands where priests could move freely, Irish colonists in search of the sacraments could more easily enjoy access to Catholic baptism, the mass, and burial than their coreligionists on the mainland. The Caribbean archipelago was a place where geopolitical and religious borders were porous, always threatening to dissolve under the pressures of illicit trade, privateering, and rebellion. In the Leeward Islands, "Irish priests from the ffrench islands in disguise" could "easily mingle themselves . . . amongst our Sloop Men and pass from Island to Island undiscovered," the governor complained.[9]

Barbados was home to a thriving community of Anglo-Irish Catholics in the seventeenth century and, as the wealthiest and most successful of the sugar colonies until eclipsed by Jamaica in the eighteenth century, attracted the attention of Catholic Church officials eager to serve this neglected population. The Vatican first resolved to send priests to the West Indies in 1638,

8. Deposition of John Mould, May 1681, *Archives of Maryland*, XV, 348; "Irish Priests in the West Indies (1638–1640)," rpt. in Aubrey Gwynne, ed., "Documents Relating to the Irish in the West Indies," *Analecta Hibernica*, no. 4 (October 1932), 190, 193; Johnston, "Papists in a Protestant World," 76, 86. Shaw's estimate of the number of Irish servants transported to English America in the second half of the seventeenth century is a bit lower, in the twenty thousand to forty thousand range (*Everyday Life in the Early English Caribbean*, 195 n. 12). Given the dismal survival rates for indentured servants, this works out to about 13 percent of the white population in the English Caribbean overall and 29 percent in the English Leeward Islands during the mid-seventeenth century; see Heather Miyano Kopelson, *Faithful Bodies: Performing Religion and Race in the Puritan Atlantic* (New York, 2014), 151. As Kopelson notes, these figures are "low, but scholars are not sure to what extent."

9. April Lee Hatfield, *Boundaries of Belonging: English Jamaica and the Spanish Caribbean, 1655–1715* (Philadelphia, 2023); copy of part of a letter sent by Col. Codrington from Saint Christopher to Antigua, Aug. 18, 1701, CO 152/4, no. 42, TNA.

when the archbishop of Tuam, Malachy O'Queely, learned that the Irish Catholics on the islands "have been deprived of all spiritual assistance . . . and that they are vulnerable to the proximate threat of perversion due to the practices of heretical ministers." To assist them, he "sent two priests . . . full of faith and zeal to go with a great number of Catholics to that place." In 1640, there were about three thousand Catholics in the Lesser Antilles, or 10 percent of the total population in the islands. Barbados received its first missionary priest in 1650, and their reports home for the next forty years constitute some of the best evidence we have of the actual practice of Catholicism in English America. The Irish Jesuit John Grace estimated the Catholic population in the Lesser Antilles in 1669 to be twelve thousand, a fourfold increase. A similar population surge occurred in Jamaica, where the five hundred or so Irish servants transported in the 1670s had so multiplied by the 1720s that the frustrated Anglican minister James White believed the "greatest number of my Parishioners" were either "absolute Recusants" or "half-Recusants."[10]

A rare but fascinating glimpse into colonial Catholic life is afforded by a cache of depositions taken on Barbados in 1689, right after James II had been deposed and the Protestant William and Mary of Orange installed on the English throne in a (mostly) bloodless coup. In the three short years when England had an openly Catholic monarch (1685–1688), the island's recusants moved out of the shadows and into the documentary light, bringing a French Jesuit from Martinique to serve them and celebrating mass openly in the homes of the wealthiest Catholic planters. This brief interlude of toleration came to a crashing halt in 1689, and the colony's governor, Colonel

---

10. "Scritture riferite nelle Congregazioni Generali," CCCXCIX (Memoriali del 1638), fol. 257, Archivio della Sacra Congregazione de Propaganda Fide, fol. 84, in Gwynne, ed., "Documents Relating to the Irish in the West Indies," *Analecta Hibernica*, no. 4 (October 1932), 188; Francis J. Osborne, *History of the Catholic Church in Jamaica* (Chicago, 1989), 126; James White to Governor Nicholas Lawes, ca. 1720s, Fulham Papers, XVIII, fols. 186–217. For the initial estimate of three thousand in 1640, see Curran, *Papist Devils*, 80–81. John Grace broke down the Catholic population in the Lesser Antilles: "On the island of Barbados are counted up to eight thousand, and on the other islands, five of which I toured—namely Antigoa, Martinique, Guadeloupe, Saint Christopher, and Saint Eustatius, from three of which the French had expelled the English—a great many live"; see "Letter of Rev. John Grace (July 5, 1669)," in Gwynne, 257. The decision to ship Irish servants to the West Indies was driven, in part, by concerns over the severe racial imbalance in the islands, where enslaved Africans had been imported in ever larger numbers as early as the 1630s. White Irish servants, it was hoped, would provide the racial ballast that would stabilize the social and political order.

Edwyn Stede, moved quickly to arrest the ringleaders of the Catholic faction, Sir Thomas Montgomery and Willoughby Chamberlain. Over the course of Stede's prosecution of Montgomery and Willoughby, dozens of witnesses testified that they attended, or knew of, the masses held in these two men's homes. Nearly fifty men in all were caught in Stede's net (though as many as five hundred reportedly gathered for mass regularly, out of the "thirteen hundred" Catholic residents on the list Montgomery and Chamberlain compiled). Shona Johnston's reconstruction of the social and economic profile of these men reveals the Barbados Catholic community to be cross-class and multiethnic, if a majority poor and Irish. We will return to these documents in later chapters, when we explore the sacramental politics of colonial Catholicism, but their value here is in the snapshot they provide of island Catholics in a moment of time. Prominent planters orchestrated the gatherings, with networks of Irish servants deployed to spread the word about when and where to the wider community. Two Irish men testified that "they did goe to several plantacons to give notice to all persons that were of the Roman Catholique perswasion that there was Mass to be said at the House of Mr. Chamberlain and that all persons should receive good entertainm't that came there." Some people came out of curiosity to hear a Roman mass, but the majority seem to have been recusants who took advantage of the loosening of restrictions on public worship and the presence of a French priest to activate their faith. Montgomery admitted that most of the people who attended mass at his house were "poor Catholiques" who had previously been "compassed by great Severities to dissemble" their true faith.[11]

Though far more modest in size than the massive influx of Irish servants to the West Indies, the growth in Irish servants on the mainland also caused concern in the seventeenth and early eighteenth centuries. In the Chesapeake, one known Irish Catholic (Francis Magnel) was among the very first settlers to set foot in Jamestown. In 1621, the Virginia Company received an offer from Captain William Newce (or Nuce) to transport 1,000 Irish settlers, though only one small consignment of servants reached the colony before Newce died. The following year, a plantation was settled in Virginia by "Mr. Gookin out of Ireland," who "brought with him aboute 50 men upon that

11. Deposition of Edward Bishop, in "A Collection of Papers Relating to Sir Thomas Montgomerie and Willoughby Chamberlayne," Mar. 13, 1689, CO 28/37, no. 7 xlvi, TNA; Deposition of John Rowe, Mar. 18, 1689, ibid., no. 7 li; Deposition of Thomas White, ibid., no. 7 xlix; Montgomerie to Lord Dumbarton, Apr. 17, 1689, ibid., no. 7 lx; Johnston, "Papists in a Protestant World," 54–56.

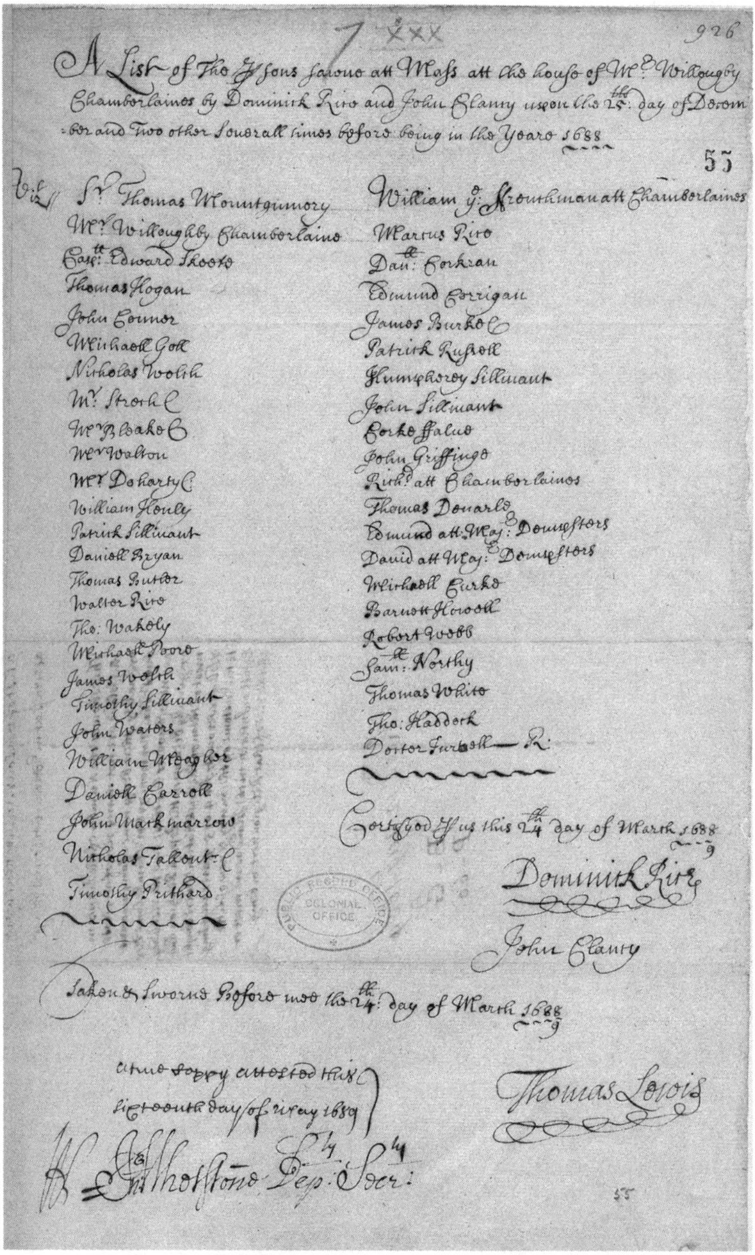

7 xxx 926

A List of The P[er]sons seane att Mass att the house of Mr. Willoughby Chamberlaine by Dominick Rice and John Clancy upon the 25th: day of December and Two other severall times before being in the Yeare 1688

55

Viz Sr. Thomas Mountgumery
Mr. Willoughby Chamberlaine
Capt: Edward Hoote
Thomas Hogan
John Connor
Michaell Goll
Nicholas Welsh
Mr. Strock
Mr. Blake
Mr. Walton
Mr. Doharty
William Honly
Patrick Silliuant
Daniell Bryan
Thomas Butler
Walter Rice
Tho: Waholy
Michaell Poore
James Welsh
Timothy Silliuant
John Waters
William Meagher
Daniell Carroll
John Markmarrow
Nicholas Talbott
Timothy Prithard

William ye Frenchman att Chamberlaines
Marcus Rice
Danll: Corkran
Edmund Corrigan
James Burke
Patrick Russell
Humphrey Silliuant
John Silliuant
Corke Falue
John Griffinge
Richd: att Chamberlaines
Thomas Donarle
Edmund att Majr: Downestors
David att Majr: Downestors
Michaell Burke
Barnett Howell
Robert Webb
Samll: Northy
Thomas White
Tho: Haddock
Doctor Furbell — R:

Certifyed by us this 24th day of March 1688/9

Dominick Rice
John Clancy

Taken & Sworne before mee the 24th: day of March 1688/9

Thomas Lewis

A true Coppy attested this sixteenth day of May 1689
W. Whetstone Dep: Secr:

FIGURE I. "A List of the Persons Sawne at Mass at the House of Mr. Willoughby Chamberlaine," in "A Collection of Papers Relating to Sir Thomas Montgomerie and Willoughby Chamberlayne," Barbados, May 30, 1689, CO 28/37, no. 7 xxx. Courtesy of The National Archives, Kew, U.K.

Adventure, besides some 36 other Passengers." From these early beginnings developed a steady trade in servants from Ireland to the region. Governor Francis Nicholson wrote the Board of Trade in 1698, warning of the "dangerous consequence" attending the arrival in Maryland of several hundred Irish servants, "who are most, if not all, Papists." The Irish, along with their countrymen in Virginia, "might make great desturbances, if not Rebellion: because these are very open Countrys, and they may have easy Communication with one an other."[12] Worse, it was suspected that some priests had been smuggled into the country under the guise of Irish servants. The Anglican clergy of Maryland wrote a letter beseeching the bishop of London to halt the importation of "great Numbers of Irish Papists, . . . many Irish priests being suspected to be coming Incognito amongst us (as having no better place of Refuge in the Kings Dominions) upon their being banished from Ireland." Farther south, the South Carolina Assembly in 1716 was alarmed at the growing importation of "Native Irish servants that are Papists, and persons taken from Newgate and other prisons" and passed a law requiring that all ship captains "shall upon their oaths declare that to the best of their knowledge none of the servants by them imported be either what is commonly called Native Irish, or persons of whom scandalous characters are predominant or Roman Catholics."[13]

12. "Francis Magnel's Relation of the First Voyage and the Beginnings of the James Town Colony," in Philip L. Barbour, ed., *The Jamestown Voyages under the First Charter, 1606–1609: Documents Relating to the Foundation of Jamestown and the History of the James-town Colony* . . . (Cambridge, 1969), I, 151–157; "Company Letter, August 21, 1621, Sent in the Marmaduke," rpt. in Edward D. Neill, ed., *History of the Virginia Company of London: With Letters to and from the First Colony, Never before Printed* (Albany, N.Y., 1869), 285, quoted in Griffin, "Catholics in Colonial Virginia," *Records*, XXII, 90–92; Governor Nicholson to Board of Trade, Aug. 20, 1698, *Archives of Maryland*, XXIII, 498. The Maryland Assembly passed acts in 1699, 1704, 1708, 1716, and again in 1717 providing for increased taxation on "Irish Papist" servants in an effort to stem the tide. In 1706, the assembly considered but rejected a bill preventing Catholics from purchasing Protestant servants (ibid., XXVI, 583, 588–589). The neighboring province of Pennsylvania issued similar warnings: the lieutenant governor vowed in the 1720s to "provide a proper law against these crowds of Foreigners who are yearly powr'd upon us . . . Irish papists and convicts." See Lt. Gov. Patrick Gordon's message to the "Representatives of the Freemen of the Province of Pennsylvania and the Three Lower Counties," Dec. 17, 1728, in Joseph L. J. Kirlin, *Catholicity in Philadelphia: From the Earlier Missionaries down to the Present Time* (Philadelphia, 1909), 28.

13. Clergy of Maryland to Bishop Compton, Annapolis, May 14, 1698, Fulham Papers, II, 100; No. 358: An Act to Encourage the Importation of White Servants into This Province, in Thomas Cooper, ed., *The Statutes at Large of South Carolina* (Columbia, S.C., 1837),

The middle and northern colonies had their share of Irish servants, too. A Catholic courtier, Edmund Plowden, proposed creating an entire colony of Irish Catholics stretching from the Hudson to the Delaware River valley in the 1630s, only to find the Swedes had already occupied the area. One can find scattered references to an Irish "papist" here and there in the more voluminous records of New York, Pennsylvania, the Jerseys, and the New England colonies. A blacksmith, John Cooley, worked at the fort in New York City in 1684 and continued to work there until 1700, despite that fact that he was a "Popish malignant." His fellow Irishman John Fenney labored as a tailor in the city (the governor called him "a Popish tailor in this City and a beggar"). In Massachusetts, a young Irish dog-handler, unnamed, arrived along with "3 woolfe doggs and a bitch" in 1633, bound as a servant for five years to John Winthrop. The Winthrops' London friend, the Reverend Edward Howes, recommended the "boy" as "a verie tractable fellowe" despite his religion. At first, Howes recounted, "he would not goe to church; nor come to prayers," but in time, "we gatt him up to prayers and then on the lords day to catachise, and afterwards very willingly he hath bin at church 4 or 5 tymes." Despite this pressure, the boy clung to elements of his faith: he "as yet makes conscience of fridayes fast from flesh, and doth not love to heare the Romish rel[igion] spoken against, but I hope with gods grace he will become a good convert."[14]

Irish names are strewn throughout the colonial records of seventeenth-century Plymouth and Massachusetts, and we can safely assume that most of these men and women were Catholics of a sort. During the Cromwellian Interregnum, some four hundred Irish servants, mostly women and children, arrived in Boston on the ship *Goodfellow* to be dispersed into Puritan households. Irish "papists" were so numerous in Boston by the early eighteenth century that the governor ordered an investigation into "the number and proceedings of Papists" in the town, which yielded twenty-seven names—all "pretended Ch[urch]men"—though this was a serious undercount, since there were "many Servants, Porters, Carters, etc. whose names at present don't

---

quoted in Richard C. Madden, "Catholics in Colonial South Carolina," *Record*, LXXIII, no. 1/2 (1962), 20. These complaints about Irish servants stem from the period 1689–1715, when the Catholic Lords Baltimore temporarily lost their charter for the colony of Maryland, which was only restored when the fifth baron, Charles Calvert, converted to Anglicanism.

14. Evan Haefeli, *Accidental Pluralism: America and the Religious Politics of English Expansion, 1497–1662* (Chicago, 2021), 187–189; Bennett, *Catholic Footsteps in Old New York*, 196–197; Howes to Winthrop, Aug. 5, 1633, in *Winthrop Papers*, III, 134. Plowden planned to call his colony "New Albion" and to rechristen Manhattan "Syon" in honor of a wealthy medieval abbey (187 n. 3).

occur." Rumors that the town's papists were scheming to celebrate St. Patrick's Day with a mass led by an Irish priest in a private home led to a plan to "set a private Guard nigh said houses and Endeavour to apprehend the whole body of 'em."[15]

But it was the fisheries in Maine and Newfoundland that became the epicenter of Irish Catholic life in the north. Few remember that Lord Baltimore, the renowned Catholic founder of Maryland, had an earlier venture in Newfoundland, where he tried to establish a Catholic colony called Avalon in 1627. The history of Avalon was—to paraphrase Thomas Hobbes—nasty, brutish, and short, and within a decade, few of the original Catholic settlers remained. (The air was "so intolerable cold, as it is hardly to be endured," one colonist grumbled. To which an Anglican retorted, "The Ayre at Newfound Land agrees perfectly well with all God's Creatures except Jesuits and Schismaticks.") Later in the century, the fisheries of Newfoundland were home to a large population of transient Irish workers who came during the summer months and, too often, outstayed their welcome. By the 1720s, English ship captains were complaining about the "great numbers of Irish Roman Catholicks" being brought to the colony every year by less scrupulous competitors; already, there were "nine of these Irish Roman Catholicks for every English man" in the ports. Scores of these seasonal workers made their way south into New England, compounding the problem. "They are of so indolent a disposition that they do not earn enough in the summer to pay their passages back again, so some go away to New England, others remain here all the winter, and are the occasion of most of the disorders that then happen." Most of the disorders of the fisheries, where drink was plentiful and life was hard, were attributed to those Irish who "remain in the winter season to the great prejudice of H.M.'s Protestant subjects who dread the consequences," another ship captain wrote to the Council of Trade. And, in fact, some forty Irishmen employed as day laborers on George's Island in Halifax ("all Roman Catholics") deserted to "the Indian Enemy" in 1751.[16]

15. R. Scott Spurlock, "Catholics in a Puritan Atlantic: The Liminality of Empire's Edge," in Crawford Gribben and Spurlock, eds., *Puritans and Catholics in the Trans-Atlantic World, 1600–1800* (London, 2015), 21–46 (*Goodfellow* on 33); *Boston Town Papers, vols. 1–2, 1637–1733*, Ms.f.Bos.7, II, 306, Boston Public Library. I am grateful to Erik Seeman for providing this reference. A local newspaper reported on March 20, 1732, "We hear that Mass has been performed in town this winter by an Irish priest among some Catholics of his own nation of whom it is not doubted we have a considerable number among us" (*Weekly Rehearsal* [Boston], Mar. 20, 1732, 2).

16. Krugler, *English and Catholic*, 102; Sir David Kirke to Archbishop Laud, Oct. 2, 1639, CO 1/10, no. 40, fol. 119, TNA; Commodore Lord Vere Beauclerk to Mr. Popple, Oxford

Clearly, colonial authorities paid most attention to the Irish servants in their midst when they were worried about internal rebellion and foreign invasion. The notion that the Irish in the English colonies constituted a "fifth column" who could be activated by their Spanish or French Catholic "masters" was a commonplace in the literature of empire. Catholics in general were "intestine enemies," and those who were not English born were doubly suspicious. New Jersey's Governor Morris fretted in 1744 that the "ten or twelve thousand" Irish and German "Papists," mostly indentured servants and redemptioners, in the Jerseys and New York could be mobilized in case of war with France, and hence were "not a little dangerous to these and neighboring colonies." The Quaker founder of Pennsylvania and supposed advocate of religious toleration, William Penn, warned repeatedly of "disguised papists ready to pull off the mask when time serves." These fears were magnified in the sugar islands and, on occasion, became a reality. On St. Christopher, an island that was divided between the French and the English, Irish servants rioted in the 1650s when they were forbidden by their English masters to travel to the French sector to hear mass. In retaliation, the English "kidnapped one hundred and twenty-five Irish Catholics who they estimated to be the most fervent and the most important, put them on a ship that cast them onto the Island of Crabes, 200 leagues distant from Saint-Christophe, and left them in this place where no one lives and which is completely destitute." Surviving only on "a few weeds and some shellfish," the exiles became "so weak that they seemed more like corpses than like living men" and even contemplated cannibalism, according to their spiritual adviser Father John Stritch. Only a handful survived their ordeal and ultimately found refuge on the French island of Tortuga, off the coast of Saint-Domingue.[17]

Forty years later, Irish Catholics rebelled throughout the Lesser Antilles in support of the deposed James II and with the aid of the French. On St. Christopher, "The bloody Papists and Irish assembled suddenly, and declaring themselves for King James, kill, burn, and destroy all that belongs to the Protestant interest," according to Colonel Stede. The Irish did more than

---

in St. John's Harbor, Oct. 14, 1729, ibid., 194/8, fols. 263–276; Capt. Philip Vanbrugh to Council of Trade and Plantations, Chatham, Nov. 6, 1738, ibid., 194/10, fols. 93–104d; *Virginia Gazette*, Aug. 29, 1751. On the history of Avalon, see Luca Codignola, *The Coldest Harbour in the Land: Simon Stock and Lord Baltimore's Colony in Newfoundland, 1621–1649* (Kingston, Ont., 1988).

17. Kirlin, *Catholicity in Philadelphia*, 55; St. Alban Kite, "William Penn and the Catholic Church in America," *Catholic Historical Review*, XIII (1927), 480–496 (quotation on 491).

just use threatening language; one eyewitness testified that "he saw the Irish flying colours, which they called King James's colours, in St. Christopher's, and saw a Frenchman at the head of the Irish." From St. Christopher, the rebellion spread to the neighboring islands, and a report reached London that "the *Irish* Planters and Inhabitants of *Montserrat* had declared for the late King, and appeared in a Body of Seven or Eight hundred Men for that Interest." Montserrat "is in far greater danger than any by reason of the few Protestant Inhabitants in that place, there being twinty Roman Catholicks to one Protestant," an English colonel warned in 1701. "Unless they quickly find out how to stop the progress of the Irish among them, who daily grow thicker, . . . they seem to be disposed, as soon as they'll find an opportunity (I mean the Papists there, who would soon overpower the others) to deliver the Island into the hands of the ffrench, or any of their Popish confederates."[18]

Such moments of high geopolitical drama aside, Irish servants are most visible in the archives when they ran away or were arrested. Scholars have long known about the allure of Spanish Florida to malcontents living on its northern border, at least some of whom were motivated by a desire to live in a Catholic colony. In 1674, four runaways from Carolina fetched up in St. Augustine, where they swore "on the sign of the Cross" that they were Catholics. James Fleming, Thomas Witty, Hugh Jordan, and Charles Miller had all come to Charleston originally from Barbados as servants and, like many other discontented servants (and enslaved Africans), made their way south to La Florida in a bid for freedom. But there was also a thriving, if less visible, escape route for Catholic servants from Virginia into Maryland in the early seventeenth century and even hints that some of this cross-border exchange was done with the willing connivance of planters who recognized the benefits of uniting Catholic servants and masters in one household. William Waters

---

The phrase "intestine enemies" was "a stock epithet for Catholics in the eighteenth century," according to Robert Emmett Curran (Curran, ed., *Intestine Enemies: Catholics in Protestant America, 1605–1791; A Documentary History* [Washington, D.C., 2017], xviii). Stritch (or Destriches) narrated the story of the Irish exiles in "De La Mission Irlandaise," rpt. in Gwynne, ed., "Documents Relating to the Irish in the West Indies," *Analecta Hibernica*, no. 4 (October 1932), 210–212.

18. Deposition of Darby Considine, July 9, 1689, in J. W. Fortescue, ed., *Calendar of State Papers*, Colonial Ser., XIII (London, 1901), 79, 95; "A Full and True Account of the Beseiging and Taking of Carrickfergus by the Duke of Schomberg (1689)," rpt. in Carla Gardina Pestana and Sharon V. Salinger, eds., *The Early English Caribbean, 1500–1700*, 2 vols. (London, 2014), II, 385; Col. Fox to Council of Trade and Plantations, Leeward Islands, July 11, 1701, CO 152/4, no. 37, TNA.

deposed in 1645 that "Mr. Yardley and Mr. Robins Fower servaunts Fugetives of myne Fled From mee at Kicoughtan to St. Maryes in Maryland and one more of myne from Rapohanocke lent by mee to Capt. Fleete Fledd thither since." The Jesuits routinely "redeemed" from Virginia Catholic servants who had "sold themselves into bondage," and some lay planters followed their lead. "Some others have performed the same duty of Charity, buying thence Catholic servants, who are very numerous in that country." In 1671, two Catholic men in St. Mary's County, Maryland, engineered a deal to redeem their brother from servitude in Virginia in exchange for a Protestant servant they purchased in a majority Protestant neighboring county for just this purpose.[19]

By the early 1700s, newspapers had begun to carry ads for runaway servants and slaves. In 1737, the *Virginia Gazette* carried an advertisement to retrieve "a white Irish Servant Man, named John Lee," who had run away; "he is by Trade a Joyner, a short thick well-set Fellow, fresh Colour'd, pitted with the Small Pox, with a Scar in his Forehead, Speaks through the Nose, and has the Brogue in his Speech. . . . He is an Irish Papist." The notice added, "It is suppos'd he was harbor'd by some of the Irish Inhabitants in those Parts." These ads became more frequent over the course of the eighteenth century and recycled the standard negative stereotypes of the Irish as unmanageable and vicious in their habits: "a Servant Girl named Bridget Burk" was described as "a professed Papist" who had "much of the Brogue, of a forward Conduct"; a "Papist Irishman, named Patrick McCue" was "very much given to strong drink, and when in liquor his eyes shine like glass"; a man "pretending to be a Roman Catholick" had an "insinuating, fawning Way of expressing himself and is much addicted to Lying."[20]

The criminal court records, not surprisingly, paint a similarly brutish portrait of Irish servants. Sarah Short and her son Henry testified in the 1660s that they were afraid of Daniel Massilloway, who, "being of Irish bloud," had

19. José Miguel Gallardo, "The Spaniards and the English Settlement in Charlestown," *South Carolina Historical and Genealogical Magazine,* XXXVII (1936), 133, quoted in Madden, "Catholics in Colonial South Carolina," *Records,* LXXIII, no. 1/2 (March/June 1962), 12–13; Susie M. Ames, ed., *County Court Records of Accomack-Northampton, Virginia, 1640–1645* (Charlottesville, Va., 1943), 440; Andrew White, *Relatio itineris in Marylandiam . . . Narrative of a Voyage to Maryland,* ed. E. A. Dalrymple (1634; rpt. Baltimore, 1874), 61; *Archives of Maryland,* V, 103. Another servant had supposedly been "inticed" to abscond by one of Governor Calvert's men.

20. Advertisements: Thomas William Irwin, *Virginia Gazette,* Mar. 11, 1737, 4; John Heed, ibid., Apr. 18, 1751, 3; John Hanna, *Pennsylvania Gazette* (Philadelphia), Dec. 22, 1763, 4; Jechonias Wood, ibid., Aug. 2, 1775, 1.

threatened to "knock [John] Ewens on the head." We don't know for sure that Massilloway was Catholic, but he was absent "on the fast day," a common form of religious noncompliance among Irish Catholics in Anglo-America. On Barbados, Patrick O'Callahan was arrested, whipped, and deported in 1657 for speaking "irreverently and profanely of the Holy Bible and uttering bad expressions of Englishmen." His fellow Irish servant, Cornelius Bryan, had received twenty-one lashes "on the bare backe by the common hangman" the year before for derisively rejecting a tray of meat with the taunt "if there was soe much English Bloud in the Tray as there was meate he would eat it." Thomas Macnemara arrived as a servant to the wealthy Carroll family in Maryland in 1703 and within a year had allegedly seduced Carroll's niece. After boasting that "A Doze of Squill would cleare his Stomach of these Oaths" he had taken declaring his fidelity to crown and church, he went on what one historian calls a "crime spree, committing several rapes, various assaults, buggery, and murder." On trial for manslaughter in 1710, Macnemara fled to England. David "alias Daniel" Sullivan was less fortunate. His body hung in chains in Annapolis after he was executed for the murder of another Irishman; he "died a Roman Catholic." A group of servants, including "a Highland Papist," "an Irish one," a "West Country Convict Woman," and "an Orphan apprentice Girl," all "of the same Communion," plotted to murder a Maryland planter by pledging their oath on "a Bible." The Sunday before the murder, "the Highlander receiv'd the Sacrament at Mass."[21]

Irish servants appear in colonial court records not just as criminals but also as victims. A troubling case of domestic and religious abuse comes to us from the Essex County, Massachusetts, court records, where Joan Sullivan lodged

---

21. *Records and Files of the Quarterly Courts of Essex County, Massachusetts,* 8 vols. (Salem, 1914), IV, 179; Minutes of the Council of Barbados 1654–1658, from the Original in Barbados, Jan. 15, 1655/6, PRO 31/17/43, I, 121, TNA; Edward Lloyd and the Council to the earl of Dartmouth, July 18, 1712, CO 5/720, fol. 116, PRO/LC, unsigned letter from Maryland to unknown, Aug. 13, 1710, CO 5/720, fol. 42, both quoted in Beatriz Betancourt Hardy, "Papists in a Protestant Age: The Catholic Gentry and Community in Colonial Maryland, 1689–1776" (Ph.D. diss., University of Maryland, College Park, 1993), 155–156; *New-York Gazette, or Weekly Post-Boy,* May 6, 1751, [2]; *American Weekly Mercury* (Philadelphia), May 8– May 15, 1746, [2]. See also Hilary McD. Beckles, "A 'Riotous and Unruly Lot': Irish Indentured Servants and Freemen in the English West Indies, 1644–1713," *WMQ,* 3d Ser., XLVII (1990), 503–522 (quotations on 513–514). Shaw notes the eucharistic connotations of Bryan's "calculated insult," situating it in the context of long-standing aspersions on the Catholic doctrine of transubstantiation as a form of cannibalism; see *Everyday Life in the Early English Caribbean,* 143–144.

a series of complaints against her master and mistress, Thomas and Naomi Maule, in 1681. In her petition to the court, she called herself "a poore Irish servant woman, now bound unto Thomas Mawle, who hath bin ever since I lived with him and unto this Tyme a cruell master unto me poore Creature, brought from another country and here destitute of any Friend." Sullivan's accusations that Maule and his wife beat her ("at least 30 or 40 blowes at a Tyme and that some tymes before my cloathes have bin on about me"), forced her to work on the Sabbath, and kicked her out of the house were corroborated by multiple witnesses, though some neighbors stepped forward in defense of the Maules. When a fellow Irish servant, Sarah Linseay, asked Sullivan why she resisted going to the public meeting, she replied, "It was a develish place for thay did not goe to mast [mass] and what shud she doe there for shee was resolved to stay out her time with her master and misteris and then goe whome to her one [own] contry againe wher shee mite go to mast." Sullivan's longing to attend mass in her own country is a poignant reminder of the desolate religious condition of Irish servants marooned in Protestant America.[22]

Most tragic of all is the case of Ann Glover, executed for witchcraft in 1688 after a trial that centered in part on her Catholicism. After badgering from the panel of judges, including the repeated insistence that Glover recite the Lord's Prayer (a common test for witchcraft in Anglo-America), the court was frustrated that they "could receive Answers from her in none but the *Irish*, which was her *Native* Language." The elderly woman "own'd her self a Roman Catholick; and could recite her *Pater Noster* in Latin very readily; but there was one Clause or two alwaies too hard for her whereof she said, *She could not repeat it, if she might have all the world.*" Based on her failure to properly recite the Lord's Prayer in English, and other evidence, Glover was convicted and sentenced to hang. A Jesuit historian argues that Glover balked not at reciting the Lord's Prayer in itself but at adding the final phrase, "For thine is the kingdom, the power and the glory," which only Protestants used.[23]

22. "Records of the Salem Quarterly Court," in George Francis Dow, ed., *Records and Files of the Quarterly Courts of Essex County Massachusetts*, VIII, *1680–1683* (Salem, Mass., 1921), 222–226. There are hints of sexual abuse as well; Sarah Cole "testified that the shoulders of the Irish maid were all black and blue and she [Sullivan] told deponent that it was a great deal worse down lower on her body" (225).

23. Cotton Mather, *Memorable Providences Relating to Witchcrafts and Possessions a Faithful Account of Many Wonderful and Surprising Things That Have Befallen Several Bewitched and Possesed Person in New-England* (Boston, 1689), 6–7, 9; Vincent Lapomarda, S.J., "Catholic in a Puritan Society," *American Benedictine Review*, XL–XLI (1989–1990),

Lord Baltimore's Colony

Only one colony was home to a sizable population of white English Catholics, and it has received the lion's share of attention from scholars of colonial Catholicism: Maryland. Though the colony was founded under the proprietorship of the first Lord Baltimore, George Calvert, who had (re)converted to Catholicism, Maryland's Catholics never comprised a majority of the population, in contrast to Montserrat, which has a far stronger claim to being the birthplace of Catholicism in English North America. But thanks to the efforts of Antoinette Sutto, Michael Graham, Tricia Pyne, Helen Kilburn, and Beatriz Hardy, we have a detailed picture of the shifting demographic and political fortunes of Maryland's Catholic population. At no point did Catholics number more than 15 percent of the total population, though in certain counties (St. Mary's and Charles) they constituted one-third to one-half. Only a handful of the original 140 passengers on the *Ark* and *Dove* who disembarked at Patowmede River in 1634 were Catholics—most were Protestant servants.[24]

Maryland does, however, merit a special place in the history of colonial Catholicism because it was the only English colony that welcomed priests—at least until 1704, when England's penal laws were introduced into the colony following the Glorious Revolution. The colony was served by the Jesuit order, which sent 113 priests and 30 brothers to Maryland between 1634 and 1776;

192–208. Cotton Mather linked another suspected witch to Catholicism when he accused Mercy Short of stealing a book on Catholic devotion from his own library for diabolical purposes; see William H. J. Kennedy, "Catholics in Massachusetts before 1750," *Catholic Historical Review*, XVII (1931), 10–28.

24. Antoinette Sutto, *Loyal Protestants and Dangerous Papists: Maryland and the Politics of Religion in the English Atlantic, 1630–1690* (Charlottesville, Va., 2015); Michael James Graham, "Lord Baltimore's Pious Enterprise: Toleration and Community in Colonial Maryland, 1634–1724" (Ph.D. diss., University of Michigan, 1983); Tricia Terese Pyne, "The Maryland Catholic Community, 1690–1775: A Study in Culture, Religion, and Church" (Ph.D. diss., Catholic University of America, 1995); Kilburn, "Catholics in the Colonies"; Hardy, "Papists in a Protestant Age." Hardy admits that she expected to find two to three hundred Catholics when she began her dissertation research. "I started compiling a list of Catholics. Some six thousand Catholics later . . . " (ii). Michael Graham concludes, "The most that can be said regarding the seventeenth century is that about one in seven of Maryland's population in 1689 was Catholic" ("Meetinghouse and Chapel: Religion and Community in Seventeenth-Century Maryland," in Lois Green Carr, Philip D. Morgan, and Jean B. Russo, eds., *Colonial Chesapeake Society* [Williamsburg, Va., and Chapel Hill, N.C., 1988], 242–274 [quotation on 247]).

even when the Anglican Church was established in the colony after the fifth Lord Baltimore's conversion in 1715, the province hosted more priests than any other English colony. "We have Popish Priests daily flocking in amongst us," one Anglican minister complained in 1724, "and the whole Province smells of Popish Superstition." To the extent that Catholics elsewhere on the North American mainland had access to priests and the sacraments, it was through the efforts of the Maryland Jesuit missions. And like their counterparts in New France, the Maryland Jesuits wrote regular reports back home to the Society of Jesus detailing their efforts to serve the recusant community and convert the local Native peoples.[25]

No congregational records for Catholic churches have survived for the colony, so scholars have turned to other sources to identify and count recusants. Wills and probate inventories are among the most promising for the seventeenth century. Some testators, such as William Smith, who died in 1635, included forthright declarations of faith in their wills: "I profess that I die a member of the Catholick Roman Church out of which there is no salvation," he dictated to the friend who wrote the will for him. The desire to avow one's Catholicism when facing the prospect of death is a recurrent theme in Maryland wills, an assertion of membership in a beloved community or a final gesture of defiance, perhaps. No one outdid Luke Gardiner for a full-throated embrace of his Catholic identity, who specified that he be buried "according to the Ceremonies of the holy Roman Catholique Church . . . in Token that I dye a Roman Catholique and so desire the prayers of the holy Roman catholick Church." Multiple testators left legacies to the Church or to individual priests, especially in the formative years of the Jesuit missions. John Shirtcliffe specified that if his children should die without heirs, his property would "go and descend to the Catholick church towards the reliefe of the Poor and Orphans." Edward Parker of St. Inigoes Manor gave his "good friend" the Jesuit Michael Boston one hogshead of tobacco "in Signe that I dye a true Roman Catholick." Even the poorest of Catholic testators made some provision for the Church; George Manners left "one red Cows Calf" to the Church in 1651. And a handful of testators instructed their overseers, as John Davies did, "to see that my Child or Children to be brought up in the Roman Catholick Church and to see that they are not abused by any Mannor of Person or Persons whatsoever."

25. Tricia T. Pyne, "Ritual and Practice in the Maryland Catholic Community, 1634–1776," *U.S. Catholic Historian*, XXVI, no. 2 (Spring 2008), 17–46; extract of letter of Giles Rainsford to unnamed correspondent, Maryland, Apr. 10, 1724, Fulham Papers, III ("Popish Priests").

Others were adamant that their children *not* be exposed to Catholic super-stition: Thomas Adams insisted in his will that "[as] for the disposal of my Children, I would not have them to live with any papist."[26]

But in many cases, we have to infer religious identity from textual clues. Colonial wills usually included a preamble that was essentially a statement of faith before proceeding to the dispersal of worldly goods. The basic formula was the same for both Protestant and Catholic testators: "I Commit Com-mend and bequeath my Soul into the hands of my Lord and Saviour Jesus Christ. Then I bequeath my body to the Earth whereof it was made to be buried at the Discretion of my Executors." Catholics expanded this formula to include some unique elements. References to the "bitter Death," "Passion," or "precious blood" of Jesus are far more common in Catholic wills, a reflection of the greater emphasis on the incarnated Christ in Catholic soteriology. A typical Catholic preamble can be found in John Davies's 1667 will:

> Being penitent and sorry from the Bottom of my heart for my sins and humbly desireing forgiveness for the same, I give and Commit my soul unto Almighty God my Saviour and Redeemer in whom and by the Meritts of Jesus Christ I trust and believe assured to be saved and to have full remission and forgiveness of all my Sins and that my Soul with my Body at the Generall Resurrection in the last Day shall rise again with Joy and through the Meritts of Christs Death and Passion possess and Inheritt the Kingdom of Heaven, which is Prepared for his Elect and Chosen.

Catholics were more likely to express assurance of their salvation through the "full remission" of sin, a form of spiritual arrogance (in Protestant eyes) made possible through the sacraments of penance and extreme unction. And references to supernatural intercessors appear only in Catholic wills:

---

26. *Maryland Wills*, I, 1 (Smith), 16 (Adams), 32 (Manners), 174 (Shirtcliffe), 276 (Davis), 631–632 (Gardiner), https://www.ancestrylibrary.com/imageviewer/collections/9068/images /007737513_00001?ssrc=&backlabel=Return. Shirtcliffe included a proviso that nullified the clause "in case an Urgent necessity by reason of alteracion or disturbance in Religion should compell them or any of them or their heirs to sell alienate or dispose of their own Proportions." William Cottershall also specified that if his children died before reaching their majority, their share of the estate "shall go and descend to the Roman Catholick Church and to the poor distressed Roman Catholickes equally to be divided between the Church and them" (ibid., 392). For Parker, see ibid., 368; others used the phrase "in Signe" or "in Token" that "I dye a Roman Catholicke" (Charles Maynard, 310; James Lindsey, 433, 1671).

Edward Cotton's 1653 will invoked "the fellowship of all [God's] holy angels and Saints," whereas Peter Bathe hoped "by the Merritts and Passions of our blessed Saviour and by the Intercession of our Blessed Virgin Mary and all the Saints in heaven that my Soul will Enjoy Eternall bliss."[27]

There are other clues in Catholic wills aside from these theological preambles. Names are one good indication: having a son named "Ignatius" (for the Jesuit founder Ignatius Loyola) is an obvious giveaway, and Catholic parents apparently favored the name "Ellinor" for their daughters. (Even the names of livestock can be a clue; Robert Joyner of St. Mary's County left to his daughter Mary two cows, one of whom was named "Shrovetuesday.") No Protestant would begin his will with the phrase "In nomine Dei Patris Amen" as Roger Shehee did in 1674, also leaving a hogshead of tobacco to "my Ghostly father Mr. Foster." Providing legacies for one's godchildren could also be an indication of recusancy. Samuel Goldsmith gave to his "Godson George" a ring and a "peece of plate," whereas John Thimblebee bestowed upon his "God Daughter Mary Brown all my Land and housing that I have." We can't be sure Goldsmith and Thimblebee were Catholic, as Anglicans also appointed godparents for their children when they were baptized, but it seems to have been a uniquely Catholic practice to honor godchildren with specific, and substantial, legacies.[28]

Patching together the evidence from colonial wills thus yields a partial portrait of Maryland's recusant population in the seventeenth century. Certain patterns are just what we would expect, namely the concentration of Catholics in the western shore counties of St. Mary's and Charles and the prominence of Irish surnames among the Catholic testators. The affective ties knitting the recusant community together also come through in these documents, especially that between godparents and godchildren. The strong bond between the lay community and the priests who served them surfaces in the many bequests left to individual Jesuits: "my well beloved friend," "my honored friend," "my good friend." Men and women facing death often entrusted the

27. *Maryland Wills*, I, 46 (Cotton), 124–125 (Bathe), 275 (Thomas Inness). The same wording was used by dozens of testators in the 1660s, 1670s, 1680s, and 1690s. Protestant testators occasionally spoke of the "passion" and "precious blood" of Christ in their wills, such as John Lawson, who directed his executors "if possible at my buriall to have read the buryall form according to the Canon of the Church of England" (ibid., 322). But it is exceedingly rare to find these phrases in non-Catholic wills.

28. Jane Fenwick's 1660 will mentions her son Ignatius (ibid., 118); for this and the bequest of Shrovetuesday, see ibid., I, 543. Graham notes that Eleanor was a common Catholic name ("Lord Baltimore's Pious Enterprise," 380). Shehee: *Maryland Wills*, I, 621–622. Goldsmith: ibid., 442–443. Thimblebee: ibid., 80.

guardianship of their young children to the local priest, the ultimate mark of respect. Priests tended the laity at their most vulnerable and reaped the rewards; in one case, a man who originally left two thousand pounds of tobacco to St. Mary's Church changed his mind and directed that the legacy go to the priest Henry Carew "for his Love to me in the time of my Sickness." There was an element of pragmatism at work here as well as affection, for the political status of the Church was always precarious in colonial Maryland, and individual bequests seemed the safer bet at times. John Londey left a portion of his estate to the Church in his 1693 will but included a clause that, "in Case the Catholicks of Talbot County should be under persecution and restrained from having Liberty of Conscience at my Decease," the bequest would revert to the three priests who served the parish.[29]

Finally, in 1708, we have the first colonywide census of "papists and reputed papists," which yielded 2,974 souls, broken down by county, out of a total colonial population of 33,833 (or around 8–9 percent). Like most such bureaucratic interventions, Governor John Seymour's desire to count Catholics was motivated by fears of insurrection, but his census nonetheless is remarkably thorough. "Observing the Roman Catholiques in this Province were very attentive to the late design's Invasion by the pretended prince of Wales," Seymour wrote to the earl of Sutherland, "I thought it might not be amiss to Inquire the Number of them in the Several Countys that I might compute their ability in case any Misfortune should befall us." Seymour ordered the county sheriffs to "take a List of the said papists names as well Masters of Familys as Inmates Servants and negros baptized in that Religion." The nearly three thousand names on Seymour's lists surely undercounted certain categories of Catholics—especially those who would have been considered "church papists" in England; crypto-Catholics, who kept their faith hidden; and the enslaved, whose religious views were often a total mystery to their owners—but it is the only census from the colonial era that recognized "Servants and negros" as constitutive members of the Catholic community. By the end of the colonial period, a 1763 census commissioned by Richard Challoner, the Catholic bishop of the English Province, found approximately sixteen thousand Catholics in Maryland and another eight thousand on the other side of the disputed border with Pennsylvania.[30]

29. *Maryland Wills*, I, 69, 183, 368, II, 260 (John Londey), 372 (Richard Moy).

30. Seymour to earl of Sutherland, Sept. 6, 1708, Seymour Papers MS 737, Maryland Historical Society, Baltimore; the actual order is in *Archives of Maryland*, XXV, 243. In a 1708 letter to the Lords of Trade, Seymour reported that "they [settlers] were last year computed to be 33,833 Souls, White and Black" in the colony, a figure that Russell Menard

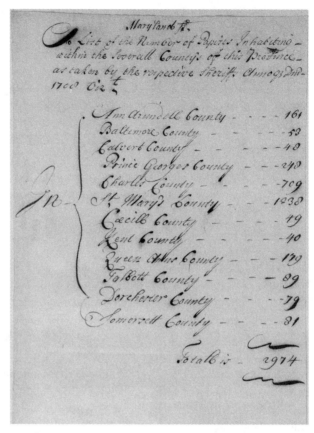

FIGURE 2. "A List of the Number of Papists Inhabiting within
the Severall County's of This Province," in Letter from Seymour
to Earl of Sutherland, Sept. 6, 1708. Courtesy of the Maryland
Center for History and Culture, MS 737: Seymour Papers

Gender and Catholicism

Seymour's 1708 census was one of the few to explicitly include women, white
or Black, in its returns. Colonial counters routinely ignored women, making them harder to spot amid the undifferentiated population of papists and
reputed papists reported by the colonial bureaucracy. The legal fiction that

---

believes represents an undercount of 5,000; Menard's adjusted population total would bring
the percentage of Catholics down from 9 percent to 8 percent. See *Archives of Maryland*,
XXV, 243, 258; and Menard, "Five Maryland Censuses, 1700 to 1712: A Note on the Quality
of the Quantities," *WMQ*, 3d Ser., XXXVII (1980), 623. There were more than 200 Irish

households were run by men who thus stood in for the other members, even to the point of extinguishing civic identity in the case of married women, makes determining the religious leanings of colonial women particularly tricky. Scholars of religion are fortunate that the doctrine of coverture did not extend to religious crimes in early modern Anglo-America: white women were held responsible for their own religious choices and punished on their own account when they transgressed in accordance with general Protestant views of individual agency. As the recusant Thomas Tresham put it when arguing he was not responsible for his wife's transgression, "The husband hath no power over the soul of his wife." But major life transitions such as servitude, marriage, childbirth, and widowhood could alter or undermine women's prior religious allegiances. A woman like Margaret Otis—a Puritan child taken captive as an infant in 1693 in an Indian raid on her town, raised in a French convent and baptized a Catholic, who married and bore two children with her Catholic first husband but (re)converted to Protestantism and remarried when she was "redeemed" from both her captivity and her papistry in 1714— went through multiple changes of faith during her lifetime. Otis's experience of conversion and reconversion was typical of women taken during the Indian wars of the northern and southern frontiers, as Ann Little's biography of perhaps the most famous of these women, Esther Wheelwright, attests. The iconic figure of the "white Indian" that so fascinated Benjamin Franklin and modern historians—an English settler who chose to remain with his or her Native American captors when offered the chance to return home—was almost always a girl or young woman, and conversion to Catholicism was a crucial step in the process of transculturation.[31]

---

servants on Governor Seymour's estate alone, although the census only listed 102 Catholics in total in Baltimore and Cecil Counties (Hardy, "Papists in a Protestant Age," 123). The 1763 census commissioned by Bishop Richard Challoner is reprinted in "Ragguaglio dello stato della religione cattolica nelle colonies inglesi d'America [An Account of the Condition of the Catholic Religion in the English Colonies of America]," *Catholic Historical Review*, VI (1921), 517–524.

31. Memorandum in the hand of Thomas Tresham, titled "Whether the Innocentt Husbande May by Law Be Bound to Pay for His Wyfe's Recusancye," 1601, Tresham Family Correspondence and Papers, II, 1598–1605, Manuscript Collections, 39829, fol. 57, British Library, London; Thomas W. Jodziewicz, "An Unexpected Coda for the Early American Captivity Narrative: A Letter from a Romish Priest," *Catholic Historical Review*, LXXXI (1995), 568–587; Ann M. Little, *The Many Captivities of Esther Wheelwright* (New Haven, Conn., 2016); William Henry Foster, *The Captors' Narrative: Catholic Women and Their Puritan Men on the Early American Frontier* (Ithaca, N.Y., 2003); James Axtell, "The White Indians of Colonial America," *WMQ*, 3d Ser., XXXII (1975), 55–88; Alden T. Vaughan and

But even without such violent disruptions as war and captivity, colonial women's religious identities often reflected their circumstances rather than their choices. Take Eleanor Stephenson: she arrived in Maryland in 1642 as the servant of a Catholic proprietor, Sir Edmund Plowden, and once free, married a known Catholic, William Braithwaite. Does this mean that she, too, was a recusant? She was labeled a Catholic by one historian of early Maryland, but the evidence is "fragmentary and anecdotal at best," Shona Johnston argues. Beyond the bare facts that Stephenson served a Catholic master and a Catholic husband, we know nothing of her personal beliefs or practices. And we know that female servants, especially young ones, were sometimes pressured to convert by overzealous masters: Luke Gardiner was accused in 1654 of detaining "one Elinor Hatton a Young Girle Daughter to the wife of Lieutenant Richard Bancks and Neice to mr Thomas Hatton" for the purpose of "trayn[ing] her up in the Roman Catholick Religion Contrary to the mind and will of her Said Mother and Uncle." When Gardiner refused to return the girl, the Maryland council authorized her forcible removal from his household. Of course, most of the nameless men who labored in Catholic households were also vulnerable to religious misidentification or manipulation, but we have greater access to men's social, economic, and religious lives through their participation in colonial institutions such as the courts and the militia and their presence in legal records such as deeds and wills. The absence of sacramental records for the seventeenth century is especially unfortunate here. For most early modern white women, the only times their names were recorded were when they were baptized, married, or buried. The loss of church records for the colonial South and the islands, combined with the devastatingly high mortality rates and the high incidence of remarriage among those men and women who outlived their spouses, make it difficult to track women's religious careers.[32]

Daniel K. Richter, "Crossing the Cultural Divide: Indians and New Englanders, 1605–1763," *Proceedings of the American Antiquarian Society*, XC (1980), 53–62. Catholic women were routinely jailed for the crime of recusancy in the Elizabethan and Jacobean eras; see Marie B. Rowlands, "Recusant Women, 1560–1640," in Mary Prior, ed., *Women in English Society, 1500–1800* (New York, 1985), 149–180.

32. Annette Laing probes the religious choices of one colonial figure, Elizabeth Ashbridge, who was born an Anglican in England, flirted with Catholicism in Ireland, explored the full spectrum of denominations available in colonial Pennsylvania after migrating as an indentured servant, and finally settled on Quakerism as her spiritual home; in Ashbridge's case, circumstances did not dictate her choices but shaped them in crucial ways (Laing, "'All Things to All Men': Protestant Religious Culture and the Anglican

Culturally, there was a powerful association in post-Reformation England between Catholics and women as subversive agents in the body politic. Constructions of Catholics as "both dangerously strange and intimately familiar— foreign and local" applied to women as well, Frances Dolan points out, as both defied easy categorization. Recusancy in particular was viewed as a woman's crime, as in many Catholic households it was the paterfamilias who conformed so his wife and children could continue to worship in the old ways. Recusant women maintained the households that harbored fugitive priests on their peripatetic journeys, outfitted and prepared the private chapels in homes wealthy enough to support one, instructed their servants in the strategies of disguise necessary to screen the household's Catholicism from prying eyes, catechized their children using the Roman missal, and led private devotions for all the household's dependents when their husbands were away. Because women were so central to the survival of the faith after the Reformation, scholars speak of the "domestication" of Catholicism in the sixteenth and seventeenth centuries. All of this essential labor was done out of sight—behind closed doors. The female servants who did most of the actual labor of maintaining recusant households were doubly burdened, especially if they did not share the faith of the master and mistress. But most gentry Catholic families hired only coreligionists for servants to reduce the risk of exposure.[33]

By all accounts, white colonial households tried to re-create this gendered structure wherever there were enough Catholic women to provide marriage partners for Catholic men and where the demographic conditions favored the formation of stable families. This was not the case in most of English

---

Mission in Colonial Pennsylvania, 1701–1750" [Ph.D. diss., University of California, Riverside, 1995], 56–75). For Stephenson, see Johnston, "Papists in a Protestant Age," 49–50. For Hatton, see *Archives of Maryland*, X, 354–355. It is not coincidental that the case occurred in 1654, when Cromwell's Protectorate had made life difficult for Maryland's Catholic community and raised confessional tensions to a boiling point.

33. Frances E. Dolan, "Gender and the 'Lost' Spaces of Catholicism," *Journal of Interdisciplinary History*, XXXII (2002), 641–665, esp. 643–644; John Bossy, *The English Catholic Community, 1570–1850* (New York, 1976); Rowlands, "Recusant Women, 1560–1640," in Prior, ed., *Women in English Society*, 149–180. Of the 1,155 recusants seized and imprisoned during one sweep of Oxford in 1612, for example, the majority were women. See "Proceedings against Recusants in Oxfordshire, 1612," in Anthony G. Petti, ed., *Recusant Documents from the Ellesmere Manuscripts*, LX (London, 1960), 209. On the pivotal role of recusant women in printing and disseminating clandestine Catholic literature, see Helen Smith, *"Grossly Material Things": Women and Book Production in Early Modern England* (New York, 2012), 162–173.

America for the first century of settlement. On the sugar islands, white recusant families who were swept up in the political deportations of the 1640s
were deliberately separated, according to the priest who ministered to the
Irish on Barbados: "They were sold, especially after it was discovered that they
were Catholics, the husband in one place, the wife in another, and the children in another place so as not to receive any solace from each other." Even
in Maryland, with its steady supply of priests and the protection of a wealthy
proprietor, Catholic families faced unprecedented rates of death and dissolution in the seventeenth century. Every marriage ended by an untimely death
(and the average lifespan of a marriage in the seventeenth-century Chesapeake was only seven years) created an opportunity for apostasy or forced
conversion when new unions were formed. The problem of "mixed marriages"
between Protestants and Catholics was not unique to the North American
colonies, but the notoriously high death rates in the southern and island colonies made these marriages a ubiquitous feature of the religious landscape.
Women were caught in the middle, the object both of orthodox fears and
recusant hopes for sustaining colonial Catholicism in such an unforgiving
environment. Catholic men sometimes used their wills to try to ensure that
their widows would continue to raise their children in the faith even if they
remarried a Protestant. Robert Gates, "Carpenter," included in his 1694 will
his fervent hope that "in case my wife be merried after my decease . . . hee and
shee doue use their utmost care and indevour in bringing up my children in
the Roman Catholick faith I now live in and hope to dye in." Gates, like many
of his peers, made his wife, Dorothy, the sole executor of his will, a sign of his
trust in her fidelity but also a reminder of her new responsibility as the head of
a recusant household. James Langworth also appointed his wife, Agatha, as
his sole executrix but included a clause that "in case my aforesaid wife should
happen either to Dye or Change her Religion . . . or marry any one that was
not a Roman Catholick," Luke Gardiner and Thomas Turloe would take her
place to ensure "that my Children be brought up Roman Catholicks." Richard
Willan likewise named two friends to take over as executors "in case my Wife
dye or should marry an ill husband" out of the same concern.[34]

---

34. Jerome S. Handler, "Father Antoine's Visit to Barbados in 1654," *Journal of the Barbados Museum and Historical Society*, XXXII (1967), 50–76 (quotation on 66); Lois Green Carr
and Lorena Walsh, "The Planter's Wife: The Experience of White Women in Seventeenth-
Century Maryland," *WMQ*, 3d Ser., XXXIV (1977), 542–571; Non-Jesuit Wills, box 25,
folder 8, MPA; *Maryland Wills*, I, 140 (Langworth), 194 (Willan). In recognition of the
unstable religious climate of Baltimore's colony in the 1650s, Langworth made provision

Mixed marriages troubled the clergy, whether Catholic or Protestant. In the Catholic stronghold of St. Mary's County, Maryland, the SPG minister Arthur Holt fought a losing battle in the early eighteenth century against what he perceived as a growing tendency to marry across confessional lines. "Many families amongst us are but half Protestant," he lamented, "the husband of one and the wife of the other Persuasion." Most commonly, this meant a Protestant husband and a "Papist" wife, and the "Women who are Papists and intermarry with Protestant Husbands make it a part of their contract that all their Daughters shall be brought up in the Romish Faith." By means of such demographic manipulation, "the Number of Papists we suppose now to exceed the protestants at least 3 to 1 in this Country." According to one study of wills in colonial Maryland, mixed marriages most often led to the conversion of the Protestant spouse to Catholicism rather than vice versa. The determination of Catholics in such mixed marriages to raise their children in their own faith occasioned bitter domestic disputes that sometimes spilled over into the colonial courts, as the authorities struggled not to lose traction in their ongoing efforts to curtail the "growth of Popery." In 1658, Francis Fitzherbert was cited to appear before the court for threatening Thomas Gerard, a Catholic married to a Protestant, with excommunication because Gerard refused to force his wife and children to come to mass with him. More than a quarter of Catholic testators in the 1660s tried to control their children's faith from beyond the grave: Robert Cole, for one, insisted that his "Children bee brought and taught in the Roman Catholic Religion as they shall [answer to] the Contrary att the dreadful day of Judgement." Luke Gardiner went further, including a clause in his will disinheriting any of his children who "should prove Irreverent and Stubborn and Change his Religion that he be no Roman Catholick."[35]

On balance, mixed marriages contributed to the growth of the Catholic, not the Protestant, population in the colonies and placed women squarely in the center of the Catholic community's fight for survival. Honor Boughton was called before the Maryland courts in the 1690s for defying her Protestant

---

to also remove Gardiner and Turloe as executors if either "should alter his Religion." His final plea was "that my Children may be surely brought up in the Roman Catholick Faith" (ibid., 140–141).

35. Arthur Holt to Rev. Samuel Smith, All Faiths, Saint Mary's County, May 21, 1734, Fulham Papers, III, fols. 174–175; *Archives of Maryland*, XLI, 145 (Fitzherbert and Gerard); Graham, "Lord Baltimore's Pious Enterprise," 91; *Maryland Wills*, I, 186 (Cole), 635 (Gardiner).

husband and the law by raising an orphan placed in the Boughton household in the Roman faith. Real power in these mixed households accrued to Catholic women, some of whom went on to establish female dynasties that endured into the eighteenth century. Henrietta Neale was a figure to be reckoned with in late-seventeenth-century Maryland: the daughter of a wealthy Catholic family, she married Richard Bennett, who was among the richest men in the colony. Bennett, like so many of the Catholic gentry, made Henrietta his executrix, and she inherited the bulk of his estate at his death. She then married another prominent planter—this time a Protestant, Philemon Lloyd, with whom she had ten more children. She raised the two children from her first marriage as Catholics, but she complied with the terms of Lloyd's will and raised their children as Protestants after he died in 1685. Henrietta herself remained a recusant her entire life, and at least one of her two estates— "Henrietta Maria's Discovery" and "Henrietta Maria's Purchase" (named, one might add, for the most famous interconfessional marriage of the era, Charles I's with Henrietta Maria of France)—housed a private chapel for the area's Catholics to gather. The most renowned woman in colonial Maryland, Margaret Brent, never married (there were rumors that she had taken religious vows at one time), but her influence in the colony reached far beyond the recusant household. Appointed by Lord Baltimore as his executrix and legal representative, Brent was in and out of the colonial courts in the 1640s and in 1648 demanded two votes for herself in the assembly: one as Baltimore's representative and one for herself as a landowner. Hailed as America's first suffragette and female lawyer, Brent can be more accurately described as a gentrywoman anchoring the kind of seigneurial Catholicism that had sustained the recusant community in England for a century.[36]

French and German Refugee Communities

High rates of mixed marriage also characterized two groups of European immigrants whose Protestant and Catholic members commingled in dangerous proximity: French Huguenots and German Palatinates. Following the revocation of the Edict of Nantes in 1695, which brutally ended a century of partial toleration in France, Huguenots fled the country by the thousands to

36. Hardy, "Papists in a Protestant Age," 71, 206; Curran, *Papist Devils*, 108. Leonard Calvert's 1644 will designated Brent "my sole Executrix" (*Maryland Wills*, I, 9). Today there is a large crucifix on Route 1 north of Fredericksburg honoring the role of the Brent family in establishing "religious liberty" in Virginia ("The Brent Family," *Virginia Places*, http://www.virginiaplaces.org/religion/brentfamily.html).

avoid massacre, forced conversion, and enslavement. Some forty thousand to fifty thousand found their way to London, from where five thousand to ten thousand took ship for North America and the East and West Indies. Though in many ways the "model" colonists, willing to work at whatever jobs needed doing while allowing England to bleed its chief North American rival of productive artisans, their religious affiliation was always suspect. When Francis LeBaron, a French survivor of shipwreck, landed in Plymouth in 1694, the townspeople didn't know what to make of him. Was he a Huguenot or a Catholic? As a descendant biography put it, "He could not speak English, the people about him could not speak French, but Dr. John Cotton, the minister of the town, talked with him in Latin, and became interested in him." At his death in 1704, he was buried with "a cross upon his breast." This might seem irrefutable proof that he was, in his heart of hearts, a Catholic, but he was probably one of those ambidextrous Christians described by Christopher Haigh. We know that Huguenot children were sometimes taken away from their parents and forcibly raised as Catholics, which might have been the case for LeBaron.[37]

After 1695, there were concerted efforts by the Protestant International to help the Huguenot exiles find new homes. In the Leeward Islands, Huguenots were welcomed, provided that "upon examination it shall be judged that the said person is what he pretends to be, and not a spy, or disguised papist," as the Antigua Act of 1702 put it. The concern that papists were infiltrating the colonies disguised as Huguenots was widespread. A general survey of St. Christopher in 1722 complained about "some pretended French Refugees, who (as pretended Sufferers for their Religion) lay Claim to several Thousand Acres" on the island. These sham Huguenots were "sometimes Protestants, and sometimes Papists; changing always their Religion, or rather the Profession thereof . . . as they found the same suit best." Thomas Hassel's report to the SPG in 1724 claimed there were "two or three 'Papists'" among the Huguenots who had settled in large numbers on the Santee River in South Carolina, "deserters from Louisiana."[38]

37. Owen Stanwood, *The Global Refuge: Huguenots in an Age of Empire* (New York, 2020); Martha H. Le Baron Goddard, "The Le Baron Family," *New England Historical and Genealogical Register*, XXV (1871), 180.

38. R. M., S. B., *A General Survey of That Part of the Island of St. Christophers* . . . (London, 1722), 24–25, quoted in Natalie A. Zacek, *Settler Society in the English Leeward Islands, 1670–1776* (New York, 2010), 165–166; David Duncan Wallace, *The History of South Carolina*, I (New York, 1934), 427, quoted in Madden, "Catholics in Colonial South Carolina," *Records*, LXXIII, no. 1/2 (March/June 1962), 22.

German emigrants posed similar problems of religious classification. In 1709, as many as thirty thousand Germans left their home in the Palatinate, about one-tenth of whom reached North America in 1710. Like their Huguenot counterparts, most of the German migrants went to Britain first, where they adopted the label "poor Palatines" and petitioned for aid as "the Poor Distressed Palatines," although nearly one-third were, in fact, Catholic. Unease quickly spread through London about the number of Catholics mixed in with the majority Protestant exiles, forcing their defenders (among them Daniel Defoe) to downplay just how "Catholic" they were: "They are far from being either Frenchifi'd or Spanioliz'd Papists, for most of them having been Protestants, or the Children of Protestants, they still retain a Tincture of their Father's Religion, which they had not forsaken, but to avoid Persecution and Contempt." The first German migrants arrived in the port town of New York and were sent en masse into the interior of the colony to work as indentured servants on one of the larger Hudson River valley manors. The resident SPG minister for the area, John Frederic Haeger, informed his employers in October 1710, "I instructed fifty-two in the fundamentals of our religion according to the Church Catechism; among them were thirteen Papists." Four years later, he reported with satisfaction that his German communicants now numbered 380, of whom only one family was still "Papist"— a dubious, and self-serving, claim. More likely the remaining "Papists" had simply melted into the community, known only to themselves and perhaps to their neighbors, but not to the SPG missionary trying to bring them into the Anglican fold.[39]

Over the next decades, the usual complaints about "great numbers" of foreigners invading the English provinces were lobbed at the Palatinates, "many of whom" were rumored to be "concealed Papists." The German Pietist preacher Henry Muhlenberg heard such rumors in Pennsylvania in the 1750s, lamenting that "a false saying has been circulating among the English to the effect that the Lutherans are secret papists." The Anglican clergy of Maryland held a special meeting in 1753 to discuss the worrisome influx of new German migrants. "These People chuse to live in a Body, care not to

39. "Queens Order, June 16, 1709," in *The State of the Palatines for the Fifty Years Past to This Present Time* . . . (London, 1710), 8–9, quoted in Philip Otterness, "The 1709 Palatine Migration and the Formation of German Immigrant Identity in London and New York," *Pennsylvania History*, LXVI (1999), 8–23 (quotation on 13); Daniel Defoe, *A Brief History of the Poor Palatine Refugees, Lately Arrived in England* (London, 1709), 18, quoted in Otterness, 15; Bennett, *Catholic Footsteps in Old New York*, 228, 232.

intermarry with or live among us, and settling in the Back Woods may from the Principles of their supposed Religion be induced to join the French in Case of a War," they warned. Putting aside the by-now-formulaic rhetoric of a Catholic fifth column hiding behind the facade of Protestantism, the insular nature of the German diaspora—who did tend to settle in discrete communities—made the task of discerning Catholics all the more difficult. By the 1750s, moreover, many of the original Palatinate migrants had married across confessional lines, forcing their ministers to confront the reality of religiously mixed families. When Israel Heinzelman's mother Margreth remarried "a certain Anthony Fricker of the Romish perswasion" after the death of his father, his uncle was worried that Israel's now-Catholic mother would try to "breed him up in the principles of the Church of Rom" and asked the courts to intervene and provide him "a Guardian of the same Religion as his said late Father."[40]

The tendency of French Huguenots and German Palatinates to marry outside the faith only enhanced the threat they posed to English Protestant hegemony in North America. The threat was both demographic and bureaucratic: mixed marriages increased the odds of a new generation of Catholics hiding in plain sight within these ethnic enclaves as they grew and prospered, while making it more difficult for colonial officials to sort their inhabitants into recognizable denominational categories.

Enslaved Catholics

No group of Catholics was more "foreign" in English America than the enslaved Africans transported to the mainland and the sugar islands in the seventeenth and eighteenth centuries. Some of these enslaved Catholics came from the Kongo, which had been a Catholic kingdom since the late fifteenth century, but most came from Spanish, Portuguese, and French territories either directly to English colonial markets or via a preliminary stay in the multinational, multilingual West Indies. The religious lives of the enslaved are concealed by layers of obfuscation, misunderstanding, and willful ignorance erected by colonial slaveowners as a barrier to acknowledging the humanity of the men, women, and children they held in bondage. To admit Africans

---

40. Theodore G. Tappert and John W. Doberstein, trans., *The Journals of Henry Melchior Muhlenberg*, I (Philadelphia, 1942), 360, 509; "Proceedings of the Parochial Clergy," *Maryland Historical Magazine*, III (1908), 376.

into the family of God was to invite a disturbing spiritual intimacy; as one slaveholding Carolina woman said plaintively, "Is it Possible that any of my slaves could go to Heaven, and must I see them there?"[41]

The earliest settlers spilled little ink describing African spiritual traditions and customs and even less energy trying to convert them to Protestant Christianity. Why would they, when founding charters such as the 1682 Fundamental Constitution of South Carolina gave every white settler "absolute power and authority over Negro slaves of what opinion or Religion whatever?" The short and dismissive answers submitted by SPG missionaries to the bishop of London's 1724 questionnaire about their congregations bear eloquent testimony to the supreme disregard for the spiritual lives of enslaved Africans in the sugar islands, where most resided. The minister of St. Michael's Church, Barbados, reported there were "about 10,000 Negroes of wch above 9000 are Infidels" in his parish. "And no means are used for their conversion." In St. Philip, "The Negroes in general are Infidels, of whom there are about 10,000 in this Parish and no means us'd for their instruction." On Jamaica, in Westmoreland Parish, "There is a vast swarm of unbaptiz'd Negros, Mulattos, Indians, etc.; and as to their Conversion, they are so strictly kept to Labour, that their Time is intirely spent that way." In the neighboring parish of St. Ann's, "Three thousand Negroe Slaves unhappy not only in being at present Infidels but in all probability doomed so to continue." And so on, in a monotonous catalogue of ecclesiastical apathy. As one Anglican in Jamaica wrote frankly in 1728, even if there were interest in baptizing some of the 100,000 slaves on the island, most chapels could accommodate only 200 congregants at any time. "And even supposing they were spacious enough, . . . the Stench would be so intolerable as not to be bor[n]e either by the Minister or the white Congregation."[42]

41. Francis Le Jau to Secretary, Sept. 18, 1711, in Frank J. Klingberg, ed., *The Carolina Chronicle of Dr. Francis Le Jau, 1706–1717* (Berkeley, Calif., 1956), 102.

42. Jon Sensbach, "Slaves to Intolerance: African American Christianity and Religious Freedom in Early America," in Chris Beneke and Christopher S. Grenda, eds., *The First Prejudice: Religious Tolerance and Intolerance in Early America* (Philadelphia, 2011), 195–217 (quotation on 204–205); answers to queries addressed to the clergy, Barbados, 1724, Fulham Papers, XVI, no. 206 (St. Michael's), 209 (St. Philip); answers to queries to the clergy, Jamaica, 1724, ibid., XVII, nos. 211–214 (Westmoreland), 226 (Saint Ann's). On the Anglican Church's deeply ambivalent relationship to the institution of slavery, see Travis Glasson, *Mastering Christianity: Missionary Anglicanism and Slavery in the Atlantic World* (New York, 2012); and Katharine Gerbner, *Christian Slavery: Conversion and Race in the Protestant Atlantic World* (Philadelphia, 2018).

In the face of this malignant archival silence, identifying the "opinion or Religion" of the enslaved has proved to be a Herculean task. There has been greater scholarly interest in the fate of Muslim slaves in English America than in the fate of Catholic ones, and we now have reasonably reliable estimates of the percentage of enslaved Africans who came to North America from Islamic regions, who might or might not have practiced the faith of their fathers in the New World. In all likelihood, the percentage of enslaved Africans in English America who were Catholics (or, to be more precise, had been baptized at the hands of Catholic slaveowners and missionaries) exceeded those who identified as Muslim by a considerable margin in the seventeenth century. The Catholic imperial powers of Spain and France made it a priority to baptize those they enslaved as a matter of course, as the first step toward incorporating them into the colonial religious regime. In contrast to the Dutch and English empires, in New Spain and Brazil baptism was the first, not the final, step in a process of religious indoctrination that would turn alienated outsiders into obedient workers by offering them circumscribed membership in the body of Christ. The baptism of slaves upon arrival had been a royal mandate in Spanish and Portuguese America since the sixteenth century. The Code Noir of 1685, which governed French imperial policy, also required the baptism of all slaves and guaranteed their right to participate in the sacramental life of the communities in which they lived and labored (a right more often honored in the breach, but an important legal marker nonetheless). In the words of Sherwin K. Bryant, slaves entering the Iberian colonial world were "baptized, grafted onto the body of Christ, and dispersed into the realm for sale. This act of spiritual redemption completed their enclosure within the realm."[43]

---

43. G. [Marquis] Duquesne to [Henry] Newman, Jamaica, May 15, 1728, Fulham Papers, XVII, fols. 248–257. Although estimates fluctuate, the consensus seems to be that between 10 and 20 percent of all enslaved Africans in North America were Muslims or came from those regions of Africa most heavily influenced by Islam; however, the lower figure seems more plausible. See Michael A. Gomez, *Black Crescent: The Experience and Legacy of African Muslims in the Americas* (New York, 2005); Sylviane Diouf, *Servants of Allah: African Muslims Enslaved in the Americas* (New York, 2013). On baptism of slaves in Iberian America, see Sherwin K. Bryant, *Rivers of Gold, Lives of Bondage: Governing through Slavery in Colonial Quito* (Chapel Hill, N.C., 2014) (quotation on 81–82); April Lee Hatfield, *Boundaries of Belonging: English Jamaica and the Spanish Caribbean, 1655–1715* (Philadelphia, 2023); Linda Newson and Susie Minchin, *From Capture to Sale: The Portuguese Slave Trade to Spanish South America in the Early Seventeenth Century* (Leiden, 2007); Herman L. Bennett, *Africans in Colonial Mexico: Absolutism, Christianity, and Afro-Creole Consciousness*

Since most of the enslaved Africans sold in English America during the seventeenth century came, not from Africa itself but through the intercoastal trade linking New Spain, the West Indies, and mainland North America, we can intuit that many, if not all, had some exposure to Catholicism before they ever arrived in English colonial ports. Not until the early eighteenth century would the Atlantic slave trade tilt decisively toward direct importation from Africa into North America thanks to the revocation of the Royal Africa Company's monopoly and the opening up of the trade to private traders. Africans thus appear in the early colonial records under a variety of Iberian names and European ethnonyms, such as "Spanish Negroes" or "ffrench Mallattoes," an indication of their mixed racial as well as religious background. Heather Miyano Kopelson traces the complicated family history of one such woman in mid-seventeenth-century Bermuda, Lucretia, whose daughters and granddaughters continued to carry Iberian names into the next generations. There were still individuals identified as "Spanish Negroes" in colonial port cities as late as the mid-eighteenth century: a man who ran away in Pennsylvania was described as "a Spanish Negro Man, named Mona of about 28 or 30 Years of Age," who spoke "broken English" and "had some Money, suppos'd to be given him by the Papist Priest." And "Spanish Negroes" figured prominently in the 1741 slave "conspiracy" in New York City that led to the brutal deaths of thirty to forty Africans and one supposed Catholic priest. One of the executed, a "Spanish negro" named Juan, "prayed in Spanish" and "kissed a crucifix" as he went to his death.[44]

Anglican ministers who served in southern colonies were most likely to take notice of the Spanish and Portuguese "Negroes" in their midst. No

---

(Bloomington, Ind., 2003); Joan C. Bristol, *Christians, Blasphemers, and Witches: Afro-Mexican Ritual Practice in the Seventeenth Century* (Albuquerque, N.M., 2007). On the Code Noir, see Brett Rushforth, *Bonds of Alliance: Indigenous and Atlantic Slaveries in New France* (Williamsburg, Va., and Chapel Hill, N.C., 2014), 122–132. Sue Peabody points out the centrality of Catholicism in the preamble and first fourteen articles of the Code Noir in "'A Dangerous Zeal': Catholic Missions to Slaves in the French Antilles, 1635–1800," *French Historical Studies*, XXV (2002), 70–71.

44. Col. Stede to Lordship, Barbados, July 16, 1689, CO 28/37, no. 16 ("ffrench Mallattoes"), TNA; Heather Miyano Kopelson, "'One Indian and a Negroe, the First These Ilands Ever Had': Imagining the Archive in Early Bermuda," *Early American Studies*, XI (2013), 272–313; *Pennsylvania Gazette*, Sept. 4, 1746, 4; Daniel Horsmanden, *The New-York Conspiracy; or, A History of the Negro Plot, with the Journal of the Proceedings against the Conspirators at New-York in the Years 1741–2*, 2d ed. (1744; rpt. New York, 1810), 320; *Pennsylvania Gazette*, Aug. 20, 1741.

missionary was more attentive to the spiritual lives of the enslaved Africans and Natives who labored in his parish than the former Huguenot Francis Le Jau. After spending eighteen months in the sugar islands, in 1706 Le Jau assumed his post in South Carolina, where he labored for the next eleven years. An astute observer of Native languages and customs, Le Jau is one of the few missionaries who was more interested in converting the Indigenous and Black "infidels" in the colony than the white parishioners he was sent to serve. He noted in 1710 that in his parish were "a few Negroe Slaves who were born and baptised among the Portuguese." Although they spoke "very good English" and expressed "a great desire to receive the H. Communion amongst us," Le Jau insisted on their "Abjuring the Errors of the Romish Church" before he could allow them to participate in the sacrament. Another of his parishioners had been "bred in Guadalupe," and he had similar hopes of her "abjuration." Living among these enslaved Africans were several Native Americans who had been "baptised by Spanish priests, and have Christian Names" and a group of "Apalachi Slaves" whom "Indian Traders" told him "were baptised;" indeed, "some Indians themselves have told me so." Scattered among these Native and African Catholics were a handful of white "papists" who occasionally found their way to Le Jau's church. In February 1709, "two Strangers that were papists came to our Church and another who is reputed also a papist and has been long settled here" joined them. So within this one Carolina parish could be found Native, African, and white Catholics worshipping together in the early 1700s.[45]

Since three-quarters of the 22,000 Africans who arrived in South Carolina between 1716 and 1746 came from Angola (which included the kingdom of Kongo), Le Jau's parish was surely not the only one in which African Catholics were present in significant numbers. There is clear evidence that the Stono Rebellion of 1739 was a revolt wrapped in Catholic ritual and symbolism. One contemporary account noted that, in Angola, where most of the enslaved came from, "Thousands of the Negroes there profess the Roman Catholic Religion." The date chosen for the uprising had special meaning for African

45. Klingberg, ed., *Carolina Chronicle of Dr. Francis Le Jau*, 57, 69, 73, 133; Le Jau to Secretary, Goose Creek, Feb. 18, 1708/9, SPG Letters "A" Series, 1702–1737, IV, fol. 96, *British Online Archives*, https://britishonlinearchives.com. A "significant number" of the enslaved in South Carolina during its earliest years had "an explicit affiliation with Catholic Christianity," Ras Michael Brown notes, and carried "Iberian names" (Brown, "The Immersion of Catholic Christianity in Kalunga," *Journal of Africana Religions*, II [2014], 246–255 [quotation on 252]).

Catholics: September 8 was the day of the Nativity of the Virgin Mary. The insurgents armed themselves with white cloth in remembrance of a fifteenth-century victory over a rival (non-Christian) tribe in the Kongo, which had been inspired by a vision "of a lady in white whose dazzling splendour blinded the enemy." That the rebels were headed to St. Augustine, where they hoped to find sanctuary in New Spain, also suggests an awareness of Catholic networks among the enslaved.[46]

In the early 1700s, the border wars between the Carolinas and La Florida (New Spain's northernmost colony), in which Spanish mission towns were targeted and destroyed, brought thousands of baptized Native peoples into the southern English colonies.[47] The proportion of Indigenous slaves among the entire enslaved population of Carolina peaked at around 30 percent, "almost all of whom were acquainted with Catholic Christianity in some form or another from their lives in the Spanish missions."[48] In the sugar islands, piracy and the English conquest of formerly French and Spanish islands (St. Christopher, Montserrat, Jamaica) transferred thousands of Africans from Catholic to Protestant households overnight. In one year alone (1671), the infamous pirate Henry Morgan sold to Jamaica planters five hundred to six hundred enslaved Africans whom he had captured in raids on Panama. The superior general of the Jesuit mission to the French West Indies described

46. Annette Laing, "'Heathens and Infidels'? African Christianization and Anglicanism in the South Carolina Low Country, 1700–1750," *Religion and American Culture*, XII (2002), 197–228, esp. 208; Allen Daniel Candler, ed., *The Colonial Records of the State of Georgia*, XXII, part 2 (Atlanta, 1904), 233 ("Thousands"); Mark M. Smith, "Remembering Mary, Shaping Revolt: Reconsidering the Stono Rebellion," *Journal of Southern History*, LXVII (2001), 513–534 ("lady in white," 530). John Thornton estimates that most of the Angolans enslaved in 1710 to 1740 came from the Kongo (Thornton, "African Dimensions of the Stono Rebellion," *American Historical Review*, XCVI [1991], 1101–1113).

47. Jon F. Sensbach, "Religion and the Early South in an Age of Atlantic Empire," *Journal of Southern History*, LXXIII (2007), 631–642. For a firsthand account of these raids, see *An Account of What the Army Did, under the Command of Col. Moore . . .* , in Bartholomew Rivers Carroll, *Historical Collections of South Carolina . . .* (New York, 1836).

48. Brown, "Immersion of Catholic Christianity in Kalunga," *Journal of Africana Religions*, II (2014), 252. As Edward E. Curtis and Sylvester A. Johnson point out, "Although most Africans under Atlantic slavery were not converted to Christianity, those who did convert were overwhelmingly affiliated with Catholicism. This means it is not Protestantism but Catholicism that constituted the majority of Black Christian experience in the Americas, a pattern that still holds true today" (Curtis and Johnson, "Black Catholicism," ibid., 245).

how the "conquest of Saint-Christophe, where I found myself twenty years ago [1690], took away six thousand blacks, all Catholics, who by this conquest became the slaves of the English." The steady exodus of enslaved Catholics from the English Caribbean to Spanish and French islands in search of religious asylum in the late seventeenth century was a constant vexation for colonial officials. Ignacio Hernandes helped lead a party of twelve escapees from Jamaica to Cuba in 1667 so that he could "be a Christian Catholic" once again, and in the 1690s twenty-one "negroes" fled Antigua to Guadeloupe, where they were welcomed by the French governor because they had been "baptised and received into the Roman Catholic Church" before being seized by the English. Thousands more, of course, remained on Protestant islands in a state of spiritual and physical subjugation.[49]

It was not lost on the English that the thousands of African and Indigenous people flooding into their parishes from La Florida and the West Indies were nominal Catholics. Anglo-American Protestants were well aware that their own, anemic efforts to Christianize the enslaved fell far short of the standard set by their Spanish and French counterparts. The Reverend William May was defensive about his lack of progress in baptizing Africans on Jamaica, acknowledging that he knew "the French and Spaniards did always Baptize New Negroes as soon as they were brought from Guinea." But, he argued in self-justification, he was determined to "never Baptize any Adults but such as cou'd answer for themselves." The governor of Barbados admitted to the bishop of London that, although "the Ministers of our Parish don't convert their own Proper Negroes nor Christen the Children of their own slaves born in their own houses," the "French, Spaniard, and Portuguese do convert, and Christen all the slaves they have." There is even scattered evidence that enslaved Africans occasionally worshipped alongside white recusants in the islands. Jenny Shaw points out that, although the depositions gathered in 1689 to document illegal Catholic masses taking place on Barbados did not identify any "Portuguese Negroes" among the fifty or so English and Irish recusants present, the minutes of the Barbados Council for that year include a reference to three Africans who "doe openly profess themselves Roman

49. Hatfield, *Boundaries of Belonging*, 90, 98, 102; [Guillaume Moreau?], "Mémoires concernant la mission des pères de la compagnie de Jésus dans les isles françoises de l'Amérique," rpt. in *Annales de la Société d'histoire de la Martinique*, XXVII (1988–1991), 74–75; Peabody, "'A Dangerous Zeal,'" *French Historical Studies*, XXV (2002), 53.

Catholick" and had been "in the time of the Jesuits . . . often seen at Mass." The council ordered the Africans to be "sold or transported and sent of[f] this Island."[50]

We have no reliable figures for how many enslaved Africans who were Catholic by birth, forced baptism, or conversion lived in the English colonies in the seventeenth and early eighteenth centuries. But we have a much clearer picture of the enslaved who labored on the Jesuit plantations in Maryland and came under the Catholic Church's sacramental authority. The Jesuit engagement with slaveholding began almost as soon as the first tobacco fields were planted, and that legacy today continues to bedevil the institutions (colleges, universities, seminaries) founded by colonial Jesuits. An inventory of the Jesuit manor at Newtown written in 1711 by William Hunter listed 15 "Negro servants," including 4 men ("Will, Jack, Kill, Peter"), 4 women ("Mary, Teresa, Clare, Pegg"), 4 "boyes—Jack, Clemm, Tomm James," and 3 "girles—Betty, Cate, Susan." In 1765, a census taken of all the enslaved residing and working on the Jesuit plantations revealed 20 Africans at St. Inigoes, 29 at Newtown, 38 at St. Thomas's, 65 at White Marsh, 26 at Bohemia, and 14 on the smaller estates, for a total of 192. The Catholic gentry, who collectively were wealthier than their Protestant neighbors, owned a disproportionate number of slaves as well—at least "300 that may be call'd Roman Catholicks" in one neighborhood alone in the 1750s. We know that by the end of the eighteenth century, slaves comprised a full one-fifth of Maryland's Catholic community and in some areas were outperforming white Catholics in the sacramental life of the church. The roots of this extraordinary flowering of Black Catholicism lie in the Jesuit plantations.[51]

50. William May to Bishop Gibson, Kingston, Nov. 19, 1725, Fulham Papers, XVII, fols. 244–245; Governor Henry Worsley to Bishop Gibson, Barbados, Mar. 3, 1723/4, ibid., XV, fols. 174–177; Lucas MSS, reel 2, fol. 383, Bridgetown Public Library, Barbados, quoted in Shaw, *Everyday Life in the Early English Caribbean*, 123.

51. Rachel L. Swarns, *The 272: The Families Who Were Enslaved and Sold to Build the American Catholic Church* (New York, 2023). Georgetown University's efforts to come to terms with and make amends for its slaveholding past has been the most notable among Jesuit institutions in the U.S.; see "Georgetown Reflects on Slavery, Memory, and Reconciliation," Georgetown University, https://www.georgetown.edu/slavery/, for an overview of the university's history and its current campaign of reparations. Hunter's inventory is in Edwin Warfield Beitzell, *The Jesuit Missions of St. Mary's County, Maryland* (Abell, Md., 1959), 64; the 1765 census figures are from "The Jesuit Farms in Maryland: Facts and Anecdotes," *Woodstock Letters*, XLI, no. 2 (1912), 195–222. By 1838, English Jesuits owned 272 slaves throughout Maryland; see Michael Pasquier, "'Though Their Skin Remains Brown,

Early denominational historians went out of their way to emphasize the "gentleness" of Jesuit slaveholding, claiming that the priests only "reluctantly" accepted the necessity of using bound labor on their farms and preferred to refer to their laborers as "servant men," "servant women," and "members of the family" rather than "slaves." One went so far as to assert that the phrase "'Priest Slave' came to mean one who was granted a large measure of freedom of movement, did not work too hard, and was well cared for." Modern historians offer a far more damning assessment of Jesuit slaveholding but concur that most slaves of Catholic owners had access to the sacraments of baptism and even marriage. What these sacraments might have meant to the enslaved will be explored in a later chapter, but the high rates of marriage, in particular, among the enslaved on Jesuit plantations do set these communities apart from their Protestant neighbors. At the very least, marriage implies that both partners were baptized or had been instructed in the Catholic faith— it was a double sacrament, in this sense. Contrary to the Jesuits' professed scruples about not separating husbands and wives who had been joined in holy matrimony, however, the sale of mission slaves did not always respect these sacramental ties. This was especially true in the late eighteenth century, after the dissolution of the Jesuit order in 1773 led the missions to liquidate their "property" by selling the enslaved to the newly settled territories west of the 1763 Proclamation Line.[52]

Lay Catholic slaveholders distinguished between the baptized and unbaptized Africans in their wills, suggesting that, in contrast to the Jesuit

---

I Hope Their Souls Will Soon Be White': Slavery, French Missionaries, and the Roman Catholic Priesthood in the American South, 1789–1865," *Church History*, LXXVII (2008), 337–370, esp. 346.

On December 9, 1755, Col. Edward Lloyd reported the arrival in Maryland of 900 French Acadians, who, together with "mine and other Negroe Slaves on this River, of which there is at least the num: of 300 that may be call'd Roman Catholicks," swelled the Catholic population of the county to 1,200 (William Hoyt, Jr., "A Contemporary View of the Acadian Arrival in Maryland, 1755," *WMQ*, 3d Ser., V [1948], 571–575, esp. 573). Curran claims that Black worshippers constituted "the vast majority of those who were baptized, as well as those married in the church on the [Eastern] Shore. And the vast majority of godparents were black, as well" (*Papist Devils*, 177). See also Joseph C. Linck, *Fully Instructed and Vehemently Influenced: Catholic Preaching in Anglo-Colonial America* (Philadelphia, 2002), 133.

52. Joseph S. Rossi, "Jesuits, Slaves and Scholars at 'Old Bohemia,' 1704–1705 as Found in the *Woodstock Letters*," *U.S. Catholic Historian*, XXVI, no. 2 (Spring 2008), 1–15 (quotations on 6–7).

missions, there was a hierarchy of sacramental belonging on these plantations. The wealthy Catholic landowner Thomas Gerrard gave "unto my Negro
Boy baptized and named Thomas one Thousand pounds of Tobacco to be
bestowed upon for his Learning and Education att the Discrecion of my
Executors" while bequeathing several unnamed "Nigros" to each of his children as part of their general inheritance. Gerrard exhibited a callous disregard for these anonymous souls: if "any of the four Nigroes dye before their
deliverys to the Severall Children," he instructed his executors to see to it
"that the Dead Nigro or Nigroes be made good by supplying of others as
good Live Nigroes as they were before their Death." The contrast between
the care lavished on "my Negro Boy Thomas" and the indifference toward the
unbaptized enslaved, dead or alive, could not be starker. Some—very few—
Catholic slaveholders provided for the gradual or qualified manumission of
their bondspeople upon death. James Pattison's will bequeathed "to my Love-
ing friend Mr John Hall one of my black Gerlls named Margaret," then aged
eight, to serve Hall until she turned thirty-nine, at which point she was to be
"free of all Service or Slavery whatsoever." Jane Fenwick's 1660 will offered a
far more circumscribed freedom to "William Payne a Negro boy," requiring
that he pay "yearly to the Roman Catholic Church for Ever one [hogshead]
of Tobacco" after his manumission. If the "said William continue not always
a Member of the said Church," she decreed "that he Shall be for ever a slave
to the foresaid Catholick Church."[53]

Some enslaved Catholics took their freedom into their own hands, elect-
ing to run away. Jacobus Van Cortlandt placed an ad in the *New-York Gazette* in 1733 to recover his "Negro man slave, named Andrew Saxon." Saxon
was described as "a tall lusty Fellow, is very black," last seen wearing a shirt
"marked with a Cross on the left Breast." He "professeth himself to be a
Roman Catholick, speaks very good English, is a Carpenter and a Cooper
by Trade." The wearing of a cross as a signifier of Catholicism shows up in
other advertisements as well, as in the ad placed in the *Saint Jago Intelligencer*
(Jamaica) for a "mulatto boy" who "goes by the name of STEPHEN BOU-
TET" and was seen "wearing a cross." The symbol "I H" (the Latin initials
for Jesus Christ) also marked a runaway as a Catholic. A "negro wench named

53. *Maryland Wills,* I, 571–572; "Some Quaint Wills of Early Catholic Settlers in Mary-
land: From the Archives of the Riggs Library, Georgetown College, Washington, D.C.,"
Records of the American Catholic Historical Society of Philadelphia, XIII (1902), 22–44, esp. 24
(Pattison), 38 (Gerrard); *Maryland Wills,* I, 117 (Fenwick).

Diana, of the Congo country" ran away from Mrs. Fussell and was described as being "marked IH on her breast."[54]

The record of Catholic slaveholding is depressingly familiar. Recusant planters and priests behaved much like other slaveholders in the colonial South when it came to buying and selling Africans and African Americans, although they did incorporate the enslaved into the sacramental life of their community to a much greater extent. As Helen Kilburn puts it, colonial Catholic slaveholders "creatively managed the practice of slave baptism and marriage and sex across the colour line" so that "neither the sacraments nor slavery were undermined." The views of one Jesuit in the 1770s were probably typical: "The Negroes that do belong to the Gentlemen of our Persuasion, and our Own, are all Xans [Christians], and instructed in every Xan duty with care. Some are good, some very bad, some docile, some very dull. They are naturally inclined to thieving, lying, and much Lechery." The true moral rot at the heart of Catholic slaveholding could no longer be ignored after the Revolution, when the domestic slave trade exploded and planters in the Chesapeake region began to sell off their surplus "chattel" in large numbers to the western and southern territories. This rush to liquidate human property— many of whom had been baptized and, on the larger plantations, worshipped side by side with their masters in private chapels—prompted some soul-searching among clerics, one of whom asked the Vatican's Congregation of Propaganda Fide in 1802: "What is to be done with masters who sell their Negroes to heretics on the condition that they will go to their church," a condition that he recognized was "not often filled?" The firm answer—"It is not permitted"—did not end the debate, and the Congregation was asked to weigh in again in 1828. "1. What is to be thought concerning Catholic Masters who having Catholic slaves sell them indiscriminately to Catholics or Heretics . . . ? 2. Can owners who have unruly slaves, given up to depraved habits, taking no account of warnings and beatings, sell them also to Heretics dwelling in far-distant regions? 3. If the abovementioned slaves so depraved and corrupt were joined in legitimate wedlock, can the Masters sell them to the first bidder even a Heretic who would take them into a region far away from

54. Jacobus Van Cortlandt, advertisement, *New-York Gazette*, Oct. 1, 1733, [3]. Jeroen DeWulf discusses the case of Andrew Saxon at more length in *Afro-Atlantic Catholics: America's First Black Christians* (Notre Dame, Ind., 2022), 1–3. "Runaway": *Saint Jago Intelligencer* (Jamaica), Apr. 16, 1768. "Diana": *Freeport Gazette, or the Dominica Advertiser* (Rousseau), July 18, 1768.

their spouses?" These were questions that cut to the heart of what it meant to bring the enslaved and the slaveholders together into a shared community of faith through the sacraments, a community that ended at the border of the plantation.[55]

Conclusion

From Maine to Maryland, from Carolina to the Caribbean, Catholics— white, Black, and Native—were everywhere in English America. Given this cumulative evidence of the presence of the transient, the unwanted, and the uncounted, the very low estimates that colonial and ecclesiastical officials consistently provided of the number of "papists" in their midst are implausible. It is inconceivable that the entire colony of New York contained *no* papists, as the Dutch Reformed minister affirmed in 1682, or "not ten papists," as the governor of New York declared to the Committee on Trade and Foreign Plantations in 1696.[56] Lord Culpeper informed the Lords of Trade that there was only one Catholic (Margaret Brent's brother George) in the entire colony of Virginia in 1681. The official line in Jamaica in 1683 was that "we have very few Papists or Sectaries, for neither Jesuits or Nonconformist Parsons do or can live among us."[57] Before he was chased out of Georgia for his rigid views on communion and baptism in the 1730s, John Wesley wrote home that "in this place, I do not know of more than one Papist remaining, except an Italian or two." Two SPG missionaries gave dramatically different

55. Kilburn, "Catholics in the Colonies," 238; Joseph Mosley to his sister, Oct. 3, 1774, in "Letters of Father Joseph Mosley, 1757–1786," *Woodstock Letters*, XXXV, no. 2 (1906), 227–245 (quotation on 235); Pasquier, "'Though Their Skin Remains Brown,'" *Church History*, LXXVII (2008), 353.

56. "We have not ten papists in the provinces, and those of no rank or fortune," Governor Fletcher wrote to William Blathwayt on May 30, 1696 ("America and West Indies: May 1696," in Fortescue, ed., *CSP*, Colonial Ser., XV [London, 1904], 8). "As to papists, there are none; or if there are any they attend our services or that of the Lutherans" (Domine Henry Selyns to Classis of Amsterdam, October 1682, quoted in Bennett, *Catholic Footsteps in Old New York,* 78). Caleb Heathcote was a little more generous in his estimation, telling Gilbert Heathcote that there were "not 20 papists and Jacobins in the whole Province" in 1701 (William Blathwayt Papers, mssBL 218–224, p. 3, Henry E. Huntington Library, San Marino, Calif.).

57. "Minutes of a Committee of Trade and Plantations, Whitehall, Nov. 26, 1681," *Virginia Magazine of History and Biography,* XXVI (1918), 41; *The Laws of Jamaica Passed by the Assembly, and Confirmed by His Majesty in Council, February 23, 1683* . . . (London, 1683), sig. C8i–D1v. As David Manning points out, only "a willingness to discount unfree peoples"

answers to London's query about the presence of Catholics in their circuits. One assured the bishop of London in 1741, "Papists are but few, not above three or four families" in his parish, whereas a neighboring minister wrote just two years later to warn that there were more "Papists" than Quakers living in his neck of the woods.[58]

The conclusion of the census commissioned by Bishop Challoner in 1763 that there was only "a Catholic here and there" in the English colonies outside of the Jesuit missions in Maryland and Pennsylvania thus doesn't hold up under scrutiny. Even Catholic historians slip into the habit of ignoring recusants who were neither white nor Anglo in their histories of the faith. Robert Emmett Curran concludes that, outside the small provincial government appointed by the Catholic duke of York, Catholics were "virtually a non-presence in the heterogeneous general population" in New York City during the 1670s and 1680s. In Philadelphia, where the recusant community was large enough to sustain a church by the 1720s, Curran finds only "a score" of Catholics in the city. Yet we know that Irish servants and African slaves were present in significant numbers in both colonial cities.[59]

Ever since John Adams quipped that Catholics in colonial America were as rare as comets or earthquakes, historians have endorsed the view that English

---

could lead to such a misleading impression; see "Reformation and the Wickedness of Port Royal, Jamaica, 1655–ca.1692," in Crawford Gribben and Scott Spurlock, eds., *Puritans and Catholics in the Trans-Atlantic World, 1600–1800* (London, 2015), 131–163, esp. 142.

58. Geordan Hammond, *John Wesley in America: Restoring Primitive Christianity* (Oxford, 2014), 162–163 (quotation on 163); Rev. Pugh, Apr. 16, 1741, in "Information about 'Popery' in Pennsylvania in Colonial Days as Given by Ministers of the Church of England," *American Catholic Historical Researches*, XI (1894), 58–64 (quotation on 62); Arthur Usher to Bishop Gibson, Philadelphia, Sept. 4, 1743, Fulham Papers, VII, fol. 309.

59. "Ragguaglio dello stato della religione cattolica," *Catholic Historical Review*, VI (1921), 517–524 ("here and there," 521); Curran, *Papist Devils*, 121 ("non-presence"), 196–197 ("a score," 197). Curran's history of Catholicism in early America is generally quite good on incorporating the Irish, in contrast to many earlier denominational studies, but he underestimates their presence outside the sugar islands. Farrelly's survey of the forging of an "American Catholic" identity in colonial America similarly claims that the number of Catholics in New York in the late seventeenth century "was so small that Jews may actually have outnumbered them" (Maura Jane Farrelly, *Papist Patriots: The Making of an American Catholic Identity* [New York, 2012], 192). Leslie Woodcock Tentler's sweeping history of American Catholicism—which focuses on the evolution of an American church after the Revolution—nonetheless excludes Irish, African, and Native Catholics almost entirely from her account of the colonial origins of the church; colonial Catholics, she writes, were a "miniscule presence" before 1763 (*American Catholics: A History* [New Haven, Conn., 2020], 47).

America was a Protestant space. That it was designed to be so is abundantly clear. But, like so many other imperial visions, the reality never matched the aspiration. To count or not count Catholics was a political choice for colonial census takers, Anglican commissaries, governors, assemblymen, militia leaders, registrars of wills and deeds, and local chroniclers. It is a methodological choice for scholars, who have to make inferences based on incomplete and sometimes misleading evidence. I've erred on the side of inclusion in this chapter, deploying the "preponderance of evidence" standard when the record is inconclusive and building certain assumptions into my choices: that Irish migrants before 1700 were most likely Catholics rather than Protestants; that a majority of enslaved Africans brought to North America from Spanish, Portuguese, and French territories in the seventeenth century were Catholic by virtue of baptism; that many of the Native servants and slaves laboring in the northern colonies as a consequence of being taken captive in the frontier wars were also Catholics; that Anglican missionaries who complained about papists and suspected papists among the English, Irish, French, and German settlers in their congregations were not always just being paranoid or reflexively resorting to the rhetoric of antipopery. What it actually meant for an Indigenous or African laborer to be a Catholic (or an Irish servant, for that matter) is a question I've put aside for now. My aim has been simple: to probe the outer limits of the Catholic presence in English America. If we look for Catholics in the interstices of the colonial order—on the wharves of bustling seaports, in the garrisons and privateering ships that defended the vulnerable coast, in the slave quarters and the households of plantations, in the ethnic refugee communities that sprang up wherever Europe's persecuted gathered in the New World—we find abundant evidence of these "people out of place."[60]

60. "A native of America who cannot read and write is as rare an appearance as a Jacobite or a Roman Catholic, that is, as rare as a comet or an earthquake," John Adams wrote in his 1765 "A Dissertation on the Canon and Feudal Law" (https://www.digitalhistory.uh.edu /disp_textbook_print.cfm?smtid=3&psid=4118).

CHAPTER TWO

"Papists in Masquerade"

Religious Passing in English America

W HEN JOSIAS FENDALL was on trial in Maryland for sedition in 1681, he quizzed each potential juror on his religious allegiance. "Are you a Catholick or a Protestant?" Fendall demanded. "It is hard to answer," responded one honest planter. Such candor is refreshing, for scholars of colonial religion if not for Fendall, who was eager to pack the jury with Protestant supporters. So, how *did* one recognize a Catholic in early English America? What were the distinguishing characteristics of "Catholicity," the telltale signs of a recusant, church papist, or crypto-Catholic? And what were the mechanisms of masking that shielded Catholics from prying eyes both official and informal? The "disguised papist" was a stock character in the arsenal of antipopery, a useful shorthand for the nested anxieties about political loyalty, moral probity, commercial credibility, and racial purity that lay at the heart of the British empire. In the eyes of their Protestant neighbors, flesh-and-blood Catholics existed in the intersection between cultural stereotype and lived religion.[1]

Although this chapter is organized around the figure of the disguised papist, my interest is less in the discourse and politics of antipopery than in the ways that men and women of indeterminate or ambivalent faith occupied the terrain of dissimulation—a term that, as we will see, enjoyed a powerful renaissance after the Reformation. Strategies of dissimulation (secrecy, deception, misdirection, concealment) helped to protect members of a minority faith from exposure in the confessional era, but they can also be read as symptoms of the underlying ambiguity that characterized post-Reformation Christianity. What

---

1. Trial of Josias Fendall at Maryland Provincial Court, Nov. 15, 1681, *Archives of Maryland,* V, 316. On antipopery as a foundational discourse of early modern British identity, see Peter Lake, "Anti-popery: The Structure of a Prejudice," in Richard Cust and Ann Hughes, eds., *Conflict in Early Stuart England: Studies in Religion and Politics, 1603–1642* (London, 1989), 72–106; Linda Colley, *Britons: Forging the Nation, 1707–1837* (New Haven, Conn., 1992).

looks like deceit in one context may be a genuine expression of uncertainty or ambivalence viewed from another perspective. Disentangling the threads of ambivalence from those of ambidexterity is a tricky enterprise. Many of the examples of people acting "in bad faith"—a phenomenon I'm calling "religious passing"—explored below can be, and have been, interpreted in different ways. Some Catholics who "passed" as Protestants did so to elude prosecution or to advance their fortunes; some moved seamlessly between identities as they transitioned from one household to another, from one phase of life to the next; still others observed all the rituals of the Reformed church while remaining loyal to traditional Christianity, without any apparent cognitive dissonance. All are "disguised papists" as I'm using the term, without prejudice or judgment. Religious passing was a ubiquitous fact of life after the Reformation, when churches and parishioners alike had to navigate unchartered fissures in the ecclesiastical landscape.[2]

Religious Identity and the Reformation

To fully grasp the problem of disguised papists, we have to take a step back and understand how religious identity was perceived in the post-Reformed world. By the late Middle Ages, Europeans had developed a taxonomy of "others" that came perilously close to religious racialism, in which the three major faiths (Christianity, Judaism, and Islam) were understood to be inheritable, rooted in blood and embodied in distinctive behavioral and cultural habits. England's treatment of its Jewish population led the way in this process of religio-racial formation; by the time they were expelled in 1290, England's Jews had already been subject to a series of race-based legal restrictions that sought to curtail their movement, their right to worship as they wished, their ability to live where they chose, to act civilly and economically, and to eat, marry, and raise children in their own way. Popular stereotypes of Jews as horned, diseased, fetid, insatiable, and bleeding at inappropriate times played on physiological and cultural notions of difference to constitute Jews as a despised racial minority.[3]

2. For an insightful discussion of the role of secrecy in enabling movement between religious categories in a very different time and place, see Paul Christopher Johnson, *Secrets, Gossip, and Gods: The Transformation of Brazilian Candomblé* (New York, 2002).

3. Geraldine Heng rehearses the long process of ethnoracial typing that constituted Jews as a separate race in late medieval England in chapter 2 of her *Invention of Race in the European Middle Ages* (Cambridge, 2018).

The bred-in-the-bone nature of religious identity was revealed most clearly when those who attempted, or were forced, to convert came up against entrenched notions of who was and who wasn't a Jew, a Christian, or a Muslim. The tragic fate of Iberian Jews who converted to Christianity (called variously *conversos, marranos,* and crypto-Jews) to escape the massacres and forced dislocations of the fourteenth and fifteenth centuries was but the most extreme example of religious racialism in late medieval Europe: conversos were never fully accepted as Christians, and the passage of *limpieza de sangre* (purity of blood) laws in the sixteenth century fixed in law what had already been established in practice. Jews were forever Jews, constituted as such explicitly by their bloodlines, and no statement of faith or ritual initiation into Christianity could change that.[4] The concept of a "crypto-[fill in the blank],″ a derogatory term applied to those who hid their true faith behind the facade of another, was developed first in reference to the problem of the converso but was extended in the early modern era to any false convert.

After the Reformation split Europe's Christians into two rival tribes that regarded each other as heretics, the problem of religious identity shifted. Distinctions of blood and lineage that had previously sorted Europe's believers into protoracial categories were an awkward fit for a people who had once understood themselves to be members of a universal family. What, exactly, distinguished a Protestant from a Catholic? Did these identities extend beyond the theological beliefs that were at the heart of the Reformation to encompass other differences—external signs of behavior and deportment, interiorized emotional and psychological states, predispositions? Even the body itself?

---

4. The literature on conversos is extensive. For a sampling, see David Nirenberg, "Mass Conversion and Genealogical Mentalities: Jews and Christians in Fifteenth-Century Spain," *Past and Present,* no. 174 (February 2002), 3–41; the essays collected in Mercedes García-Arenal and Yonatan Glazer-Eytan, eds., *Forced Conversion in Christianity, Judaism, and Islam: Conversion and Faith in Premodern Iberia and Beyond* (Leiden, 2020); Yosef Kaplan, ed., *Religious Changes and Cultural Transformations in the Early Modern Western Sephardic Communities* (Leiden, 2019); Richard L. Kagan and Philip D. Morgan, eds., *Atlantic Diasporas: Jews, Conversos, and Crypto-Jews in the Age of Mercantilism, 1500–1800* (Baltimore, 2009). Just how "racial" were these medieval ways of categorizing different faiths is debated; for two good discussions, see Nirenberg, "Was There Race before Modernity? The Example of 'Jewish' Blood in Late Medieval Spain," in his *Neighboring Faiths: Christianity, Islam, and Judaism in the Middle Ages and Today* (Chicago, 2014), 169–190; and Kathryn Burns, "Unfixing Race," in Margaret R. Greer, Walter D. Mignolo, and Maureen Quilligan, eds., *Rereading the Black Legend: The Discourses of Religious and Racial Difference in the Renaissance Empires* (Chicago, 2007), 188–202.

And were these post-Reformation identities inheritable, passed along to children by virtue of shared blood or inculcated in them by virtue of rigorous programs of religious discipline? These were questions that had to be sorted out in the centuries following the split with Rome, and the answers provided by Reformed theologians and churchmen varied depending on the geopolitics of place. A German community caught between warring princes who followed the principle of *cuius regio, eius religio* ("he who governs the territory decides its religion") faced different challenges placing people in confessional boxes than a French village after the 1695 Revocation of the Edict of Nantes upended a century of partial toleration, or an English parish after the 1559 Act of Uniformity created a single national church for the entire kingdom. In Germany, one was (officially) a Catholic or a Protestant—a loyal subject or a rebel—depending on which principality one resided in. In France, a Protestant was a protected member of a religious minority one year and an outlaw the next. In England, after Elizabeth I, everyone was presumed to belong to the established church unless he or she made a deliberate choice not to conform. Under such shifting conditions, maintaining a uniform, and stable, set of standards by which a person's religious identity could be ascertained was difficult in post-Reformation Europe.

Categories of identity were further complicated by the incomplete nature of the Reformation in those European countries that embraced variations of Reformed theology as the basis of a new national church. The whipsaw effect of three regime changes within little more than a decade in England magnified the problem of fixing religious identity in this fluid new world. The rapid succession of religious regimes from the Protestant Edward VI in 1547 to the Catholic Mary in 1553 and the Protestant Elizabeth I in 1558 meant that men and women who had grown up as traditional Christians and came of age during Henry VIII's tumultuous reign had to change their faith (or pretend to) at least four times in one lifetime. As the Separatist minister Roger Williams put it, "When *England* was all *Popish* under *Henry* the seventh, how esie is conversion wrought to half Papist halfe-Protestant under *Henry* the eighth? From halfe-Protestantisme halfe-Popery under *Henry* the eight, to absolute Protestan[t]isme under Edward the sixth: from absolu[te] Protestation under *Edward* the sixt to absalute Popery under Quegne *Mary,* and from absolute Popery under Quegne *Mary* (just like the Weather-cocke, with the breathe of every Prince) to absolute Protestantisme under Queene *Elizabeth*." With the exception of those fervent Reformers and traditionalists who were uncompromising in their faith, the majority of the English laity were "ambidexterous" Christians whose personal beliefs combined elements of Protestantism and Catholicism in a mixture dictated as much by pragmatism as by theology.[5]

In Elizabethan England, where behavior and not belief was the measure of conformity to the established church, efforts to discern the orthodox from the heterodox were hampered by the external similarities between the new state church and the old. The Church of England had retained many of the trappings of the Catholic liturgy, which is why it was so often criticized by dissenters like the Puritans as insufficiently reformed. In their personal lives, Protestants and Catholics shared a common understanding of the parameters of faith. An Anglican woman and a Catholic woman both attended worship services regularly, took communion (at least three times a year for the Anglican, at least once for the Catholic), married in the church, baptized their children in the font and underwent the ritual purification of "churching" after the birth, and were buried in holy ground after their deaths. An Anglican man and a Catholic man mediated between the church and the family as heads of household, provided both with material and financial support, went to worship services probably less frequently than their wives, chose godparents to serve as proxy spiritual guardians for their children, and took responsibility for the religious health of the entire household, servants included. Catholics in England, male and female, who chose to outwardly conform (church papists) did not have to abandon much of this sacerdotal system under the Elizabethan settlement. What they thought about each of these spiritual activities is a different matter, but a matter beyond the purview of the state's ecclesiastical arm. This made church papists "far 'more dangerous and hurtfull'" in Protestant eyes than "symple recusants" who wore their religion openly. How, then, to tell the Catholic from the Protestant?[6]

By the time the first English colonies were being planted in the early seventeenth century, the religiopolitical landscape had (in the eyes of the Church establishment, at least) been settled for a half century. But the effects of this earlier turbulence still lingered, especially within the recusant community,

5. Roger Williams quoted in Steven Mullaney, *The Reformation of Emotions in the Age of Shakespeare* (Chicago, 2015), 9. Christopher Haigh describes the "ambidexterous religious life" of most believers in "The Church of England, the Catholics, and the People," in Haigh, ed., *The Reign of Elizabeth I* (London, 1984), 195–219 (quotation on 200).

6. Clare Talbot, ed., *Miscellanea: Recusant Records* (London, 1961), 66, quoted in Alexandra Walsham, "England's Nicodemites: Crypto-Catholicism and Religious Pluralism," in Walsham, *Catholic Reformation in Protestant Britain* (Farnham, U.K., 2014), 85–101 (quotation on 100).

who had long memories of the betrayal they felt when the brief resurgence of Catholicism under Mary was extinguished by her Protestant sister. The ascension of the Stuarts following Elizabeth's death in 1603 reignited these hopes of a Catholic restoration, and in fact both James I and his son Charles I gave mixed signals during their reigns that encouraged recusants to hope for a more tolerant future. In some important respects, the years surrounding the ascensions of James in 1603 and Charles in 1625 resembled the reign of Mary, as Catholics who had been practicing their faith in secret came into the open once again. The chapels maintained by the Catholic wives of James and Charles, and those attached to the foreign embassies of France and Spain in the nation's capital, became the central nodes of a revived recusant community whose branches spread from London into the northern provinces, where seigneurial Catholicism had taken deep root in the sixteenth century. During the first three decades of the seventeenth century, then, the problem of distinguishing between Protestants and Catholics was again at the forefront of national conversations about identity and belonging.

An important strand of this conversation concerned the practice of dissimulation. All religious minorities living under a national church system in post-Reformation Europe, whether tolerated or proscribed, had to dissemble to some degree, to protect themselves and their loved ones. And the closer the orthodox and the heterodox were in terms of their beliefs and practices, the greater the possibilities for dissembling. It was much easier for a recusant to "pass" as an Anglican than for a Jew or Muslim to pass as a Christian. In England, the phenomenon of Nicodemism (named for the Pharisee Nicodemus, who concealed his faith in Christ out of fear of Jewish reprisal [John 3:1–2]) encompassed both Protestants living in Catholic lands who betrayed their faith by participating in Catholic rites and church papists at home who continued to practice their faith secretly while conforming to the established church. Nicodemism was denounced by Protestant and Catholic authorities alike as spiritual cowardice if not outright treachery, but laymen and -women (along with the local pastors who served them) were often more generous in their assessment of religious passing. Dissimulation (pretending not to be what one really is, as opposed to simulation, or pretending to be what one really is not) was the better part of discretion for early modern believers and as such had a valuable, and recognized, role to play in maintaining peace during the confessional age.[7]

7. For a general discussion of the problem of dissimulation, see Perez Zagorin, *Ways of Lying: Dissimulation, Persecution, and Conformity in Early Modern Europe* (Cambridge,

The prevalence and clandestine nature of dissimulation in early modern environments marked by a powerful state church and substantial populations of dissenters meant that there was a constant argument between those in power and those on the margins about religious identity. This was very much a two-way conversation, involving everyone from imperial policymakers and colonial magistrates to the humblest parishioner in the pew. How those conversations played out in early English America is the subject of the remainder of this chapter.

Clerical Disguises

Trained in the arts of deception by the penal laws imposed in the late Elizabethan era, Catholic priests and the congregations who sheltered them in the British Isles developed a repertoire of disguises to mask their beliefs, practices, and persons. This repertoire was for the most part easily adaptable—indeed, was ideally suited—to colonial conditions of extreme mobility, dispersed settlement patterns, and the social anonymity of servitude, but the disconcerting religious and racial heterogeneity of English America required new habits of disguise and rendered old ones more risky.

Priests, in particular, were masters of deception because they had to be. Jesuits were the dissemblers par excellence in early modern Protestant controversial literature, and the very name "Jesuit" became a synonym for deception, secrecy, casuistry, and manipulation. Pamphlets with titles like *The Jesuite in Masquerade* and *The Protestant Mask Taken off from the Jesuited Englishman* poured from the English presses in the seventeenth century. It can be easy to forget that disguises were a matter of life and death, not merely a polemical device in the discourse of antipopery; every Jesuit who traveled to England after 1585 did so under penalty of death. The first step toward self-preservation was assuming an alias. There are directories of the aliases assumed by Jesuit

---

Mass., 1990). Zagorin sees dissimulation and simulation as two sides of the same coin, though he recognizes that "in a strict sense dissimulation is pretending not to be what one actually is, where simulation is pretending to be what one actually is not" (3). In contrast, William B. Taylor, in *Fugitive Freedom: The Improbable Lives of Two Impostors in Late Colonial Mexico* (Oakland, Calif., 2021), argues that dissimulation carried more legitimacy than its "evil twin," simulation, in the early modern world; in his words, simulation was merely lying to save one's own skin, whereas dissimulation was sometimes understood to be "a morally grounded, positive kind of pretense in which actors protected their own well-being and the well-being of others, allowing different beliefs and attitudes to coexist unacknowledged for their mutual benefit" (14).

missionaries in the archives; one resides in the Maryland Province Archives of the Society of Jesus in Georgetown University Library. Changing one's name was only the first step. Jesuits traveled in disguise, usually under an assumed occupation: merchant, physician (a popular choice since it provided cover for the Latin texts and sacramental unguents carried by priests), courtier, bookseller, clerk, or simply "gentleman." It was risky for a priest to pretend to be a tradesman or laborer, since it would raise immediate suspicion should the Catholic lay gentry (their primary protectors) be seen paying deference to someone in humble garb.[8]

Detecting priests began with outward appearance and deportment. The black robes of a priest were said to hide many sins in popular cultural discourse, including lechery, gluttony, and avarice, but like all forms of attire, clerical garb was, in fact, very revealing. It's difficult to overstate the importance of clothing as a marker of status in the early modern world, where sumptuary laws spelled out in detail what different social groups were entitled to wear and punished those who transgressed. Anxieties about status inversion underwrote these laws—the prospect of a servant masquerading as a gentlewoman or a vagabond as a man of property—but fear of gender inversion was at play as well when it came to clerical dress. Monastic garb was notoriously ambisexual with its long gown that hid the contours of the human body, and the long-standing critique of the medieval clergy as either sexual predators or eunuchs made their clothing the object of satire. As one antipapist warned, "If about Bloomsbury or Holborn thou meet a good snug fellow in a gold-laced suit, a cloak lined through with velvet, one that hath good store of coin in his purse, rings on his fingers, a watch in his pocket, which he will value at £20, a very broad laced band, a stiletto by his side, a man at his heels, willing (upon small acquaintance) to intrude himself into thy company, and still desiring to insinuate himself with thee, then take heed of a Jesuit of the prouder sort of priests." Jesuits were often described as "wolves in sheep's clothing," their chaste robes betraying the "wolvish" nature underneath. Thomas Gage, who converted from Catholic priest to Protestant

---

8. *The Jesuite in Masquerade* . . . (London, 1681); [Thomas Comber], *The Protestant Mask Taken off from the Jesuited Englishman* (London, 1692); *The Jesuite in the Pound; or, Father Peters in Disguise, Taken by Vice Admiral Herbert* (London, 1688); H[enry] F[oley], *English Province S.J.: Alphabetical Catalogue of Members of the English Province S.J. Who Assumed Aliases or By-Names, together with the Said Aliases* (London, 1875), box 2, folder 14, MPA. The *Early English Books Online* database lists more than three thousand publications with the keywords "Jesuit" and "disguise" in the period 1535–1700, with the number spiking in the second half of the seventeenth century.

minister in the early seventeenth century, described casting off his "Fryers weed"—the "sheepskin, which covers many a wolvish, greedy and covetous heart under it; which doubtlesse is the ground, why in *Germany,* in the Protestant and *Lutheran* Towns, when the boyes and yong men see a Fryer go along their streets, they cry out to the neighbours, saying, a Wolfe, a Wolfe, shut your doors." Shedding the "hypocriticall cloak and habit" of a Catholic priest, Gage converted to Protestantism, preached a "Recantation Sermon" at St. Paul's in London, married, and threw his lot in with the parliamentary cause during the English Civil War.[9]

A century later, the Old Bailey trial of a suspected priest, Francis Archangel Monford, turned on Monford's clothing, as well as the gestures of his body and those of his auditory, to settle the question of his true identity. John Kettle testified, "I went the Saturday before *Easter Sunday* to the Romish Chapel in *Warwick-Street,* and I saw the Defendant there in a white Surplice, cross'd down the Back." When asked, "Do you know any thing else of his being a Popish Priest? Was there any distributing of Bread and Wine? . . . In what Posture was he when he had the Cup; was he standing up by the Communion-Table; was any of the Congregation near him?" Kettle responded, "Some of them were down upon their Knees; and he took the Cup and he held it as high as his Head." Despite this damning evidence, the case against Monford unraveled when another witness admitted "no" when pressed, "Do you know what the Dress of a Popish Priest is?" There was, in truth, little to distinguish the vestments of a Catholic from an Anglican priest: both wore a long, black gown and a surplice, a loose white tunic worn over the cassock, while conducting religious services. It is not surprising that the witnesses in Monford's trial did not have a clear idea of what a Catholic priest customarily wore.[10]

Although missionary priests in the colonies were part of the same administrative Vatican unit as their counterparts in England (the English Province

9. William P. Treacy, *Old Catholic Maryland and Its Early Jesuit Missionaries* (Swedesboro, N.J., 1889), xi; John Gee, *The Foot out of the Snare: With a Detection of Sundry Late Practices and Impostures of Priests and Jesuits in England* (London, 1624), 23; Thomas Gage, *A New Survey of the West-India's; or, The English American His Travail by Sea and Land,* 2d ed. (London, 1655), 202–203, 211. For a sampling of the history of sumptuary laws in Europe, see Giorgio Riello and Ulinka Rublack, eds., *The Right to Dress: Sumptuary Laws in a Global Perspective, c. 1200–1800* (Cambridge, 2019).

10. Trial account, Francis Archangel Monford, Apr. 9, 1746 (t17460409-44), *Old Bailey Proceedings Online,* www.oldbaileyonline.org.

of the Society of Jesus, which assumed its own institutional status in 1623), the conditions of their work led them to make different sartorial choices to enhance their effectiveness and limit their political liability. Donning the garb of a gentleman or a courtier was as likely to draw unwanted attention as deflect suspicion. It's hard to imagine a would-be colonial layman getting away with sporting a "ruffling suit of apparel, gilt rapier, and dagger hanging at his side" or "gay feathers in their hats" and "scarlet cloaks over crimson satin suits," as Jesuits posing as "worldlings" did in Britain. In a province like Maryland, where the proprietary government acknowledged (often begrudgingly) their authority, priests could safely act and dress like gentlemen. Because the Jesuit order could not own property in its own right, individual priests served as proxy landholders under the title of "gentleman." A deed transferring property from one priest to another in 1726 records an "Indenture made . . . between George Thorold late of St. Marys County now of Portobacco in Charles County Gentleman of the one part and Peter Attwood . . . Gentleman of the other Part." And they dressed the part: when Father Pierron visited Maryland in the 1670s, he found "two of our Fathers and a Brother, who are English, the Fathers being dressed like gentlemen, and the Brother like a farmer; in fact, he has charge of a farm, which serves to support the two missionaries."[11]

As "gentlemen," moreover, priests had cover for their Latin skills—very much a marker of elite education in early modern England. To those on the lookout for Catholics, the use of Latin could be a clue that Jesuits were afoot. Mary Hemsley testified before the Governor's Council in Maryland that a book she had lent the priest William Hunter was returned to her with a letter hidden "amongst the Leaves" that contained "some Latin and dark expressions." The Dutch ministers in New York complained to the Classis of

11. "Disguises and Aliases of the Early Missionaries," *Woodstock Letters*, XV, no. 1 (1886), 72–73; George Thorold deed to Peter Attwood, May 9, 1726, Materials re. Little Bretton and St. Thomas Manor, box 27, folder 9, MPA; Reuben Gold Thwaites, ed., *The Jesuit Relations and Allied Documents: Travels and Explorations of the Jesuit Missionaries in New France, 1610–1791*, 73 vols. (Cleveland, 1896–1901), LIX, 73–75. Account books concealed the rich materials needed to make priestly garments under different labels. A 1742 inventory from a Jesuit manor included no cassocks, though one Jesuit historian noted a discrepancy in the cost of the materials listed for a "fustian coat" and the breeches that accompanied it; the far more expensive coat, he concluded, was most likely a cassock. See Joseph Zwinge, "The Jesuit Farms in Maryland: Facts and Anecdotes," *Woodstock Letters*, XLI, no. 1 (1912), 53–77 (quotation on 59–60).

Amsterdam in 1698 that the Jesuits "built a school here under the pretense to teach the youth the Latin Language, to which some even of the most influential had already sent their children." The bell in the Dutch Reformed church in the colonial city, in a final insult, chimed every morning to mark the beginning of the Jesuit school day. The other professional disguise priests adopted, that of physician, similarly gave them a screen for their seminary training. Father Schneider "travel[led] under the guise of a physician in Pennsylvania" and "was more generally known and received as a medical doctor than as a priest." Under cover of his advanced literary training, Schneider "wrote out, entire, in legible hand, two copies of the Roman Missal" for his rural parishioners. Being too "learned" was an occupational hazard for disguised missionaries. When a suspected Jesuit ("a violent Roman Catholic") was observed lurking around Charleston, South Carolina, the governor asked John Butler, a local trader, "Do you know Anthony Dean? What kind of a man is he? Do you take him to be a Jesuit?" Butler demurred: "He is reckoned a very learned man." Pressed again—"Do you think him a Jesuit?"—Butler repeated, "They say he is a very learned man."[12]

Outside the urban centers, posing as a gentleman of any kind was risky. A "young man" in Barbados was suspicious when he first spied Father Antoine Biet because he was dressed too finely. Biet recalled, "He said to himself: 'Is this Monsieur Biet, or is it not? He is a priest, this man does not have the appearance of one': for I was dressed in the clothing of a gentleman." A fellow missionary was unmasked on the island when "the People here conclude[d] him Rather a Spy than a Priest, hee appearing altogether in publique as a Gent'l traveler." Some priests tried to blend in by dressing, and working, as merchants, farmers, mariners, and common tradesmen. Laurence Starkie (or Sankey/Sanchez) used "every species of disguise" to "evade his enemies" in the late 1640s. "When he wished to visit the gentleman in his manor, or the Indian in his hut, he was obliged to dress as a farmer, or a soldier, and wear

12. *Archives of Maryland*, Feb. 13, 1715/16, XXV, 331; William Harper Bennett, *Catholic Footsteps in Old New York: A Chronicle of Catholicity in the City of New York from 1524 to 1808* (New York, 1909), 201; "Historical Sketch of the Mission of Gosenhoppen, Now Churchville," John Gilmary Shea Papers, box 19, folder 24, MPA; Richard C. Madden, "Catholics in Colonial South Carolina," *Records of the American Catholic Historical Society of Philadelphia*, LXXIII, no. 1/2 (1962), 24. Jean Pierron was initially suspected of being a Jesuit "owing to the unusual knowledge that he displayed" (Thwaites, ed., *Jesuit Relations*, LIX, 73).

a beard that covered his breast." John Stritch took on the persona of a wood merchant on his first mission to the Leeward Islands in 1650.[13]

> The Father, who knew they would not allow a priest on their island, disguised himself as a merchant, and went there under the pretext of wanting to purchase wood. As soon as he arrived he made himself known to several of the Irish, and through them to all the others. They choose a place in the woods where the missionary went every day to say mass and to bestow the sacraments. The whole morning was employed in the cultivation of souls, and afterwards they in fact went to cut wood, which the Father had these good Catholics haul, in this confirming the English in their belief that he had only come for this purpose.[14]

The association of Jesuit missionary work in the colonies with trade and commerce is a recurring motif in the sources. The official report of the Jesuit superior George Hunter in the 1760s referred to congregants as "customers," and another Jesuit referred to his order as "our *Factory*." Henry Neale, the first priest assigned to the Pennsylvania portion of the Maryland mission, assured his superiors, "We have at present all liberty imaginable in the exercise of our *business*." Henry Warren wrote in code to a fellow priest in 1690 who was "desirous to know how things are with us in these troublesome times, since trade [religion] is so much decayed," reassuring him that there were "three public shops [chapels] open in Oxford." Without the full institutional apparatus of the Roman Church behind them, itinerant priests had to peddle their religious wares to customers who met them not in the hushed splendor of a cathedral but in private homes and rural outbuildings. The circumstances of their mission automatically put priests and their parishioners on a more equal footing. If anything, priests were now the supplicants of the laity on whose goodwill and generosity they depended for their very survival. Their detractors scoffed at the "priests and Jesuits" who "wander up and down in England" and the colonies "apparrelled as Tradsmen." These "blake spirits

13. Jerome S. Handler, "Father Antoine Biet's Visit to Barbados in 1654," *Journal of the Barbados Museum and Historical Society*, XXXII, no. 2 (May 1967), 56–76 (quotation on 58); Lt. Gov. Stede to earl of Sunderland, Barbados, Sept. 1, 1688, CO 1/65, no. 54, TNA; "Historical Points Connected with New-Town Manor and Church, St. Mary's County, MD. (Continued.)," *Woodstock Letters*, XIII, no. 2 (1884), 112.

14. Pierre Pelleprat, "De La Mission Irlandaise," from "The Mission of Father John Stritch, S.J., (a. 1650–1655)," in Aubrey Gwynn, ed., "Documents Relating to the Irish in the West Indies," *Analecta Hibernica*, no. 4 (October 1932), 208–214 (quotation on 209).

dispers themselves all over the Country in America," a black market of a peculiar kind.[15]

In a religious environment in which even clergymen of the Church of England had dubious credentials (and worse reputations) and unlicensed preachers circulated freely, some Catholic missionaries masqueraded as clergy of other denominations. Ministers of all stripes complained endlessly about the scourge of unlicensed preachers who seemed to roam the colonial countryside with impunity—those "wandering Pretenders to preaching" who seduced those "that have their Religion still to choose." Early Massachusetts was so plagued by clerical impostors, according to Cotton Mather, that the Puritan Commonwealth was in danger of being *"Besotted,* not to say, *Bejesuited"* by these wolves in sheep's clothing. The bishop of London complained about the "growing evil" of fake ministers presenting "counterfeited letters of orders under my hand and seal" on Jamaica in the early 1700s. Colonial assemblies repeatedly passed laws prohibiting any *"Vagrant* Preacher . . . or disguised *Papist"* who wandered into their province, as a New York law put it. It was difficult to tell the genuine article from the imposters, leaving the door open to clerical misdirection. Father Greaton, one of the first priests to serve the fledgling Catholic congregation in Philadelphia, "was accustomed to assume the garb of a Quaker, whenever he visited the City."[16]

15. Thomas Hughes, *History of the Society of Jesus in North America: Colonial and Federal, Documents,* I, part 1 (1605–1838) (London, 1908), 337, 342; "Letter of Lt. Col. Alexander T. Knight to J. Glimary Shea, LL.D.," Apr. 28, 1883, in "Letters of Father Joseph Mosley," *Woodstock Letters,* XXXV, no. 1 (1906), 37; "'We Have . . . All Liberty Imaginable in the Exercise of Our Business': Growth of the Catholic Community in Penn's Colony, 1741," in Robert Emmett Curran, ed., *Intestine Enemies: Catholics in Protestant America, 1605–1791; A Documentary History* (Washington, D.C., 2017), 189; Fr. Henry Warren of Maryland, Oxford, May 2, 1690, in "Disguises and Aliases of Early Missionaries," *Woodstock Letters,* XV, no. 1 (1886), 74 (brackets in original); "Complaint from Heaven," *Archives of Maryland,* V, 147. Black was the ubiquitous color of clerical robes in Anglo-America, and as late as the early 1800s, priests in New York were still wearing brown instead of black robes to hide their identity. See "New York Catholic Historical Notes," *American Catholic Historical Researches,* I (1905), 184.

16. Clergy of Maryland to Bishop Compton, Annapolis, May 14, 1698, Fulham Papers, II, fol. 100; Dublin, Aug. 25, 1711, ibid., Compton 2, fols. 94–95; *Boston Evening-Post,* Jan. 21, 1745, 2; "Annals of St. Joseph's Church, Philadelphia, Part First," *Woodstock Letters,* II, no. 1 (1873), 19; Cotton Mather, *A Warning to the Flocks against Wolves in Sheeps Clothing* (Boston, 1700), 8. As Thomas Harward wrote in 1731, "Abundance of Mischief has been often done in this Country by Persons coming over pretending to be Clergymen" (Harward to Bishop Gibson, Boston, May 24, 1731, Fulham Papers, V, fol. 35). For a good

Ironically, some preachers had the misfortune of being mistaken for Catholic priests: in the late 1670s, two Labadist ministers, Jasper Dankers and Peter Sluyter, visited New York City on their way through Pennsylvania, where they were (in their words) besieged by Catholics eager for the sacramental presence of a priest. "We are in everyone's eye and yet nobody knows what to make of us. Some declared that we were Jesuits traveling over the country to spy it out, some that we were Recollects designating the places where we had held Mass and confession. The Papists believed we were Priests and we could not get rid of them, they would have us confess them, baptize their children and perform Mass, and they continued in their opinion." There was a persistent strain of anxiety in Church of England circles about the possibility of Catholic priests masquerading as Anglicans—who, after all, shared the title of "priest" and whose liturgical practice more closely resembled the Roman Church than any other Protestant denomination. An anonymous cleric wrote to Bishop Gibson in 1723 to inquire "whether Any Popish Priests go in Clergymen's habits and perform offices in the Church of England?"[17]

The suspicion was not entirely misplaced. A surprising number of Protestant ministers in the colonies were, in fact, converts from the Church of Rome. On the island of Nevis, William Simpson, a "Proselite from the Church of Rome," was appointed by the governor to serve as the parish minister, although he reverted to his true colors upon his deathbed—"He dyed professing himself a Roman Catholick." Albert Pouderous, the SPG minister in St. James Santee Parish in South Carolina, was "a learned divine and convert from the Church of Rome," as were his fellow missionaries Gabriel d'Emillian (Maryland), John Urmston (Carolinas), Michael Houdin (Pennsylvania), Charles Delamotte (South Carolina), and Joseph O'Hara (Pennsylvania and Rhode Island). D'Emillian was an attractive choice for Maryland because of his religious past; he "knows that some are of Opinion that he can do some considerable good among the papists there hav[ing] Been formerly a Romanist himself." In O'Hara's case, certificates had to be obtained

discussion of the phenomenon of clerical impostors, see Thomas Kidd, "Passing as a Pastor: Clerical Imposture in the Colonial Atlantic World," *Religion and American Culture: A Journal of Interpretation*, XIV (2004), 149–174.

17. Joseph L. J. Kirlin, *Catholicity in Philadelphia: From the Earliest Missionaries down to the Present Time* (Philadelphia, 1909), 19. The Labadists were a seventeenth-century Protestant religious movement founded by a French Pietist. "Any Popish Priests": Letter to Bishop Gibson, June 6, 1723, MS 1471, fol. 36, Letters to Edmund Gibson, bishop of London, Lambeth Palace Library.

from members of his former flock in Ireland attesting that he had indeed "renounced the errors of Popery" and been inducted into the Church of Ireland before he could be sent to the colonies by the Society.[18]

That so many colonial priests were of Scots or Irish heritage further muddied the Anglican/Catholic boundary. Colonial posts were not particularly attractive to English ministers for a host of reasons, ranging from poor and unreliable pay to primitive living conditions, profane congregants, and weak institutional support, and the SPG had trouble filling its positions with reputable clergy. The image of the colonial clergy as exceptionally dissolute may be exaggerated, but there is no doubting the struggles of the missionary societies to field reliable priests. Irish and Scots priests—some of whom had converted from Catholicism and all of whom faced prejudice in English parishes—were an obvious choice. "Of those who are sent from hence, a great part are of the Scotch and Irish," admitted Bishop Sherlock, "who can get no employment at home, and enter into the Service more out of necessity than Choice." Even so eminent a minister as the SPG commissary Gideon Johnston could not escape the stigma of his Scottish origins: he complained that his adversaries in South Carolina had lobbed the epithets "Irish Rapparee, and Scotch Irish Lyllibolaro" at him during his tenure in the colony. But whatever their ethnic or class origins, ministers of any denomination faced skepticism about their motives for volunteering to serve in colonial outposts.[19]

Wigwam Chapels and Ghost Churches: Liturgical Space

The colonial clergy labored under conditions befitting their dubious reputation. Whereas some officiated in parishes lucky enough to have an actual church, others had to make do with crude structures thrown up hastily and

18. Governor William Matthew to Bishop Gibson, Saint Christopher, Sept. 22, 1735, Fulham Papers, XIX, fols. 237–238. On Pouderous, see "A Short Memorial on the Present State of the Church and Clergy in South Carolina, by William Tredwell Bull, Aug. 10, 1723," ibid., IX, South Carolina, 1703–1734, nos. 118–121; on Urmston, see Brian Hunt to Bishop Gibson, Oct. 30, 1723, ibid.; on O'Hara, see "Certificate of Francis Ormsby and James Crofton, Rhode Island, Jan. 30, 1727/8," ibid., VIII, Pennsylvania and Rhode Island, fols. 224–226; on d'Emillian, see Nov. 12, 1702, *Archives of Maryland*, XXV; on Houdin, see Bennett, *Catholic Footsteps in Old New York*, 291; on Delamotte, see Mr. Marson to Dr. Bray, Charles Town, Feb. 2, 1702/3, SPG Letters "A" Series, 1702–1737, I, no. 60, *British Online Archives*, https://britishonlinearchives.com.

19. Bishop Sherlock to Doctor Doddridge, London, May 11, 1751, Fulham Papers, XIII, fols. 41–42. For an even-handed assessment of the reputation of the colonial clergy, see

with no expectation of permanency. This was not a problem for the more radical Protestant dissenters such as the Puritans and Quakers, who disdained the material trappings of faith, but for Anglicans and Catholics, the lack of a suitably reverential liturgical space was a source of cultural and theological anxiety. (Lutherans, too: Henry Muhlenberg recalled in disgust that his first pulpit in Philadelphia was in a "leaky slaughterhouse.") The first brick Anglican churches date only from the 1680s, and it was not until the eighteenth century that the landscape of colonial America was truly "sacralized," in Jon Butler's words, by the spread of Anglican ecclesial structures throughout the middle and southern colonies. Most seventeenth-century colonial structures were multipurpose: homes functioned as taverns and courtrooms, villagers congregated in barns and other large outbuildings for town meetings or worship services. The iconic New England meetinghouse was the exception, and even there, the point was to dissolve the visual distinction between church and home. Buildings, too, "passed" in English America.[20]

Colonial Catholics had to tread cautiously in creating liturgical spaces of their own given the legal proscriptions on public worship in every colony except for Pennsylvania and pre-1704 Maryland, and, like the priests who served them, most were disguised in some fashion. The first settlers in Maryland celebrated mass in a longhouse the Piscataway sold to Father Andrew White in 1634. "You would call this the first chapel in Maryland, though it is fitted up much more decently than when the Indians lived in it," White wrote. Chapels in Native villages were thereafter known as "wigwam chapels" by the Jesuits. Subsequent chapels would share the rudimentary form of these first structures. The chapel at Newtown, Maryland, was built to resemble a

---

Patricia U. Bonomi, *Under the Cope of Heaven: Religion, Society, and Politics in Colonial America* (New York, 1986), chap. 3, "The Clergymen," 39–72. For Gideon Johnston, see Johnston to Secretary, Jan. 27, 1710/11, in Frank J. Klingberg, ed., *Carolina Chronicle: The Papers of Commissary Gideon Johnston, 1707–1716*, XXXV (Berkeley, Calif., 1986), 84. According to the *OED*, "rapparee" was a seventeenth-century term meaning "An Irish pikeman or irregular soldier, *esp.* one fighting on the Jacobite side during the Williamite War of 1689–91. Hence: an Irish bandit, robber, or freebooter"; and "Lyllibolaro" ("lilli burlero") was "Part of the refrain . . . of a song ridiculing the Irish, popular about 1688" (*OED* Online).

20. Theodore G. Tappert and John W. Doberstein, trans., *The Journals of Henry Melchior Muhlenberg*, III (Philadelphia, 1958), 36; Jon Butler, *Awash in a Sea of Faith: Christianizing the American People* (Cambridge, Mass., 1990), chap. 4, "The Renewal of Christian Authority," 98–128. For an architectural history of the Anglican parish, see Dell Upton, *Holy Things and Profane: Anglican Parish Churches in Colonial Virginia* (Cambridge, Mass., 1986).

FIGURE 3. Detail from drawing depicting St. Mary's City. Ca. 1634. By Cary Carson. Collection of the Maryland State Archives

tobacco barn to hide its real purpose. The first dedicated chapel in Philadelphia, built in the 1730s, was "a room eighteen feet by twenty-two, which had very much the appearance of an out-kitchen, . . . adorned with a chimney instead of a cross." As late as 1837, St. Joseph's maintained a low profile. Its resident pastor, Father Etienne Dubuisson, described the church as "a rather poor affair. . . . It is a low depressed-looking edifice, having nothing on the outside that indicates its purpose, so that one might think it an old storehouse at the farther end of the court."[21]

21. Andrew White, *Relatio itineris in Marylandiam . . . Narrative of a Voyage to Maryland,* ed. E. A. Dalrymple (1634; rpt. Baltimore, 1874), 39; P. F. Dealy, "The Struggles and Sufferings of Our First American Missionaries," *Woodstock Letters,* XXI, no. 2 (1892), 210–227 (quotation on 225); "Annals of St. Joseph's Church, Philadelphia: Part First," ibid., II, no. 1 (1873), 21; Joseph C. Linck, *Fully Instructed and Vehemently Influenced: Catholic Preaching in Anglo-Colonial America* (Philadelphia, 2002), 99; Dennis C. Kurjack, "St. Joseph's and St. Mary's Churches," *Transactions of American Philosophical Society,* XLIII (1953), 199–209 (quotation on 200).

Only in Maryland did a Catholic chapel stand proud and tall—the "great brick chapel" (as it was commonly referred to) built in St. Mary's City in 1667 and, until its forced closure in 1704, the most prominent physical structure in the colony.[22] A census of Catholic and Quaker places of worship commissioned by Governor Nicholson in 1698 reported nine Catholic chapels in all, most attached to Jesuit manors, and two more were constructed before the first penal laws were enacted in 1704.[23] They were scattered far and wide across the Maryland backcountry, much to the dismay of the itinerant priests who served them. "You must not imagine our chapels lie as yours do," Joseph Mosely wrote his brother Michael, who was chaplain to a wealthy recusant family in England; "they are in great Forrests some miles from any House or Hospitality." The Jesuit chapels were built with the financial support of the lay community and deliberately adopted the architectural style of Protestant churches, excising much of the "pomp and ceremony" associated with the Catholic mass. As Tricia T. Pyne describes, chapels were "small and plain" both inside and out. No stained glass windows, no statuary, no incense, no pews. Nothing, in other words, to draw the eye of disapproving Protestants.[24]

22. John D. Krugler and Timothy B. Riordan trace the rise and fall of the great brick chapel in "'Scandalous and Offensive to the Government': The 'Popish Chappel' at St. Mary's City, Maryland, and the Society of Jesus, 1634 to 1705," *Mid-America*, LXXIII (1991), 187–208. The grandeur and prominence of the brick chapel was a defiant departure from Baltimore's plan to keep the practice of Catholicism in Maryland as private as possible, as Krugler notes in his *English and Catholic: The Lords Baltimore in the Seventeenth Century* (Baltimore, 2008), 226. There was one other Catholic chapel in seventeenth-century English America—on the island of Jamaica, which was seized by the English from Spanish control. John Taylor reported in 1687 that there was "a Romish chappell" in Port Royal, along with an Anglican church, a Presbyterian meetinghouse, and a "Quackers' meeting house and a Jewe's sinagog." See David Buisseret, ed., *Jamaica in 1687: The Taylor Manuscript at the National Library of Jamaica* (Kingston, Jamaica, 2000), 240.

23. In 1689, Nicholson ordered "the several Constables [to] go about from house to house . . . and take an exact Acco[unt] of all men women and Children and what religion and perswasion they are of also what ministers or priests Noncomformists Speakers or others they have residing within their several hundreds and what Churches Chapels meeting houses and other publick places of Devotion they have" (*Archives of Maryland*, XXV, 9).

24. Joseph Mosley to Michael Mosley, July 30, 1764, in "Letters of Father Joseph Mosley, S.J.," *Records of the American Catholic Historical Society of Philadelphia*, XVII (1906), 192–196 (quotation on 195); Tricia Terese Pyne, "The Maryland Catholic Community, 1690–1775: A Study in Culture, Religion, and Church" (Ph.D. diss., Catholic University of America, 1995), 45. In 1662, William and Temperance Bretton deeded an acre and a half of land to the "Roman Catholick Inhabitants and their Posterity" in New Towne to build "a Church or Chappel . . . Likewise for a Church yard wherein to bury their dead" (*Archives of Maryland*, XLI, 531).

FIGURE 4. Reconstruction of the "great brick chapel," St. Mary's City. Built ca. 1667. Photo by author

FIGURE 5. Sketch of St. Joseph's Church, Talbot County, Maryland. By Joseph Mosley, S.J. Archives of the Maryland Province of the Society of Jesus, box 1, folder 15, on deposit at the Booth Family Center for Special Collections, Georgetown University Library, Washington, D.C.

The simplest way to hide Catholic worship services, of course, was to perform them in a Protestant church. The practice of biconfessionalism—two different faiths sharing the same church building—was never officially sanctioned in Britain, though it was a common arrangement in Dutch and French communities that housed sizable populations of both Catholics and Protestants.[25] But in England's overseas possessions, biconfessionalism was an occasional feature of the colonial religious landscape, a pragmatic adaptation to reduced circumstances and geographical remoteness. Biconfessionalism was more likely to occur between different Protestant denominations: Anglican and Dutch Reformed congregations shared the church inside the fort in New York after the English conquest of New Amsterdam; Boston's Third Church hosted both Anglican and Puritan services in the 1680s; and German Lutherans and Dutch Reformed worshiped together in Pennsylvania (not always harmoniously).[26] There are fewer references to Protestants and Catholics sharing sacred space, but we know that the first Lord Baltimore allowed Protestants and Catholics to worship together in his house in Avalon (his ill-fated venture in Newfoundland), and the practice continued in his far more successful second plantation in Maryland. It seems reasonable to assume that similar arrangements were in place wherever there were Catholics numerous enough to assemble and the colonial authorities were willing to turn a blind eye to their presence—for example, in the sugar islands.[27]

25. Benjamin J. Kaplan's study of *simultaneum*, or biconfessionalism, in early modern Europe includes no examples drawn from the British Isles (*Divided by Faith: Religious Conflict and the Practice of Toleration in Early Modern Europe* [Cambridge, Mass., 2007]).

26. Governor Dongan wrote, "The great Church which serves both the English and the Dutch is within the fort, which is found to be very inconvenient" (Dongan to Lords of Trade and Plantations, New York, March 1687, CO 1/61, no. 75, fol. 309, TNA). Samuel Sewall complained repeatedly about the shared arrangements at the Third Church in his diary; see the entries for March 25, May 10, June 1, and June 12, 1687, and June 10 and 23, 1688, in *Diary of Samuel Sewall, 1674–1729*, I, *1674–1700* (Boston, 1878), 171, 176–177, 179–180, 216–218. On Lutheran and Dutch Reformed, see Tappert and Doberstein, trans., *Journals of Henry Melchior Muhlenberg*.

27. Thomas Hughes, *History of the Society of Jesus in North America: Colonial and Federal, Documents*, I, part 1 (London, 1908), 196; G. Alan Tar, "Church and State in the States," *Washington Law Review*, LXIV (1989), 73–110, esp. 77. By canon law, consecrated churches were not permitted to be used for "common or profane purposes"; see A. J. Schulte, "Consecration," in *The Catholic Encyclopedia* (New York, 1908), http://www.newadvent.org/cathen/04276a.htm. By the 1760s, biconfessionalism would become the official policy of the English in the newly conquered territory of Quebec; the archbishop of York's plan for managing interconfessional relations included a clause "That the Churches in the said

Purpose-built chapels were exceedingly rare in English America, and most Catholic houses of worship were private homes, or rooms in homes, during the seventeenth and eighteenth centuries. After the brick church in St. Mary's was closed and the public worship of Catholicism outlawed in 1704, colonial Catholics had to develop a "tactical and adaptive relation to space," as Frances Dolan put it in her study of the "lost spaces" of early modern English Catholicism. Like their English counterparts, Maryland Catholics created a new sacred geography centered on the household. Private chapels attached to the estates of wealthy Catholics proliferated in Maryland, numbering more than fifty by midcentury. These were for the most part very modest affairs, as a survey of such private places of worship in 1698 confirms: a "Wooden Chappell at Mr Goulicks Plantation," a "Clabboard house att Doncaster Towne," a simple room "in the dwelling house of Keystone." In Philadelphia, before the first Catholic church was erected in 1732, the city's resident priest, Father Joseph Greaton, "followed the custom of his predecessors and celebrated Mass in the house of some of the faithful, attended by the other members of the congregation. This custom was known to all the city naturally, as there was no need of secrecy, and hence tradition has marked certain sites in the city as 'chapels,' which were in reality the houses of the Catholics in the early days, who were privileged to have Mass celebrated beneath their roof."[28]

But, in fact, there was considerable need for secrecy, and the operation of private chapels outside Maryland was usually a clandestine affair, shrouded in mystery and rumor. The Irish were particularly familiar with clandestine chapels, since in the seventeenth century the majority Catholic population in Ireland worshipped in "semisecret chapels, which the English called mass-houses" and which were designed to be as "unobtrusive" as possible in the

Province of Quebec be used for the public Worship of Almighty God, as well by those who profess the Church of England as by the Roman Catholics; and the times of service in the said Churches according to the Rites of each Religion respectively to be so settled as to prevent any Interferings or Dispute." See Heads of a Plan for the Establishment of Ecclesiastical Affairs in the Province of Quebec, ca. 1764, Shelburne Papers, LIX, 27, Clements Library, University of Michigan, Ann Arbor.

28. Frances E. Dolan, "Gender and the 'Lost' Spaces of Catholicism," *Journal of Interdisciplinary History*, XXXII (2002), 641–665 (quotation on 641); Reports of Sheriffs, in A Collection of Papers Brought to the Council of Trade, by Sir Thomas Laurence, Maryland, May 28, 1698, CO 5/714, no. 47v, TNA; Kirlin, *Catholicity in Philadelphia*, 31. Beatriz Betancourt Hardy's dissertation, "Papists in a Protestant Age: The Catholic Gentry and Community in Colonial Maryland, 1689–1776" (Ph.D. diss., University of Maryland, College Park, 1993), lists the private chapels in Maryland in appendix B.

landscape; in the cities, most were "converted stables or warehouses located on narrow lanes behind other buildings." Even Montserrat—the demographic center of Catholicism in the English Atlantic—had no formal churches at all until the nineteenth century, leaving recusants no option but to worship covertly in private homes. In the colonies, we have fewer archival traces of these secret chapels outside of the oral histories collected by nineteenth- and early-twentieth-century antiquarians. On Antigua, the Anglican minister reported that the island's Catholics "have mass performed in some private houses in this Island but so secretly that tis almost impossible to discover them." A chapel "capable of holding 300 persons" was apparently maintained in the house of the Spanish asiento agent Don Santiago de Castillo after the English conquest of Jamaica, when "there was no liberty of conscience" for Catholics. Santiago's church came to an end when an English clergyman on the island denounced him and his priests as traitors; the chapel was broken into, and the priests "had to seek safety in hiding." A Jesuit historian concluded, "This church must have been somewhere in Spanish Town, but we have no further record of its existence."[29]

A story recounted in a commemorative biography of St. Joseph's Church, however embellished by sentimental prose, captures the confused geography of Catholic liturgical practice in the colonial city and the longing of recusants for consecrated spaces of their own.

> An old lady of mixed English and German descent, then more than four-score years and ten . . . delighted to tell, how one Sunday morning, her father, mother, sisters, and two elder brothers with herself were gathered, according to custom, in the "best room" while the father read the prayers for mass, when a friend, stopping at the window, said: "Why don't you go to hear mass?" "Father and Mother both replied; O, if we only could!" The tears would run down the dear old lady's cheeks, as she told how

29. Kaplan, *Divided by Faith*, 184; Francis Byam to Bishop Gibson, Antigua, June 16, 1744, Fulham Papers, XIX, fols. 275–276; Francis X. Delaney, *A History of the Catholic Church in Jamaica, B.W.I., 1494–1929* (New York, 1930), 24–25. April Lee Hatfield provides a good account of Castillo's chapel and its travails in *Boundaries of Belonging: English Jamaica and the Spanish Caribbean, 1655–1715* (Philadelphia, 2023), 144–159. She points out that, if Castillo's church really was big enough to hold three hundred people, it would have been one of the largest buildings on the island. Those who attended might have included "Spanish, English, Irish, French, or Black seamen or residents, or enslaved Africans awaiting transshipment" (145).

mass was said for years in the very next house, "and we knew nothing of it." This old lady told me that her mother had often been present at mass and instructions, in an old frame house that stood at the S. W. Corner of Front and Spruce Streets, and whenever she passed that house, she would make a profound courtesy, for she said it was holy ground.[30]

Over time, certain sites became associated in memory, if not in historical fact, with private chapels or churchyards. The burial site of a suspected priest, Philadelphian Dr. Browne, was referred to as "The Priest's Lot" and a century later was "still pointed out as such by the old residents of the neighborhood." The home of another Philadelphia resident, Paul Miller, was known as "The Chapel" for the remainder of the eighteenth century even after it had been replaced by St. Joseph's as the meeting place for the city's Catholics. When it was put up for sale in 1780, the advertisement in the *Pennsylvania Packet* described the lot as "fifteen acres . . . known by the name of the Chapel," and "with a large two story brick tenement."[31]

The memories recorded by a nineteenth-century chronicler of Philadelphia, John F. Watson, show that these associations ran deep. A lot on the northeast corner of Front and Walnut Streets was reputed to be "holy ground" that had been "consecrated as a chapel"; an elderly resident of the city "remembered to have seen a neighbouring man often passing the house to the Green Tree pump for water, who always made his genuflexion in passing, and on being questioned, said he knew it was consecrated ground." Another site, at the corner of Second and Chestnut Streets, had a similar reputation. A woman born around 1760 told Watson that "she had often heard her parents say it was built for a Papal chapel, and that the people opposed its being so used in so public a place." And a building "in ruins" on the road connecting Nicetown to Frankfort was rumored to be the site of an early chapel frequented by "Irish papists"—it was called, fittingly, "the haunted place." These echoes of a colonial Catholic past in the republican city evoked complicated narratives of loss, longing, and half-remembered ritual habits that are difficult to de-code from our vantage point. Were Watson's nineteenth-century informants recalling actual sites of worship or voicing the Victorian nostalgia for colonial

30. "Annals of St. Joseph's Church, Philadelphia, Part First," *Woodstock Letters,* II, no. 1 (1873), 17–18.

31. Kirlin, *Catholicity in Philadelphia,* 69; *Pennsylvania Packet* (Philadelphia), Apr. 4, 1780, 3.

precedents that characterized their generation? In either case, their memories reflect the deep-seated association of Catholicism with local places that marked the faith from its inception.[32]

Ghosts both spectral and material also haunted those colonial communities where the English displaced previous Catholic residents and their religious structures. The 1655 conquest of Jamaica, originally a Spanish colony, entailed a dismantling of the former Catholic ecclesiastical buildings on the island. These sites of Spanish Catholicism continued to exert an uncanny power over the new Protestant inhabitants, even after the sites were demolished or repurposed. A fanciful account of the "inchanting" of Jamaica by its former Spanish Catholic residents can be found in the narrative of a convicted felon transported to the island in 1687. John Taylor enumerated the "inchanted places" he encountered on Jamaica: the "secret caverns and bowels of the earth" where the fleeing Spanish hid their treasure, the mirage of a "well-built Spanish house" into which a "frier of the order of St. Francis by his garbb" lured the English before vanishing into thin air. After the English victory, the smaller hermitages and chapels that had given architectural shape to the capital of Spanish Town (or St. Jago de la Vega) were all demolished or secularized. The "hermitages of Our Lady of Bethlehem, St. Lucy, St. Jerome and the Calvary, all very decent and venerable," were razed. The hermitage of Our Lady of Belén was turned into a sheep pen, the cathedral known as the "White Church" was destroyed in the fighting, and the second most prominent church—the Dominican friars' "Red Church"—was taken over by the Anglicans. These Catholic sites might have "ceased to serve as local landmarks" for the English conquerors, in James Robertson's view, but the main residential streets retained their Spanish-era names: White Church Street, Red Church Street, and Monk Street.[33]

The process of naming, and renaming, colonial sites created layers of meaning and memory that defy easy disentanglement, as scholars of Native

32. John F. Watson, *Annals of Philadelphia, and Pennsylvania, in the Olden Time*, 3 vols. (Philadelphia, 1884), I, 427, 453.

33. James Robertson's study of Spanish Town, Jamaica, during the transition from Spanish to English rule highlights the presence of "ghosts" (Catholic sites, objects, and associations) that "clustered in the towns where the Spanish imprint remained strongest"; see Robertson, "Re-writing the English Conquest of Jamaica in the Late Seventeenth Century," *English Historical Review*, CXVII (2002), 813–839 (quotation on 833). For a wonderful discussion of "uncanny" sacred spaces—landscapes or buildings that exude a numinous power beyond their material presence—see Jon P. Mitchell, "How Landscapes

America have shown, and we can add religion to this cultural sedimentation. Catholic place-names were not unknown in English America, but as a rule Protestant settlers avoided saints' names and other Catholic references wherever possible. John Winthrop insisted that a settlement in Massachusetts called Hue's Cross be renamed Hue's Folly because of the idolatrous connotations of the word "cross." Anglican officials also eschewed using saints' names as toponyms for colonial towns, even though many of their parishes carried the name of a saint. In sharp contrast, Lord Baltimore's colony aggressively turned Native names into Catholic ones. Yaocomico was the Indigenous name of the community that became St. Mary's City. In March 1634, Leonard Calvert and other "Gentlemen adventurers, and their servants" arrived at Patowmede River, where "they began to give names to places, and called the *Southerne* point of that River, Saint *Gregories;* and the *Northerne* point, Saint *Michaels.*" They anchored at an island "which they called S. *Clements.*" "Almost every Place that they came to they called by the Name of a Saint," an early settler grumbled. When the proprietor lost his colony in 1694 after the ouster of James II, the capital was moved from St. Mary's to the town once known as Anne Arundel's Towne, after a prominent English Catholic laywoman, now renamed Annapolis in a symbolic renunciation of Maryland's Catholic roots. The battle over names further muddied the ability of colonial authorities to create legible and stable maps of religious belonging in their provinces.[34]

Remember," *Material Religion,* XVI (2020), 432–451. For John Taylor, see Buisseret, ed., *Jamaica in 1687,* 128–129. On the hermitages, see Robertson, "Late Seventeenth-Century Spanish Town, Jamaica: Building an English City on Spanish Foundations," *Early American Studies,* VI (2008), 346–390 (quotations 359, 361). Jamaica's confessional history in the 1650s and 1660s, when it underwent a rapid succession of regime changes—from Spanish Catholicism to Cromwellian Puritanism to Restoration Anglicanism in the space of five short years—represents a telescoped version of England's larger Reformation; see David Manning, "Reformation and the Wickedness of Port Royal, Jamaica, 1655–c. 1692," in Crawford Gribben and Scott R. Spurlock, eds., *Puritans and Catholics in the Trans-Atlantic World, 1600–1800* (London, 2015), 131–163.

34. Christine M. DeLucia explores layered sites of meaning in *Memory Lands: King Philip's War and the Place of Violence in the Northeast* (New Haven, Conn., 2018). Winthrop: James Kendall Hosmer, ed., *Winthrop's Journal, "History of New England," 1630–1649,* Original Narratives of Early American History (New York, 1953), I, 94. Calvert: Francis L. Hawks, ed., *A Relation of Maryland, Reprinted from the London Edition of 1635* (New York, 1865), 4–5. "Name of a Saint": *A Short Account of the First Settlement of the Provinces of Virginia, Maryland, New-York, New-Jersey, and Pensylvania, by the English* (London, 1735), 12.

The Laity

Another kind of absence haunts the scholar of early American Catholicism: the thousands of men, women, and children who may be entirely lost to our view because of their invisibility in the archives. Served by fugitive priests in disguise, gathering in chapels camouflaged as tobacco barns or in a private room on an isolated plantation, the Catholic laity lived a furtive religious existence that is difficult to reconstruct. The colonial records reviewed in the previous chapter provide a useful starting point, telling us how many people came to the attention of constables, sheriffs, and justices of the peace for behavior that fit the stereotypical "Catholic" or who left clues as to their religious allegiance in their personal and legal documents. The cumulative evidence points to the existence of a sizable recusant population interspersed throughout the North American colonies, with concentrated pockets in certain places (Maryland and the sugar islands), living largely incognito, or at least undisturbed, among their Protestant neighbors except when political crises forced them into public view. In these circumstances, religious "passing" was a ubiquitous feature of colonial life.

Colonial authorities were well aware that identifying *any* religious affiliation for their subject populations was challenging because of the unsettled conditions of colonial life and the wide diversity of opinions that seemed to prevail. The indentured servants, convict laborers, and diasporic refugees who made up the bulk of European immigration to the English colonies in the seventeenth and eighteenth centuries were drawn from a multitude of religious backgrounds. The lament of the much-harried governor of the Leeward Islands, Colonel Stapleton, in 1677 was echoed by many of his peers: "There is noe question but there are (Considering the number of people) as many Various Religions as at home, but as all, or most doe frequent the Churches when they like the parson or when a fitt of Devotion comes over them, some, when Comon prayer is over, I cannot tell the Variety of their Religion." Complaints about the "mixed multitude" of faiths in the provinces were as routine as complaints about smuggling and debt—just part of the background noise in the flow of correspondence between the colonies and the metropole.[35]

35. "Answer to Inquiries sent to Colonel Stapleton, Governor of the Leeward Islands . . . ," Nov. 22, 1677, CO 1/38, no. 65, TNA. Historians of the Irish in the West Indies have largely endorsed Stapleton's views; as Donald Harman Akenson puts it, the Irish on Montserrat practiced a religion that was "flexible and equivocal. Rather than professing either a Catholic or a Protestant faith, many Irish planters adhered to both—either at separate

Clues about lay religious identity were hard to come by. Outward dress provided no help in unmasking ordinary papists as it did for priests. Nor did the display of specialized skills such as Latin or deep theological knowledge. Apart from those lay Catholics wealthy enough to have a private chapel or a dedicated room in their house for the celebration of the mass, there was nothing in the social or economic lives of the vast majority of laymen and -women to indicate their religious "perswasion." Deference in the presence of a priest or suspected priest could indicate an instinctive preference for the Roman religion, but it could also indicate the habitual deference of laboring men (many of whom had once been, or still were, indentured servants) toward a man of obvious learning and genteel bearing. Scorn for the established church—whether manifest in disruptive behavior or simple avoidance—could certainly raise suspicions, as could unguarded declarations of support for the pope or the Stuart cause, or the possession of Catholic books or objects. And sometimes Catholics could be revealed by the color of their skin.

Since priests were so scarce in English America, the reaction of ordinary Catholics when they came face-to-face with one for the first time could be very telling. One such encounter was recorded in the journal kept by Antoine Biet of his mission to Barbados in the 1650s. "I went for a walk alone in a se-cluded spot, between the orange and lemon trees, . . . when I was surprised by a large man who came up to me. He was of the Irish nation." Addressing Biet in "a corrupt language intermixed with Italian, Portuguese, and Provençal" (the lingua franca of the Mediterranean), the man declared himself "a servant of your Lady." Biet tried to deflect the overture, responding (in the same patois), "What do you mean, I am not a priest." But the Irishman persisted. He "started to show me a great deal of tenderness, making the sign of the cross to let me know he was Catholic." Still rebuffed by the wary priest (who "feared that he was someone who came to expose me and reveal me as a priest in court"), the man "almost fell to his knees in front of me, once again making the sign of the cross, and recited the Lord's Prayer in Latin, the Hail Mary, the Credo and the De Profundis to certify that he believed in the prayer for

---

times, or, in some cases, simultaneously" (Akenson, *If the Irish Ran the World: Montserrat, 1630–1730* [Montreal, 1997], 46 n. 137). Evan Haefeli traces the adaptability of the Irish on Montserrat to their experiences as a clandestine faith in Ireland in Haefeli, *Accidental Pluralism: America and the Religious Politics of English Expansion, 1497–1662* (Chicago, 2021), 185–186. That the Irish lived "intermingled with the English and Scottish heretics" on the islands abetted their flexible religiosity; see Gwynn, ed., "Documents Relating to the Irish in the West Indies," *Analecta Hibernica,* no. 4 (October 1932), 187.

the dead, and he told me he was Catholic, Apostolic, and Roman." Here are all the standard hallmarks of lay Catholicism: extreme deference to a priest, using the sign of the cross, and the ability to recite by memory (and in Latin) the key prayers of the faith.[36]

Such frank displays of Catholic belief and practice were more common in a place such as Barbados, where—as Biet would learn in his three short months on the island—on "Sundays, when each one is free to do as he wants on the plantation . . . no one bothers with what one is doing." A similar freedom of religious expression reigned on nearby St. Christopher, where John Stritch described the "joy" of the island's Catholics, who "came in droves and without concealing themselves" to greet him. "Some took his hands to kiss them, others threw themselves at his feet to receive his benediction." First-time encounters between priests and lay Catholics on the mainland were far more circumspect and rarely recorded, though we have one story from colonial New York. During his 1643 visit to New Amsterdam, the Jesuit Isaac Jogues took the confession of an "Irish Catholic" who had just arrived from Virginia and encountered a "good lad" ("a Pole," he later learned), who met him "in a retired place" and "fell at his feet—taking his hands to kiss them, and exclaiming 'Martyr, Martyr of Jesus Christ!'"[37]

For a handful of unfortunates, the first time they encountered a priest was in prison, awaiting execution. Prisons functioned as important communication nodes for England's recusant population as the laity flocked to see, hear, and touch the hundreds of missionary priests caught in the judicial net under Elizabeth and the early Stuarts. From their cells, the soon-to-be-martyred priests heard confessions, distributed devotional objects, and even performed the sacrament of the mass, turning prisons into de facto churches. But prisons served another purpose for the Catholic felons who found themselves incarcerated after being convicted of a capital crime: providing last rites. For many poor and vagabond recusants, this might have been the first time they had sacramental access to a priest. Thanks to the voluminous records of the Old Bailey in London, especially the ordinary's accounts, we can eavesdrop on the conversations between convicted felons and their priests as the former sought

36. Handler, "Father Antoine Biet's Visit to Barbados," *Journal of the Barbados Museum and Historical Society*, XXXII, no. 2 (May 1967), 60–61.

37. Ibid., 62; Pelleprat, "De La Mission Irlandaise," in Gwynn, ed., "Documents Relating to the Irish in the West Indies," *Analecta Hibernica*, no. 4 (October 1932), 209; Thwaites, ed., *Jesuit Relations*, XXXI, 99.

absolution before mounting the scaffold. Executions were prime opportunities for religious conversion—or for moments of religious unmasking. A man who "declar'd himself a Protestant" when arrested might reveal his true colors while awaiting death, as did John Cross, who "immediately became a Papist" when he was visited by "a Gentleman of the *Romish* Perswasion."[38]

We can't extract lessons about colonial recusants directly from these stories, but they do give us an entry point into the conversations about religious identity taking place in situations when the stakes were high and desperate men and women had one last chance to show their "true" faith. And what we find by listening in on these conversations is that the line between Protestant and Catholic was considerably blurred for many laymen and -women. Alexander Carroll, condemned to hang for the murder of Thomas Fenwick, "did at first pretend to be a *Protestant*, and born of *Protestant* Parents; but at last confess'd that he was a *Papist*, and all his Ancestors were of that perswasion, and therefore he was resolved to die in it." Carroll's beliefs did not fall neatly on one side of the confessional divide, however, as further questioning revealed: "He said, he rely'd only upon Christ's Merits for the Pardon of his Sins and the Salvation of his Soul; and that he did not depend upon the Prayers that might be made for him after his Death, but thought it most Safe for his eternal Welfare to do what he could to repent and be reconcil'd to God, before he left this World." The ordinary (or prison chaplain) was dismissive of Carroll's equivocating—he did not appear "much versed in any Religion"—but we can more charitably, and more accurately, describe Carroll as ambidextrous in his faith. Another flexitarian was the convicted felon Gabriel Laurence, "a Papist" who "did not make many particular Confessions." The ordinary was confused as to how to categorize Laurence. "He kept the Chapel with the rest, for the most part, . . . and said the Lord's Prayer and the Creed after me. He own'd himself of the *Romish* Communion, but said he had a great liking to the Church of *England*, and could communicate with them, but this I would not allow unless he renounc'd [his e]rrors." We are firmly in the world of Protestant/Catholic hybridity here, of men like the accuser in Katherine Curtis's 1717 trial for theft, who presented "so indifferent a Character on several accounts, and especially as having in a little time chang'd his Religion

38. Lisa McClain, *Lest We Be Damned: Practical Innovation and Lived Experience among Catholics in Protestant England, 1559–1642* (New York, 2004), 144; Ordinary of Newgate's Account, Oct. 18, 1749 (OA17491018), *Old Bailey Proceedings Online*.

from a Protestant to a Papist, and then again from a Papist to a Protestant" as to lose all credibility. (Curtis was acquitted.)[39]

Some of these convicted felons found their way to the colonies. One such religious chameleon surfaced in Jamaica during the 1680s. William Hicks, once the curate at a London parish, was convicted of a capital crime in 1687 and "caryed in a cart with a halter about his neck to Tibourne." Hicks earned himself a last-minute reprieve by an opportunistic conversion to Catholicism while in jail. A priest, no less a personage than "Father Peters the King's confessor," "perswaided him from the Protistant religion (or rather from noe religion) to be a Roman Catholick, by which means he obtained the benefitt of transportation." The transported Hicks fetched up on Jamaica, where he came to the attention of John Taylor. And executions were occasions for religious unmasking in the colonies as well as in London. In Georgia, a man awaiting execution admitted he "had been of different Sects of Religion, conformable to the Country he was in: a Presbyterian in the Northern Provinces, and at Augustin a Papist, as it was generally thought he died; though he received the Sacrament at the Hands of a Divine of the Church of England."[40]

The colonial gentry as well as transported felons contained within their ranks those who had converted to (or from) Catholicism for pragmatic reasons and occupied a middle ground of belief. A prominent planter on Barbados, Irish emigrant Richard Hackett, played a dangerous game of religious roulette during the politically volatile decade of the 1640s, when an influx of Puritan settlers disrupted the island's uneasy coexistence of Catholics and Protestants. Hackett's Anglo surname and propertied status provided "cultural camouflage" at first—"if indeed he was Catholic," Kristen Block and Jenny Shaw caution. But in 1642, Hackett and a crew of "Hibernian Christians" numbering in the hundreds fled Barbados to nearby Guadeloupe, where they petitioned for religious asylum. Greeting the Spanish governor (in Latin), Hackett described how the refugees, "sick and wretched," had fled persecution at the hands of English heretics. Block and Shaw suggest Hackett might have "feign[ed] his Irish Catholic heritage to gain the governor's trust," though we will never know for sure. In the event, Hackett—like many

39. Ordinary of Newgate's Account, Jan. 28, 1708 (OA17080128), May 1726 (OA17260509), Trial of Katherine Curtis, Jan. 11, 1717 (t17170111–33), all in *Old Bailey Proceedings Online*.

40. Buisseret, ed., *Jamaica in 1687*, 18; William Stephens, *A Journal of the Proceedings in Georgia, Beginning October 20, 1737*, in Allen D. Candler, ed., *The Colonial Records of the State of Georgia*, IV, *Stephens' Journal, 1737–1740* (Atlanta, 1906), 382.

other ambidextrous Christians—"played with multiple religious and national identities to achieve his goals."[41]

The religious allegiance of the governor of the Leeward Islands himself, Sir Nathaniel Johnson, was hotly disputed during the turmoil of the 1680s. A seasoned imperial administrator, Johnson enjoyed a reputation for latitudinarianism in the islands because of his willingness to cultivate good relationships with local Catholics and with neighboring French Martinique. After James II was ousted and William and Mary took the throne in 1689, however, he found his Protestant credentials challenged. Johnson's somewhat tortured defense of his religious orthodoxy reveals just how tricky it was for ambitious men of ambiguous faith to navigate the unstable religious landscape of the late seventeenth century. "I have allwaies professed and owned my self a Protestant, and so far from being a Dissembler in that particular, that I never during the late indulgence in England to the Roman Catholicks once went, as I believe many good Protestants out of curiositie may have done, to hear Mass." Since his arrival in the islands, "I doe not remember that there hath bin any Roman Catholick Priest in my Companie above 2 or 3 times and that in Publick." Johnson maintained he had always been a faithful communicant of the Church of England, even during James II's rule, when Catholics could openly practice their faith; "if I were a Roman Catholick why should I not have publickly professed it when with safety and to the advancement of my Interest I might have done it[?]" During Charles II's reign, "there might be good reason for such dissimulation in Papists in any office, because without it they could not qualifie themselves for a Continuation therein," but under the openly Catholic James II, papists had no need to hide their faith. Johnson's forthright acknowledgment of the politics of religious identity is a rare glimpse into a world where ambition and "curiositie" could drive men to explore switching faiths.[42]

---

41. Kristen Block and Jenny Shaw, "Subjects without an Empire: The Irish in the Early Modern Caribbean," *Past and Present,* no. 210 (February 2011), 39–41. Block explores the stratagems and "performances" of northern European Protestants caught up in the Spanish Inquisition's net in *Ordinary Lives in the Early Caribbean: Religion, Colonial Competition, and the Politics of Profit* (Athens, Ga., 2012), part 2. Those who professed to convert to Catholicism to spare themselves from the Inquisitors were "religious chameleons," in her words, who had learned to act the part of Catholics from their exposure to the multiconfessional, multilingual world of Atlantic trade and privateering (103).

42. Governor Sir Nathaniel Johnson to Lords of Trade and Plantations, July 15, 1689, CO 152/37, no. 19, TNA.

On the island of Barbados, a supposed Catholic "plot" to overthrow the colonial regime in 1688 led to a series of interrogations that yield valuable insight
into the vernacular understanding of lay piety. The colony had been roiled by
the news of James II's ouster, which upended a half century of tentative peace
among the Protestant and Catholic settlers on the island. Amid the turmoil
of 1689, as the island awaited news of the Glorious Revolution's outcome, a
handful of prominent Catholic planters were arrested for conspiring with the
island's numerous Irish servants to support the Stuart cause. Thomas Montgomery tried to convince the vengeful governor, Colonel Stede, that he had
always been a true Protestant at heart by distancing himself from all the
standard markers of Catholicism: "He knows not by wrote [rote] any one
Prayer used in the Church of Rome or ever kept the fast of the said Church
or did ever use beads or know their meaning, or is acquainted with any of
the ceremonys soe as to know anything thereof." His seeming embrace of
the Roman Church was "out of complaisance and to oblidge the said Jesuit."
(The "said Jesuit" was the French priest Father Michael, whom Montgomery
and his coreligionist Willoughby Chamberlain had brought over from Martinique themselves to minister to the island's Catholic community.) Only a
desire to be "civill and curteous" to the visiting priest, who spoke only Latin
and French and therefore needed a translator, induced Montgomery to invite
the Jesuit to stay at his house. The "Jesuit made me do it" defense didn't work,
since Montgomery had already been seen multiple times at mass, receiving
the eucharist from the hands of the priest and even assisting the priest during
the sacrament. One witness's testimony that he heard Chamberlain "declare
that the Reason of his being of the Popish Religion was onely for his Interest
sake" confirmed Stede's judgment of the two as rank "hypocrites." Another
witness dismissed Chamberlain as "an Ambitious, fatt foole" who "changed
his religion on that very day his Ma'ties Landed in England." Dissembling
was never a valid defense for accused recusants, since deceit was the hallmark
of Catholicism in the eyes of Protestants.[43]

In Maryland, the shifting fortunes of the Catholic elite—who held most
of the positions of trust and authority in the colony under the first three
Lords Baltimore—led to opportunistic renunciations and conversions as men

43. Col. James Kendall to earl of Shrewsbury, Barbados, June 26, 1690, CO 28/1, no. 41,
TNA. Chamberlain himself insisted "he never was a Roman Catholique in his heart" and
volunteered "for his fault to stand publiquely in a white Sheet," the standard punishment
for ecclesiastical crimes; see "A Collection of Papers Relating to Sir Thomas Montgomerie
and Willoughby Chamberlayne," May 30, 1689, CO 28/37, nos. 7 xx, 7 xxxi, 7 liii.

shifted their religious allegiances to advance their careers. Maryland's Catholic elite faced two civil wars in the 1640s and the 1650s that forced them temporarily from power, the loss of their proprietary status in 1694 after James II's ouster, the adoption of harsh new penal laws that outlawed the public practice of Catholicism in 1704, and the proprietor's pragmatic conversion to the Church of England in 1715 in a successful bid to regain his province. Their hold always precarious, many in Baltimore's circle found that discretion was the better part of valor. Henry Darnall, the colony's attorney general in the mid-eighteenth century, was one such religious careerist. He faced a series of charges in the 1750s from Maryland's assembly that were aimed at uncovering his true identity. Though Darnall was "brought up and educated at St. Omer's [the Jesuit seminary in France]" and "professed the Popish Religion," he had to make strategic adjustments to his religious practice when he began to practice law and take on government positions. At that time, he publicly declared he was a Protestant, but one neighbor testified that "Mass was said in his House after such Appointment." He himself, however, "was never present," and the religious service was apparently "for Mr. Darnall's Family" only. On the other hand, he did not act like a good Protestant, either: another testified that "he never saw Mr. Darnall at any Protestant Church, nor ever heard any of his Neighbours say they ever did see him, Mr. Darnall, at any." Avoiding services both at the parish church and his own private chapel, Darnall placed himself in religious limbo. Darnall's brother John also tried to walk a fine line between recusancy and conformity, educating his children "as Papists" while making an occasional appearance at his parish church.[44]

Planters of ambiguous religious identity often presided over mixed households of Catholics and Protestants. Thomas Gerard was described variously in the colonial records as a "pretended" Catholic whose "life and conversion was not agreable to his profession" and as a Protestant householder who mistreated his Irish Catholic servants. Gerard's inconsistent religious policy within his own household landed him before the courts in the 1650s. Though Gerard "professed himselfe a Roman Catholique," Robert Slye testified, he "brought not his Wife and children to the Roman Catholique Church." The Jesuit Francis Fitzherbert allegedly told Slye that Gerard had "beaten an Irish Servant of his . . . because shee refused to bee a Protestant, or goe to prayer wth those of his family tht were soe." (Slye himself stood accused of "beating his Irish servants, because they refused to bee of the same Religion of him,"

44. "Report Delivered by Col. Hooper, from the Committee of Grievances and Courts of Justice," June 17, 1752, *Archives of Maryland*, L, 52–53.

so his testimony was not disinterested.) Filtered as it is through the intense religious partisanship of the Cromwellian era, the testimony in Gerard's case suggests a household in which the religious allegiances of the master, his family, and his servants were unclear and contested.[45]

In another case, a Maryland man told multiple stories of his upbringing in order to avoid punishment as a deserter. William Marshall, "alias Johnson," confessed before the Governor's Council in Annapolis that he was born "of protestant parents, and I have also been brought up in that Religion." But others testified that "Johnson" had been "brought up in the Romish Faith" in a border town in Pennsylvania and now resided in Baltimore County among other "Roman Catholicks." Mobilized into the Maryland militia at the beginning of the Seven Years' War, Marshall deserted and found refuge with a band of French and Indians. When discovered, he "pretended that I had been taken Prisoner by a party of Indians" but later—while "very drunk"— admitted that "I was not taken prisoner but went off voluntarily to the French being incited thereto by several Roman Catholics who corresponded with the Enemy." Since he "knew some of that profession," he "framed such a Story as I thought would be believed" of his life as a Catholic, including regularly attending mass at the Jesuit chapel of Henry Neale. Now, his ruse discovered, he "solemnly declare[d] that I never was at Mr. Neal's, or any other Mass House in my Life." If the various reports are to be believed, Marshall "passed" as both a Protestant and a Catholic, depending on which identity best served his purposes.[46]

An illuminating case of ambiguous or mixed identity was John Tatham, "alias Gray," who at his death in 1700 left an estate worth £3,765, including more than 500 books, making his the largest library outside New England. Tatham was a former Benedictine monk who apparently married and started a family before emigrating to Pennsylvania in the 1680s. In the late 1670s, he served as a missionary priest in England at considerable risk to life and limb, given the heightened hysteria over Catholic spies sparked by the "Popish Plot" of 1678. We don't know when he left the priesthood, but in 1685, he came to the attention of William Penn, who wrote his agent, Thomas Lloyd, about the man he knew as Gray. "Pray be carefull of thy carriage to one Gray, a

45. "Thomas Gerard Esquire," ibid., XLI, 145.

46. The confusing story of Marshall, alias Johnson, can be found in several places in the Maryland Archives; see Horatio Sharpe to Lord Baltimore, Nov. 1, 1756, ibid., VI, 501–504, 512; "At a Council Held in the City of Annapolis," Nov. 29, 1756, ibid., XXXI, 174, 178–179.

Rom. Cath. Gent. that comes over now, he is subtile and prying and lowly . . . but not such a bottom in other things, he is a Scholar, and avers to the Calvanists." Despite his doubts, Penn directed his stewards to provide Tatham with a generous land grant (five thousand acres) in Bucks County. Attracting financially solvent settlers in these early years of the colony's existence was more important than creed. "Remember me . . . to J. Gray the R.C.," he wrote James Harrison. "Keep things well with such Persons, for our Genll credit."[47]

Tatham went on to have a prosperous career in Pennsylvania and the Jerseys, amassing a fortune and serving in several important governmental positions. Yet suspicions about his true religious identity dogged him throughout his life; he was a frequent litigant in the colonial courts, and in 1698, he filed a slander suit against Christopher Wetherill for "Scandalizing [him] by Saying that he is a Papist." Although Tatham "passed" as a Protestant in the colonial world for most of his life, the scholarly consensus was that he was a crypto-Catholic, as revealed by his estate inventory: alongside his library, which contained more than 200 Catholic titles, were listed numerous devotional items, such as a silver box containing relics, some pieces of gold church plate, and two crucifixes. But when we look more closely, we see that his library—like the man himself—presented two faces; shelved alongside numerous Catholic instructional manuals on such topics as *How to Hear the Mass* were treatises on religious cohabitation, such as *A Method for Uniteing Cathol. and Protestts.* and *The Way to Convince without Dispute.* On one "low shelf" in Tatham's study, close at hand, a copy of the Thirty-Nine Articles of the Church of England sat next to Lithurgie of the Mass—a small but telling example of the religiously mixed world men such as Tatham inhabited.[48]

---

47. Henry H. Bisbee, "John Tatham, Alias Gray," *Pennsylvania Magazine of History and Biography,* LXXXIII (1959), 253–264 (quotations on 254).

48. Ibid., 259. The inventories of John and Elizabeth Tatham, along with a full catalog of Tatham's library, can be found in Thomas C. Middleton, "John and Elizabeth Tatham of Burlington, N.J., A.D. 1681–1700," *Records of the American Catholic Historical Society of Philadelphia,* VI (1895), 61–135 (quotations on 117, 118, 125–127). At his death in 1700, Tatham owned 554 individual book titles, and of these, 203 were by Catholic authors or were "pro-Catholic" in subject, according to Shona Helen Johnston, "Papists in a Protestant World: The Catholic Anglo-Atlantic in the Seventeenth Century" (Ph.D. diss., Georgetown University, 2011), 155–159. Although, as Susannah Monta points out, devotional texts written by Catholic authors had wide cross-confessional appeal in the seventeenth century; see Monta, "Uncommon Prayer? Robert Southwell's *Short Rule for a Good Life* and Catholic Domestic Devotion in Post-Reformation England," in Lowell Gallagher, ed., *Redrawing the Map of Early Modern English Catholicism* (Toronto, 2012), 247–271.

Despite the efforts of some recusants to downplay their beliefs for strategic purposes, there were times when they threw caution to the wind. The periodic attempts by the exiled Stuarts to restore their right to the English throne prompted Catholics in the American colonies to raise toasts to various Stuart "Pretenders" and other Catholic monarchs. A gathering of recusants at the home of the Popes in 1693, which included some notables (a ship captain, an attorney, a merchant, the commander of a troop of horse) and "several others of the Irish Nation," began with drink and ended in criminal charges of sedition. A "Coll. Sayer" "began to discourse of the late Revolution both at home and here and . . . swore God damn em all for a Company of heretick Dogs Especially the Church of England who were the worst of all the Seperatists from the Church of Rome and again Swore by God that the Turkish Religion was better than the Protestant Religion and that he had rather see that Religion flourish in England then that damn'd Protestant Religion." And then the entire company "drank King James's health." An inquiry was opened five years later into the doings of "Major Walter Smith" to see "if he kept an house for people to drink King James health in." The Irish who congregated at the home of Willoughby Chamberlain in Barbados were encouraged to "Drinck the King and Prince's health as also the Governor's health," with "severall Gunns fired upon the same healths" to drive the point home. A young schoolteacher in Ulster County, New York, in the 1740s found himself imprisoned when, drinking with friends, he defiantly "drunk the health of King Philip of Spain" rather than of King George. "It was recalled that, although a man of marked intellectual attainments, he preferred the company of Irish Catholic servants in the neighborhood."[49]

At other political moments, the colonial authorities forced recusants into the open. After their victory in one of the few pitched battles between Protestants and Catholics in colonial North America—the Battle of the Severn, in which Catholic forces under the command of Governor Stone were defeated by a much larger Protestant army in 1655 (at the cost of twenty-three lives)— the Protestant-dominated assembly in Maryland paraded a series of Catholics before the court to confess their religious allegiance to Rome. "Robert Clarke gent hath openly in Court Confessed himself to be a Roman Catholick owning the Popes Supremacy" and was fined ten thousand pounds of tobacco. His

49. "The Deposition of William Wheeler, Aged Fifty Years or Thereabouts," in *Archives of Maryland*, VIII, 560–561; July 22, 1698, ibid., XXIII, 469; "Papers Relating to Montgomerie and Chamberlayne," May 30, 1689, CO 28/37, no. 7 xxix, TNA; Bennett, *Catholic Footsteps in Old New York*, 265.

coreligionists Thomas Matthewes, William Boreman, John Dandy, and John Pyle all made similar declarations "openly" in court and were likewise punished. Moments of intense political strife can thus reveal both those Catholics who might have preferred to remain hidden and those who made calculated decisions to play both sides against the middle.[50]

It is no surprise that many recusants, poor and rich alike, were able to straddle the porous border separating Anglicanism from Catholicism, sometimes falling on one side, sometimes on the other. Nor is it particularly newsworthy that the established church recognized the porousness of this border and took steps to shore it up by mandating attendance and ritual compliance at the local parish for metropolitan and provincial Christians alike. After all, Nonconformists such as the Puritans and (later) the Quakers had been complaining for years that the Church of England was only a thinly veiled version of its Roman predecessor. But what may be more surprising is that in the North American colonies, a variety of Protestant *dissenters* came under suspicion of being covert Catholics. Hostility to the Church of England— a trait shared by Puritans, Quakers, Moravians, and a host of sectarian offshoots—was sometimes conflated with recusancy in the law and in the eyes of churchmen. This says more about the political fears and motives of the establishment than it does about the instability of religious identity in the post-Reformation Anglo-American world, but the persistent temptation to collapse all varieties of dissent into the single formula of the disguised papist speaks to the cultural power of this category.

Anglican rectors, for example, reported having difficulty discerning Quakers from Catholics who, they feared, were taking cover for their Nonconformity under the cloak of Quakerism—quite literally in one case, as some "reputed" papists in Chester, Pennsylvania, donned "quaker garb" to hide their true identity. In the 1690s, a harried Anglican official complained that the Quakers "are all Jacobites, and many of them Papists in Masquerade." Some "come to our Church in the Morning, and goe to the Quakers meeting in the Afternoon"; others were "not Christened themselves nor are their Children nor when Dead are they given them Christian Buriall." When the Quaker Thomas Story encountered James Burtell, a Huguenot, on Jamaica in 1709, Burtell accused Story of "favour[ing] the Popish Doctrine rather than the Protestant" and "also reported me to be a Jesuit." Sixty years later, the backcountry residents of South Carolina presented a petition to the legislature to restrain the spread of dissent, "as we are a mix'd People and many

50. *Archives of Maryland*, X, 425–429.

concealed Papists among us (especially in the Disguise of Quakers)." Colonies like Maryland, Pennsylvania, and Barbados, which had large populations of *both* Quakers and Catholics, created big headaches for colonial officials trying to keep a lid on dissent, especially since "many of our Church people are mixed with them." Between "the ʾRoman priests cunninge and the Quakers bigatry," fumed the SPG missionary Hugh Jones, "religion was in a matter turned out of doors."[51]

It may seem implausible to us that any observant Anglican could mistake a Quaker (dressed demurely, using archaic language, abstemious in habits) for a Catholic, especially a stereotypical Irish one (dressed in the rough clothing of the servant or laborer, using profane language, and given to drink). And the trope of the "disguised papist" was too widespread, and too indiscriminately applied, to give much credence to tales of Catholics masquerading as Quakers. But there were important liturgical, theological, and cultural similarities between Catholics and a host of dissenting Protestant groups that occasionally led to denominational confusion—or at least the opportunity for a recusant to take advantage of the confusion to elude churchwardens.[52] Quakers and Catholics shared a disdain for the established church, a more welcoming attitude toward female religiosity, and a preference for the oral over the written word in their public worship. Both refused to swear oaths and chafed at the civil and legal disabilities they endured in the colonies.[53] Both had suffered grievously for their faith and spoke in martyrological terms

51. The Reverend Mr. Backhouse to SPG, Dec. 9, 1738, quoted in "Information about 'Popery' in Pennsylvania in Colonial Days as Given by Ministers of the Church of England," *American Catholic Historical Researches*, XI (1894), 58–64 (quotation on 62); Gov. Kendall's letter, July 11, 1693, CO 28/37, no. 51; *A Journal of the Life of Thomas Story: Containing, an Account of His Life and Convincement of, and Embracing the Principles of Truth, as Held by the People Called Quakers* . . . (Newcastle upon Tyne, 1747), 439; "Copy of Remonstrance Presented by Inhabitants of Back Country to Governor Charles Greville Montago and Legislature," 1767, Fulham Papers, X, 168–185; Jacob Henderson to Bishop Gibson, Maryland, June 5, 1733, ibid., III, fols. 166–167; Rev. Hugh Jones to Rev. Dr. Benjamin Woodroffe, January 1698, Misc. Colonial Manuscripts, MS 2018, box 3, 1695–1708, 372, Maryland Historical Society, Baltimore.

52. Numerous pamphlets were published in England in the 1650s, 1660s, and 1670s accusing Quakers of being papists in disguise; see, for example, William Prynne, *The Quakers Unmasked, and Clearly Detected to Be but the Spawn of Romish Frogs, Jesuites, and Franciscan Fryers: Sent from Rome to Seduce the Intoxicated Giddy-Headed English Nation*, 2d ed. (London, 1665); Prynne, *A New Discovery of Some Romish Emissaries, Quakers* . . . (London, 1656).

53. Both, for example, were "much dissatisfied" with the £40 poll tax imposed on dissenters in Maryland in 1698, leading to speculation that, if the Quakers could successfully

of their persecution at the hands of the Church of England. William Penn himself came to believe that Quakers and Catholics were united in a "bond of suffering," despite his earlier vehemence against "papists." As he said in his address to Parliament in 1678, "I have not only been supposed a Papist, but a seminarist, a Jesuit, an emissary of Rome and in the pay of the Pope . . . I am far from thinking that Papists should be whipped for their consciences, because I exclaim against the injustice of whipping Quakers for Papists."[54]

Of more direct relevance, members of both groups maintained a principled distance from the liturgical and sacramental reach of the established church. In the late seventeenth century, "Quakers" and "other Sectaries" in Barbados (by which we can infer recusants, the only other dissenters present in significant numbers on the island) "doe not christen nor Register the births of their Children," prefer to "take one anothers word" in private ceremonies rather than participate in church marriages, and bury their dead "in fields and hedges and so [are] not taken notice of in the Register of the Church." The clergy in Maryland believed that the "Sole Opposers of th' Establishment of our Church and Clergy in that Province are the Quakers and the Papists," with the "Papists" constituting the greater threat because they "do not publickly appeare," unlike the Friends. The periodic campaigns to require all members of the community to register their births, marriages, and burials in their local parish were directed at Quakers and Catholics alike, suggesting that both groups routinely ignored these laws. And in at least one case, we have evidence of active collusion between Quakers and Catholics to thwart the established church, when the Quakers in Chester, Pennsylvania, hired "a rigid, virulent Papist, to set up School" in order to "oppose and impoverish the said Protestant teacher."[55]

---

petition to be exempt from the tax, "the Papists might all pretend to do so too" (William Stevens Perry, *Historical Collections Relating to the American Colonial Church*, IV, *Maryland* [Hartford, Conn., 1870–1878], 11).

54. On oath-taking, see Paul Douglas Newman, "'Good Will to All Men . . . from the King on the Throne to the Beggar on the Dunghill': William Penn, the Roman Catholics, and Religious Toleration," *Pennsylvania History*, LXI (1994), 459; Penn quoted in Kirlin, *Catholicity in Philadelphia*, 9, 11.

55. "Answer to the Several Heads of Inquiry Made in This Island Given to Sr Rich. Dutton by Order of the Lords of Trade and Plantations," Barbados, June 11, 1691, CO 29/3, fols. 80–81, TNA; Perry, *Historical Collections*, IV, 35–36; "The Quakers of Chester, Pa., Employ 'a Rigid, Virulent, Irish Bigotted Papist,' Schoolmaster in 1741," *American Catholic Historical Researches*, XVI (1899), 185–186. The 1698 Maryland law ordered the attorney general to "make Report whether Popish Priests Quakers etc. may marry people without

Moravians were another "Catholic-like" sect who aroused suspicion, and in their case, the linkage is not as far-fetched. According to Linford Fisher, when English and German Moravians, "with their mystifying blend of pre-Reformation and Protestant religious sensibilities," began to proselytize among the Native villages of New York and western Connecticut, "local colonial officials, settlers, and ministers feared that these rather mysterious individuals might be Catholics in disguise." The baroque "blood-and-wounds" theology for which Moravians were infamous in the mid-eighteenth century evoked the sensuous world of the crucified Christ with a fervor matched by the Catholic veneration of the eucharist. Moravians and Catholics were frequently lumped together in laws aimed at suppressing dissent, such as the New York law passed in the aftermath of the 1745 Stuart rebellion, which prohibited any *"Vagrant* Preacher, *Moravian* or disguised *Papist"* from preaching "either publickly or privately in that Province." The future Methodist leader John Wesley found himself accused of being both a Moravian and a Catholic on his ill-fated journey to Georgia in the 1730s.[56]

---

their Banns published or License Granted and whether Such persons are not obliged to register their Births Marriages and Burials etc. according to the Act of Assembly" (*Archives of Maryland*, XXV, 31). Hardy, "Papists in a Protestant Age," claims Quakers and Catholics "regularly ignored this law" (57).

56. Linford D. Fisher, "Colonial Encounters," in Paul Harvey, Edward J. Blum, and Randall Stephens, eds., *The Columbia Guide to Religion in American History* (New York, 2012), 49–68 (quotation on 63). Moravians were not the only Pietist sect to adopt Catholic-like spiritual practices; Philip Lockley explores the affinities between a variety of radical sects in the eighteenth century and Catholicism in "'With the Papists They Have Much in Common': Trans-Atlantic Protestant Communalism and Catholicism, 1700–1850," in Crawford and Spurlock, eds., *Puritans and Catholics in the Trans-Atlantic World*, 217–234. *"Vagrant* Preacher": *Boston Evening-Post*, Jan. 21, 1745, 2. On the Moravians' baroque theology, see Paul Peucker, *A Time of Sifting: Mystical Marriage and the Crisis of Moravian Piety in the Eighteenth Century* (University Park, Pa., 2015); Aaron Spencer Fogleman, *Jesus Is Female: Moravians and the Challenge of Radical Religion in Early America* (Philadelphia, 2007); Craig D. Atwood, *Community of the Cross: Moravian Piety in Colonial Bethlehem* (University Park, Pa., 2004).

Wesley was suspected of being a papist, according to a contemporary pamphlet, because he allegedly performed the sacraments of "Confession, Penance, and Mortifications, mixed wine with water in the Sacrament," and "caressed" known Roman Catholics as "First-rate Saints"; see Geordan Hammond, *John Wesley in America: Restoring Primitive Christianity* (Oxford, 2014), 162. As for Moravians, Wesley did travel and worship with members of the German sect in Georgia, though he later distanced himself from their more radical ideas.

For all their worries about "disguised" papists passing as Quakers or Moravians, the Catholic who most eluded the colonial authorities was the one who hid his beliefs entirely while maintaining outward conformity to the Church of England. Long-nurtured habits of private devotion and mental reservation had protected recusants in the British Isles and were the most easily transportable elements of their faith as they established new homes across the Atlantic. The concept of "mental reservation" first developed around the practice of oath-taking, a fraught area of contention between the state and British recusants who tried to find ways to evade the requirement of denouncing allegiance to the pope and accepting the supremacy of the crown in all things ecclesiastical without abjuring their faith. The Yorkshire Catholic community asked John Mush, the Jesuit confessor to Margaret Clitherow (one of three women executed by Elizabeth I for harboring priests), "What if, when the magistrate doth tender us the oath, we pray him that we may hear it read, or that we may privately read it ourselves, without making any sign or show or swearing, or reverence at all: and after we have heard it read say 'This oath containeth many difficult points which we do not understand . . . but to so much of it only as doth truly concern our temporal allegiance to the king, we will and do swear sincerely and willingly' and without more ado, kneel down and lay our hand upon the book?" Such evasive tactics were a favorite target of anti-Catholic literature. The *Jesuite in Masquerade* (1681) warned, "We have long laboured under the difficulty of Jesuites slipping their necks out of the Collar of the Laws by Equivocations, Mental Reservations and Evasions."[57]

The oaths, and the long-simmering history of recusant resistance to them, carried over to the English colonies. When the Test Act was adopted by the Maryland Assembly in 1699, all potential officeholders not only had to swear that they renounced the doctrine of transubstantiation; they also had to affirm that "I do make this Declaration and every part thereof in the Ordinary Sence of the words now read unto me, as they are Commonly understood by English protestants without any Evasion Equivocation or Mentall reservation

---

57. Yorkshire community quoted in McClain, *Lest We Be Damned*, 287. As McClain argues, the legitimacy of practicing mental reservation while taking oaths was never fully endorsed by the Catholic hierarchy and remained a divisive topic among the clergy. Perez Zagorin reviews the debates over mental reservation in chapter 9 of his *Ways of Lying*. "We have long laboured": *The Jesuite in Masquerade, or the Sheriffs Case Uncas'd, in Some Brief Observations upon the Taking Oaths Otherwise Than According to the Plain and Literal Meaning of the Imposers* (London, 1681), 7.

whatsoever." Recusants who disavowed their faith were required to swear, as Christopher Gilmer did on Barbados in 1734, that they did so "according to the Comon sense and meaning of the words now by me spoken, without any reserve, exception, equivocation or qualification whatsoever."[58]

Oaths were only the most public occasions for Catholics to engage in imagined acts of disobedience and devotion. One of the most important consequences of the Reformation's assault on the material edifice and ideology of medieval Christianity was the renewed emphasis among Tridentine Catholics on imaginative communion with the divine. Deprived of the ability to see, touch, taste, and hear Christ in the world in the same way their ancestors had, Europe's Catholics were invited to interact with God through a variety of mental exercises. Rather than physically consume the body of Christ at communion, for instance, Catholics could enjoy "spiritual reception": the knowledge that others were receiving communion on one's behalf as a substitute for the real thing. More radically, some lay Catholics imagined their own bodies as the sacrifice being offered at the mass, an extreme version of spiritual reception. In the absence of a chapel or a shrine in which to praise God and his saints, Catholics were instructed by the Jesuit Robert Southwell to dedicate each room in their homes to a particular holy figure: "In every roome of the house where I dwell, imagin in some decent place thereof, a throne or chaire of estate, and dedicate the same and the whole roome to some Saint, that whensoever I enter into it, I enter as it were into a chappell or church that is devoted to such a Saint, and therefore in minde doe that reverence that is due to them." Not just the house but the surrounding grounds—the "wallkes, gardens, and orchards about the house"—were to be reimagined by the recusant as holy space inhabited by the saints. As they went about their daily business recusants could perform a series of "short pilgrimages" without ever leaving home.[59]

The Jesuits who served colonial recusants schooled them in these disciplines of imagined communion. A sermon delivered by Charles Sewall advised laymen and -women who could not "visit the chapels so often"—which

58. *Archives of Maryland*, XXV, 68. "Renunciation of the Roman Catholic Church and Declaration of Acceptance of Church of England by Christopher Gilmer, Read in St. Michael's, Bridge-Town," July 14, 1734, Fulham Papers, XVI, fols. 56–57.

59. McClain explores these imaginative exercises in *Lest We Be Damned*, 118–132. For Robert Southwell, see his *Short Rule of Good Life to Direct the Devout Christian in a Regular and Orderly Course* (Saint-Omer, France, 1622), 162, 165.

was, in truth, a majority of lay Catholics in English America—to envision the "Blessed Sacrament" and pray to the crucified Christ "in your private chambers, or when you are at work or walking about." This notion of a papist secretly adoring the eucharist while at home, at work, or simply "walking about" captured what was most threatening about Catholicism in a Protestant society. To visualize the "Blessed Sacrament" while engaged in daily routines was not merely a matter of nostalgic longing but a rigorous form of spiritual discipline encouraged by the Catholic clergy to compensate for the loss of regular access to the sacraments. With no way to police the imagination, Protestant authorities were helpless to detect, let alone control, recusancy in the face of such mental techniques.[60]

"Motly-Complexion'd": Race and Religious Identity

But if the mind of the disguised recusant was inaccessible, their physiognomy was not. The deepening association of Catholicism with Native Americans, Africans, and Europeans of suspect whiteness—Spanish, Portuguese, the Irish—gave Protestants another tool in unmasking secret papists in their midst: skin color. The polemical literature of anti-Catholicism circulating in post-Reformation England had already portrayed the "Jesuite disguis'd" as "a motly-complexion'd Saint," a cultural hermaphrodite whose multicolored disguises hid the black soul underneath.[61] This inner spiritual blackness became overtly racialized in the seventeenth and eighteenth centuries as Protestant settlers in the colonies came face to face with Indigenous and African Catholics whose racial otherness extended to the white ethnic recusants who worshipped with them. Dark-hued strangers sometimes confused the early settlers, who found it difficult to pigeonhole them either ethnically or religiously. A person "skulking in Town, under the Character of a Jew practicing Surgery and Physick" was taken and examined by the magistrates in Georgia in 1739. The "principal Jews" of the town were asked to interrogate the

---

60. Linck, *Fully Instructed and Vehemently Influenced*, 127 n. 118.

61. *The Character of a True-Protestant Ghostly Father* (London, 1683), broadside, Milton House Archives, box 4, folder 23, p. 2, MPA. A 1603 anti-Catholic tract denounced the "motly visards" of the Jesuits and the devils they consorted with: *A Declaration of Egregious Popish Impostures, to With-draw the Harts of Her Majesties Subjects from Their Allegeance. . . . Practised by Edmunds, Alias Weston a Jesuit and Divers Romish Priests His Wicked Associates* (London, 1603), 49.

prisoner; they reported that "he was not of that Religion." The magistrates moved on to ethnicity: when they "ask[ed] him what Country he was of, he said, of Germany. But his Complexion not agreeing with that Climate, we could not presently give Credit to it." Finally, the man was forced to "confess" he was "born in old Spain" and was hence Catholic. "It was plain that he had gone by several Names; and in short there was sufficient Reason for suspecting strongly that he was no better than a Spy." The man was committed to jail for the combined offense of being Spanish and Catholic. Benjamin Franklin's infamous "Observations concerning the Increase of Mankind," published in 1755, offered a typology of phenotypes that contrasted the "purely white People" of English America with the "swarthy Complexion" of the Spanish, Italians, French, and Germans, who, along with the "black and tawny" Africans imported into the colonies, were irreparably damaging the racial purity of the New World. "Why should we in the Sight of Superior Beings," he asked, "darken its People? why increase the Sons of Africa, by Planting them in America, where we have so fair an Opportunity, by excluding all Blacks and Tawneys, of increasing the lovely White and Red?" Franklin's stark contrast between the "purely" white English and their Black slaves has captured the attention of historians of racial formation ever since, but less noted is his categorization of continental Catholic peoples as inhabiting a middle register of racial otherness, as "swarthy."[62]

Irish Catholics also inhabited this middle ground of darkness. The so-called "Black Irish" were the supposed offspring of Gaelic women and the Spanish invaders who were shipwrecked along the Irish coast during the armadas of the late sixteenth century, but the derogatory label cast a much wider shadow in popular culture. By virtue of the Catholicism they shared with continental Europeans, all Irish—even those without black hair and black eyes—were "black Irish" in an important sense. Charles Gawen, a shoemaker sentenced to death for smuggling, was "nicknamed the Papist, from the dark Cast of his Countenance, which bore no small Resemblance to the Complexion of the People on the Continent of *France* and *Spain*." The "Papist from Beccles," as he was known within the criminal confraternity, died insisting he was "bred a Protestant," but his "dark Cast" said otherwise to those who judged him. The legislative council of Barbados told the Colonial Office in 1697 that "we

62. *Stephens' Journal*, 378–379; Benjamin Franklin, "Observations concerning the Increase of Mankind, 1751," *Founders Online*, National Archives, Washington, D.C., https:// founders.archives.gov/documents/Franklin/01-04-02-0080.

desire no Irish rebels may be sent to us" because "we want not labourers of *that colour* to work for us, but men in whom we may confide, to strengthen us."[63]

In the Chesapeake, Irish servants and African slaves were often lumped together in the same breath, as when the governor of Maryland wrote in 1697 of his concern about the influx of foreign elements into his colony. "By the middle of next month I hope to know certainly the number of servants imported, which may be six or seven hundred, chiefly Irish. If next year, or within two or three years, the like number of inhabitants should die and as many Irish and negroes be imported (especially the first, who are most if not all papists) it may be of dangerous consequence to Maryland." The Irish servants, Nicholson feared, "may confederate with the negroes." It is surely not coincidental that the one interracial marriage from colonial Maryland that has received the most attention from scholars is the union of Eleanor Butler, "Irish Nell," with "Charles the Negro" in 1681, over which the "Roman Priest" William Hubbard presided.[64]

63. Ordinary of Newgate's Account, Mar. 26, 1750 (OA17500326), *Old Bailey Proceedings Online;* Hilary McD. Beckles, "A 'Riotous and Unruly Lot': Irish Indentured Servants and Freemen in the English West Indies, 1644–1713," *WMQ*, 3d Ser., XLVII (1990), 503–522 (quotation on 521). On the association of Irish Catholics with Blackness, see Helen A. Kilburn, "Catholics in the Colonies: Nation, Religion, and Race in Seventeenth-Century Maryland" (Ph.D. diss., University of Manchester, 2018), esp. chap. 3, "Religion, Race, and the Life Cycle in Maryland."

64. Governor Nicholson to Council of Trade and Plantations, Aug. 20, 1698, in J. W. Fortescue, ed., *Calendar of State Papers,* Colonial Ser., XVI (London, 1860), 390–391. The marriage was described by numerous deponents in an eighteenth-century freedom suit filed by Nell and Charles's descendants. William Simpson recalled that he "heard his father talk of one Wm Hubberd being a Roman Priest"; another deponent testified that Nell herself identified Hubbard as the priest who had performed her marriage ceremony to Charles; see "Depositions from *Butler v. Boarman,*" folio 242 (Simpson) and 243 (James Jameson), https://msa.maryland.gov/megafile/msa/speccol/sc5400/sc5496/000500/000534/html/00534sources.html. Martha Hodes explores the story of Nell and Charles, and other Irish servants who married enslaved Africans in Hodes, *White Women, Black Men: Illicit Sex in the Nineteenth-Century South* (New Haven, Conn., 1997), 19–38. For a nuanced reading of Nell and Charles's marriage in the context of white Catholic Marylanders' efforts to recognize enslaved Catholics as coreligionists while preserving their own imperiled whiteness, see Kilburn, "Catholics in the Colonies," 206–214. Nell and Charles's marriage was the proximate cause of the 1681 Maryland Act concerning Negroes, which punished the masters of servants and slaves who married across the color line, as well as the clerics (Protestant and Catholic alike) who performed the ceremonies; see *Archives of Maryland,* VII, 203–205.

Fears of covert alliances between Irish and African Catholics were realized in the sugar islands, where the two groups worked and lived so closely together as to form one indistinguishable body at times. The specter of "one unholy entity" (in Jenny Shaw's phrase) comprised of Black and white Catholics arose whenever servants and slaves rebelled together. Barbados faced several conspiracies of Irish and Africans in the mid-seventeenth century, most probably imagined rather than real, but no less telling for that. The council reported, "There are severall Irish servants and negroes out in rebellion in the Thickets" in 1655, and thirty years later, rumors again surfaced that "some Irish servants" were involved in "the late intended riseing of the Negroes to destroy all Masters and Mistresses of families." And in 1691, Joseph Crisp recalled how "Negroes, French and Irish gathering and making up together a formidable Body, discended from the Mountains armed" to attack the "poor planters" on Barbados. On neighboring St. Christopher, the embattled governor, Edwyn Stede, decried the collusion between "those bloody Popish Irish Rebells" and the "ffrench Mallattoes, Mustees and Negroes, that are Imbodyed with the Irish."[65]

The association of Catholicism with blackness could cut both ways, ensnaring those who wished to distance themselves from the degraded status of the enslaved. The Catholic governor of New York, Colonel Thomas Dongan, received a petition from two brothers, Philip and Dego Dequa, who claimed to be free Spaniards sold unjustly into slavery. The "poore petitioners" insisted they were "free born subjects to our King" who had been "brought up in the wayes of Christianity and in the Roman Catholique Religion" but now found themselves in bondage, their African ancestry compounded by the stigma of Catholicism. A half century later, in the 1740s, a "Spanish Negroe fellow"

---

65. Minutes of the Council of Barbados 1654–1658, from the Original in Barbados, Nov. 6, 1655, PRO 31/17/43, 108, TNA; Journal of the Proceedings of the Governor and Council of Barbados, Mar. 16, 1685, CO 31/1, 677; "Deposition of Joseph Crisp, Gent., 2 July 1691," CO 28/37, no. 31, fols. 148–150; Col. Stede to Lordship, Barbados, July 16, 1689, ibid., no. 16. For a discussion of the rumors about Irish joining with Africans, see Jerome S. Handler, "Slave Revolts and Conspiracies in Seventeenth-Century Barbados," *NWIG: Nieuwe West-Indische Gids/New West Indian Guide*, LVI (1982), 5–42. To suggest that Irish servants and enslaved Africans were often joined together in the minds of colonial authorities is not to endorse the "white slavery" argument that some Irish writers have proposed. Both legally and practically, Irish servants were accorded privileges never granted to African slaves. For a good historical overview and refutation of the "white slavery" thesis, see Handler and Matthew C. Reilly, "Contesting 'White Slavery' in the Caribbean," ibid., XCI (2017), 30–55.

who had run away from his master in Pennsylvania was described as a "cunning fellow" who mocked "all religious worship, except that of the Papists." But although proud of his religion, the man was insulted by the implicit linking of religion and race—he "dislikes to be called a Negroe," insisting on his Spanish (white) identity.[66]

Conclusion

Contemporary accounts of Anglo-American Catholics abound in such ambiguities. Religion might no longer have been a matter of blood and genealogy after the Reformation, but it continued to be a fundamental, and deeply entrenched, social identity. Modern scholars are accustomed to invoking the holy trinity of identity categories—race, class, and gender—when they describe the multiple positions that human beings occupy, and religion has always been an awkward addition to this list. Because we think of religion as primarily the product of culture rather than birth, we assume that religious identity is chosen rather than inherited. But this way of thinking is a by-product of the Reformation, which (for Europe's Christians, at least) made faith a matter of choice. This is an overly simplistic way of describing the effect of religious schism on confessional identities, which were always circumscribed by external conditions, including most powerfully the formation of new national churches, but there is truth to the axiom that Protestantism opened the door to a less essentialist understanding of religious identity.

The continued presence of Catholics in Protestant countries troubled the emerging paradigm of religious voluntarism. The Catholic Church did not agree that religion was purely a matter of choice. Its members belonged to the universal Roman Church, whose rituals and sacraments created a material web of belonging that could not be undone by a monarch's decree or penal legislation. The laity, too, often spoke of their indissoluble bond with the mother Church. "I was born in such a time when holy mass was in great reverence," Cecily Stoner told her judges in 1581, and, despite three regime changes in her own lifetime, "I hold me still to that wherein I was born and bred; and so by the grace of God I will live and die in it." Yet in order to survive, Catholics like Stoner had to act as if they accepted this new order. The growing split between their public behavior (swearing oaths of allegiance to the Protestant monarch, sometimes attending the Anglican Church and

66. Bennett, *Catholic Footsteps in Old New York*, 96; *Pennsylvania Gazette* (Philadelphia), June 23, 1748, [3].

participating in its rites, paying taxes for the support of the clergy) and their private beliefs created a gap in which dissimulation and suspicion thrived. This chapter has focused on that gap, sifting through the available evidence to explore the terrain of dissimulation from the perspective of both those who "passed" as members of other faiths and those who wanted to unmask them.[67]

The metaphor of passing is an imperfect one, admittedly; unlike members of racial minorities who "pass" as white, colonial Catholics did not have to deny fully either their true ethnic or national identity. Anglo-Irish Catholics were still subjects of the British empire, however much their loyalty was questioned; they were still "free" men and women insofar as they were not enslaved; they were still, in some important sense, members of the universal Christian family, even if they behaved like heretics. But the phenomenon of "passing" does capture something important to the experience of surviving as a Catholic in a Protestant world that viewed them as inherently "other." And, like those who risk their families, their livelihoods, their reputations, and sometimes their lives by passing as a member of a different race, crypto-Catholics faced serious penalties if caught.[68]

That the penal codes did not transfer intact to the English colonies and that their enforcement was always at the whim of colonial authorities who were far from home did mitigate the risks of recusancy. But what provided the most cover for fugitive Catholics was their skill at dissimulation and their near resemblance to orthodox Anglicans. The contrast with Quakers is illustrative. Quakers faced a wave of persecution from Barbados to Massachusetts in the second half of the seventeenth century, which saw hundreds fined, jailed, whipped at the tail end of a cart as they were paraded through the streets, dismembered, and—in four cases—executed. Meanwhile, in these same places, Catholics quietly went about their business, even worshipping openly in Barbados and the nearby islands. Quakers courted infamy and reveled in their sufferings, to be sure, whereas Catholics sought anonymity. But the stark difference in their public fates has as much to do with the ability of Catholics to pass in ways unavailable to Quakers. Quaker meetings were radically simplified, with none of the sensory or material richness that marked an Anglican or a Catholic service. The role of the minister was minimized, as well (Quakers themselves rejected the term "minister" in favor of "Public

67. Christopher Haigh, "The Continuity of Catholicism in the English Reformation," *Past and Present*, no. 93 (November 1981), 37–69 (quotation on 37).

68. For a good overview of passing, see Allyson Hobbs, *A Chosen Exile: A History of Racial Passing in American Life* (Cambridge, Mass., 2014).

Friend" to signify that any Friend who felt so moved, including women, could assume a leadership role), and there were no sacraments to administer. The itinerancy forced on Catholic priests was the preferred mode of operation for Quaker missionaries. Flaunting their disdain for sacred time or space, Quakers were a far more visible target than recusants, which only amplifies the irony of the Anglican tendency to conflate the two for polemical purposes. Quakers, in other words, could not have passed even if they had wanted to.[69]

We will never know how many Catholics chose a quiet life of domestic devotion while passing as conforming churchmen. Colonial authorities feared such crypto-Catholics numbered in the thousands while simultaneously insisting, as we saw in the last chapter, that there were no papists to speak of in their jurisdictions. The disjuncture between the exaggerated fears of throngs of disguised papists descending upon unsuspecting Protestant communities and the repeated denial of actual Catholics residing in these same communities is one of the central paradoxes of recusant history. Wildly varying estimates of the actual number of Catholics present in a particular community at any one time speak to political, not confessional, agendas. When colonial officials wanted to whip up public sentiment against "intestine enemies" infiltrating their communities, they spoke of Catholic hordes (often allied with savage Indians or enslaved rebels) on their borders. When they wanted to assure the crown that they were good governors presiding over peaceful settlements of godly Protestants, they insisted no papists or "suspected papists" were tolerated. The truth lies somewhere in between. Their numbers relatively small outside Maryland, Pennsylvania, Newfoundland, the mainland port cities, and the sugar islands, colonial Catholics were a convenient target for political scapegoating. Beneath the overheated rhetoric of Catholic disloyalty and invasion, however, lay an equally potent social reality: many of the inhabitants of English America lived religiously ambidextrous lives that eluded detection.

In the next chapter, we turn to an exploration of material culture as another vector of ambiguity in the religiously plural Atlantic world. On the one hand, religious objects held out the promise of piercing the veil of dissimulation, exaggeration, and secrecy surrounding Anglo-American Catholics. Frustrated

---

69. There is a large literature on Quaker "sufferings" in the seventeenth century, much of it written by Quakers themselves. For a good specimen, see Joseph Besse's *Collection of the Sufferings of the People Called Quakers, for the Testimony of a Good Conscience, from the Time of Their Being First Distinguished by That Name in the Year 1650 . . . to the Time of the Act of Toleration* (London, 1753).

by the elusiveness of Catholic belief and practice, Protestants often looked to the tangible signs of Catholicity for confirmation of their suspicions: the altar vessels, sacramentals, rosaries, crucifixes, statuary, devotional medals, and other material paraphernalia of traditional Christianity possessed by those who refused to accept the Reformed world. But all too often, the material emblems that colonial officials and ministers uncovered in their search for clandestine Catholics proved just as slippery to categorize as colonial subjects themselves. Objects had their own stories to tell, though not always the ones imagined or intended.

CHAPTER THREE

"A Set of Beads and a Crucifix Make a Good Catholic"

Object Lessons

W HEN, IN THE 1590S, a recusant noblewoman in Elizabeth's court wished to attend the chapel royal, she pledged to wear "some sygne about her necke, as a peare of beades a crucifyx or the lyke wherby she might be knowne to be a catholyke." A century and a half later and a world away, enslaved Africans on the island of Jamaica were marked by the same "sygnes": the rosaries and small crucifixes their former Spanish masters had bestowed upon them at baptism. "Among the French and the Spanish they are obliged to christen their Slaves; but they give them not the least Instruction; and they are Christians only in Name," the Anglican missionary on the island scoffed. "A set of Beads and a Crucifix make a good Catholic. But I hope we have not so learned Christ; for this is rather mocking God." Material "sygnes" were the most indelible markers of Catholicism in Protestant eyes: tangible, visible in public, accessible to both the highborn and the lowly.[1]

The association of Catholicism with the material world has a long and complex history that goes back to the artistic vibrancy of the religious culture of late medieval Europe and the theological battles of the Reformation. Protestantism was born out of revulsion for the gross materiality of the medieval Church and came of age in the iconoclastic campaigns of the sixteenth and seventeenth centuries, which destroyed centuries of religious art and architecture throughout northern Europe. The revisionist historian Eamon Duffy has

---

1. "An Answere to a Comfortable Advertisement" (ca. 1588), quoted in Alexandra Walsham, *Church Papists: Catholicism, Conformity, and Confessional Polemic in Early Modern England* (Woodbridge, U.K., 1993), 66. Metropolitan priests rejected her request after six months of deadlocked debate. "Set of Beads": John Venn to Bishop Sherlock, June 15, 1751, Fulham Papers, XVII, fols. 45–52.

called iconoclasm "the central sacrament of the reform," and by "iconoclasm," he meant not just the ritualized vandalism of hard-core Reformers in France, the Netherlands, and England but the theological assault on the entire incarnational edifice of the medieval Church, which began with the crucified Christ. The deep hatred of objects ("idols," to the Reformers) nurtured by John Calvin and his theological heirs spread "rhizome-like" to tarnish a range of material, liturgical, and devotional practices in the aftermath of the official assault, authorized by the Tudors, on "abused" objects such as spurious relics. Within a remarkably short period of time, everything from the towering market crosses of provincial England to the rood screen of the local chapel, the bone of a dead saint encased in a reliquary, the holy oil used in the (former) sacrament of extreme unction, and even the simple act of crossing oneself had become "idols" to be destroyed, either by legislative fiat or popular rage. Under Elizabeth, even the most commonplace of devotional objects such as the rosary had been criminalized: the 1571 Act against Bulls prohibited "any token or tokens, thing or things called by the name of an *Agnus Dei,* or any crosses, pictures, beads or suchlike vain and superstitious things"—a clause so broad as to cover almost any object a lay Catholic might own or use.[2]

Theological debates over the nature of images and the need to destroy them peaked in the decades leading up to the English Civil War, as the early Stuart monarchs reintroduced many of the ceremonial aspects of the English church that had languished under the austerities of the Elizabethan settlement. The 1603 coronation of James I (whose Catholic mother, many recalled, had met a martyr's death at the hands of Elizabeth) sparked a devotional revival, including the creation of new churches, chapels, and images, along with the restoration of as many ecclesial objects as could be salvaged from the wreckage of the past century. To the disgust of the godly, "many papisticall

---

2. Eamon Duffy, *The Stripping of the Altars: Traditional Religion in England, c. 1400 to c. 1580* (New Haven, Conn., 1992), 480; James Simpson, *Under the Hammer: Iconoclasm in the Anglo-American Tradition* (New York, 2010), 64; 13 Eliz. 1. c. 2, quoted in Aislinn Muller, "Catholics and the Underground Devotional Market in Post-Reformation England," in Kristin M. S. Bezio and Scott Oldenburgh, eds., *Religion and the Early Modern English Marketplace* (New York, 2021), 76–99 (quotation on 81). For a discussion of the theological and discursive history of iconology and iconoclasm during the English Reformation, see Susan Juster, *Sacred Violence in Early America* (Philadelphia, 2016), 194–218. For a brilliant introduction to the role of "holy matter" in late medieval thinking and practice, see Caroline Walker Bynum, *Christian Materiality: An Essay on Religion in Late Medieval Europe* (New York, 2015).

pictures, medailes, and crucifixes have beene publikely sold, and endured amongst us, with much outfacing and ostentation" in the wake of the Stuart ascension. During the 1630s, the regime of Archbishop Laud provocatively waged a public offensive to restore much of the material edifice of high Anglicanism, prompting Puritan outcries against alleged crypto-Catholics masquerading as orthodox churchmen and renewed calls for popular resistance. This was more than just another front in the ongoing battle between radicals and conservatives for the soul of the English church; the offensive against all idolatrous images, both imagined and real, succeeded in changing the terms of the debate. No religious object, not even the simplest wooden cross, could avoid carrying a polemical message in the seventeenth century.[3]

Thus by the time the first English settlers arrived in North America, the meaning of so small a thing as a rosary was overdetermined by a century of overwrought theological argument about the dangers of idolatry. The colonizers carried this legacy with them to their new world and, over the first century of settlement, reenacted (on a much smaller scale) some of the iconoclastic battles of the Reformation. Puritan ministers doctored the "Horne books" sent over to help teach the Indians to read and write by "blott[ing] out all the crosses of them, for feare least the people of the land should become Idolaters." In 1634, the zealous residents of Salem, Massachusetts, ripped out the red cross of Saint George embroidered in the royal ensign—this "badge of the Whore of Babelon," in Captain John Endicott's fighting words. The Bay Colony's own version of the Glorious Revolution featured the vandalism of the Anglican church in Boston: the Quaker Thomas Maule accused his fellow Bostonians of "breaking the Church Windows, tearing the service Book, making Crosses of Mans Dung on the Doors, and filling the Key-holes with the same." More orchestrated acts of iconoclasm occurred during the raid on the Acadian settlement at Port Royal in 1690, when the Catholic chapel was

3. *Something Written by Occasion of That Fatall and Memorable Accident in the Blacke-Friers on Sonday, Being the 26. of October 1623. . . .* (London, 1623), 17; Peter Lake, "The Laudian Style: Order, Uniformity, and the Pursuit of the Beauty of Holiness in the 1630s," in Kenneth Fincham, ed., *The Early Stuart Church, 1603–1642* (Basingstoke, U.K., 1993), 161–186; Fincham, "The Restoration of Altars in the 1630s," *Historical Journal,* XLIV (2001), 919–940. No cross would top a Protestant church in the part of North America that became the United States until the nineteenth century, a remarkable testament to the bred-in-the-bone hostility of the Reformation to that hated symbol. See Ryan K. Smith, "The Cross: Church Symbol and Contest in Nineteenth-Century America," *Church History,* LXX (2001), 705–734.

burned along with the houses of royal officials and the town's warehouse. As the official report of the expedition boasted, "We cut down the Cross, rifled the Church, Pu'lld down the High-Altar, breaking their Images." In Boston, the merchant Samuel Sewall celebrated by composing a poem: "The bawdy bloudy Cross, at length / Was forc'd to taste the flame: / The cheating Saviour, to the fire / Savoury food became." Sewall is mocking both the idolatrous cross and the discredited Catholic doctrine of transubstantiation here, in which the body of Christ becomes "savoury food" in the form of the eucharist.[4]

Into this fraught theological and cultural context stepped the first colonial Catholics and the material baggage they brought with them. This chapter traces the material history of Catholicism in early English America, from the large cross planted in 1634 by the first settlers in Maryland to the "wigwam chapels" furnished from native materials, the sacramentals carried by missionaries on their spiritual travels, the "church stuff" pillaged from chapels and rescued from shipwrecks, the personal devotional objects owned by lay Catholics and passed on in their wills to loved ones, and the very features of the landscape that became sites of spiritual power in North America. The interplay of the old and the new, the inherited and the found, the vestigial and the created, is especially important to the story of the transplantation and adaptation of sacred things in early America. So much of the material

---

4. Juster, *Sacred Violence in Early America*, 192–241; Thomas Morton, *New English Canaan; or, New Canaan, Containing an Abstract of New England*. . . . (London, 1637), 153, 164; Papers on the State and Government of New England, 1675, Egerton MSS 2395, 1627–1699, fols. 396, 397, 414, 522, British Library, London; Thomas Philathes [Thomas Maule], *New-England Pe[r]secutors Mauld with Their Own Weapons*. . . . (New York, [1697]), 51; *A Journal of the Proceedings in the Late Expedition to Port-Royal*. . . . (Boston, [1690]), 6; Lt. Governor Usher to the Council of Trade and Plantations, June 28, 1708, CO 5/864, no. 225, enclosure 3, TNA; *Diary of Samuel Sewall, 1674–1729*, II, *1699–1714* (Boston, 1878), 143. See also C. D., *New-England's Faction Discovered; or, A Brief and True Account of Their Persecution of the Church of England*. . . . (London, 1690), 4; Abstract of a Letter from Samuel Myles, Minister at Boston, Dec. 12, 1690, CO 5/855, no. 127; Owen Stanwood, *The Empire Reformed: English America in the Age of the Glorious Revolution* (Philadelphia, 2011), 158–159. John Winthrop narrated the affair of the desecrated ensign in his diary; see James Kendall Hosmer, ed., *Winthrop's Journal: "History of New England," 1630–1649*, I, Original Narratives of Early American History (New York, 1908), 137, 151, 182. For a good discussion of the red cross episode in the context of Puritan views on symbols, see Francis J. Bremer, "Endecott and the Red Cross: Puritan Iconoclasm in the New World," *Journal of American Studies*, XXIV (1990), 5–22.

landscape of European Christianity was doubly lost: first to the iconoclasts' hammers and then to the act of overseas migration. But things as well as people migrated from the Old to the New World, and in encountering a new land and new peoples, the European settlers encountered new things, as well.

The material world that Catholics made for themselves in North America was composed of elements from three human cultures (Indigenous, European, African) and one ecological one (the natural environment of North America) whose varied habitats provided much of the raw material out of which religious objects were fashioned. The meanings these objects carried were invariably unmoored from their original contexts. My aim in this chapter is twofold: to uncover the material remnants of colonial Catholicism in archives and the archaeological record while exploring the shifting meaning these objects carried for those who made, owned, used, and abused them. We begin with those religious objects most widely associated with early modern Catholicism—crosses and liturgical vessels—then move progressively to consider altered, adulterated, or hybridized forms of material religion, such as portable altars, rosary beads strewn across the landscape, and pillaged Catholic statues adorning Anglican churches.

Planting Crosses: Global Catholicism in the Americas

In 1605, a group of Catholic investors in England financed George Weymouth's exploratory voyage to the North Atlantic coast. On board Weymouth's ship was a Catholic priest, James Rosier, who published an account of the journey that same year. According to *A True Relation*, the crew "set up a crosse on the shoreside upon the rockes" after landing. The cross-planting ceremony was repeated wherever they set foot: "We carried with us a Crosse, to erect at [each] point . . . [and] set it up in maner as the former." Rosier was struck, as were so many European adventurers, by the absence of any visible sign of "civilized" presence in the New World, observing that "in no place, either about the Islands, or up in the maine, or alongst the river, we could discerne any token or signe, that ever any Christian had beene before; of which . . . by . . . setting up Crosses (a thing never omitted by any Christian travellers) we should have perceived some mention left." Rosier was, in fact, mistaken. Other European voyages to the Atlantic fisheries had preceded Weymouth's, and as early as the 1570s, Martin Frobisher's men had marked their arrival in the Arctic by erecting "a Columne or Crosse of stones heaped uppe of a good heigth together in good sorte." Catholics and Protestants alike used crosses to announce their arrival and, it was hoped, intimidate the

Native inhabitants of these remote shores. Even in staunchly Anglican James-town, Virginia, John Smith and his motley crew of soldiers and gentlemen adventurers "set up a Crosse at Chesupioc Bay" and another "Crosse" at the head of the James River in their initial scouting of the area.[5]

So when, thirty years later, a company of settlers headed by the Jesuit Andrew White planted a "great cross" on the shores of Maryland, the ritual was an established facet of English exploration and settlement of North America. Yet this time, the erection of the cross was accompanied by the sacrifice of the mass. "On the day of *the Annunciation of the Most Holy Virgin* Mary in the year 1634," White recounted, "we celebrated the mass for the first time, on this island. This had never been done before in this part of the world. After we had completed the sacrifice, we took upon our shoulders a great cross, which we had hewn out of a tree, and advancing in order to the appointed place, with the assistance of the Governor and his associates and the other Catholics, we erected a trophy to Christ the Saviour, humbly reciting, on our bended knees, the Litanies of the Sacred Cross, with great emotion." (White, too, was mistaken: Spanish missionaries had celebrated mass in the Chesapeake area in the 1560s and 1570s.) Catholic variants on the English "ceremony of posses-sion" typically included these sacramental elements of ritual and prayer, turn-ing a generically Christian rite into a specifically Roman one. The unifying element of all these rituals, however, Catholic or Protestant, was the material transposition of an indigenous entity—a tree, stone, or natural spring—into a European "token or signe." The colonial encounter was as much a material as a cultural and political one, a collision of two different environments and ecosystems that both destroyed and created something anew.[6]

5. James Rosier, *A True Relation of the Most Prosperous Voyage Made This Present Yeere 1605, by Captain George Waymouth* (London, 1605) (quotations on [21], [39]); [George Best], *A True Discourse of the Late Voyages of Discoverie, for the Finding of a Passage to Cathaya, by the Northweast, under the Conduct of Martin Frobisher General: Devided into Three Bookes* . . . (London, 1578), book 2 (quotations on 9–10); "George Percy's *Discourse:* Observations Gathered out of a Discourse of the Plantation of the Southerne Colonie in Virginia by the English, 1606" ([1608?]) [before Apr. 12, 1612], in Philip L. Barbour, ed., *The Jamestown Voyages under the First Charter, 1606–1609* (London, 1969), I, 129–146 (quotations on 135, 141). See also Laura M. Chmielewski, *The Spice of Popery: Converging Christianities on an Early American Frontier* (Notre Dame, Ind., 2012), 44. For a fuller discussion of the use of crosses as English symbols of possession and the distinction between a Protestant cross and a Catholic crucifix, see Susan Juster, "Planting the 'Great Cross': The Life, and Death, of Crosses in English America," *WMQ*, 3d Ser., LXXIV (2017), 241–270.

6. Andrew White, *Relatio itineris in Marylandiam . . . Narrative of a Voyage to Mary-land,* ed. E. A. Dalrymple (1634; rpt. Baltimore, 1874), 26 ("*Palm*"), 29–30 ("*Locust*"), 32

The large crosses that Catholic conquerors erected in the Americas were not brought with them but carved out of native trees. As they might or might not have been aware, the wooden cross of Christianity was originally an appropriation of pagan "tree worship," and Catholic missionaries who hoped to Christianize the pagan Americas in like manner searched the New World's topographical features for sacred meaning. Many of the crosses erected by Spanish colonizers were "natural crosses discovered in living trees and rocks," according to William Taylor. White believed that American trees carried scriptural associations that organically linked the ancient and the new worlds. During a brief stay in Barbados, White reported with excitement the discovery of native flora that seemed to have biblical roots: "the *Palm of Christ*" and "the *Locust tree,* which is supposed to have afforded sustenance to St. John the Baptist." The collapsing of primitive (in the sense of reaching back to biblical times and the early days of the church) and present times was a common strategy for the agents of global Catholicism seeking to incorporate the Americas into a Christian narrative of world history. The discovery and conquest of the Americas provided an unprecedented opportunity for Catholic conquistadors to relive the excitement of the church's founding, to imagine themselves as apostles who were, quite literally, retracing the steps of Christ's first followers, some of whom had allegedly made their way across the Atlantic to this new world in their miraculous travels.[7]

("*Annunciation*"), 33 ("great cross"), 32–33 ("we celebrated"); Patricia Seed, *Ceremonies of Possession in Europe's Conquest of the New World, 1492–1640* (New York, 1995).

7. Alexandra Walsham, *The Reformation of the Landscape: Religion, Identity, and Memory in Early Modern Britain and Ireland* (New York, 2011), 29, 78; William B. Taylor, "Placing the Cross in Colonial Mexico," *Americas,* LXIX (2012), 154. As Taylor notes: "What was unusual, if not unique, about colonial American crosses was . . . the extent of their presence in the colonial landscape as objects alive with the sacred" (ibid.). Liesbeth Corens suggests that, whereas the Book of Exodus was the primary scriptural text for early modern–era Calvinist expatriates, who saw themselves as modern-day exiles suffering persecution in the manner of the ancient Jews, the Book of Acts served that function for Catholic migrants, who were more apt to see themselves as modern-day apostles than exiles; see Corens, *Confessional Mobility and English Catholics in Counter-Reformation Europe* (New York, 2019), 25–29. On the apostolic paradigm for missionary work, see Kenneth Mills, "Mission and Narrative in the Early Modern Spanish World: Diego de Ocaña's Desert in Passing," in Andrea Sterk and Nina Caputo, eds., *Faithful Narratives: Historians, Religion, and the Challenge of Objectivity* (Ithaca, N.Y., 2014), 115–131; Karin Vélez, *The Miraculous Flying House of Loreto: Spreading Catholicism in the Early Modern World* (Princeton, N.J., 2019). One Dominican missionary believed that the famous wooden cross in Oaxaca that predated his arrival had been planted by one of the apostles, possibly Saint Thomas; see Taylor, "Placing the Cross," *Americas,* LXIX (2012), 155.

Styling themselves modern-day Romans, Spanish conquistadors were the first to reprise the choreography of conversion that had turned early medieval Europe from a pagan wilderness to a Christian garden by making the cross the centerpiece of their ceremonies of possession. In carving crosses out of indigenous flora, conquistadors did more than flex their imperial muscle: they performed an act of exorcism to expel demons from Satan's last refuge on earth. The tactic of placing crosses across the landscape wherever Native "idols" were found was a form of "topographical exorcism." Spanish missionaries deployed a variety of indigenous and Christian resources, including native plants with cross-shaped leaves and relics of the "True Cross," to drive the devil out of his habitat. The French soon followed suit, though they were not as interested in the demonological possibilities of the indigenous landscape. In New France, Jesuits tied bundles of twigs together in a cruciform shape, which they held above their heads to announce their arrival, carried relics of the "True Cross" with them as they traveled the waterways of North America, and erected towering crosses in the Spanish style. Claude Allouez recounted one such ceremony in the Illinois country in 1677: "We planted in the middle of the village a Cross 35 feet in height . . . in the presence of a large number of ilinois of all the nations. . . . The children even came devoutly to kiss the Cross, while the grown-up people Earnestly entreated me to plant it there so firmly that it might never be in danger of falling."[8]

These cross plantings were interactive affairs, involving both European and Indigenous participants. When Jacques Cartier arrived on the shores of

---

8. Taylor, "Placing the Cross," *Americas*, LXIX (2012), 156; Claude Allois, "Narrative of a 3rd Voyage to the Ilinois," in Reuben Gold Thwaites, ed., *The Jesuit Relations and Allied Documents: Travels and Explorations of the Jesuit Missionaries in New France, 1610–1791*, LX (Cleveland, 1900), 163, quoted in Tracy Neal Leavelle, "Geographies of Encounter: Religion and Contested Spaces in Colonial North America," *American Quarterly*, LVI (2004), 913–943 (quotation on 922). The Dominican Francisco de la Asuncion used his relic of the true cross to cast out demons in Mexico, while Philip II's royal physician, Francisco Hernandez, performed an exorcism of the *"caragna* tree" in the 1570s, whose leaves were reputedly shaped like a cross; see Jorge Cañizares-Esguerra, *Puritan Conquistadors: Iberianizing the Atlantic, 1550–1700* (Stanford, Calif., 2006), 111–112 ("True," 112), 126 (*"caragna"*). The Benedictine monk Claude Martin sent the Ursulines in Montreal "a particle of the True Cross encased in crystal, hermetically sealed" (quoted in Julia Boss, "Writing a Relic: The Uses of Hagiography in New France," in Allan Greer and Jodi Bilinkoff, eds., *Colonial Saints: Discovering the Holy in the Americas, 1500–1800* [New York, 2003], 211–233 [quotation on 214]).

Gaspé Bay in July 1534, he "had a cross made thirty feet high, which was put together in the presence of a number of savages on the point at the entrance to this harbour. . . . We erected this cross on the point in their presence and they watched it being put together and set up. And when it had been raised in the air, we all knelt down with our hands joined, worshipping it before them." According to Cartier, the intent of the act was immediately apparent to, and contested by, the local Indian "captain": "pointing to the cross he made us a long harangue, making the sign of the cross with two of his fingers; and then he pointed to the land all around about, as if he wished to say that all this region belonged to him, and that we ought not to have set up this cross without his permission." This encounter reminds us that Native peoples had their own understandings of the sacred objects Catholic missionaries brought into their communities or constructed out of indigenous materials.[9]

The cross was not merely a European import, however, but an Indigenous American ritual form as well. The Jesuits who lived among the the Mi'kmaqs along Gaspé Bay in present-day New Brunswick called them "Cross-bearers," not only for the depth of their devotion to the Christian cross but for their ancient traditions and stories that centered on an indigenous cross. Father Chrestien Le Clercq relayed an origin story he was told in his 1677 *New Relation of Gaspesia*. At a time when their country "was afflicted with a very dangerous and deadly malady," a vision of a "beautiful" man appeared "with a Cross in his hand. He told them to take heart, to go back to their homes, to make Crosses like that which were shown them, and to present these to the heads of families with the assurance that if they would receive the Crosses with respect they would find these without question the remedy for all their ills." The cross halted "this torrent of sickness and death," and ever since then, the Mi'kmaqs had revered the cruciform shape. "They wear it pictured upon their clothes and upon their flesh: they hold it in their hands in all their voyages, whether by sea or by land: and finally they place it both outside and inside their wigwams, as a mark of honour which distinguishes them from

9. *The Voyages of Jacques Cartier* (Toronto, 1993), 26. Modern historians have noted the congruence between Christ's crucifixion and Indian traditions of captivity, in which the true warrior suffers nobly while being tortured to death by his enemies. See Jane T. Merritt, "Dreaming of the Savior's Blood: Moravians and the Indian Great Awakening in Pennsylvania," *WMQ*, 3d Ser., LIV (1997), 723–746; Merritt, *At the Crossroads: Indians and Empires on a Mid-Atlantic Frontier, 1700–1763* (Williamsburg, Va., and Chapel Hill, N.C., 2003).

the other nations of Canada." They even displayed the cross at their burial places, which gleaned the title of "cemeteries" from the Jesuit chronicler.[10]

The striking similarity between the Mi'kmaq and Catholic use of the cross as a devotional object facilitated the global missionary project, at least in Le Clercq's telling, as the "Gaspesians" responded eagerly to his call to replace the "pagan" worship of the indigenous cross, which had withered over time, with the symbols and rituals of the Catholic Church. The Jesuit missionaries, he boasted, "have laboured successfully to cause to be re-born in the hearts and minds of these Indians the love and esteem which they ought to preserve inviolably for this sacred sign of their salvation." Where once the Mi'kmaqs gathered in a circle around the ancient cross in their council meetings, now they gathered together under the shadow of the large cross erected in the village or under the crucifix displayed at the altar in the Jesuit chapel ("which they called the wigwam of JESUS").[11]

The self-serving tone of Le Clercq's narrative is evident, and we have to read his version of the origins and displays of Mi'kmaq cross worship through the distorted lens of his own, Christocentric view. But what is equally striking about Le Clercq's account is his focus on the *materiality* of the Mi'kmaq cross, which he explicitly connects to the material culture of Catholicism: "The swaddling-clothes and the cradles of their infants are always adorned with it, while the barks of their wigwams, their canoes, and their snowshoes are all marked with it. The pregnant women work it in porcupine quills upon that part of their garment which is over the womb, in order to place their offspring under the protection of the Cross. In fact, there is scarcely one of them who does not preserve very carefully in his privacy a little Cross made with wampum and beadwork, which he keeps and esteems much as we do the relics of the Saints, and even to such a degree that these people prefer it to all the richest and most precious things which they possess." The layering of Native and European material cultures here in the service of religion—crosses made from wampum—would become a defining characteristic of French colonial Catholicism.[12]

10. Chrestien Le Clercq, *New Relation of Gaspesia: With the Customs and Religion of the Gaspesian Indians*, ed. William F. Ganong, Publications of the Champlain Society, V (Toronto, 1910), 145–147.

11. Ibid., 134, 144, 152. On the Mi'kmaq cross, see Kenneth M. Morrison, "The Solidarity of Kin: The Intersection of Eastern Algonkian and French-Catholic Cosmologies," in Morrison, *Solidarity of Kin: Ethnohistory, Religious Studies, and Algonkian-French Religious Encounter* (Albany, N.Y., 2002), 165–168.

12. Le Clercq, *New Relation of Gaspesia*, ed. Ganong, 149–150.

FIGURE 6. Ink drawing, probably by Father Le Clercq or Father Jumeau. In Chrestien Le Clercq, *New Relation of Gaspesia: With the Customs and Religion of the Gaspesian Indians*, ed. William F. Ganong, Publications of the Champlain Society, V (Toronto, 1910), 31. Internet Archive

In central Africa as well, the cross wielded extraordinary visual and material power before the arrival of Europeans. With remarkable consistency, from the eleventh through the sixteenth century, rock paintings, textiles, and engravings in the Kongo displayed the distinctive geometry of a diamond-shaped cross, and the cross featured prominently in the initiation ceremony of the Kimpasi, a ritual society, in which the symbolic death and resurrection of the candidate was staged. As it did for Europe's medieval Christians, the Kongo cross marked those places on the physical landscape where the worlds of the living and the dead met—"empowered spaces," in Cécile Fromont's words. The conversion of the kingdom of Kongo to Catholicism in the 1490s was accomplished in large part through this shared iconology of the cross in

African and European religious traditions. Enslaved Kongolese brought the distinctive material emblems of their brand of Catholicism with them to the plantations of the New World. These material traces surface in moments of ritual and revolt, at the burial sites of the enslaved and in the sacred objects they repurposed as weapons of rebellion. The Kongolese who led the Stono Rebellion, the largest slave uprising in colonial North America, for instance, armed themselves with the white cloth and drums associated with both the Virgin Mary and a fifteenth-century victory over a non-Christian tribe in the Kongo. On Saint-Domingue, the African "conjurer" Mackandal organized a plot in the eighteenth century to poison the island's water supply, using *ouanga* (charm) packets that contained ritual elements from both traditional African and Catholic sources: the ground-up roots of the *figuier maudit* tree (apparently an African transplant), the bones of baptized children from a cemetery, nails, holy water, holy candles, holy incense, holy bread, and cruci-fixes. This ritual amalgam was supposedly activated by a chant invoking both the Islamic and Christian gods, a marvelous illustration of the hybridization of religious cultures wrought by global Catholicism.[13]

In English America, we have very little documentary evidence of how Christian settlers interacted with the environmental and indigenous habitats of the New World to fashion new or modified ritual cultures. This is largely because Protestant adventurers remained tone-deaf to the echoes of spiri-tual power in the American landscape. One intriguing story from colonial Maryland, however, opens a window into possible material transpositions. In the spring of 1698, a controversy developed between the predominantly Catholic residents of St. Mary's County and the Protestant governor. A group of settlers noticed "some Extraordinary Cures lately wrought at the Could

13. Cécile Fromont, *The Art of Conversion: Christian Visual Culture in the Kingdom of Kongo* (Williamsburg, Va., and Chapel Hill, N.C., 2014), 175. For a more focused discussion, see Fromont, "Under the Sign of the Cross in the Kingdom of Kongo: Religious Conversion and Visual Correlation in Early Modern Central Africa," *RES*, nos. 59/60 (Spring/Au-tumn 2011), 109–123. Christopher Fennell similarly emphasizes the resonance of shared ideographic elements in Christianity and African religions, such as the crossed-line motifs displayed on numerous archaeological artifacts found in colonial sites; see Fennell, "Early African America: Archaeological Studies of Significance and Diversity," *Journal of Archae-ological Research*, XIX (2011), 1–49. On the Stono Rebellion, see John K. Thornton, "African Dimensions of the Stono Rebellion," *American Historical Review*, XCIV (1991), 1101–1113; Mark M. Smith, "Remembering Mary, Shaping Revolt: Reconsidering the Stono Rebel-lion," *Journal of Southern History*, LXVII (2001), 513–534. On Mackandal's use of poison, see Gwendolyn Midlo Hall, *Africans in Colonial Louisiana: The Development of Afro-Creole Culture in the Eighteenth Century* (Baton Rouge, 1992), 164–165.

FIGURE 7. Kongo cross. Ca. 18th–19th century. From the Metropolitan Museum of Art Collection, New York. https://www
.metmuseum.org/art/collection/search/318320

Springs," a freshwater spring on the estate owned by Captain John Dent that local residents believed to have once been a site of Indigenous power. Soon rumors that "severall poor people flocked thither to recover their healths and Lymbs" reached the governor's ears. He swiftly dispatched a Protestant arsenal to combat this embarrassing resurgence of popish superstition: ten Bibles, "a Book of Homilyes Two Books of Family Devotions and a Book of Reformed Devotions written by Dr. Theophilus Dorrington," along with a "sober man . . . to read prayers there twice a day." Despite this orthodox offensive, reports of miraculous cures continued to circulate among "the poor people," and by the fall the governor had come up with an ingenious plan: he ordered "an Hospital" to be erected at the site of "the Coole Spring." The story of how an Indigenous sacred spring became first a Catholic shrine for miraculous cures, then a makeshift Protestant place of prayer, and finally a hospital where Catholics and Protestants together could be healed is a prime example of how different Christianities converged on the American frontier.[14]

That the New World would become the site of a new miracle was proof to Catholic settlers that the very land itself was blessed. Planted on land redeemed (appropriated) from its original pagan inhabitants under the spiritual guardianship of her namesake and patron saint, Saint Mary, the colony of Maryland was "hallowed" ground for its Catholic inhabitants. In the eyes of colonial Catholics and their denominational historians, the land around the Chesapeake had been "sanctified" ever since the first Catholic chapels had been planted by the Spanish in the sixteenth century. "Dedicated itself to the Virgin Mother, nearly all its rivers and creeks, its farms and villages, its roads, woods, and hills have been placed under the protection of saints and angels," one nineteenth-century Catholic chronicler enthused. "The Mass bell has been heard for more than two centuries in all its hamlets, and the *Clean Oblation,* which was foretold by the prophet, has been offered up in hundreds, aye, in thousands of its devout old homes. It has been sanctified by the labors and sufferings of devoted missionaries, and by the faith and charity of a pious and truly Catholic people." In this one passage is encapsulated the entire process by which a place becomes sacred space: the fusion of the natural landscape with the numinous power of supernatural agents and the human labor of thousands of "old hands." Nature, God, and man work together to "hallow" the land.[15]

14. Minutes of Council Meetings, Maryland, June 4, 1698, CO 5/741, 518 ("Extraordinary Cures"), 646 ("an Hospital"), TNA. A historical marker for "Ye Coole Springs" in St. Mary's County explains that "Legends of healing waters in St. Mary's came from the Native Americans and the colonists" ("Ye Coole Springs Three Notch Trail," HMDb.org, The Historical Marker Database, https://www.hmdb.org/m.asp?m=135329). On "converging Christianities," see Chmielewski, *Spice of Popery.*

15. Henri de Courcy and John Gilmary Shea, *History of the Catholic Church in the United States . . .* (New York, 1879), 182, quoted in Martin I. J. Griffin, "Catholics in Colonial Virginia," *Records of the Catholic Historical Society of Philadelphia,* XXII (1911), 84–100 (quotation on 85); "Historical Points Connected with New-Town Manor and Church, St. Mary's County, Maryland," *Woodstock Letters,* XIII, no. 1 (1884), 69–76 (quotation on 69).

Traveling Chapels and Saddle Chalices:
Catholic Liturgical Culture

From the forests and coastal habitats that surrounded them, European Catholics brought the native North American world and its spiritual power into their chapels. All sorts of flora and minerals, in addition to wood, were used to fashion a colonial Catholic sacramental culture. The Jesuits at the Huron-Wendat mission were "the first to make wine from native grape, wax for candles from the wild laurel, and incense from the gum-tree . . . they were the first to work the copper mines of Lake Superior for ornaments for the altars at the Sault." The altar at Jacques Bigot's chapel at the Abenaki mission was adorned with Native-made ornamentals—"a great number of Collars, made in all sorts of designs; Bugle beads and strings of porcelain; and articles worked with glass Beads and porcupine quills." To these were added "the most beautiful ornaments that we have in our Church." These collars and strings of beads were most likely fashioned by Native women, according to Ann Little.[16]

Rather than a one-way process by which native elements were transformed into European ones by the consecrating power of the priest, the missionary chapels in New France and New Spain represented the nodal point of a bilateral system of exchange in which sacramentals flowed in both directions across the Atlantic. Relics and sacramentals came to North America from the missionary centers in England, France, and Spain, but Native sacred objects made their way to Europe as well. In the late seventeenth and early eighteenth centuries, the Huron-Wendats of the Jesuit Mission of Lorette sent at least five beaded ceremonial wampum belts as gifts to Catholic communities on the continent. The Jesuit Pierre-Joseph-Marie Chaumonot suggested in 1673 that the Lorette Wendats donate a wampum belt to their namesake community in Loreta, Italy, and the "votive gift" was decorated with words as well as beads in a highly unusual departure from traditional custom. The belt displayed "well-formed letters in black, saying [in Latin] Hail Mary, Grace." As Karin Vélez explains, wampum belts were "a pictorial art, and rarely depicted words, much less prayers, in Latin." The Catholic communities in France

16. "The Struggles and Sufferings of Our First American Missionaries," *Woodstock Letters*, XXI, no. 2 (1892), 210–227 (quotation on 226–227); "Journal of What Occurred in the Abnaquis Mission from the Feast of Christmas 1683 until October 6, 1684," in Thwaites, ed., *Jesuit Relations*, LXIII, 27; Ann M. Little, *The Many Captivities of Esther Wheelwright* (New Haven, Conn., 2016), 76.

and Italy reciprocated, sending as thanks to the Wendats (in the case of the cathedral of Notre-Dame des Ardeilliers) an image of Our Lady of Samur, and (in the case of the cathedral chapter at Chartres) a silver reliquary "in the shape of their famous relic the *Sancta Camisia,* and engraved with scenes of Mary's Annunciation."[17]

These ceremonial belts circulated not only between Old and New France but among Native convert communities in North America as well. In 1677, the Iroquois of Sault-St.-Louis hung from the beams of their new chapel the wampum belts the Wendats had sent them. As narrated by the resident Jesuit, "This year will be remarkable for a celebrated present which was sent from Lorette to the Sault. It was a hortatory collar which conveyed the voice of the Lorette people to those of the Sault, encouraging them to accept the faith in good earnest, and to build a chapel as soon as possible; and it also exhorted them to combat the various demons who conspired for the ruin of both missions. This collar was at once attached to one of the beams of the chapel, which is above the top of the altar, so that the people might always behold it and hear that voice." Woven into the center of the belt was an image that resembled a chapel with a cross on top. The belt was preserved by the Iroquois as one of the treasured "Indian relics" housed at the old mission.[18]

In English America, the situation was quite different. Jesuit missionaries did not live among their Indigenous congregations, and unlike their French counterparts, they were a tiny fraction of the European population in these colonies. Outnumbered and isolated from Native America for the most part (only in Maryland did the Jesuits make a concerted effort to convert the local Nanticokes, Piscataways, and Pocomokes), Jesuits created a sacramental culture in their chapels that was far more European than Native. The rudimentary "wigwam chapels" of Maryland's early years might have resembled French mission churches, but once purpose-built structures were erected in the latter half of the seventeenth century, colonial Catholicism in English America presented a largely European face to its Protestant neighbors. If we peered into the Jesuit chapels in St. Mary's City and St. Inigoes, we would not find wampum belts hanging from the rafters or altar vessels adorned with

17. William Lonc, trans., *Pierre Joseph Marie Chaumonot, S.J.: Autobiography and Supplement* (Halifax, N.S., 2002), 24, quoted in Karin Vélez, "'A Sign That We Are Related to You': The Transatlantic Gifts of the Hurons of the Jesuit Mission of Lorette, 1650–1750," *French Colonial History,* XII (2011), 31–44 (quotations on 36, 38).

18. "Narration annuelle de la Mission du Sault St-Louis depuis la fondation jusqu'à l'an 1686," in Thwaites, ed., *Jesuit Relations,* LXIII, 193–195.

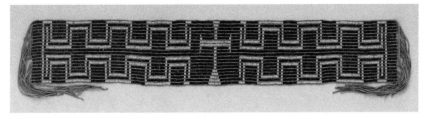

FIGURE 8. Replica of the wampum belt given in 1677 to the Kahnawake Mohawks by the Hurons of Lorette. Reproduction and photo courtesy of Darren Bonaparte

copper beads. Beyond the chapels, a more diverse material culture of personal and sacramental devotional items grew up around recusant communities, especially after enslaved Africans and their ritual habits began to make their presence felt in North America. Liturgical space, however, was English space.

A rare inventory from Lancaster, Pennsylvania, in the early 1800s gives us some clues as to what a typical English mission chapel might look like on the inside. There was the usual assortment of altar vessels that were supposed to be found in any Catholic church, though in reality few colonial chapels were so well equipped: a silver ciborium (a cup to hold the consecrated wafers), communion cloths, pewter candlesticks, and a baptismal font. Other sacramentals, however, were adapted to fit the itinerant lifestyle of the missionaries attached to the station. The two silver chalices were described as "very convenient to unscrew and pack up," and the altar cloths were "small [in order] to carry in a Saddle bag." The chapel possessed two "Altar Stones, Portable," "1 Tin box for carrying the bread in the Saddle Bags," 5 crucifixes (one "very large" and the rest "small"), two small bells, one large "Mass Book" and one "Small mass Book very small." In order to serve the multilingual congregation that gathered on Sundays, the priests had access to a German prayer book and a Roman missal printed in both Latin and English. The mix of the traditional with the modified was a characteristic of missionary Catholicism. These modifications did not dilute the sacramental efficacy of the liturgical objects, but they did affect the sensory experience of those kneeling in the pews or taking communion. The small bell would struggle to reach the ears of those sitting in the very back, and it probably sounded a tinny rather than a resonant call to prayer. The baser metal of the eucharistic box (tin, not silver) might affect the taste of the wafer, especially after being stored for so many days in musty saddlebags. The break in the center of the chalice that allowed the two halves to be unscrewed was more than a physical imperfection—it was an emblem of the fractured and episodic nature of sacramental life in recusant communities. The Roman Church preferred to use precious metals and jewels in liturgical vessels to signify the majesty and awe of the sacraments they performed, but mission chapels made do with tin, wood, and plain cloth.[19]

From their manors, the Jesuits dispersed over the colonial countryside, bringing the sacraments to their far-flung parishioners in the form of "traveling chapels," which consisted of a portable altar and some sacred utensils. A Jesuit described his missionary labors in a report to the Society in 1642:

> This is the manner of conducting our excursions. We enter a boat or canoe: . . . We carry with us a chest of bread, butter, and cheese, of corn cut and dried before it is ripe, and another for carrying bottles of wine for the holy Sacrifice one, and six of consecrated baptismal water; also a chest with the vestments, and a moveable altar, and another full of little things to make presents to the Indians and gain their favour, such as little bells, combs, knives, fish hooks, needles, thread, and the like.[20]

Little had changed by the early eighteenth century, where "saddle chalices" (which could be disassembled to fit inside a saddlebag) were used by itinerant missionaries on horseback. Mary Xavier Greene remembered that, when the missionary arrived in her village in Prince George's County, "the front yard would be crowded with men, women, babies and children of all ages and sizes. . . . When the season was fair, we erected a temporary altar in the yard." Protestants, too, had to use the materials they found at hand as they built their first churches. "I well remember wee did hang an awning (which is an old saile) to three or foure trees to shadow us from the Sunne," John Smith recalled; "our walles were rales of wood, our seats unhewed trees till we cut plankes, our Pulpit a bar of wood nailed to two neighbouring trees.

19. Inventory of furniture and other articles, R. Catholic Church and Presbytery of Lancaster, 1804, Materials re. Pennsylvania, box 34, folder 3, MPA. In another example of frontier modification, the altar of St. Francis Xavier Church, a modest brick chapel built in 1766 at Newtown, was not elevated and railed off as was typical in most Catholic churches, and it sported a distinctive blue backdrop; see Tricia Terese Pyne, "The Maryland Catholic Community, 1690–1775: A Study in Culture, Religion, and Church" (Ph.D. diss., Catholic Univ. of America, 1995), 47–48.

20. Father Le Moyne is described as carrying a "traveling chapel" with him when he visited New Amsterdam to administer the sacraments to the local Catholics in the 1640s; see William Harper Bennett, *Catholic Footsteps in Old New York: A Chronicle of Catholicism in the City of New York from 1524 to 1808* (New York, 1909), 54. For the Jesuit's report, see Province Notes on the Mission of Maryland, 1633–1874, box 3, folder 7, p. 32, MPA.

. . . This was our Church, till wee built a homely thing like a barne." The baptismal font was made from a hollowed tree trunk. So the first Protestant and Catholic churches in the Chesapeake resembled one another due to frontier exigencies. But in keeping with the Reformation's exiling of the sacred from the material world, these wooden pulpits and fonts carried no spiritual power of their own. The inside of a Protestant church, like its exterior, was not (in theory, at least) sacred space but a functional place where believers came together to worship and hear the word of God.[21]

For Catholics, by contrast, every place of worship was sacred space, made so by a discrete act of consecration. The concept of consecration is key to understanding the differences between a Protestant church and a Catholic chapel, a Protestant cemetery and a Catholic churchyard, a Protestant communion table and a Catholic altar. Consecration not only confers sacred power on a material object; it connects individual sites and objects to a universal Catholic world presided over by a centralized ecclesiastical hierarchy. The power of consecration flowed from God, through the pope, down to bishops—it did not extend to the missionary or parish priest, who by himself could not turn a slab of stone into an altar or an Indian longhouse into a chapel.[22]

The absence of a bishop in the English colonies was a long-standing impediment to the successful transplantation of the Catholic Church onto North American soil (as it was for Anglicans), and colonial priests, like their English counterparts, had to find creative ways to skirt the letter of the law. When Governor Seymour hauled the Jesuit William Hunter before him in September 1704 on charges of continuing to offer mass in another location after Seymour closed the "great brick chapel" in St. Mary's City, Hunter

21. Robert R. Grimes, "The Emergence of Catholic Music and Ritual in Colonial Maryland," *American Catholic Studies*, CXIV, no. 2 (Summer 2003), 1–35 (quotation on 24); Mary Xavier Greene, *Grandma's Stories and Anecdotes of ye Olden Times* (Boston, 1899), 40, quoted in Pyne, "Maryland Catholic Community, 1690–1775," 36; John Smith, *Advertisements; or, The Path-Way to Experience to Erect a Plantation* (London, 1631), in Philip L. Barbour, ed., *The Complete Works of Captain John Smith, 1580–1631* (Williamsburg, Va., and Chapel Hill, N.C., 1986), III, 295. On the baptismal font, see James Horn, *A Land as God Made It: Jamestown and the Birth of America* (New York, 2005), 183.

22. A. J. Schulte, "Consecration," in *The Catholic Encyclopedia* (New York, 1908), http://www.newadvent.org/cathen/04276a.htm. The Catholic Church distinguishes between consecration, a higher form of power reserved to bishops, and blessing, which ordinary priests can administer. Holy oil is used in consecrations, holy water in blessings. And most important, consecration elevates persons or things to a new, permanent state of sanctity that requires a separate ritual process to undo. Consecration is required for certain objects: churches, fixed altars (though not portable altar stones), chalices, and patens.

(disingenuously) acknowledged that, although "very sorry for any annoyance in his Conduct," he could not be guilty of "consecrating the Chappel," for "that is an Episcopal Function and that no body was present but himself in his common Priests vestments." Hunter might not have formally consecrated the new chapel, but he certainly treated it as consecrated space by celebrating the sacraments inside it, as missionary priests had done in private homes and chapels for some time.[23]

Alternative forms of consecration had to be found in colonial environments, and one of the most potent was to imagine direct lines of material connection between Catholic communities residing on both sides of the Atlantic. The portable altar stones used by the Jesuits in Maryland were transported to North America on the same ships that brought the missionaries, as were their chalices, holy oil, and other sacramentals. The very bricks used to build the great chapel in St. Mary's City came from recusant communities in England, and when that chapel was demolished after being closed by order of Governor Seymour in 1704, the bricks were disassembled and used to construct a new chapel at the Jesuit plantation of St. Inigoes some four miles away. The reuse of sacred materials from one Catholic site to another was thus in its own way an act of consecration, spreading the salvific power of the incarnate Christ to each new chapel, each new community. A Jesuit researching the history of St. Inigoes in the 1940s argued, "The St. Inigoes Manor as a *house* is sacred: a) Because it was directly fashioned from the bricks of St. Mary's Chapel." There is an enduring oral tradition among Maryland Catholics that connects the "old mulberry tree" in St. Mary's City—under which the first mass was celebrated, the colonial charter was first read aloud, and the first treaty between the English and the Natives was signed—to the succession of chapels erected on the site. As described in one early-twentieth-century account, "On the site of St. Mary's City, where stood the old mulberry tree under which Calvert and the Indians held their negotiations, is . . . Trinity Church, built of bricks from the first state house. The altar, communion rail, lectern, and reading desks of Trinity Church were made of wood from the famous mulberry tree."[24]

23. *Archives of Maryland*, XXVI, 44–45.

24. Handwritten MS, "Fr. Morgan's Research, 1942," Materials re. St. Inigoes, box 15, folder 10, MPA. Edwin Beitzell explores the different scenarios by which Jesuit scholars have imagined the consecrated bricks from the original St. Mary's chapel as the basis for new additions or new chapels after its destruction in Beitzell, *The Jesuit Missions of St. Mary's County, Maryland* ([Abell, Md.], 1959), 54–55. "On the site": *St. Mary's Beacon*, May 21, 1926, Materials re. St. Thomas, St. Inigoes Manor, box 26, folder 14, MPA.

FIGURE 9. Replica of the wrought iron cross mounted on a
stone pedestal at Old Bohemia Manor, Maryland. Oral history has it that the cross was fabricated in 1634 in St. Mary's
City and brought to Old Bohemia around 1704 by Father
Thomas Mansell. Photo by author

From St. Mary's City to St. Inigoes to St. Thomas to Bohemia, each new
Jesuit plantation borrowed elements from its predecessors. When the Jesuits
acquired St. Thomas Manor in Little Bretton in 1649—the "Jerusalem of
Maryland," according to a Jesuit newsletter—it housed some of the "sacred
relics" used by the missionaries in their first decades in the colony: "Here is
kept a sacred relic, the tabernacle in which was kept the Blessed Sacrament
in the early days of the church. Among other valuable possessions of the
Manor is a Bible and commentator bearing date of 1643." The wrought iron
cross that the original settlers brought from England in 1634 graced the brick
chapel at St. Mary's before it was transported to the newest outpost on the

Eastern Shore, Bohemia, in 1704. Legend has it that the cross was "beaten from horseshoes contributed by the first settlers of Maryland before they left England." The cross greeted worshippers at Old Bohemia "for generations" before being transferred, along with other colonial relics, to Georgetown University Library.[25]

Today, the Jesuit manors function as shrines for modern-day Catholics who seek a tangible connection to their heroic past, a past they associate with modern ideals such as religious liberty and freedom of conscience. But for laymen and -women in the seventeenth and early eighteenth centuries, the chapels were active sites of sacramental practice, and they invested their time, labor, and wealth in outfitting them. Wealthy Catholics used their transatlantic connections to import sacramental objects from abroad, further strengthening the material ties between the Old and the New Worlds. Philip Calvert thanked Richard Nicolls in 1667 for sending him "the Chalice and the seaven books you were pleased to recommend to my patronage," assuring him, "They shall only be employed to the sacred use they were first consecrated for." From England came a bell for the chapel at Newtown Manor in 1691; from Rome came "a Madonna and a Crucifixion" for St. Joseph's, the first dedicated church in Philadelphia. The "Silver Chalice" and silver baptismal spoon that served St. Thomas Manor also presumably came from wealthy donors, along with the "hand-carved tabernacle" that housed the liturgical vessels.[26]

Imported objects cemented the material link to recusant communities back home and thus created sacramentality in the absence of formal mechanisms

---

25. News clipping, "'Jerusalem of Maryland' Gains Influence since 1649 Opening," Materials re. St. Inigoes, box 15, folder 18, MPA; "Wrought Iron Cross from Bohemia Manor Mission 1704," Materials re. White Marsh and Bohemia, ibid., box 16, folder 3; Joseph S. Rossi, "Jesuits, Slaves, and Scholars at 'Old Bohemia,' 1704–1756, as Found in the *Woodstock Letters*," *U.S. Catholic Historian*, XXVI, no. 2 (Spring 2008), 1–15 (quotation on 4).

26. Nineteenth-century denominational historians first embraced the notion that the Maryland mission was the birthplace of religious liberty; see, for example, Rev. John McCaffrey's "Oration Delivered at the Commencement of the Landing of the Pilgrims of Maryland," delivered in 1842: "The sun, which shone on her [the colony's] origin," he enthused, "enlightened the birth-day of equal rights and genuine liberty. . . . The first cross, which was reared within our borders, was indeed the sign of universal love." "Our celebration therefore," he concluded, "is the festival of religious liberty" (box 3, folder, 2, pp. 5–6, MPA). "The Chalice and the seaven books": Philip Calvert to Richard Nicolls, Maryland, Mar. 22, 1667/8, William Blathwayt Papers, 1657–1770, mssBL 1–423, box 1, Henry E. Huntington Library, San Marino, Calif. "A Madonna and a Crucifixion": Materials re. Little Bretton and St. Thomas Manor, box 27, folder 2, MPA.

of consecration. But it is the objects left to the church in the wills of ordinary men and women that did the most to turn frontier buildings into consecrated space. As many as 60 percent of the Catholic testators in Maryland between 1660 and 1670 left legacies to the church, and of the ninety or so colonial wills dating from the last third of the seventeenth century reprinted in a historical records publication, 13 percent included bequests of land and/or religious objects to the Catholic church. The bequeathed objects range widely in size and value, from the "Chappell built of Lime and Brick" by Frances Sayer in 1698 to mark the burial site of her husband, Peter, to the pound of "nailes toward the Pailing in of the Church yard" left by Edward Clark to the Newtown chapel in 1675. Dr. Lowrey bestowed "twenty pounds Sterling to buy a Callice" and a "Small Marble pillar with a holy water pott of Marble" on the church, whereas Peter Bathe left "all the Pictures and other things in the small and great boxes" to be "disposed of to the Church for my Souls Sake." These bequests served a ritual purpose, to be sure, usually to pay for prayers for the soul of the deceased, but they also forged tangible material links between the laity and the institution of the church in ways unmatched in Protestant communities. These links proved indispensable in Maryland after 1690, when the locus of Catholic worship moved from the public chapels to the private mass-houses built by the gentry.[27]

Some of these objects can be found today, housed at Jesuit universities and local museums, a testament to the material legacy of colonial Catholicism. The University Art Collection at Georgetown once housed a number of colonial relics, including "a picture of Ignatius Loyola brought over by Andrew White, a pewter chalice and paten used at the first mass celebrated in Maryland, the

---

27. Michael Graham, "Lord Baltimore's Pious Enterprise: Toleration and Community in Colonial Maryland, 1634–1724" (Ph.D. diss., University of Michigan, 1983), 123; "Some Quaint Wills of Early Catholic Settlers in Maryland," *Records of the American Catholic Historical Society of Philadelphia*, XIII (1902), 22–44 (quotations on 24 [Bathe], 37 [Clark], 39 [Sayer], 40 [Lowrey]). Graham found that Catholic testators supported the church far more often in proportion to their numbers than Quakers or Anglicans in Maryland ("Lord Baltimore's Pious Enterprise," 374). Thomas Hughes compared the bequests made to their respective churches by Catholic and Protestant testators in Maryland between 1635 and 1685; the fifty or so legacies left to the Catholic church far outnumbered the ten bequests made to Protestant churches (Hughes, *History of the Society of Jesus in North America: Colonial and Federal, Documents*, I, part 1 [London, 1908], 218). Shona Helen Johnston argues that the number of bequests to the Catholic church rose sharply after 1690; see "Papists in a Protestant World: The Catholic Anglo-Atlantic in the Seventeenth Century" (Ph.D. diss., Georgetown University, 2011), 176.

chapel bell, and a cross made of mulberry wood." (Only the mulberry cross remains today.) A "saddle chalice" from the colonial era is on display at Port Tobacco, whereas the liturgical vessels used by Father Sebastian Rale at his mission in Norridgewock reside in the Maine Historical Society, and the Maryland Historical Society includes items donated by descendants of the families who maintained chapels in their homes. St. Francis Xavier Shrine, at the site that was once Bohemia Manor, maintains a modest museum of relics from eighteenth-century missionaries, including frayed vestments, old shoes, and an iron host press, which was used to make communion wafers.[28]

The private chapels that proliferated after 1704 as attachments to gentry homes were attenuated versions of the Jesuit chapels. Designed to hold a small number of worshippers at a time, who accessed the chapel by a separate entrance, the altar typically displayed a crucifix and perhaps some cut flowers. Paintings, stained glass windows, and statues were "conspicuously absent," Tricia Pyne notes (as indeed they were in the Jesuit chapels). The archival traces of these private sacramentals are faint indeed. Only a handful of colonial estate inventories include items that might have been used by an itinerant priest in a chapel: Leonard Calvert's 1647 inventory featured "3 small bitts of Sylver plate," "A gold Reliquary case," and "A kneeling desk and a picture of Paules." Dr. John Michael Brown of Philadelphia bequeathed to his sister "a suit of priestly vestments and a silver chalice," giving rise to speculation that he was a disguised priest, though it's more likely he was a lay Catholic who hosted mass at his house. Only one mass-house in colonial Maryland was equipped as richly as the Jesuit manor chapels: the private chapel of the wealthiest Catholic family in the province, the Carrolls, which in 1723 housed "a monstrance, ciborium, sprinkler, bread box, water cup, thurible, two crucifixes, tabernacle, four vestments, and ten chairs." More often, the estate inventories of Catholic laymen with chapels or mass-rooms hid sacramentals under the obscure phrase "church stuff." A widow in Virginia, Jane Green, left "all my Church Stuff" to the Jesuit chapel at Port Tobacco in 1699.[29]

---

28. Grimes, "Emergence of Catholic Music," *American Catholic Studies*, CXIV, no. 2 (Summer 2003), 1–35 (quotations on 19, 24). For Rale's vessels, see Chmielewski, *Spice of Popery*, 192.

29. Tricia T. Pyne, "Ritual and Practice in the Maryland Catholic Community, 1634–1776," *U.S. Catholic Historian*, XXVI, no. 2 (Spring 2008), 22; Henry S. Spalding, *Catholic Colonial Maryland: A Sketch* (Milwaukee, 1931), 113; "An Inventory of Lands, Goods, and Chattells Belonging to Mr. Leonard Calvert Esqr.," June 30, 1647, *Archives of Maryland*, IV, 320–321; "Annals of St. Joseph's Church," *Woodstock Letters*, II, no. 1 (1873), 16–17 (quotation

The phrase "church stuff" is maddeningly opaque, a fitting note on which to conclude this survey of Catholic liturgical material culture in English America. Although the evidence suggests that the chapels maintained by the Jesuits in Maryland on their own manors and in the homes of wealthy planters were modest spaces without the exotic touches of indigenous metals and beads that adorned the French chapels to the north, we simply don't know what most of their interiors looked like. The most important lesson that colonial recusants had learned from their clerical leaders and their own years of experience as a minority faith, however, was that ordinary things could be turned into sacred ones by the power of imagination, memory, and the tangible threads connecting them to the communities they had left behind. A single tin cup or woolen cloak was as powerful a sacred object as a silver chalice or lace surplice.

Sacramental Booty: Destruction and Reappropriation

The potency of colonial Catholic sacramentals was not lost on their neighbors. In the ongoing war between global Catholicism and the Protestant International for control of the Americas, the vessels and furnishings of Catholic chapels were a favorite target. One of the earliest skirmishes on record between Catholics and Protestants in North America occurred during the 1560s, when English adventurers attacked and looted the Spanish Jesuit mission in the Chesapeake region, seizing "a missal, and devotional books, rosaries, images, hair cloth, disciplines and a sacred crucifix." A century later, religious war came again to the Chesapeake, this time in the form of civil war. The two battles fought by Protestants and Catholics in Maryland in the mid-seventeenth century claimed as collateral damage much of the Jesuit missions' material property. The Jesuit plantation at St. Inigoes was plundered during the 1640s, and among the spoils of war were the altar vessels. The inventories

---

on 16); Beatriz Betancourt Hardy, "Papists in a Protestant Age: The Catholic Gentry and Community in Colonial Maryland, 1689–1776" (Ph.D. diss., University of Maryland, College Park, 1993), 201; "Some Quaint Wills of Early Catholic Settlers in Maryland," *Records of the American Catholic Historical Society of Philadelphia*, XIII (1902), 42. Jesuits, too, used the phrase "church stuff" to conceal sacramentals, as in the deed granted by William Hunter to Thomas Jameson, Sr., in which he granted Jameson "all and every the goods, Church stuff, plate, household stuff . . . and all other things whatsoever now on or belonging to [the] dwelling plantation of Britton's Neck" (deed dated Jan. 30, 1717/18, in Hughes, *History of the Society of Jesus*, I, 222).

submitted to the Admiralty Court in London for reimbursement after the rebellion listed five large "double gilt" bowls, one "great Diamond" and three other pieces of jewelry made of diamonds and rubies, a silver basin, two rich cloaks "lined with plush and thick lace," and four Arras tapestries. The total value was a stunning £1,598. Clearly, these were no ordinary jewels, furs, and tapestries for austere Jesuit priests living on the edge of empire. Most likely, these luxury items were euphemisms for liturgical vessels: the five golden bowls probably represented chalices, for example, whereas the plush cloaks referred to the outer liturgical vestment worn by priests. Even the chapel itself was referred to as a "house" in the document. After the Battle of the Severn in 1655, where the Catholics were thoroughly routed, the victors destroyed "all their consecrated Ware," including "Pictures, Crucifixes, and rows of Beads, with great store of Reliques and trash they trusted in."[30]

In colonies where territory was disputed between English, French, and Spanish authorities, church furnishings became the target of iconoclastic violence. The 1654 invasion of Jamaica by Oliver Cromwell's forces was accompanied by wholesale vandalism of Catholic churches and statuary. One account hailed the troops' assault on "a chappell furnisht with a good store of popish trumperie, which wee wasted." Another soldier recalled storming a monastery from which the "Ballpated friors" had fled, leaving behind "all thayer Imedges." The invaders assaulted a statue of the Virgin Mary: they "did fall a flinging of orringes att her, and did sodainelly deforme her." The multiple raids on Spanish mission towns in La Florida by troops from Georgia and Carolina in the early 1700s brought Catholic sacramentals to English settlements to be distributed as war trophies. "Many times the sacred vessels of the altar came back to Charles Town as plunder, distributed as spoils to the raiders and shown as trophies to the stay-at-homes. Catholics with a vestige of reverence in them could not have witnessed this sacrilege without pain," concludes one denominational historian.[31]

30. Henry F. Dupuy, "An Early Account of the Establishment of Jesuit Missions in America," *Proceedings of the American Antiquarian Society*, XXX (1920), 62–80 (quotation on 67–68); "The Jesuit Farms in Maryland," *Woodstock Letters*, XL, no. 1 (1911), 65–77 (quotations on 70, 73); Beitzell, *Jesuit Missions of St. Mary's County*, 15 ("a house"); Timothy B. Riordan, *The Plundering Time: Maryland and the English Civil War, 1645–1646* (Annapolis, 2004), chap. 11, "Burn Them Papists Divells"; Roger Heaman, *An Additional Brief Narrative of a Late Bloody Design against the Protestants in Ann Arundel County, and Severn, in Maryland in the Country of Virginia* (London, 1655), 11.

31. C. H. Firth, ed., *The Narrative of General Venables: With an Appendix of Papers Relating to the Expedition to the West Indies and the Conquest of Jamaica, 1654–1655* (London, 1900), app. D, "Letters concerning the English Expedition into the Spanish West Indies

When the Massachusetts troops returned to Boston in 1690 after sacking the Catholic chapel at Port Royal, they were loaded with sacramental booty, including "surplices, communion wafers, and priestly vestments." We can only imagine the impact these looted objects might have made in this Puritan stronghold, where the Anglican Church (with its liturgical and material similarities to Catholicism) had only recently established a foothold, to the dismay of the orthodox. Whatever the afterlife of the stolen objects, the presence of "consecrated Ware" in the heart of the Puritan commonwealth is a salutary reminder that the material worlds of Protestantism and Catholicism sometimes coexisted in disturbing proximity. This was especially true in Anglican colonies, where imperial politics sometimes placed Protestant and Catholic objects in the same space. In colonial New York, the Catholic governor, Thomas Dongan, arrived in 1683 with two Jesuits in tow and proceeded to construct a chapel in the city's fort, which had previously housed the Anglican church. Oloff Stevensen van Cortlandt wrote to his daughter Maria van Rensselaer, "The image maker is making an altar—they intend to build a popish church over it." During Leisler's Rebellion in 1689, when zealous antipapists ousted the Catholic regime and took over the fort, the chaplain, Father Harvey, managed to save the altar vessels before fleeing. But after Leisler's defeat, the new governor, Francis Nicholson, returned the sacramentals to the chapel, to the disgust of the antipapist party. As two local workmen, Andries and Jan Meyer, testified, after the revolt was crushed, "there was a cry that all Images erected by Col. Thomas Dongan in the fort should be broken down and taken away." While "working in the fort with others" to repair the damage incurred during the rebellion, the pair learned that, contrary to their expectations, Nicholson had commanded the crew to "help the priest John Smith [i.e., Harvey]" remove the objects to "a better room in the fort, and ordered to make all things for Said Priest, according to his will, and perfectly and to erect all things, as he ordered." Even after the return to Protestant rule, the Catholic sacramental vessels remained in the fort.[32]

---

in 1655," 128–129 ("a chappell furnisht with a good store of popish trumperie"), app. E, 152 ("Ballpated friors"). English privateers routinely targeted Catholic churches and convents during their raids on Spanish islands in the seventeenth-century "age of piracy," seeking gold and silver ornaments and displaying their Protestant bona fides; see Kristen Block, *Ordinary Lives in the Early Caribbean: Religion, Colonial Competition, and the Politics of Profit* (Athens, Ga., 2012), 215. "Sacred vessels": Richard C. Madden, "Catholics in Colonial South Carolina," *Records of the American Catholic Historical Society of Philadelphia*, LXXIII, no. 1/2 (1962), 10–44 (quotation on 17).

32. Owen Stanwood, *The Empire Reformed: English America in the Age of the Glorious Revolution* (Philadelphia, 2011), 158; A. J. F. van Laer, ed. and trans., *The Correspondence of*

Of still greater interest are those occasions when the material cultures of Protestantism and Catholicism blended during acts of destruction and appropriation. Saint John's Anglican church in Antigua boasted a silver communion set as well as two life-size lead figures of saints, prizes seized from a French ship hailing from Martinique. The "communion plate" used in one of the Anglican churches in St. Jago de la Vega, Jamaica, was "plundered from a Roman catholic church some years ago," according to Edward Long, who sniffed, "It has more of grandeur than elegance in its fashion." Some two hundred pounds' worth of "Church plate" seized by Colonel Moore's troops when they invaded St. Augustine and burned the town and its convent was "promise[d] to our Carolina churches and Meeting Houses" in 1703. In the West Indies, the English appropriated the chapels of the Spanish when they invaded Jamaica and turned them into Anglican churches, in a process reminiscent of the material repurposing that had marked the early English Reformation. A "small church . . . built by the Spaniards called St. Paul's" had been "butified and adorn'd by the English" by 1687. In St. Ann's Parish, the Anglican minister reported to the bishop of London, "Here was in the time of the Spaniards, a free Church and an abby built by Peter Martyr who was abbot here, the same Peter Martyr who writ the decades. A great part of the Church remains and is in a little time to be rebuilt." The rebuilt church was to be used for Anglican services, with the "inscriptions" on the old Spanish church still visible: "Tho' the weather has effac'd some words," the missing inscriptions "may be easily supplyed." These colonial sites of worship echoed the defaced church walls in the British Isles that offered a palimpsest of Protestant and Catholic figures during the upheavals of the Reformation era, with texts imprinted on whitewashed walls that imperfectly covered the ghostly outlines of saints' faces.[33]

Maria van Rensselaer, 1669–1689 (Albany, N.Y., 1935), 83; Bennett, *Catholic Footsteps in Old New York*, 147; Deposition of Andries and John Meyer, New York, Sept. 26, 1689, in J. W. Fortescue, ed., *Calendar of State Papers*, Colonial Ser., XIII (London, 1901), 151; "New York Mission—1683–1689," *Woodstock Letters*, XV, no. 2 (1886), 175–183 (quotation on 182).

33. Natalie A. Zacek, *Settler Society in the English Leeward Islands, 1670–1776* (New York, 2010), 127; Edward Long, *The History of Jamaica: Reflections on Its Situation, Settlements, Inhabitants, Climate, Products, Commerce, Laws, and Government* (1774; rpt. Montreal, 2002), II, 5; Mr. Marson to Dr. Bray, Charles Town, Feb. 2, 1702/3, SPG Letters "A" Series, 1702–1737, I, no. 60, *British Online Archives*, https://britishonlinearchives.com; Anthony Milton, "A Qualified Intolerance: The Limits and Ambiguities of Early Stuart Anti-Catholicism," in Arthur F. Marotti, ed., *Catholicism and Anti-Catholicism in Early Modern English Texts* (New York, 1999), 85–115. For a discussion of how Catholic objects were repurposed during

The reaction of the Anglican laity to these Catholic material intrusions is rarely recorded, but in Jamaica, the parishioners of one of the repurposed Spanish churches, St. Catharine's, expressed their displeasure at the "fine ornaments and decorations" that remained in place, including the statues of Moses and Aaron that flanked the altar. Several "weak but well meaning people would not approach the altar, for fear of bowing to those images." Divine intervention took care of the problem, in the form of the 1722 hurricane that "flung them down and broke up noses and arms." The relieved minister had the remains of the "gaudy" statues removed to the vestry room, out of sight and mind.[34]

In another borderland region, northern New England, poverty often dictated pragmatic reuse rather than destruction of sacred objects. Laura Chmielewski describes the "frontier recycling program of religious material culture" that occurred during the many skirmishes between French and English settlers in the region during the eighteenth century. Since Anglicanism and Catholicism shared, to a large extent, a common material sacramental culture, English raiders of French missions conducted "a lively trade in church objects" with local Protestants. The marble baptismal font in St. John's Anglican church in Portsmouth, New Hampshire, had a remarkable transatlantic journey: first crafted in Senegal for a Catholic church in New France, it was seized by privateers off the New England coast and ultimately landed in a Protestant church. "Some of these war trophies found their way to the heart of Boston," Chmielewski notes; the cherubim surrounding the organ at Christ Church "were reputed to have come from a looted Quebec convent."[35]

Colonial churches were thus sites where the material cultures of Protestantism and Catholicism sometimes blended, on occasion harmoniously (or at least without comment in the historical record). Did the Anglican worshippers in the pews look upon the once-Catholic baptismal fonts and

---

the Reformation, see Sarah Tarlow, "Reformation and Transformation: What Happened to Catholic Things in a Protestant World?" in David Gaimster and Roberta Gilchrist, eds., *The Archaeology of Reformation, 1480–1580* (New York, 2003), 108–121. "Small church": David Buisseret, ed., *Jamaica in 1687: The Taylor Manuscript at the National Library Jamaica* (Kingston, Jamaica, 2008), 244. "Here was in the time of the Spaniards": "The State of the Church in Jamaica," [post-1722], Fulham Papers, XVIII, fols. 228–233.

34. "The State of the Church in Jamaica," Fulham Papers, XVIII, fols. 228–233.

35. Philippe Halbert, "A Curious Font of Porphyry," *The Junto: A Group Blog of Early American History*, July 12, 2018, https://earlyamericanists.com/2018/07/12/a-curious-font -of-porphyry/; Chmielewski, *Spice of Popery*, 239–241 (quotation on 239).

statuary that adorned their parish churches as the spoils of war? As vestiges of a superstitious past they wished to distance themselves from? Did they even recognize the objects' Roman origins, or did the act of transplantation in orthodox space exorcise their heterodox meanings and turn them into familiar objects? Did the material encounter of Protestantism and Catholicism reinforce the "mnemonic power of a Catholic past" that could not be eradicated by violence or appropriation, as Chmielewski puts it? There is no one answer to such questions. An Irish servant sitting in the back of the church would presumably have a different response than her Anglican mistress who occupied a prominent box up front or an enslaved African in the upper gallery who might have been baptized in just such a font in the Spanish Indies before being sold to an English planter. A newly arrived émigré from the heart of seigneurial Catholicism in northern England would have a much keener sense of the ritual significance of these looted objects than a second-generation colonial with a dim knowledge of the secret masses his parents once attended. Material objects do not have single or stable meanings, even in such highly ritualized and structured environments as a church. The best we can do is imagine different scenarios, alert to the many factors of time, place, memory, and circumstance that shaped colonial Americans' response to the material "signes" of Catholicism in their midst.[36]

"Badge or Token": Personal Objects of Devotion

However multivalent and ambiguous, the chalices, altar crosses, baptismal fonts, and saints' figures found in churches were at least recognizably religious artifacts. What of the highly portable devotional objects that English men and women packed into their trunks (surreptitiously, perhaps) as they prepared to voyage overseas—the "token or tokens" outlawed since the Elizabethan era? Some, such as the "set of beads and a crucifix" given to enslaved converts on Jamaica, were easily identifiable as Catholic in form and purpose. But others, such as the small medals or pilgrim badges that laymen and -women possessed and sometimes wore, could be more easily concealed and even mistaken for ordinary objects. In the sixteenth and seventeenth centuries, personal items of devotion proliferated both on the continent and in England, one plank in the Catholic Reformation's campaign to counter the more individualized and interiorized thrust of Protestantism by crafting

36. Chmielewski, *Spice of Popery*, 212.

a counterculture of devotional habits and resources operating alongside the church, the traditional locus of Catholic worship. Post-Tridentine Catholicism preferred that lay Catholics encounter the mysteries of faith in a church under the watchful eye of an ordained priest, but authorities sanctioned a much wider range of devotional acts in recognition that not all believers had regular access to a priest or a church. Alexandra Walsham has even suggested that English Catholicism "was a religion less reliant on sacraments than on sacramentals." There was a thriving, if clandestine, market for these objects in the larger towns and villages of England. An inventory of a large sack confiscated from a Lewes peddler in 1582 included Bibles and books of Catholic controversy, a green box containing "certain white cakes broken printed with *agnus dei,*" crucifixes, dozens of pairs of rosary beads (some broken, some with the names of their owners inscribed on them), "a little paper with a piece of old satin and written upon Queen of Scots," and three saints' relics, among them the bones of St. William and Mary Magdalene.[37]

How did these sacramental objects find their way from the Old World to the New? They came on the same ships carrying migrants (both voluntary and forced) from ports in Ireland, Scotland, and England, as well as from the European continent. Their presence is usually unmarked on shipping manifests or lading papers, though sometimes the vagaries of the sea brought them to the surface. A Spanish ship seized by privateers off the coast of Rhode Island yielded "solid Plate for the Use of a Church," along with many "rich Brocades, etc." (for use as altar decorations). A fleet of ships carrying colonial troops, including several Scots, was wrecked in the St. Lawrence River in the 1750s, and among the "spoils" recovered by French scavengers were "articles of Catholic devotion."[38]

No devotional object did more cultural and theological work than the simple rosary. By the end of Elizabeth's reign, it had become the signature "badge or token" of Catholicism to recusants and the orthodox alike. When

---

37. Alexandra Walsham, "Beads, Books, and Bare Ruined Choirs: Transmutations of Ritual Life," in her *Catholic Reformations in Protestant Britain* (New York, 2014), 379; Lisa McClain, *Lest We Be Damned: Practical Innovation and Lived Experience among Catholics in Protestant England, 1559–1642* (New York, 2004), 114; Muller, "Catholics and the Underground Devotional Market," in Bezio and Oldenburgh, eds., *Religion and the Early Modern English Marketplace,* 76–99.

38. William Stephens, *A Journal of the Proceedings in Georgia, Beginning October 20, 1737,* in Allen D. Candler, ed., *The Colonial Records of the State of Georgia,* IV, *Stephens' Journal, 1737–1740* (Atlanta, 1906), 477; Bennett, *Catholic Footsteps in Old New York,* 236.

churchwardens in Coventry were ordered in 1565 to "diligently note and mark them that wear any beads," an old devotional habit was turned into a polemical statement by ecclesiastical authority. Rosaries had the advantage of being small and easily hidden and, once blessed, could be used anywhere, at any time, by anyone, under any circumstance. The rosary was not just a sacramental object but a cycle of prayers, with each bead representing either the Paternoster (Lord's Prayer) or Ave Maria (Hail Mary), that could be recited in whatever combination the believer chose. Encapsulated in this prayer cycle was the entire theological edifice of post-Tridentine Catholicism, which focused on the incarnation of Christ and the special role of the Virgin Mary as the primary intercessor for and protector of the laity. For those recusants who could not attend mass or the sacraments, the rosary was the primary instructional aid available—the "unlearned man's booke," as the Jesuit Henry Garnet put it. The ultimate in stealth technology, the rosary offered "endless possibilities for the subtle and subversive undermining of Protestant authority and teaching," Anne Dillon has argued, by creating sacred space wherever it was used: in the home, the magistrate's court, the marketplace, the street, the prison, even places of Protestant worship. Protestant controversialists understood the danger of the rosary as both ritual and prayer and mocked its use. "What shall I say of their much mumbling of *Masses* and jumbling of *Beads?*" the seventeenth-century polemicist John Gee scoffed. "They must have *beads,* to pray by number, or else their prayers want weight. They are commanded to say somtimes in one day an hundred and fifty *Pater-nosters,* as many *Ave-Marias;* forty *Creeds;* and, if they misse but one of the right number, all is vaine and effectlesse."[39]

39. Bishop Bentham, quoted in Peter Marshall, *Heretics and Believers: A History of the English Reformation* (New Haven, Conn., 2017), 480 ("diligently note"). The rosary was, according to Henry Garnet, "a manifest badge or token of the Romane Religion" (*The Societie of the Rosary, wherin Is Conteined the Begining, Increase, and Profit of the Same . . .* [London, 1593], 10, 94). "Endless possibilities": Anne Dillon, "Praying by Number: The Confraternity of the Rosary and the English Catholic Community, c. 1580–1700," *History,* LXXXVII (2003), 451–471 (quotation on 470–471). See also McClain, *Lest We Be Damned,* 81–82; Erminia Ardissino, "Literary and Visual Forms of a Domestic Devotion: The Rosary in Renaissance Italy," in Maya Corry, Marco Faini, and Alessia Meneghin, eds., *Domestic Devotions in Early Modern Italy* (Leiden, 2019), 342–371. "Much mumbling": John Gee, *The Foot out of the Snare: With a Detection of Sundry Late Practices and Impostures of the Priests and Jesuits in England* (London, 1624), 16–17.

The flexibility of the rosary was highlighted in manuals and sermons encouraging its use. John Bucke's 1589 *Instructions for the Use of the Beades* advised his readers (of whatever "good trade, occupacion, or qualiue") to pray the rosary "whiles you goe about your necessarie businesse in your vocation, or whiles you are travaling by the waye or in tillinge or plowing the grownd." The image of the rosary included in Bucke's book could serve as a substitute for the real thing if no rosary was available, yet another example of the imaginative devotional economy of recusants. A sermon delivered by John Lewis in colonial Maryland echoed Bucke in extolling the rosary as "a devotion suited to all capacities and states: for a traveler may perform it on the road, a laborer at his work, a tradesman in his shop, a gentleman in his walks . . . and a sick man confined to his bed." Perhaps just as important, rosaries were cheap and seemingly for sale everywhere. In Lisa McCain's words, rosary beads were "readily available to most Catholics with half a mind to locate a pair" in seventeenth-century England. An Irishman arrested in London in 1639 on charges of begging was discovered to be a peddler of Catholic wares, with thirty-one strings of rosary beads in his knapsack and more than £3 in profits from earlier sales. All it took to manufacture a rosary, for those too poor to afford even the few shillings required to purchase one, was a pile of beads and a string. The truly resourceful could even manufacture a rosary out of scraps, as the imprisoned Jesuit John Gerard did in 1597, when he cut an orange peel into small crosses, then "stitched the crosses together in pairs and strung them on to a silk thread, making them into rosaries."[40]

Unfortunately for the modern scholar, these very attributes—the smallness, portability, and sheer *ordinariness* of rosaries—made them fragile. Very few rosaries appear in colonial inventories, and even fewer have been uncovered at archaeological sites. A late-seventeenth-century burial site in St. Augustine unearthed a jet rosary with a crucifix attached, and a small palm rosary was recovered from archaeological excavations at Historic St. Mary's City, the site of the first capital of Maryland and the home of the "great brick chapel." But although rosaries may be hard to find in the records, beads are everywhere.

---

40. John Bucke, *Instructions for the Use of the Beades: Conteining Many Matters of Meditacion or Mentall Prayer, with Diverse Good Advises of Ghostly Counsayle; W[h]ere unto Is Added a Figure or Forme of the Beades Portrued in a Table* (Leuven, Belgium, 1589), 84; Joseph C. Linck, *Fully Instructed and Vehemently Influenced: Catholic Preaching in Anglo-Colonial America* (Philadelphia, 2002), 96; McClain, *Lest We Be Damned,* 91; Philip Caraman, trans., *John Gerard: The Autobiography of an Elizabethan* (London, 1951), 117.

We have account books from the Jesuit missions listing large quantities of beads, presumably for the purpose of constructing rosaries for sale or distribution to the laity. George Hunter's Daybook Memoranda from 1766–1767 recorded numerous purchases of beads over a six-month period—"20 dozen" on August 2, "4 dozen" in September, and another "3 dozen" in December, as well as some "chained beads." During Leisler's Rebellion in New York following the ousting of James II, the victorious antipapist party seized an "old chest" of goods, formerly belonging to a Jesuit, that contained "22 Bunches of black Beads, also some loose ditto." A pamphlet celebrating the routing of the Catholic forces at the Battle of the Severn (1655), an earlier civil war in Maryland, described the battlefield as "strewed with Papist beads." Once unstrung, beads could be put to a variety of profane purposes. Father Andrew White recorded a story of "sacrilegious playfulness" in his narrative *Relatio itineris in Marylandiam,* in which an apostate mocked the Catholic attachment to the rosary by grounding his "prayer-beads" to a powder and smoking them in his pipe, "often boasting that he had eaten up his 'Ave Marias,'" for so he called the beads." (The man suffered a grim end, being eaten by a "huge fish" while swimming in the river, so that "he who a little while before boasted that he had eaten up his 'Ave Maria beads' should see his own flesh devoured, even while he was yet living.")[41]

Beads were also a commonplace item of the Indian trade and can be found in abundance in those sites inhabited by both Natives and Europeans. Glass beads have been recovered from several locations in St. Mary's City: at the missions, where Jesuits conducted a strategic trade with the Native

41. George Hunter's Daybook Memoranda, 1763–1768, box 46, folder 6, fol. 17, MPA; "Minutes of Proceedings Begunn in Albany This 17th Day of March 1689," in Peter R. Christoph, ed., *The Leisler Papers, 1689–1691: Files of the Provincial Secretary of New York Relating to the Administration of Lieutenant-Governor Jacob Leisler* (Syracuse, N.Y., 2002), 111; *Virginia and Maryland; or, The Lord Baltamore's Printed Case, Uncased and Answered . . .* (London, 1655), 17; White, *Relatio itineris in Marylandiam,* ed. Dalrymple, 79. On the jet rosary, see Kathleen A. Deagan, *Artifacts of the Spanish Colonies of Florida and the Caribbean, 1500–1800* (Washington, D.C., 1987), 182; author's observation of rosary, St. John's site (Koch, 1980). The "palm rosary" recovered from the home of John Lewger is a small, ten-bead version of the standard rosary, intended to be used while concealed in the palm of one's hand; Arthur Pierce Middleton and Henry M. Miller speculate that the rosary might have been placed in the ground while Lewger's house was being constructed, to bless the home and its residents. See Middleton and Miller, "'Mr. Secretary': John Lewger, St. John's Freehold, and Early Maryland," *Maryland Historical Magazine,* CIII (2008), 132–165 (palm rosary on 159).

FIGURE 10. Rosary found in St. John's site. Ca. 1638.
Courtesy Historic St. Mary's City

communities they hoped to convert, at the home of the wealthy Maryland planter Charles Carroll in Annapolis, and at sites dating from 1680 to 1720 in nearby Prince George's County.[42] William Clayborne, an Indian trader and perennial thorn in the side of the proprietary party in Maryland, had a "parcell of blue beads" weighing nearly four pounds confiscated during one of their periodic skirmishes. Jet and stone beads have been recovered from colonial sites throughout Spanish America and the Caribbean. Surprisingly, few archaeologists entertain the possibility that at least some of these beads may

42. John D. Krugler and Timothy B. Riordan, "'Scandalous and Offensive to the Government': The 'Popish Chappel' at St. Mary's City, Maryland and the Society of Jesus, 1634 to 1705," *Mid-America*, LXXIII (1991), 197; Mark P. Leone and Gladys-Marie Fry, "Conjuring in the Big House Kitchen: An Interpretation of African American Belief Systems Based on the Uses of Archaeology and Folklore Sources," *Journal of American Folklore*, CXII (1999), 372; Michael T. Lucas, "Empowered Objects: Material Expressions of Spiritual Beliefs in the Colonial Chesapeake Region," *Historical Archaeology*, XLVIII (2014), 106.

have come from, or been intended for, rosaries, despite the known practice of distributing small devotional items such as "beads, crucifixes, and little painted images" to Native converts in missionary stations throughout New France and New Spain. Beads are considered trade items first and foremost, evidence of substantial cultural, but not necessarily religious, mingling between Indigenous and European peoples in the scholarly literature.[43]

There has been much more scholarly interest in the varied religious functions of the artifacts discovered in colonial sites where enslaved Africans lived. Beads featured in the domestic and Atlantic markets in Africa as well as in Native America and were used in a variety of secular and religious arenas, from rites of passage to ceremonies of statecraft, personal adornment, treatment of illness, and conjure/magic. In some areas of West Africa, beads tied on a string functioned as an amulet worn around the neck, arm, waist, or ankle to ward off evil and protect the soul—much as the rosary did for some laymen and -women. An African American gravesite in South Carolina active in the eighteenth and nineteenth centuries yielded 3,481 glass beads in one pit alone, with two more "bead-filled pits" located on a nearby plantation that dated back to the seventeenth century. In the African Burial Ground in New York (Burial 340), one enslaved woman, presumed to have been African-born because of the ritual modification of her teeth, was buried with a bracelet of 41 glass beads around her right wrist and a string of 70 greenish-blue beads around her hips. One of the most extensively documented colonial burial sites for enslaved Africans is Newton Plantation on Barbados, where more than 30 different types of glass beads were found.[44]

43. *Archives of Maryland*, V, 173; Edward Randolph to Lords of Trade and Plantations, May 29, 1689, CO 5/855, no. 8 ("beads, crucifixes"), TNA. Jet was a popular substance in Spain for the manufacture of various devotional items, including rosaries and crucifixes. Deagan, *Artifacts of the Spanish Colonies*, chap. 7 provides a good overview of the archaeological evidence and analysis of glass beads in colonial sites. As she points out, function is much more difficult to determine than provenance, given the lack of contextual information available for most artifacts (161). Objects of mixed origin and mixed use, such as glass beads, tend to escape the conventional categories of interpretation that archaeologists attribute to artifacts; Stephen W. Silliman argues that archaeology of Native sites "does not handle well the sharing of object types across cultural/ethnic boundaries." See Silliman, "Change and Continuity, Practice, and Memory: Native American Persistence in Colonial New England," *American Antiquity*, LXXIV (2009), 211–230 (quotation on 213).

44. Robert Farris Thompson, *Flash of the Spirit: African and Afro-American Art and Philosophy* (New York, 1983), 57; Linda France Stine, Melanie A. Cabak, and Mark D. Groover, "Blue Beads as African-American Cultural Symbols," *Historical Archaeology*,

The fragmentary evidence we have from the Atlantic slave trade suggests that beads were among the material techniques of enslavement itself. One account of a slave sale on Barbados noted that some of the captives "were decorated with beads, given to them by their captors, and bracelets round their wrists and ancles." These beads were not just worn passively by captive Africans but at times actively manipulated to their own ends. An officer on board an English slaver "observed the females had all a number of different coloured glass beads hung around their necks. The master of the ship told me the chief employment, and indeed amusement, they had was in new-stringing their beads, and that very frequently [they] broke the string on purpose to set them to work." Given what we know of the religious significance (in both a European and African ritual context) of strings of beads in West African societies, the deliberate breaking apart and reassembling of the beads by the captives takes on a very different meaning from that ascribed by the captain—a way of reconsecrating what was desecrated, or of making one's own out of what was imposed by force. Colonial planters spoke of the continued attachment of their slaves to the beads that might have decorated their bodies since their arrival on the island; in the 1730s and 1740s, Griffith Hughes wondered at the "universal custom of adorning their bodies, by wearing strings of beads of various colors," despite the fact that there were people from "so many nations intermixed" on his plantation. "These beads are in great numbers twined around their arms, necks, and legs."[45]

With few exceptions, the beads recovered in archaeological sites associated with Africans in America have been presumed to reflect African rather than Christian ritual practices—even when found in sites inhabited by known Catholics.[46] We have no firm evidence that the glass beads unearthed at the

---

XXX (1996), 49–75, esp. 62; Erik R. Seeman, "Reassessing the 'Sankofa Symbol' in New York's African Burial Ground," *WMQ*, 3d Ser., LXVII (2010), 119; Jerome S. Handler and Frederick W. Lange, *Plantation Slavery in Barbados: An Archaeological and Historical Investigation* (Cambridge, Mass., 1978).

45. Handler and Lange, *Plantation Slavery in Barbados*, 147.

46. The glass beads unearthed at Charles Carroll's house in Annapolis were categorized as African charms or ritual objects by Leone and Fry, who conclude, "No Christian items" were found at the site ("Conjuring in the Big House Kitchen," *Journal of American Folklore*, CXII [1999], 384). Christopher C. Fennell points out that alternative explanations for these objects rooted in English religious culture are also possible; see Fennell, "Conjuring Boundaries: Inferring Past Identities from Religious Artifacts," *International Journal of Historical Archaeology*, IV (2000), 281–313. For a good discussion of how individuals, as

burial sites where enslaved Africans were laid to rest came from rosaries or any other Christian ritual object. But we know that a considerable proportion of the enslaved who labored in these plantations and households came from Spanish and French islands in the Caribbean and that bestowing a rosary upon a newly arrived African was one of the techniques of enslavement. So it does not seem far-fetched to suggest that at least some of these beads might have once belonged to rosaries or other Catholic devotional objects.

We have more evidence for the presence of crucifixes and religious medals among the enslaved population in North America. A "black Virgin Mary" was found by the invading English on Jamaica in 1655 among the detritus of the Spanish church, supposedly "to enveigle the blackes to worship." A century later, another visitor to Jamaica reported that it was customary for Catholic missionaries in the French and Spanish islands (the point of origin for many of the Africans sold in the English Caribbean) to provide their enslaved converts with "store of crosses, relicks, and consecrated annulets." In the town of Gracia Real de Santa Tersa de Mose, settled by converted free Africans north of St. Augustine in the 1730s, numerous religious artifacts were uncovered by archaeologists, including amber rosary beads, metal rosary pendants and chains, and a handmade pewter St. Christopher's medal. As Jane Landers suggests, the iconography on the medal can be read in different ways: St. Christopher is the Catholic patron saint of travelers and also the patron saint of Havana, Cuba, making it a fitting emblem for someone who had perhaps traveled the Atlantic circuit from West Africa to Cuba to Florida. On the reverse side of the medal is a compass rose, "also an appropriate symbol for these world travelers."[47]

---

well as the objects buried with them, defy easy attempts to categorize them by ethnicity or race, see Julia A. King and Edward E. Chaney, "Passing for Black in Seventeenth-Century Maryland," in Mary C. Beaudry and James Symonds, eds., *Interpreting the Early Modern World: Transatlantic Perspectives* (New York, 2011), 87–112.

47. Firth, ed., *Narrative of General Venables*, 130; Long, *History of Jamaica*, II, 430; Jane Landers, *Black Society in Spanish Florida* (Urbana, Ill., 1999), 55. On the archaeological excavation of Gracia Real de Santa Tersa de Mose, known as Fort Mose, see Kathleen Deagan and Darcie MacMahon, *Fort Mose: Colonial America's Black Fortress of Freedom* (Gainesville, Fl., 1995). Laurie A. Wilkie argues that the crucifix and medal more likely represent "syncretic religious beliefs rather than pure Spanish Catholicism," a valid point, but one that discounts the degree to which global Catholicism itself was a blended religion in Spain as well as in the Americas (Wilkie, "Secret and Sacred: Contextualizing the Artifacts of African-American Magic and Religion," *Historical Archaeology*, XXXI [1997], 81–106 [quotation on 96]).

FIGURE 11. Handmade silver St. Christopher medal. Ca. 1750–1770. Gracia Real de Santa Teresa de Mose (known as Fort Mose), Florida. Courtesy of Florida Museum of Natural History

The paucity of intact sacramentals in colonial archaeological sites is not surprising. Only fifty-eight religious medals, for example, have been found so far in sites scattered throughout British America. The ten medals traced to the Maryland mission stand out for their Jesuit-themed iconography; rather than traditional Catholic Reformation images of Mary or other members of the Holy Family, the Maryland medals were more likely to depict St. Ignatius or some other Jesuit symbol. In archaeological digs around English America, there are precious few crucifixes belonging to Catholics of any ethnicity, a testament to how small and ephemeral these personal devotionals were and how loath colonial recusants were to publicize their religious identity. Personal devotional objects tend to appear only in truncated form in colonial archives, without elaboration or explanation. Among the nearly fifty inventories detailed in Maryland's records during the seventeenth century, only prominent Catholic landowners seem to have owned even the most rudimentary religious objects such as Leonard Calvert's "bone Crosse." A Barbados settler "made provision in his will for 'a crucifix of silver' to be given to his sister-in-law" in 1668, and John Tatham's 1700 probate inventory included "1 round large Silver Crucifix" and "1 wooden Cross wth the Image of Christ." Another "silver Crucifix" was at the heart of a dispute between Stephen Charlton and one of his customers in 1630s Virginia when the former never received the sixty pounds of tobacco he was due for payment. Among the handful of religious artifacts found at Historic St. Mary's was a small silver crucifix, along

FIGURE 12. Crucifix. N.d. Courtesy Historic St. Mary's City

with some medallions—this from a site that served for more than sixty years as the center of Catholic worship on the mainland.[48]

More surprising, archaeological excavations of the original Jamestown settlement have uncovered a number of Catholic objects, including several unique jet crosses engraved with a stick-figure Christ, rosary beads, and a St. Nicholas medallion. Fashioned in the workshops of the Catholic Low Countries out of materials commonly found in Spain, these devotional objects speak to the transnational lives of many of Virginia's earliest settlers. In this

48. Timothy B. Riordan, "'To Excite the Devotion of the Catholics': The Use and Meaning of Catholic Religious Medals in the Colonial Period," *Historical Archaeology*, XLIX (2015), 71–86 (Riordan surveys the data from a total of forty-five sites); Johnston, "Papists in a Protestant World," 129, 143–144; Susie M. Ames, ed., *County Court Records of Accomack-Northampton, Virginia, 1632–1640* (Washington, D.C., 1954), 144–145. Calvert's estate also included a "gold Reliquary case"; see "An Inventory of Lands, Goods, and Chattells Belonging to Mr Leonard Calvert. . . . ," [July 5], 1647, in *Archives of Maryland*, IV, 320–321.

sense, their presence is unremarkable: adventurers like John Smith straddled the Protestant, Catholic, and Ottoman worlds in their travels. But on another level, the crucifixes and religious medals unearthed in Jamestown are a startling anomaly that pierces the facade of Protestant hegemony overlaying the religious history of the first colonies. The simple stick figures on the jet crucifixes suggest economizing on the part of the artisan who crafted them; their miniature size speaks to the need for concealment. Easily hidden in the palm of one's hand, each cross is both an object of numinous power and a stratagem of survival. These archaeological finds give material substance to the scattered references in the records of the Virginia Company to suspected Catholics lurking in Jamestown—one Chanterton, a winemaker, "smells too much of Roome [Rome]" and "attempts to worke myracles wth his Crucyfixe," whereas the first man executed in Jamestown was rumored to be a Catholic spy. Ever since the discovery of the Catholic objects was announced in 2015, there has been speculation about how they found their way to Virginia and in whose hands. But whether carried by gentlemen-adventurers, itinerant artisans, indentured servants, or Native converts trading with the English, these devotional objects are a palpable reminder of early Virginia's religious pluralism.[49]

Relics came to the colonies as well. And like the rosaries and pocket crucifixes found in the Chesapeake, they were highly portable devotionals. Jesuit missionaries carried "sacred relics of the most holy cross" in "casket[s]" hung around their necks, the weight of which left red marks that resembled "wound[s]," or stigmata. Andrew White used his relic to heal one Native man, who thereafter displayed similar scars on either side of the healed wound. Leonard Calvert and John Tatham owned reliquaries made of precious metals, and among the items found buried under the Jamestown church was a hexagonal silver box, containing several fragments of bone, that had been placed on top of Gabriel Archer's coffin. Scratched on the lid of the silver box

49. William M. Kelso, *Jamestown: The Buried Truth* (Charlottesville, Va., 2006), 187–188; "John Pory: A Letter to Sir Edwin Sandys," June 12, 1620, in Susan Myra Kingsbury, ed., *The Records of the Virginia Company of London* (Washington, D.C., 1933), III, 300–306 (quotation on 304); Philip L. Barbour, "Captain George Kendall: Mutineer or Intelligencer?" *Virginia Magazine of History and Biography*, LXX (1962), 297–313; Nicholas Fandos, "Unearthing Jamestown's Leaders, and a Mystery," *New York Times*, July 29, 2015, A13; Ed Simon, "Will This Relic Change Our Whole View of Early American History?" *Religion Dispatches*, Aug. 7, 2015, https://religiondispatches.org/will-a-newly-discovered-relic-change-our-whole-view-of-early-american-history.

FIGURE 13. One of six jet crucifixes found at Jamestowne. Courtesy Jamestown Rediscovery Foundation (Preservation Virginia)

FIGURE 14. Copper alloy religious medallion. Ca. 16th–17th century. Found at Jamestowne. On the front is the image of St. Nicholas; on the back is the image of the Virgin Mary and child. Courtesy Jamestown Rediscovery Foundation (Preservation Virginia)

was the letter "M," which, Christopher Allison argues, refers to the name of the saint whose bones presumably resided within—Cuthbert Mayne, the first Jesuit missionary to be executed under Elizabeth I. In the pockets of the enemy dead following the 1655 conquest of Jamaica were found "some reliques" along with "an Agnus Dei."[50]

All of these relics were miniaturized versions of the bones, skulls, and skin of saints that once populated the religious landscape of pre-Reformed England. Like rosaries but unlike crucifixes, the bodies of saints could be disarticulated into smaller pieces, in an almost endless process of replication and dispersal. The tendency of relics to proliferate—to reproduce via both natural and artificial means—infuriated Reformers, and in the wake of iconoclastic attacks on fraudulent relics, the Tridentine Catholic Church went to great lengths to police the creation and use of relics. But it was a losing battle, especially in Protestant lands, where so much of Catholic ritual life took place in private homes, beyond the oversight of priests. Stories of abused, neglected, and forgotten relics circulated in post-Reformation England, such as the head of the Irish martyr John Cornelius, which had been hidden in a cupboard only to be exposed and fall to the ground when workmen were clearing away the rubble from the Great Fire of London in 1666. These "skeletons in the cupboard," to use Alexandra Walsham's pithy phrase, were both a symptom of the "domestication" of English Catholicism after the break with Rome and an opportunity for creative lay appropriation. Situated as they were at the tail end of this long chain of relic-making, colonial Catholics often had to make do with singular atoms of sanctity: a single bead, a sliver of bone. This process of reduction did not in any way lessen the spiritual power of these sacramentals. A bone fragment does the same work as an entire skeleton of a saint.[51]

In the hierarchy of Catholic religious objects, relics ranked at the very top, since they were tangible remnants of God's saving grace in the world. A relic

50. White, *Relatio itineris in Marylandiam*, ed. Dalrymple, 87–88; Province Notes on the Mission of Maryland, 1633–1874, box 3, folder 7, p. 36, MPA; Christopher M. B. Allison, "Jamestown's Relics: Sacred Presence in the English New World," *Conversations: An Online Journal of the Center for the Study of Material and Visual Cultures of Religion* (2016), https:// mavcor.yale.edu/conversations/essays/jamestown-s-relics-sacred-presence-english-new-world; Adrienne LaFrance, "A Skeleton, a Catholic Relic, and a Mystery about American Origins," *Atlantic*, July 28, 2015, https://www.theatlantic.com/national/archive/2015/07/a-skeleton-a -catholic-relic-and-a-mystery-about-americas-origins/399743/?UTM_SOURCE=yahoo; Firth, ed., *Narrative of General Venables*, 132.

51. Alexandra Walsham, "Skeletons in the Cupboard: Relics after the English Reformation," *Past and Present*, no. 206, issue supplement 5 (July 2010), 121–143, esp. 129.

connected believers directly, without ritual or priestly mediation, to the saints and hence to God himself. Relics served an essential function in the mission field, since they consecrated the private chapels constructed by the Catholic gentry in Maryland during the eighteenth century. Each portable altar stone was made of slate, with a cavity fewer than two inches square to hold a relic of the saint to whom the altar was dedicated. In the mission communities of New France, the martyrdom of several Jesuits created new relics for their Native converts: the skull of Jean Brebeuf was preserved in a Quebec convent, encased in a "silver bust" that his family sent from France to serve as a reliquary. This was a form of glorification denied to their English brethren in North America. No Jesuit died for his faith in Maryland, though several were arrested and sent in chains back to England during the upheavals of the 1640s and 1650s. So the opportunity for relic-making was lost, as well as the martyr's crown.[52]

But if we widen our understanding of relics—as indeed English recusants did during the penal era—to include the everyday objects touched by holy men and women who, though still living, had suffered for their faith, then we can detect a similar process of relic-making in the English colonies. The impulse to turn everyday things into holy relics was one of the most powerful subversive currents of the Catholic Reformation. The Catholic tradition's long entanglement with the material world began, after all, with the polemical actions of Jesus himself, who turned water into wine and spun parables around the spiritual meaning of lamps, bushels, old cloaks, fishing nets. The Catholic Reformation reinvigorated this radical tradition in the face of new persecutions. The crowds gathered at Tyburn to witness the execution of priests engaged in relic-taking as a form of protest: anything, no matter how small or insignificant, was "fair game." The dirty handkerchief used by the hangman to wipe the mud from Robert Southwell's face before he mounted the scaffold in 1595 was snatched up by the crowd after he flung it away. Moments of high drama like executions aside, below the public surface of life in post-Reformation England, a quiet process of transubstantiation occurred in

52. Hardy, "Papists in a Protestant Age," 196. Hardy points out that, although church altars were normally made of heavy stone, canon law required that "the furnishings of family chapels be easily removable, because the private chapels often reverted to secular use" (197). After the 787 Council of Nicea, all portable altar stones originally contained a relic; see Sarah Luginbill, "The Medieval Portable Altar Database," *Material Religion*, XVI (2020), 683–685. "Silver bust": "Struggles and Sufferings of Our First American Missionaries," *Woodstock Letters*, XXI, no. 2 (1892), 224.

the households of recusants who treasured as a holy relic each scrap of materiality that had been worn, touched by, or was in the presence of the fugitive priests who visited on their periodic journeys. The same process occurred in colonial households and mission stations. The old shoes and frayed liturgical vestments displayed in the museum at the St. Francis Xavier shrine at Old Bohemia are not just reminders of the colonial past but relics in the true sense of the word: material objects that retain the sanctity of the men whose bodies they once adorned.[53]

The concept of a relic also provides a crucial point of connection between Native, African, and European religious material cultures. The hortatory wampum collar gifted to the mission at Sault-St.-Louis is venerated today as a relic, but the notion that objects can hold sacred power was a long-standing cosmological principle in Native American and African cultures rather than a Christian import. Ritual objects like *minkisi*, misunderstood and mislabeled as "fetishes" by European travelers and missionaries, similarly were active spiritual agents in traditional African religions. The material world, in fact, did much of the heuristic and tangible work of knitting together colonial Catholicism. In Karin Vélez's words, the Catholic tradition is "powerfully accretive: it is always in flux and reinvention, never frozen or static." This was especially true in frontier regions, the borderlands where Protestantism and Catholicism collided and converged, where Native and African converts brought their own beliefs, practices, and objects to the ritual complex developing in colonial communities and plantations.[54]

Conclusion

Religious objects, like the people who possessed them, migrated from the Old to the New World, the end point in what was often a long chain of transmission stretching between the hamlets and metropolitan centers of Europe, the Native villages of North America, and—in time—the interior and coastal forts of Africa. The material world of colonial Catholicism was as ambivalent

---

53. Maureen Miller, "Introduction: Material Culture and Catholic History," *Catholic Historical Review*, CI (2015), 1–17; McClain, *Lest We Be Damned*, 152–156 (quotation on 164).

54. Karin Vélez, *The Miraculous Flying House of Loreto: Spreading Catholicism in the Early Modern World* (Princeton, N.J., 2019), 33. On the "fetish" and its African and European meanings in the colonial South, see Jason R. Young, *Rituals of Resistance: African Atlantic Religion in the Kongo and the Lowcountry South in the Era of Slavery* (Baton Rouge, 2007), chap. 3, "*Minkisi*, Conjure Bags, and the African Atlantic Religious Complex," 105–145.

and polyphonic as the religious lives of its human residents. Objects and people alike inhabited more than one religious identity in the post-Reformation era, and decoding them is no simple, hermeneutic task. As Alexandra Walsham reminds us in her analysis of English domestic objects such as mugs, plates, and pots that displayed religious images or inscriptions, "It would be wrong to approach these objects as if they provide a transparent window into the souls and a clear imprint of the religious mentalities of their owners and users. The meanings they carried must also have shifted as they traveled down the generations from parents to children and as they were bought, borrowed, pawned, and sold. They circulated in a multiconfessional society in which particular iconographies were never the monopoly of any single religious community." Her caution applies even more strongly to the colonial world, where vagrant objects circulated in a highly mobile community that hailed from four continents. English settlers brought remnants of their religious culture with them in the form of liturgical and devotional items, and much was lost, broken, discarded, or altered in transit. Captive Africans were forcibly separated from the spirit objects, cosmograms, and ancestral graves that constituted their spiritual legacy; they endured the imposition of a new material culture comprised of the instruments of enslavement. Native peoples experienced unprecedented levels of displacement and resettlement that presented material as well as spiritual challenges to their sacred traditions. With every remove, every arrival, the meaning of objects shifted.[55]

In such a fluid semiotic environment marked by rupture and loss, memory was the key to preserving *and* reimagining religious habits and habitats. Many English Catholics had survived with little more than the memories of traditional ways of worship for decades before they set sail for North America, memories that they called upon to turn their domestic spaces into private chapels, as we explored in the last chapter. In recusant households, memory helped turn profane objects (tin cups, wooden sticks, and tables) into sacred ones (chalices, crucifixes, and altars) and transformed ordinary rooms into sites of imagined pilgrimage and worship. Even in Reformed households, memory could be subversive by throwing up unwanted or unanticipated reminders of the Romish past. Wealthier families who had compiled storehouses of personal and decorative items might stumble across a religious medal or a crucifix buried in a chest when it came time to inventory their

55. Alexandra Walsham, "Domesticating the Reformation: Material Culture, Memory, and Confessional Identity in Early Modern England," *Renaissance Quarterly,* LXIX (2016), 566–616 (quotation on 580–581).

possessions at the death of the patriarch. In time, a distinct material culture emerged within Protestantism—vernacular Bibles, hymnals, the Book of Common Prayer, wall inscriptions, household items engraved with biblical scenes—around which new memories accrued, subject to the same vagaries of time and emotion as they passed from generation to generation.

But memory was more than a mental exercise that shaped the relationship of people to the things they touched, owned, and used; memory itself was understood to be part of the physical, material world in early modern Anglo-America. Organized into physical spaces (a room, a storehouse, a palace, a church) into which people placed images of the objects they encountered in their daily lives as mnemonic devices, memory was part of the material and sensory landscape of early modern Christianity. The great theorist of the "art of memory," Saint Augustine, wrote of the "fields and vast mansions of memory," wherein are stored "innumerable images brought in there from objects of every conceivable kind perceived by the senses." From this "huge repository of the memory, with its secret and unimaginable caverns," medieval and early modern Christians (the illiterate and the learned both) constructed mental maps that would guide them through the prayers and rituals of their faith. Sixteenth- and seventeenth-century followers of the Augustinian tradition wrote manuals instructing the laity how to enter a church, fix their attention on the statues, stained glass, and altars inside, and commit each corner, each object, to memory along with its corresponding virtue or doctrine. By returning again and again to these mental images, forged through contact with the physical world, lay Christians learned their faith. The iconoclasts of the Reformation tried to smash these memory palaces along with the stained glass windows and saints' pictures that adorned Europe's churches, replacing the "art of memory" with book learning as the pedagogy of choice. But the "vast inner memory cathedrals of the Middle Ages," in Frances Yates's wonderful phrase, could not be destroyed so easily. And, in fact, the late medieval tradition of "artificial memory" was reinvigorated by Tridentine Catholicism's need to replace actual sacramental practice with imagined reconstructions in Protestant lands.[56]

Thinking of memory as material allows us to consider more holistically the world of objects that colonial recusants inhabited. There was much that was strange and unfamiliar in the Americas, from the native trees and minerals

56. Quoted in Mary Carruthers, *The Book of Memory: A Study of Memory in Medieval Culture*, 2d ed. (New York, 2008), x–xi; Frances Yates, *Selected Works*, III, *The Art of Memory* (New York, 1999), 101.

to the Indigenous artifacts that found their way into colonial households and chapels, all of which had to find a place in their mental landscapes as well. Contact with the physical and sensate environment was the key to forming new memories, according to the theories of the day. But just as important, those memories had a corporeal dimension of their own. To the many contact zones of English colonization, we can add the zone of memory formation, where old mental storehouses were filled with new material objects that left their imprint on the very structures of feeling and remembering that were so crucial to colonial self-fashioning.

To bring this discussion back down to earth, let's return to the rosary and the crucifix, the devotional workhorses of post-Reformation Catholicism. On one level, rosaries and crucifixes were unambiguous symbols of Catholicism. As John Venn, the SPG minister for Jamaica, put it, "A set of beads and a crucifix make a good Catholic." By "make," he meant "mark"—as in, these objects *marked* indisputably the bearer as Catholic. (And by "good," he really meant "bad.") The mere presence of a rosary or crucifix was enough to label someone a recusant, a shorthand for the theological, cultural, political, and racial otherness that all Catholics inhabited. When the governor of Barbados told the crown in 1667 that he wanted only those servants "without a crucifix about [their] neck" to be sent to the island, there was no need to elaborate on his concerns. A servant who wore a crucifix was also one who would defy his master, join in rebellion with other discontented laborers, scorn the established church, and raise heretic children.[57]

But in colonial America, these tokens of Catholicism inhabited different material and mental frameworks, and thus their meaning was much more fluid. The "Wooden Cross" that a servant on Montserrat insisted on carrying during his wife's funeral procession, for example, was carved on the island from a mental image he had formed beholding and handling crucifixes in his native Ireland. By using indigenous materials and crafting it with his own hands, he turned an Old World artifact into a New World one and rearranged his memory storehouse to accommodate this new object. A sacramental that in Ireland might have been a family heirloom as well as a powerful aide-mémoire for the Roman liturgy now carried different or additional meanings as a symbol of spiritual resilience and resistance to English colonial rule. The "Strange Indian" whom a company of English soldiers encountered in Maryland in 1705 wore a "Crusifix and Beads . . . about his Neck," baptismal gifts

57. John Venn to Bishop Sherlock, June 15, 1751, Fulham Papers, XVIII, fols. 45–52; Francis Willoughby to king, Sept. 16, 1667, BL, Stowe MS 735, fol. 19.

he had been given by the French who kidnapped him from his village years before; in this context, the crucifix and rosary were simultaneously symbols of faith and tokens of captivity. The admission of a French prisoner in Cartagena (Huguenot or Catholic, depending on which story he told) that the rosary pressed upon him by his jailers was "no good" because "those in his land were different" reminds us that early modern Catholics understood this semiotic fluidity just as well as modern theorists.[58]

However resourceful Catholics were in transforming the material detritus of colonial settlement into familiar devotional objects through acts of salvage or creative adaptation, they continued to inhabit religious half-lives without access to priests and the sacraments. Mere possession of a rosary or crucifix did not "make a good Catholic," John Venn's taunt notwithstanding. Good Catholics, in the eyes of the Church at least, went to church, where they were instructed by the priest in the essentials of faith and received the sacraments of baptism, penance, communion, confirmation, marriage, and—at the end of life—last rites at his hand. Gauging the degree of ecclesiastical compliance among lay Catholics in North America, where priests were scarce and barriers of language, race, ethnicity, and class impeded the formation of a cohesive religious culture, is far more challenging than counting the number of rosary beads, liturgical vessels, crucifixes, or relics found in colonial sites.

Did the Irish servant who served in the Barbados militia with a crucifix around his neck attend mass when an itinerant priest was on the island? Did he and his family observe the feast and fast days of the liturgical calendar, pray for the souls of their dead loved ones, and recite the Roman missal at home, even after attending the local parish church under the watchful eye of their master? Did he long for the consolation of last rites and burial in consecrated ground after his death? It is time to turn to the sacramental lives of colonial Catholics.

58. Samuel Waad to Oliver Cromwell, Dec. 6, 1654, CO 1/12, no. 31 iii, TNA; *Archives of Maryland*, Feb. 21, 1704/5, XXV, 183–185 (quotations on 184–185); Block, *Ordinary Lives*, 98.

PART TWO

Sacramental Politics

Introduction

IN THE MID-EIGHTEENTH CENTURY a Jesuit priest reported with great satisfaction the conversion of Adam Livingston of Virginia. The tale, a moral fable wrapped up in an entertaining ghost story, may be apocryphal, but it speaks to the intimate relationship between ritual and faith for Anglo-American Catholics. Soon after Livingston settled in the colonies, "he was much disturbed by an unknown person that haunted his house, his property was destroyed, his barn was burnt, his cattle all died, his clothes were cut all to pieces, his beds all burnt or cut." As generations of colonial men and women had done before him, Livingston turned to the occult for help. He "applied to three conjurers, who gave him some herbs and a book and a riddle to catch the devil, but the first night the books and herbs were put in the chamber pot and covered with riddles." The offending book, it turns out, was "a Church of England prayer book." His wife suggested he send for a Catholic priest instead, another kind of "conjurer," who came and "blessed some water and sprinkled it about the house" to great effect. Livingston was converted when, after dreaming of a "beautiful church" and a "Catholic priest dressed in sacerdotal robes," he later saw this very same man in a Catholic chapel he visited in Shepherdstown.[1]

Livingston's journey from Protestantism to Catholicism began with a vision and ended in a supernatural tutorial in the proper use of the sacraments. "After he had heard Mass two or three times he saw a light and heard a voice frequently which instructed him in the sacraments of penance and the Holy

---

1. Livingston's Conversion, John Gilmary Shea Papers, box 14, folder 4, MPA.

Eucharist. The voice ordered him and his family to keep a fast of forty days and three hours prayer every day. . . . The voice also commanded them to keep the 4th of March annually as a holy day of obligation in thanksgiving for their conversion which was always observed." Livingston and his spiritual guide "frequently said the beads" together, with the "voice" taking the opportunity to taunt Livingston's wife, who had refused to convert with her husband: "When it came to the latter part of the Hail Mary, it said (on account of the wife as I supposed she was a little stubborn as she was a Presbyterian) Holy, Holy, Holy Mary Mother of God etc." An ordinary man with "little education in the English tongue," Livingston enjoyed a special relationship with the divine rooted in the sensorium of ritual.[2]

As converts like Adam Livingston learned (usually through more conventional means), sacraments lay at the heart of what it meant to be a *practicing* Catholic in Anglo-America. The relationship of recusants to the sacraments went deep—deeper than their relationship to the pope, the Church he headed, the parish in which they (had once) lived and worshipped, and the creed they espoused. The sensory dimension of late medieval Christianity was most palpable in the sacramental life of believers. To participate in the sacraments was to partake of the incarnate materiality of Christ: to taste him in the eucharist, to be washed in his blood during baptism, to be joined in passionate union with him as well as one's spouse in the sacrament of marriage, to share a grave with him after death, and to have one's earthly body restored at the Day of Judgment as his was in the Resurrection. All the senses—taste, touch, sight, smell, sound—were activated during the sacraments. In Matthew Milner's words, "Sensation made traditional medieval religious life happen."[3]

In eliminating five of the seven traditional sacraments and stripping the remaining two of their salvific power, the Reformers struck at the very heart of traditional Christianity. For good reason, scholars of recusancy have devoted considerable energy and imagination to exploring what life *without* the traditional sacraments might have looked like for early modern Catholics in Protestant lands.[4] The expanding sphere of domestic ritual replaced church sacraments for many recusants in post-Reformation England. The sacred calendar

2. Ibid.

3. Matthew Milner, *The Senses and the English Reformation* (Farnham, U.K., 2011), 3. See chapter 4 ("Sensing Pre-Reformation English Liturgy"), in particular, for a rich analysis of the sensory dimension of traditional English sacramental life.

4. The fullest treatment of what it meant for English Catholics to live without regular access to the sacraments is Lisa McClain, *Lest We Be Damned: Practical Innovation and Lived Experience among Catholics in Protestant England, 1559–1642* (New York, 2004).

of feasting and fasting, in particular, which required no priest or consecrated space, became a focal point of devotion for recusant households. The domestication of Catholicism meant that ordinary spaces, such as the kitchen and the parlor, stood in for the sanctuary as the site of ritual practice. The acts of preparing fish on days of abstinence and gathering the household together for an improvised private "mass" were sacramental substitutes, no less potent for being performed out of the Church's sight. But they too often remain out of our sight. In place of the traditional records of congregational life (baptismal, marriage, and death registers; account books; minutes of episcopal visitations) that document the steady hum of Christian ritual through the generations, we have snapshots of a secret mass here and there, a furtive visit by a priest to a dying woman to administer last rites, a hasty baptism performed by an itinerant missionary on his way through town. We have glimpses only, in other words, not a full portrait of the sacramental life of Anglo-American Catholics. Because these rare archival sightings tend to unearth conditions of extreme political stress, when religious minorities faced greater scrutiny, they can give a distorted view of the divisive role the sacraments sometimes played in colonial communities. But the very incompleteness of the records captures the reality on the ground, where access to the sacraments was at best intermittent and at worst impossible.

Following the lead of English historians of recusancy, Part One put the question of sacramental practice aside to investigate the demographic, cultural, and material traces of the varieties of Catholicism found in colonial records. It is much easier to track people who were tagged as recusants by census takers or punished for the twin crime of being Irish and Catholic in colonial courts than to know anything about the ritual lives of these men and women. Bringing sacramental practice out of the shadows is the task of Part Two. In so doing, we will encounter colonial Catholics at the most intensely *Catholic* moments of their lives—when they sought out (often at considerable trouble and expense) the sacerdotal comforts of the church and its priests. The blurry and porous boundary between confessional identities that we traced in Part One through the lives of individuals, communities, and objects comes into clearer focus in this section. Choosing to seek out a priest to receive communion or baptize one's child was an assertion of confessional allegiance amid the welter of religious options on hand, an opportunity to affirm an identity that might be considerably more fluid or ambiguous in other contexts. Those colonial recusants who passed as Protestant in their public lives or who embraced the freedom of ambidexterity had a difficult choice to make if they wanted to commune, marry, baptize, or bury in the Roman Church.

A lot was at stake. The public exercise of the sacraments defined recusants in the eyes of the law: Catholics in Protestant countries were never more exposed than when they were attending mass, receiving communion, or burying their dead. The authorities used attendance at mass to "out" recusants, in keeping with their focus on the detested doctrine of transubstantiation as the sine qua non of heresy.[5] In England, the campaign to expose secret conventicles of papists waxed and waned with the shifting politics of the Stuarts, who made periodic efforts to enforce the penal laws to quiet rumors about their suspected Catholicism, but at no time after 1559 was the act of attending mass risk-free for ordinary laymen and -women. To receive the eucharist at mass, one needed a priest. And priests needed consecrated spaces in which to perform the sacrifice of the mass.

The sacraments were thus always *political* as well as devotional acts in the Reformed world. They were political, first and at the highest level of abstraction, because they involved a transfer of power from the divine to the human world. Who could exercise that power and what form it would take were questions hotly debated during the religious wars of the early modern era. Reformers devoted so much energy to deriding the sacramental power of priests as "magic" (a term that denoted superstition, ignorance, and the foolishness of old women) precisely because they understood how sacraments worked. To break the hold of the Roman Church over its deluded adherents, they had to break the spell of the priest's power of transubstantiation. But the sacraments were also political in a more concrete sense: as the object of law. Those who practiced the wrong sacraments or the right sacraments in the wrong way were subject to civil and ecclesiastical prosecution. Criminalizing the act of performing and hearing mass drove home the central message of the Reformation that sacred power was vested in the state and its established church, not in the hands of priests.

The culmination of the campaign to politicize the sacraments was the Test Act of 1673. Often lumped together with the various Oaths of Supremacy and Allegiance enacted after 1534 as loyalty tests for English recusants, the Test

---

5. Under the Six Articles Act adopted by Henry VIII in 1539 (31 Henry VIII cap. 14), denial of transubstantiation—the belief that the bread and wine are *materially, substantially* transformed in the act of consecration into the body and blood of Christ—was the only false doctrine for which burning at the stake was mandated, without the opportunity to recant. Henry's heirs Edward and Elizabeth did not always agree on how far to go in dismantling the theological and ritual edifice of the old Church, but they were united in their opposition to the doctrine of transubstantiation.

Act was fundamentally different from the other oaths imposed on dissenters in early modern England. The thrust of the previous oaths was political
loyalty: recusants were required to swear that they owed allegiance to the
English crown alone, not to the pope, and to renounce any attempts by the
Roman Catholic Church to depose or kill the monarch. (It's no accident that
the 1606 Oath of Allegiance was passed in the aftermath of the Gunpowder
Plot of 1605, in which a group of Catholic conspirators tried to blow up Parliament.)[6] The Test Act, in contrast, required a statement of theological orthodoxy, and the focus of this declaration was the eucharist. All officeholders
were required to affirm, "I do believe that there is not any transubstantiation
in the sacrament of the Lord's Supper, or in the elements of the bread and
wine, at or after the consecration thereof by any person whatsoever." The
startling specificity of the oath has generally escaped scholarly notice, though
early modern recusants were well aware of the Test Act's radical intrusion into
the realm of doctrine—a violation of the Elizabethan principle of conformity
in behavior, not belief, which had guided the established church for more
than a century. The Test Act was adopted throughout the English colonies
in the late seventeenth century, ensuring that arguments about the eucharist
would remain central to colonial politics as well.

Beyond the theological and the juridical, sacramental politics had an important local dimension. Anglo-American congregations had a well-deserved
reputation for fractiousness in the seventeenth and eighteenth centuries: quick
to take offense at clerical overreaching and loath to surrender local customs
in the name of episcopal conformity. A cursory read-through of the minutes
of any Anglican vestry or Nonconformist chapel meeting will yield numerous instances of parishioners fighting with their pastors and with each other
over the rules of sacramental behavior: how frequently to administer communion, whether a funeral mass needed to be said before burial, whether women
who had just given birth needed to be churched before being readmitted to
communion, whether couples could be married without the banns' having
been called three times in their home parish. Christian ritual was supposed
to provide the thread that knit a group of individuals into a community of
believers—the mystical body of Christ—but it could just as easily divide as
unite. For church papists and crypto-Catholics, the micropolitics of ritual

6. On the controversial Jacobean 1606 Oath of Allegiance, see Michael Questier,
"Catholic Loyalism in Early Stuart England," *English Historical Review*, CXXIII (2008),
1132–1165.

unfolding in countless Anglican parishes across the Anglo-American land-scape took on added meaning. As they sat in the pews and listened to fellow parishioners debate the propriety of communion in both kinds (bread and wine) or the role of godparents, they were reminded anew of what they had lost in the Reformation's dismantling of traditional Christianity's sacramental regime.

Local congregational politics in the North American colonies departed in significant ways from the English pattern, exacerbating the potential for fric-tion. The severe shortage of clergy of every denomination outside the Puritan strongholds of southern New England created an economy of ritual scarcity in which unscrupulous and fraudulent actors could thrive, selling their services to the highest bidder. Even those ministers with proper credentials and secure posts struggled to survive on inadequate salaries that were often reluctantly paid. Fees for providing sacramental services became a ubiquitous feature of the colonial religious landscape, and a never-ending source of irritation and frustration for pastors and parishioners alike. A sacramental service economy turned rituals into commodities, and the effect was to resurrect Reformation-era battles over the selling of indulgences with the reformed rituals now standing in for the object of scorn. For colonial recusants, deprived, for the most part, of *any* access to the traditional sacraments, the choices were bleak.

The sacramental landscape of English America, in its broadest contours, was as variegated, fractious, and improvisational as the lives of its inhabitants. Among the diverse creeds and ethnicities that jostled against one another in Anglo-America, the sacraments were often the central meeting ground of rival religious cultures. Disputes over the proper way to baptize and bury did not just separate Protestant from Catholic but also Huguenot from Angli-can, Anglican from Puritan, Puritan from Quaker, Quaker from Moravian, Moravian from Lutheran, Lutheran from Dutch Reformed. And, in time, white Christians from Black Christians. Situating Catholic ritual culture in its wider denominational context can help us to better understand sacramen-tal politics as both a generalized phenomenon common to the post-Reformed world and a specific instantiation of the precariousness of inherited identities on the colonial periphery.

For the sake of organizational clarity, I have divided Part Two into separate chapters on "rituals of life" (baptism, godparentage, communion, feasting and fasting, marriage) and "rituals of death" (last rites, burial, prayers for the dead). But this is an artificial distinction that subverts one of the fun-damental premises of Catholic soteriology: the bond between the living and the dead in the quest for salvation. The living and the dead did not inhabit separate ritual or material worlds in medieval Christendom and its Catholic successor, as they did in Protestant lands after the Reformers had exiled the souls of the dead from purgatory, purged the charnel houses, deconsecrated the cemeteries, and outlawed all forms of intercession by which the living could assist those souls on their journey to heaven (indulgences, pilgrimages, chantries, prayers). Within every sacrament is the duality of life and death: in baptism, one is buried in water before being reborn; in penance, forgiveness follows the death of sin; in the eucharist, the death of Christ becomes the agent of resurrection.[7]

7. Peter Marshall, *Beliefs and the Dead in Reformation England* (New York, 2002); Craig M. Koslofsky, *The Reformation of the Dead: Death and Ritual in Early Modern Germany, 1450–1700* (New York, 2000). Steven Mullaney explores the emotional terrain of loss and trauma occasioned by the Reformist "rage against the dead" in Mullaney, *The Reformation of Emotions in the Age of Shakespeare* (Chicago, 2015), esp. 11.

"Here Is Every Thing Which Can Lay Hold of the Eye, Ear, and Imagination"

Rituals of Life

T
HOMAS SOCKWELL was on trial for his life. The testimony gathered by the London court in 1746 to determine whether he was indeed a disguised "papist priest" offers a remarkably detailed description of how the Protestant laity imagined a Catholic mass to unfold. Edward Addison testified that he saw Sockwell "act with Crucifixes" in "a Room of his own House in Penitent-Street" before "a Parcel of People come in of a Sunday Morning." As the congregation filed in, Addison said, "they dipp'd their Hands" in a "Bason of Water," and afterward "I have seen them kneel down, and they have taken Beads out of their Pockets, and there was a Parcel of Images, and they seem'd to me to be made of Wax. Their Beads hung upon their Arms." Meanwhile, the accused walked "backwards and forwards with a Crucifix in his Hand. He read in an unknown Tongue, that I could not understand a Word that he spoke. It seem'd to me as if it was all Latin." Before the mass began, Sockwell allegedly baptized a newborn: "There was a Male Child brought in to be christen'd. . . . He took the Child into his Arms naked, and there was a little Gallypot that stood upon the Table, and he cross'd the Child several Times, and said some Expressions in an unknown Tongue." Whether the pot was filled with "Water or Oil," Addison could not determine.[1]

At the same time that Sockwell was fighting for his life in London, another suspected popish priest—John Ury—was on trial in colonial New York. The so-called 1741 conspiracy that unleashed a reign of terror on the city's enslaved community also revealed Protestant fantasies of Catholic worship in

---

1. Trial of Thomas Sockwell, Jan. 17, 1746 (t17460117-40), *Old Bailey Proceedings Online*, www.oldbaileyonline.org.

the figure of the hapless Ury. Numerous witnesses testified that they saw Ury perform the sacraments of communion, baptism, and penance at makeshift masses held either in private lodgings or in John Hughson's tavern, the supposed epicenter of the plot. A confectioner, Elias Debrosse, relayed that Ury had "come to his place of business and asked him if he could sell any sugar bits or wafers." Debrosse had no wafers to sell that met Ury's requirements and advised the "priest" that "he might get a mould made by any joiner for that purpose." According to another witness, Ury derided the Protestant form of the sacrament, which used ordinary bread instead of wafers. Joseph Hildreth testified that Ury "told me they received the wafer instead of bread, and white instead of red wine: I asked, why the wafer? because, says he, the wafer is most pure; and no bread he thought pure enough to represent the body of our Lord." (Hildreth then went on to claim that Ury offered him "a piece" of a wafer so he could "taste it if you will," something no Catholic priest would ever do, though this glaring discrepancy made no difference to the court.) Ury was also accused of baptizing many of the "negroes" involved in the plot and offering them the false assurance of full pardon for the sins they were about to commit. One baptism stood out in the recollections of several witnesses for its peculiar form: the christening of a child at the home of "one Coffin, a pedlar," during which Ury "put salt into the child's mouth, sprinkled it thrice, and crossed it." Ury pressed his accusers on the specific details of the sham baptism:

> Prisoner—You say you saw me christen a child in New-street, how was the child drest, and what ceremony did I use, and who was present there then?
>
> Kane—The child was not naked, it was dressed as usual; and you put it on your left arm, and sprinkled it with water three times, and put salt in its mouth, and crossed it, as I said before; there were about nine persons present.
>
> Prisoner—Did I use any thing besides salt and water?
>
> Kane—Not that I saw.[2]

The unmasking of covert Catholic sacramental practice turned on a confusing welter of such small details. By the 1740s, when both trials took place, most Anglo-American Protestants had not seen a Catholic mass in person.

2. Daniel Horsmanden, *The New-York Conspiracy; or, A History of the Negro Plot, with the Journal of the Proceedings against the Conspirators at New-York in the Years 1741–2 . . .* , 2d ed. (1810; rpt. New York, 1969), 281–282 (Debrosse), 293–294 (Kane), 307 (Hildreth).

Out of fear of what John Adams would call the sensory "bewitchment" of the Roman ritual—"Here is every Thing which can lay hold of the Eye, Ear, and Imagination," he wrote upon observing a Catholic mass—Protestant magistrates and ministers constructed a phantasm of lurid ceremonies that they presented to their audience as authentic portrayals of Catholic practice.[3] The trial accounts of Sockwell and Ury trafficked in anti-Catholic stereotypes, from the unintelligible Latin liturgy to the gross materiality of the setting (the sugar wafers, wax images, rosary beads, holy salt, holy water, baptismal oil, and crucifixes), but in the absence of congregational records, such tainted sources offer one avenue for piercing the veil of secrecy that surrounds the actual practice of Catholicism in post-Reformation England and its colonies.

This chapter probes what we know about Catholic ritual practice in early English America around the existential, life-giving experiences of birth (baptism, godparentage), eating (communion, feasting and fasting), and sexuality (marriage). I start each section with an overview of the ways these rituals were enacted and contested in Protestant churches to set the stage and allow us to see how Catholic sacramental practice took shape in an environment of endemic scarcity and friction. My goal is to explore the contact zone between sacramental cultures from multiple angles in order to highlight the areas of convergence and divergence between Protestant and Catholic ritual practice. Protestant and Catholic clergy faced common problems when they attempted to shoehorn colonial congregations into ritual compliance—too few clergy, too many denominational options, too little spiritual instruction and too much lay indifference (if not outright contempt)—and sometimes they reached for common solutions despite their doctrinal and liturgical differences. The result was a sacramental landscape that borrowed ritual elements from numerous faith traditions in ways reminiscent of the hybridizing of beliefs and objects that we saw in Part One. The everyday practice of baptism, communion, and marriage in colonial communities could be strikingly similar across the confessional divide. This was especially true for Anglicans and Catholics, whose church services shared many liturgical elements, but the process of colonial adaptation that every faith experienced in North America led to new ritual combinations and modifications. And when the enslaved and

---

3. Adams, speaking about the mass he observed in St. Mary's Church in Philadelphia, continued, "Every Thing which can charm and bewitch the simple and ignorant. I wonder how Luther ever broke the spell" (quoted in Joseph J. Casino, "Anti-Popery in Colonial Philadelphia," *Pennsylvania Magazine of History and Biography*, CV [1981], 279–309 [quotation on 283 n. 8]).

the Native peoples of North America came to participate in this sacramental culture, they did so on their own terms, in their own ways.

Baptismal Battles

Baptism was one of only two sacraments that the Reformers retained from the medieval Church. No matter how insistent Luther, Calvin, and their confreres were that salvation was by faith alone and that every individual stood naked before God with no inherited immunity from sin or promise of grace, they could not imagine a church that did not welcome each new generation into its fold via a ritual mechanism of some sort. Water replaced holy oil, and the ceremony was reimagined as an initiation rather than as a cleansing. In the medieval Church, baptism involved the exorcism of demons; this element was eliminated from the Reformed rite. Vigorous debates about whom to baptize (children or adults?), when and where to baptize (immediately after birth or a few weeks later to safeguard the health of mother and infant? at home or in the church?), and how to baptize (sprinkling? full immersion?) broke out in Protestant churches, leading to new denominational formations in the Reformed constellation, but baptism itself was an important rite of passage few religious communities wanted to do without.[4]

Because the baptizing of children was the one ritual that almost all Protestant congregations participated in on both sides of the Atlantic, it was the subject of more internecine debate than any other religious ceremony.[5] In the English colonies, conflicts over baptism in Protestant churches revealed

4. Here again, Quakers were the exception: the "sprinkling of Infants" was "no other than a Popish Relict," Thomas Story informed an Anglican churchman. See *A Journal of the Life of Thomas Story: Containing, an Account of His Remarkable Convincement of, and Embracing the Principles of Truth, as Held by the People Called Quakers . . .* (Newcastle upon Tyne, 1747), 174. Among the various sacramental misdeeds John Wesley was accused of committing during his brief stint in Savannah in the 1730s was "refusing to christen otherwise than by Dipping"; see Alexander Garden to Bishop Gibson, Charlestown, S.C., Dec. 22, 1737, Fulham Papers, X, 48–49.

5. David Cressy provides a good overview of the divergent Protestant views over baptism in Cressy, *Birth, Marriage, and Death: Ritual, Religion, and the Life-Cycle in Tudor and Stuart England* (Oxford, 1997), esp. chaps. 5 ("Baptism as Sacrament and Drama") and 6 ("Crosses in Baptism"). For a discussion of debates over baptism among Anglicans, Quakers, and Baptists in colonial Virginia, see Lauren F. Winner, *A Cheerful and Comfortable Faith: Anglican Religious Practice in the Elite Households of Eighteenth-Century Virginia* (New Haven, Conn., 2010), 45–55.

the unfinished nature of the Reformation by highlighting vestigial "papist" elements in the ritual. Dissenters such as the Puritans and the Quakers were particularly incensed by the Anglican use of "the cross" in baptism (by which they meant the priest's gesture of making the sign of the cross with his hands over the child during the ceremony), a sure sign of popish superstition in their eyes. An SPG missionary in rural New York reported that some of his parishioners who were "prejudicely averse" to the sacrament of baptism "absented themselves, Calling the Cross in Baptism Popery and downright Idolatry: Others, our Liturgy the Gaggling of Geese." Despite their own opposition to the practice, the Nonconformists who founded the Somers Island Company instructed their governor in 1639 to ensure that the island's parishes use the "Decent Ceremony of signing with the Crosse in Baptism" as well as the "Reverent Posture of kneeling" when receiving communion to avoid jeopardizing their charter.[6]

The diary of the Boston merchant Samuel Sewall narrates the running battle between Puritans and Anglicans over "the Cross in Baptism" during the late seventeenth and early eighteenth centuries and Sewall's own gradual accommodation to the practice. In 1699, the moderate Congregational minister Benjamin Colman, who advocated a policy of nonconfrontation with the newly established Anglicans, visited Sewall, who "Warn'd him of the Cross in Baptisme, . . . I told him meerly saying *Conform*, did not express such an Aprobation of the N.E. way as I desired: Many in England conform'd to things they professedly disliked." The "great end" of the original Puritan migration, after all, had been "to fly from the Cross in Baptisme." By the 1720s, however, the Anglicans were there to stay in the Bay Colony, and Sewall reluctantly came around to Colman's position. "For my part," he confided to his diary, "I had rather have Baptisme administered with the incumbrance of the Cross, than not to have it Administered at all."[7]

The practice of appointing godparents to serve as spiritual guardians at baptism was another "popish" relic, according to dissenting Protestants. One Anglican minister in Connecticut was sympathetic to the scruples of those of his congregants who skewed puritan and recommended they "might be a little indulged." "Their present circumstances are so confused that generally they declare themselves ready to joyn with the Church of England, excepting

6. Mr. Pritchard to Secretary, Rye, N.Y., [Nov. 1?], 1704, SPG Letters "A" Series, 1702–1737, II, no. 42, *British Online Archives*, https://britishonlinearchives.com; Somers Island Company to the Governor and Council, Sept. 14, 1639, CO 1/10, no. 36, fol. 92, TNA.

7. *Diary of Samuel Sewall, 1674–1729*, 3 vols. (Boston, 1878–1882), I, 207, 507, III, 298.

only in the Instances of Submitting to the Sign of the Cross in Baptism and of having sponsors for their Children, other than their natural Parents." Farther south, Brian Hunt ran into trouble with some "French Protestants" (Huguenots) in his parish who "began to cry down Godfathers and Mothers, to despise Churching, and to deny Bishops." They threatened "to have their next child baptized by a Presbyterian Minister," provoking Hunt to write "a Letter to a sensible French parishioner pleading for Godfathers etc." His fellow Carolina minister John Urmston reported, "People are mighty averse to God Fathers and God Mothers and therefore in anywise will not have their children baptized." Godparents were a vestige of a soteriological system that understood salvation to run through bloodlines, through the kin (real and fictive) who bound the newborn to the universal church, past and present. Such a genealogical understanding of faith was anathema to radical Protestants.[8]

Samuel Sewall's Boston pastor, the preternaturally prolific Cotton Mather, expressed alarm about another "mongrelized" form of baptism: the incorporation of "Papist Idolatry" into the customs of the sea. Seafarers, he noted with irritation, were "a very *numerous* People, in my Congregation," and they exhibited an annoying attachment to such Catholic habits as "praying to the Madonna to save them during storms." Sailors were notorious in early modern Anglo-America for their irreligiosity, but modern scholars have taken a more nuanced view of maritime customs as a cultural mélange of folk, pagan, and Christian elements. What Mather called "the horrid Baptisms used among Sailors, at their Passing the Line," colloquially known as "equatorial baptism," was a water rite of initiation for sailors who had crossed the equator for the first time. Rather than "stripp[ing] baptism of its religious meanings," as Marcus Rediker has argued, the sailors' baptism allowed the crew (a mix of men from many nations and religious cultures) to find common ritual ground.[9]

8. Henry Caner to Bishop Gibson, Fairfield, [Conn.], Apr. 18, 1732, Fulham Papers, I, fol. 252; Brian Hunt to Bishop Gibson, Common Prison [jailed for debt since his SPG stipend was stopped], Charleston, Feb. 20, 1727/8, ibid., IX, fols. 206–213; "Mr. Urmston's Letter," July 7, 1711, in Stephen B. Weeks, ed., *The Colonial Records of North Carolina*, I, *1662 to 1712* (Raleigh, N.C., 1886), 767.

9. Stephen J. J. Pitt, "Cotton Mather and Boston's 'Seafaring Tribe,'" *New England Quarterly*, LXXXV (2012), 222–252 (quotations on 227, 237); Marcus Rediker, *Between the Devil and the Deep Blue Sea: Merchant Seamen, Pirates, and the Anglo-American Maritime World, 1700–1750* (Cambridge, 1987), 189. Stephen R. Berry's analysis of the "sailor's baptism" also notes its sacrilegious and bawdy nature, but much of the evidence he draws upon comes from the observations of missionaries and ministers on board these transatlantic

In the southern colonies and the sugar islands, where Anglicanism held sway, the use of the cross in baptism was apparently uncontroversial. Perhaps because the parishes were filled with so many Irish servants who chose to conform, the Anglican version of the ritual was comfortingly familiar. What did occasion bitter debate was the preference of the laity for home baptisms, which violated both the official rubrics of the Church and the clerical expectation of fees for officiating at the rite. Home baptisms, in fact, had been commonplace in England for centuries, but the Book of Common Prayer condemned private baptisms as a violation of the communal purpose of the rite to induct new members into the "body of Christ" and proscribed them except "when need compelled." Rural congregants throughout the British Isles argued that it was too inconvenient to travel long distances in often inclement weather and too risky to the health of mother and child, an argument that colonial parishes (which were ten times larger than those in the home country) seized upon to justify home baptism. Behind these pleas was an invidious elitism: the desire for home baptism was a form of gentry self-display, a way to set oneself apart from the common run of Christians by limiting the guest list to social peers.[10]

When home baptism made its way to the colonies, it carried the legacy of social elitism while acquiring new meanings of exclusion in a slave society. There was a practical impediment to church baptism in North America, given that there were only three consecrated baptismal fonts in Anglican America during the colonial era, but ministers could and did improvise: John Bragg of St. Ann's in Virginia admitted, "There is no font in the churches, and I generally baptize at the communion table." Most of Bragg's peers acquiesced to the lay preference for home baptisms, where they used the fonts owned privately by the laity, an important colonial modification to the Anglican ritual. We know how prevalent the practice was from the many complaints registered in the correspondence of Anglican missionaries. Alexander Garden, the SPG missionary in South Carolina and a stickler for protocol, saw the "insolent and disorderly" practice of private baptism everywhere in the colony. By the 1720s, it had infiltrated his own parish. His fellow missionary, John Lapierre,

journeys. See Berry, *A Path in the Mighty Waters: Shipboard Life and Atlantic Crossings to the New World* (New Haven, Conn., 2015), chap. 5, "Crossing Lines" (quotation on 140).

10. Louis P. Nelson, *The Beauty of Holiness: Anglicanism and Architecture in Colonial South Carolina* (Chapel Hill, N.C., 2008), 185–188. Home baptisms grew in popularity among English Protestants after the Restoration; see David Cressy, *Birth, Marriage, and Death: Ritual, Religion, and the Life-Cycle in Tudor and Stuart England* (New York, 1997), 188–194.

was the culprit. Garden wrote to Lapierre, "I have often heard of your insolent and disorderly practices in other parishes, but little suspected that I should have experienced them in my own." Not only did Lapierre "administer the holy sacrament of baptism to a child of one of my parishioners without either my consent or privity"; he "administer[ed] it in a publick form and in a private house." Such insolence was the act of "a thief and a robber."[11]

Ministers like Garden felt "robbed" by the preference for a private baptism at home because they were then deprived of the fees they customarily collected or had to negotiate their fees on a case-by-case basis, a posture of weakness for a class of men accustomed to deference.[12] One Maryland woman was so angered by her minister's demand for payment that she swore off the sacrament altogether. "You refused to baptize my five Children, unless I would give a Hogshead of Tobacco for every one of them," she railed at John Lillingstone, "and, now, I don't care one Farthing for your Baptism." More discerning ministers like Francis Le Jau were aware of the harm inflicted upon their mission by the commodification of the sacraments. He confided to Philip Stubs in 1707 that "a vast number of Children are not baptised because the Parents had no money. I have taken care to let them know that our Church do[e]s not teach us to sell Sacraments."[13]

The plague of unlicensed (and, in some cases, fraudulent) ministers that so bedeviled orthodox churchmen in the middle and southern colonies turned the sacramental service economy into a free-for-all, entirely unregulated in certain back corners of the colonies. A group of Anglicans in Maryland circulated a petition in 1715 against William Tibbs, charging that "he demands and receives money for Administering the Sacrament of the Lord's Supper when [he] gives it in Private houses." Mary Merriman testified that Tibbs refused

11. Nelson, *Beauty of Holiness*, 183; answers to queries addressed to the clergy, 1724, Fulham Papers, XII, fols. 41–45 (John Bragg); Alexander Garden to Bishop Gibson, Charleston, May 24, 1725, ibid., IX, South Carolina, 1703–1734, fols. 176–177, 178–179. On private baptismal fonts, see Winner, *Cheerful and Comfortable Faith*, chap. 1 ("With Cold Water and Silver Bowls: Becoming an Anglican in Eighteenth-Century Virginia").

12. Anglican churches were supposed to post tables of clerical fees for various sacramental services in the local church—though, judging from the numerous complaints by colonial commissaries about noncompliance, the practice was erratic at best. One table of fees from colonial South Carolina states, "The Fees for Christnings in private Houses depend on the Benevolence of the People" (further notes attributed to Charles Martyn, Apr. 11, 1762, Fulham Papers, X).

13. Story, *Journal of the Life*, 229; Frank J. Klingberg, ed., *The Carolina Chronicle of Dr. Francis Le Jau, 1706–1717* (Berkeley, Calif., 1956), 24.

to give the sacrament to a dying woman until her kinsman paid him twenty shillings. When asked "for what[?]" he replied, "There was ten shillings for his Visit and ten shil's for his medicine." Overhearing the exchange, the elderly patient "seemed to weep crying Lord have Mercy on us I never heard that the Sacrement was bought and sold before." (It didn't help that Tibbs had a reputation for too often being "drunk" when officiating at communion, even before the "bread and Wine is dijested in his Stomach.") The German Pietist Henry Muhlenberg found himself besieged in Pennsylvania by clerical imposters out to make a quick profit from recently arrived German immigrants who didn't understand how the system was supposed to work. By 1744, he made "two announcements" to his congregation on the subject: "(1) They were not to pay anything when they had their children baptized, and also (2) at the Lord's Supper there was to be no offering of money at the altar for the pastor." "Since those vagabonds are concerned only to get a few shillings for a Baptism and the offerings at the Lord's Supper and thus produce much strife," Muhlenberg "abolished the abominable custom" altogether. He would spend much of the next two decades sparring with preachers who traveled around the country in order to "carry on [their] trade with the Holy Sacraments."[14]

Baptisms were expensive not just because of clerical fees but because they were social events that required the entertaining and feeding of guests. On Barbados, Arthur Holt complained to the bishop of London, "There are Parents who neglect the holy Sacrament of Baptism, till they have several Children to be Baptiz'd together; and the common reason they give for so doing is, that they may avoid the expence of so many different feasts." In one household where Holt was called to "a woman in Childbed," he found "several of her Children of a considerable age unbaptiz'd" gathered around for the mother and newborn for a family baptism. Over time, the luxury of a home baptism and its attendant social display was increasingly reserved for white settlers in those colonies where plantation slavery was entrenched. White gentrywomen, in particular, preferred a home baptism because it allowed them to preside over the social gathering in a manner befitting their status. The family dinner, under the watchful eye of the mistress of the household, became an occasion for domestic sacraments; as Ann Ashby Manigault noted in her diary, "Dined at my sons. The children were baptized." By privatizing

14. "A Petition agt Mr. Wm. Tibbs, Feb. 15, 1715," Misc. Colonial MSS, MS 2018, box 4, 1710–1729, Maryland Historical Society; Theodore G. Tappert and John W. Doberstein, trans., *The Journals of Henry Melchior Muhlenberg*, I (Philadelphia, 1942), 68, 84.

these rituals of faith, white settlers effectively relegated church baptism (and, as we will see, marriage and burial) to servants and slaves who lacked homes of their own. In the year 1715 in Bridgetown, Barbados, fifteen people were baptized in St. Michael's Church, whereas ninety-two were baptized in houses. Among those baptized in the church were Barbara Hayman, "'a Parish child,' and an unnamed 'child of Irish Margaret's a poor woman.'"[15]

Against this backdrop of persistent dissatisfaction over how and where baptism should be administered in Protestant congregations, colonial Catholics found a variety of ways to baptize their own children within and without the church. Before they even set foot on North American soil, they had participated in a vicarious baptism of sorts already: a baptism by seawater. English Catholic promoters sold emigration to the colonies as a form of mass baptism. Baltimore's *Declaration*, supposedly compiled by Calvert himself from various travelers' reports to encourage settlers to join his Maryland venture, advertised for "fit men to instruct the inhabitants in saving doctrine, and to regenerate them in the holy font" of overseas travel. Migrants were to be "washed in the saving waters" as they journeyed to America. Expatriate Catholic communities had a long history of turning mobility into a sacralizing agent, making a virtue out of a necessity in post-Reformation Europe, where the traditional means of worshipping God were absent. Rather than physically visit a shrine, for example, Catholics in Protestant lands could perform a "virtual pilgrimage" by reciting the prayers of the rosary or saying the "stations of the cross," a devotional practice that gained popularity in the seventeenth century as part of the Counter-Reformation. Making a circuit around a room or garden in which each stop along the way was associated with a different stage in Christ's journey through death to life became an alternative form of pilgrimage. In the same way, overseas migration became an alternative form of baptism for colonial recusants. Like other rites of passage, transatlantic migration involved the three stages of ritual separation, liminality, and reintegration. And like the sacrament of baptism, water was the medium of transformation.[16]

15. Arthur Holt to Bishop Gibson, St. Michael's, Barbados, Apr. 30, 1725, Fulham Papers, XV, fols. 215–216; Nelson, *Beauty of Holiness*, 188; Nicholas M. Beasley, "Domestic Rituals: Marriage and Baptism in the British Plantation Colonies, 1650–1780," *Anglican and Episcopal History*, LXXVI (2007), 327–357 (quotation on 350).

16. Henry Foley, *Records of the English Province of the Society of Jesus*, III (London, 1878), 331; Martin Elbel, "Pilgrims on the Way of the Cross: Pilgrimage Practices and Confessional Identity in Early Modern Bohemia," in Eszter Andor and István György Tóth, eds.,

On a less metaphorical level, for Catholics—as for Anglicans—baptism was the one sacrament that could most easily escape the domain of the Church. Under canon law, situations of "extreme necessity" allowed the laity to perform certain sacraments without a priest present. The perils of childbirth, experienced by many early modern women and feared by all, placed parturient women almost by default in the condition of "extreme necessity." Anyone present to assist in the birth, but particularly midwives, could perform a "conditional baptism" for a dying woman and the baby she delivered using unconsecrated water. In England, lay Catholics learned how to apply the water and the proper order of prayers in emergency situations, and presumably the Jesuits in Maryland trained their congregations to perform conditional baptisms. Recusants such as Robert Gray sometimes admitted they couldn't remember whether their children had been baptized by "a midwief or by a priest," since both were equally valid. A Catholic midwife known as Dr. Peggy Thompson boasted she "never allowed an infant to die on her hands without first making of it a christian by the administration of lay baptism."[17]

The vast majority of Catholic baptisms in England, however, involved a priest. Since Catholic chapels were few and far between, especially outside the cosmopolitan enclave of London, priests were more likely to perform baptisms in private homes or in the manor chapels attached to these homes. Although a 1606 act prohibited private baptism by levying a hefty fine on recusant parents who illicitly secured the services of a priest to christen their children, the custom was already too widely entrenched for the ban to be effective. The domestication of Catholic sacramental life in post-Reformation England anticipated the trend toward home baptism evident in Protestant communities by the seventeenth century, a trend that only accelerated in

---

Frontiers of Faith: Religious Exchange and the Constitution of Religious Identities, 1400–1750 (Budapest, 2001), 275–283. See Liesbeth Corens, *Confessional Mobility and English Catholics in Counter-Reformation Europe* (Oxford, 2019) for a good discussion of the phenomenon of sacralized mobility.

17. Cressy, *Birth, Marriage, and Death,* 118, 120 (ideally, these lay baptisms would later be sanctified by a priest in a church); Examination of Imprisoned Recusants, April 1593, in Anthony G. Petti, ed., *Recusant Documents from the Ellesmere Manuscripts* (St. Albans, U.K., 1968), 44; Tricia T. Pyne, "Ritual and Practice in the Maryland Catholic Community, 1643–1776," *U.S. Catholic Historian,* XXVI, no. 2 (Spring 2008), 17–46 (quotation on 35–36). The example of Thompson comes from post-Revolutionary Kentucky, where many Maryland Catholic families settled in the late eighteenth century.

the colonies. We could even say that, in this respect, Protestant practice was Catholicized as certain rituals moved out of the church and into the home.[18]

What was a matter of choice for Protestant families, however, was a matter of necessity for Catholic ones. The financial structure of ritual practice was, moreover, fundamentally different in the Catholic Church. Priests did not charge for their sacramental services, though a gratuity might have been welcome at weddings and funerals and even expected if the household could afford it. Priests were "hired" (that is, assigned) by the central Catholic Church, not by individual congregations. The element of financial uncertainty and constant negotiation that poisoned lay-clerical relations in so many Protestant parishes was thus absent in recusant communities. Lay Catholics might have had many reasons to complain about their priests, but they did not have to pay their salaries or fork over so many shillings for every sacrament performed.

English Catholics had their own sacramental economy, but it was not a monetized one. Rather, the currency that fueled sacramental transactions was grace: the "treasury of merit" accumulated by Christ's sacrifice on the cross and all the good deeds of the saints who came after him that was remitted, drop by drop, to sinners every time they said their rosary, took communion, prayed for the dead, or performed an indulgence. Grace flowed out of this treasury via the transmitting power of ritual (and ritual objects), with priests serving as the middlemen. This is not to say that commercial metaphors didn't serve a heuristic and polemical purpose in Catholic discourse as they did in Protestant circles. Lay Catholics, too, spoke of the "merchandizing" of faith and decried the avarice that made a mockery of some clerical vows of poverty. Beneath the rhetoric of money and trade, however, was a different understanding of just what was being sold, bartered, or stolen by bad sacramental actors. Salvation itself was the ultimate commodity. Good Catholics could legitimately "purchase" it by faithful performance of the sacraments; corrupt priests sold them a false bill of goods when they offered sacramental shortcuts or tried to bribe them with worldly inducements.[19]

The long-running controversy over the selling of indulgences that was well under way in Europe before Luther and Calvin made it a centerpiece of their campaigns to reform the church had not dissipated by the time the first English and Irish settlers came to North America. Ever since the

18. Alexandra Walsham, "Beads, Books, and Bare Ruined Choirs: Transmutations of Ritual Life," in Walsham, *Catholic Reformation in Protestant Britain* (Farnham, U.K., 2014), 387.

19. John Bossy, *Christianity in the West, 1400–1700* (New York, 1985).

Catholic Church had monetized the awarding of indulgences in the later Middle Ages, the sale of indulgences without performance of a penitential act was contested. In post-Reformation Anglo-America, indulgences were a frequent target of antipopery literature. As John Sidway put it in *The Pope's Cabinet Unlocked* (1680), from indulgences flowed most of the other corrupt practices of the Roman Church: "Wouldest thou know wherefore [Catholics] invocate and adore Saints, the Host, the Crucifix, Holy Relicks and Images, 'tis because of indulgences." A Catholic who accumulated years (centuries, even millennia) of purgatorial relief due to indulgences had a false sense of soteriological security, Protestants argued, and therefore considered himself pardoned in advance for any sins he might commit—an intolerable situation from the perspective of maintaining public order. There was a disturbing similarity between selling indulgences and selling sacraments: both turned acts of grace into commodities to be bought and sold in a largely deregulated market. Where Tridentine Catholics had repudiated the selling of indulgences, Anglo-American Protestants were enlarging the sacramental market in the colonies.[20]

Where did that leave recusants who believed the Anglican rite was insufficient, if not heretical, and chose not to pay for a debased version of the real thing? The desire for a proper baptism surfaced everywhere Catholic missionaries visited English America. Virtually the first thing an itinerant priest did upon arrival in a recusant enclave was baptize—infants, children, mothers and fathers, even grandparents if need be. On Jean Pierron's journey through New England, Virginia, and Maryland in the 1670s, the French Jesuit met "persons 30 and 40 years old, and even as many as ten and twelve persons in a single house, who had not received baptism" and whom he exhorted to submit to the sacrament. Some overzealous missionaries were accused of sweeping up Protestant children in their haste to baptize; in the 1620s, settlers in Newfoundland complained, "[The child of] one William Poole a protestant was baptized according to . . . the Church of Rome . . . contrary to the will of the sayd Poole" by the Jesuits brought to the colony by Lord Baltimore. Colonial recusants, like their English counterparts, maintained a principled distance from the liturgical reach of the established church; Anglican ministers on the islands complained repeatedly that the Irish and other "popishly

---

20. John Sidway, *The Pope's Cabinet Unlocked* . . . (London, 1680), quoted in Michael S. Carter, "A 'Traiterous Religion': Indulgences and the Anti-Catholic Imagination in Eighteenth-Century New England," *Catholic Historical Review*, XC (2013), 52–77 (quotation on 54).

inclined" members of their parishes refused to bring their young to church for baptism, preferring to wait however long it took for a priest to show up. Their caution was warranted. When the Irish on Nevis (who numbered more than six hundred, according to the Irish Jesuit John Grace) sought "the churches of the French to . . . bring their young to baptism," they were assaulted by their English neighbors. Grace himself reported that, on his travels through Martinique, Guadeloupe, and Antigua, he "received in excess of three hundred general confessions" in preparation for the sacrament of baptism, presumably among older children and adult converts. Participating publicly in a Roman rite was risky, even in the more freewheeling religious environment of the Lesser Antilles. Did those Irish who performed baptisms at home in secret use the old Irish custom of tying "a little peece of silver to the Corner of the Cloth wherein the Chylde is wrapped" and putting salt "in the Chyldes mouth"? We have no way of knowing.[21]

The close proximity of Protestant and Catholic in the sugar islands generated tensions over sacramental politics, even within the same household. Isabella Cryer, the wife of Benjamin Cryer, the rector at St. Philip's Church in Barbados, testified that she tangled with Willoughby Chamberlain (a wealthy planter and purported recusant) over who should baptize his child. She told Chamberlain that her husband had "promised Madam Chamberlain to Christen her child privately" in order to "prevent the Jesuit or any other Romish priest from Christening of itt." Chamberlain retorted "Merrily" that "if they had Done soe he would have his Child Drest as a fryed Pigg was which was then at the table and eat itt." Chamberlain's anticipation of Jonathan Swift's famous "Modest Proposal," which put forward thirty years later that English Protestants should cook Irish children like "roasting pigs" as a form of population control for the prolific Irish "Papists," is striking and

21. Reuben Gold Thwaites, ed., *The Jesuit Relations and Allied Documents: Travels and Explorations of the Jesuit Missionaries in New France, 1610–1791*, 73 vols. (Cleveland, 1896–1901), LIX, 73; "The Examination of Erasmus Stourton Gent. Late Preacher to the Colony of Ferryland in Newfoundland," Oct. 9, 1628, CO 1/4, no. 59, TNA; "Mission of Father John Grace (a. 1667–9)," in Aubrey Gwynne, ed., "Documents Relating to the Irish in the West Indies," *Analecta Hibernica*, no. 4 (October 1932), 139–286 (quotations on 254, 259); Graham Kew, ed., "The Irish Sections of Fynes Moryson's Unpublished Itinerary," ibid., no. 37 (1998), 1–137 (quotation on 109). Fewer than thirty Irish parents in Barbados baptized their children in the parish church from 1650 to 1715, in a population that numbered in the thousands; see Jenny Shaw, *Everyday Life in the Early English Caribbean: Irish, Africans, and the Construction of Difference* (Athens, Ga., 2013), 114.

suggests that Swift was tapping a deep well of cultural associations linking sacraments to sacrilege.[22]

English Catholics who were more secure both financially and politically sometimes resorted to double baptism for their children, first in the Anglican church and again in a Roman chapel. This happened with some frequency in Maryland, the only colony to have public chapels before the eighteenth century. Joshua and Jean Jarboe registered the births of their sons Bennett and Charles twice, in their parish church and in the Jesuit chapel in Newtown. A second church baptism was also warranted when an emergency baptism had been performed at home; Father Grassi of the Maryland mission noted, "When Mass is over, . . . infants are baptized, or the ceremonies are supplied in the case of those already baptized in danger." But it was far more common for white colonial recusants—who as a group were wealthier than their Protestant neighbors—to baptize their children at home, as their English counterparts did, rather than in a church of any kind, especially after 1704. One of the very few surviving baptismal registers from colonial Maryland lists many more baptisms (and burials) at home than in the Jesuit chapels. On December 6, 1767, Father Robert Mosley reported, "I baptised in a private baptism Edward Carman at Wye."[23]

Among those baptized by Mosley in the 1760s and 1770s were "a negro child of Mr. Wetherstrand," a "Negro child of Solomon Clayton," and "a negro child of Widow Seth." On one day alone, he christened one white and six Black children. Mosley's inclusion of enslaved Africans in his baptismal register raises questions for us about what this sacrament might have meant to the "Negro" children in the mission and their parents. Scholars of African

22. Deposition of Isabella Cryer, in "A Collection of Papers Relating to Sir Thomas Montgomerie and Willoughby Chamberlayne," Jan. 27, 1689, CO 28/37, no. 7 liv, TNA; Jonathan Swift, *A Modest Proposal for Preventing the Children of Poor People in Ireland from Becoming a Burden on Their Parents or Country, and for Making Them Beneficial to the Publick* (Dublin, 1729), https://www.gutenberg.org/files/1080/1080-h/1080-h.htm.

23. Beatriz Betancourt Hardy, "Papists in a Protestant Age: The Catholic Gentry and Community in Colonial Maryland, 1689–1776" (Ph.D. diss., University of Maryland, College Park, 1993), 57 n. 34; Pyne, "Ritual and Practice," *U.S. Catholic Historian*, XXVI, no. 2 (Spring 2008), 35; 1760 St. Joseph's and St. Mary's County Christenings, box 31, folder 1, MPA. Robert Emmett Curran notes that in England, even those recusants who chose to baptize their children at home "frequently had their names entered in the local parish books, either through a second Anglican baptism or through a parson willing to record a Catholic baptism as though he himself had performed it" (Curran, *Papist Devils: Catholics in British America, 1574–1783* [Washington, D.C., 2014], 9).

and African American religion often point to water rituals as a principal node of connection between the different faith traditions that met in the transatlantic slave trade. Water rites were a common feature of many traditional African religions in those regions from which the slave trade drew most of its captives. In the Kongo, where the conversion of the kingdom to Catholicism in the late fifteenth century was primarily the work of the nobility and the political elite, the laity experienced Christianity primarily through the sacrament of baptism. As Jason Young describes, the ritual "principally involved the conferring of salt sacrament." Traditional Catholic baptism involved salt as well as water; the priest placed a small amount of salt on the tongue before using holy water to sprinkle the forehead of the child. The use of salt, an important element in African ritual practice, was key to building a conceptual vocabulary through which villagers could translate one religion into another. Although they had little luck in persuading the Kongolese to participate in the Catholic sacraments of marriage or burial, local priests "were successful with baptism, or the eating of salt, *yadia mungwa,* as it was called locally." The purported "salt and water" baptisms performed by the supposed Catholic priest John Ury at the center of the 1741 New York slave "conspiracy" may reflect insider knowledge of the ritual practices of enslaved Africans, lending a ring of truth to the account fabricated by the authorities to justify their brutal suppression of the ringleaders. We don't need to accept the charges against Ury at face value, in other words, to recognize their use in providing insight into the ritual complex that surrounded white and Black New Yorkers in the mid-eighteenth century.[24]

We have even fewer accounts of actual sacramental practice among enslaved Africans than we do for white recusants in colonial North America. A rare account of the christening of enslaved Africans in the former Spanish and French islands comes from SPG missionary Gabriel Duquesne in 1728. Many of the enslaved on the island of Jamaica had some knowledge of Catholic ritual practice, he reported: "If they can, [they] speak a few Words [in Latin] to recommend themselves to the Virgin Mary and the Saints." Duquesne had no respect for a religion that "consist[ed] chiefly in Show and outward Ceremonies . . . perform'd in a Tongue unintelligible to the greatest part of the Congregation," but he grudgingly acknowledged that the Spanish

24. 1760 St. Joseph's and St. Mary's County Christenings, box 31, folder 1, MPA; Jason R. Young, *Rituals of Resistance: African Atlantic Religion in Kongo and the Lowcountry South in the Era of Slavery* (Baton Rouge, 2007), 52; Horsmanden, *New-York Conspiracy,* 293–294.

had a better track record when it came to baptizing their slaves. "And as for what relates to their christening, they do it immediately after their first landing, hanging at the same time Relicks around their Necks." Duquesne's account of the perfunctory ceremonies conducted by priests in the Catholic Caribbean upon the arrival of a slave ship is corroborated by the report of a fellow Frenchman, the Jesuit Jean-Baptiste le Pers. "When they arrive in my district [of Saint-Domingue] I have them make the sign of the cross as I demonstrate, in order to take possession of them in the name of Jesus Christ and his Church. They do not understand what they are doing, but through an interpreter I repeat the words of Saint Peter, 'You do not know now what I am doing but you will eventually.'" The missionary orders thought it was imperative to bring captive Africans into the body of Christ as quickly as possible by some sort of ritual sealing in case they did not survive the brutal Caribbean plantation system. Le Pers might have worried that the Africans were merely parroting his gestures, but he could not "allow a man to die without baptism" because of his "scruples."[25]

The kind of mass public baptism of Africans practiced in Catholic colonies was necessarily absent in English America. Father Antoine Biet recorded encounters with both Anglo-Irish and African Catholics during his three-month sojourn on Barbados in the 1650s. The enslaved, he wrote, "content themselves by baptising their children in the house, and if any of them have any tinge of the Catholic religion, which they received among the Portuguese, they keep it the best they can, doing their prayers and worshipping God in their hearts." By "the house," it's not clear whether Biet meant the plantation house of the slaveholder or the living quarters of the enslaved, though, given what we know of the aversion many white planters had to sharing intimate ritual space with Black people, the latter is more likely. Catholic priests elsewhere in the Americas expressed open skepticism that slave baptisms performed outside the domain of the Church were legitimate. In La Florida, where scores of fugitive slaves from the Carolinas (many, if not most, Catholic) fled in the eighteenth century, parish priests often rebaptized runaway Africans who had either received conditional baptisms "in extremis" from colonial recusants or been baptized in their home countries before being enslaved. And of course, for the enslaved themselves, the kind of mass baptisms performed upon arrival in the Americas was inextricably bound up

25. G. [Marquis] Duquesne to [Henry] Newman, Jamaica, May 15, 1728, Fulham Papers, XVII, fols. 248–257; Sue Peabody, "'A Dangerous Zeal': Catholic Missions to Slaves in the French Antilles, 1635–1800," *French Historical Studies*, XXV (2002), 53–90 (quotation on 75).

with the violence of capture and enslavement; it is hard to imagine that, under these circumstances, baptism could serve as an unalloyed "spiritual cleansing and rebirth."[26]

One impediment to slave baptisms in the early English Atlantic was the difficulty of finding sponsors (godparents) who would be acceptable to both the enslaved and their masters. Godparents introduced a third party to the transaction, one whose allegiance lay both to the Church and to the larger community. The choice of godparents for a newly baptized African child was a moment of reckoning for white recusants, who had to decide just how far their commitment to a unified sacramental community went. Among Catholics, godparents were supposed to be chosen—not assigned—by the parents from among their friends and family, whom they trusted to serve as spiritual guardians in case of their own incapacity. Godparents had to be active members of the Catholic community and well versed in the doctrines and rituals of the faith. Among whites, hierarchies of status played out in the choice of godparents, as some poor recusants sought the protection of wealthier and politically connected patrons for their children. By and large, however, godparents tended to come from the same social milieu as the mother and father; the ritual was meant to bind individual members of the community together into a new, enlarged family unit, not highlight differences of rank and birth.

Enslaved Catholics understood godparentage to be a vital community resource in an environment that denied them so many other forms of social belonging. Whenever the choice lay in their own hands, enslaved Africans selected sponsors who could best protect their children, even if that meant a white patron. Evidence for this comes primarily from the archives of Catholic empires, where Black converts are more visible. The Black Catholic community of Gracia Real de Santa Teresa de Mose (known colloquially as Fort Mose), created by free and enslaved Africans north of St. Augustine, Florida, in the early eighteenth century, offers the best window we have into how enslaved Catholics elsewhere in North America might have used sacramental politics for their own ends. Jane Landers's reconstruction of the baptismal and godparentage patterns for Fort Mose reveals enslaved parents' preference for godparents of a higher status: "Whites, free persons of color, or even slaves who were well connected." Parents didn't always get their first wish; more African children were sponsored by the lowly priest's assistant than by the planter class, Landers notes. Yet for Black converts, especially, baptism

26. Jerome S. Handler, "Father Antoine Biet's Visit to Barbados in 1654," *Journal of the Barbados Museum and Historical Society*, XXXII (1967), 56–76 (quotation on 67); Jane Landers, *Black Society in Spanish Florida* (Urbana, Ill., 1999), 113; Young, *Rituals of Resistance*, 66.

created a "system of reciprocal obligations between the *ahijado*, the baptized, and his or her godparents, and between the *compadres*, or parents and godparents." Adult converts, who tended to be uprooted and kinless *bozales*, were most in need of the protective umbrella extended by godparentage over the most vulnerable members of the Catholic community.[27]

Sacramental records for the African community in eighteenth-century New Orleans provide another opportunity to gauge the important role that baptism and godparentage played in sustaining Black Catholicism. From the unpromising beginnings of the French settlement in the malarial swamp that was the Mississippi Delta, colonial authorities and planters had been outnumbered by the Native and African slaves they relied on for survival. The Capuchin priests (and, in time, Ursuline nuns) who served the colony recognized early on that their primary mission lay with the enslaved rather than the slaveholders. Breaching the settlement's social and ideological defenses to bring the sacraments to the enslaved, priests embarked on an ambitious program of mass baptism. The desire for baptism outstripped the clergy's ability to provide the sacrament on an individual basis, so large group baptisms of adult slaves on major holy days such as Easter became the norm. One baptism on Easter Eve saw 112 catechumens baptized, a ceremony that "must have lasted hours," Emily Clark and Virginia Meacham Gould point out. Each candidate for baptism stepped forward, accompanied by the required pair of godparents, so on this one day well over 300 lay Catholics—almost certainly all Black—participated together in the ceremony, presenting a striking African face to the assembled congregation. The speed with which the African Catholic community took control over their own sacramental lives is impressive; from the 1730s to the 1770s, the percentage of Black Catholics serving as godparents for enslaved children in one parish rose dramatically, from only 2 percent in 1733 to nearly 90 percent in 1775. By the end of the century, Clark and Gould conclude, "Godparenting was the most formal way people of African descent laid claim to the resources and spaces of one of the city's chief institutions and made them their own."[28]

In the Catholic Atlantic, Black enclaves like Fort Mose and New Orleans

---

27. Landers, *Black Society in Spanish Florida*, 121–122. Stephen Gudeman and Stuart B. Schwartz find the same pattern in eighteenth-century Brazil; see Gudeman and Schwartz, "Cleansing Original Sin: Godparenthood and the Baptism of Slaves in Eighteenth-Century Bahia," in Raymond T. Smith, ed., *Kinship Ideology and Practice in Latin America* (Chapel Hill, N.C., 1984).

28. Emily Clark and Virginia Meacham Gould, "The Feminine Face of Afro-Catholicism in New Orleans, 1727–1852," *WMQ*, 3d Ser., LIX (2002), 409–448 (quotations on 425, 428).

offered enslaved Africans the opportunity to participate on their own terms in the robust baptismal culture of the Church. Enslaved Catholics in the English colonies had far fewer options when it came to initiating their children into the faith. The very idea of extending Christian membership to slaves via baptism was anathema in much of English America. White settlers, Protestant and Catholic, were acutely aware that Christian baptism was associated with freedom among the servants and slaves who labored in their homes and fields; the determination of colonial legislatures to repeatedly disavow any relationship between baptism and freedom is evidence that the notion was widespread. One Anglican in North Carolina reported, "As I was about this good work" of baptizing the parish's enslaved, "the enemies to the conversion and baptism of slaves, industriously and very busily buzzed into the Peoples Ears, that all slaves that were baptized were to be set free, and this silly Buckbear so greatly scared Esqu'r Duckenfield that he told me plainly I should Baptize no more of his slaves 'till the Society had got a Law made in England." Even those few Anglican ministers who actively encouraged white parishioners to baptize their slaves faced the additional obstacle of their reluctance to stand as sponsors. Arthur Holt asked the bishop of London what to do about "the Infant Negros born on the Society's Plantations, whether they ought not to have at least private Baptisms; publick Baptisms wo[ul]d indeed be impracticable because of the want of Suretyes."[29]

From missionary complaints, we know that some Catholic planters shared their Protestant neighbors' disinclination to baptize the enslaved. One way to assuage that anxiety while still fulfilling the sacramental obligations incumbent on slaveholders was to sponsor a Black child in baptism, ensuring that she would learn the proper lessons of subservience and service from her faith. Evidence from those recusants living within the orbit of the Jesuit manors suggests there was considerable uneasiness over the joining of white and Black as fictive kin. To be sure, there are scattered references to Catholic

29. On the complicated legal and political relationship between baptism and freedom in English America, see Rebecca Anne Goetz, *The Baptism of Early Virginia: How Christianity Created Race* (Baltimore, 2012); Katharine Gerbner, *Christian Slavery: Conversion and Race in the Protestant Atlantic World* (Philadelphia, 2018). "As I was about this good work": Mr. Taylor to the Secretary, Apr. 23, 1719, in William L. Saunders, ed., *The Colonial Records of North Carolina*, II, *1713 to 1728* (Raleigh, N.C., 1886), 331–332. "Plantations": Arthur Holt to Bishop Gibson, Christ Church, Barbados, Mar. 7, 1728/9, Fulham Papers, XV, fols. 266–267. Holt's fellow SPG missionary James White cautioned against baptizing the enslaved "unless Godfa'rs and M'rs be found"; see White to Gibson, Kingston, June 3, 1726, ibid. XVII, fols. 246–247.

slaveholders entering into what one scholar calls "spiritual partnerships" with the enslaved, serving as godparents together in the baptism of African children. But these interracial sponsorships were the exception rather than the rule: among the nearly one thousand baptisms recorded for St. Mary's County in Maryland from 1759–1776, those of Black and "mulatto" children (which accounted for 30 percent of the total) were more likely to have two white sponsors than two Black ones, and only a handful (fewer than forty) of baptisms paired a white and Black sponsor. Hellana, baptized on John Smith's plantation in 1760, was one of these few: her godparents were John Smith, Jr., and Judith, "a Smith family slave." St. Mary's County was the most Catholic county in Maryland, the only one in which white recusants were a majority. In the heavily Protestant county of Talbot, by comparison, nearly all (more than 90 percent) of the sponsors for the Black children baptized by Jesuits were themselves Black. When white Catholics were few and far between, in other words, enslaved Africans might have been freer to choose godparents from within their own community for their children. Only one white Catholic in Maryland appears to have broken the color line by asking a Black coreligionist to sponsor his child. Richard Jarboe, an officer in the St. Mary's County militia, asked two "negroes" to be godparents to his oldest daughter, Rachel. Jarboe's case is unique in the archives: it stands as a marker of the outer limits of sacramental fellowship between whites and Black Catholics in English America.[30]

From internecine tussles within Protestant denominations over "popish" rituals and extortionate fees to the universal tug-of-war between clerics (Protestant *and* Catholic) and the laity about the latter's preference for home baptisms, the rite of baptism was contested ground in the North American colonies. The theological debates that preoccupied Reformers and traditionalists

---

30. Maura Jane Farrelly, *Papist Patriots: The Making of an American Catholic Identity* (New York, 2012), 154–155; Pyne, "Ritual and Practice," *U.S. Catholic Historian,* XXVI, no. 2 (Spring 2008), 36; as Pyne notes, we don't know if the decision to select sponsors for enslaved children was "usurped" by slaveholders in St. Mary's County or if white recusants had been asked to serve in that role by the enslaved parents themselves. The case of Hellana can be found in Hardy, "Papists in a Protestant Age," 339–340. On Jarboe, see Farrelly, "American Slavery, American Freedom, American Catholicism," *Early American Studies,* X (2012), 69–100 (quotation on 91). Even in the Spanish Caribbean, where Black and white Catholics were supposedly part of one sacramental family, Africans never served as sureties for white children; see David Wheat, "Biafadas in Havana: West African Antecedents for Caribbean Social Interactions," in Ida Altman and Wheat, eds., *The Spanish Caribbean and the Atlantic World in the Long Sixteenth Century* (Lincoln, Neb., 2019), 166.

in Europe over the meaning of the ritual—was baptism an act of exorcism? Did it imprint an indelible seal of belonging or confer salvation? Was it the first or final step on the road to Christianization for adult converts?—receded in the face of the practical impediments to finding clergy and fonts enough to baptize a sprawling, fractious population. Other questions rose to the fore: was baptism a ritual of inclusion that brought the enslaved into the body of Christ or an affirmation of whiteness in a slave society? Did baptism at the hands of a priest mean that enslaved Catholics were also entitled to the sacraments of communion and marriage? Did it matter that the rite itself seemed to lose some of its confessional specificity as it traversed the space between church and home? There were no easy answers, and colonial Christians found themselves confronting the same dilemmas when it came time to communing and marrying within their faith communities.

Sacred Feasting

First if not foremost, the eucharist was a feast. On this, early modern Protestants and Catholics agreed. A feast is a special meal, an enlarged occasion for communal eating that involved *more:* more food, more drink, more guests, more pomp and ceremony. Before we delve into the politics of the eucharist, it's important to recognize this shared understanding of the sacrament as a meal that created—in the moment—a community of faith. Like baptism, it was one sacrament the Reformers could not abandon. Baptism and communion are rituals of initiation that share a scriptural origin in the New Testament. But whereas baptism is intended to be performed only once in the life of a believer, the sacrament of communion is meant to be experienced over and over again, year in and year out. Just how frequently communion should be performed was a constant bone of contention between the clergy and the laity (in this, too, Protestants and Catholics were united), but repetition was the key to its efficacy in either doctrinal system. Just as human bodies needed to eat regularly to survive, so, too, did souls need the replenishing of spiritual nutrients in the communion feast. This was not mere metaphor. Without the wellspring of regular communion, a community of faith would wither and die—as indeed many did in the spiritual wilds of North America.

The reformation of the eucharist began with a redefinition of just what was being consumed in the ritual: the bread and wine. Rejecting the medieval Christian notion of transubstantiation as little more than cannibalism ("papal anthropophagy," in John Milton's phrase) tarted up as doctrine, the early Reformers threw a barrage of satirical and scatological darts at the eucharist in an effort to demystify it. Behind the often crude polemics was the same material revulsion that underlay the iconoclastic attacks on religious art and sacramental objects. Scripted acts of defiance recalled the deliberate defiling of sacred images by iconoclasts; Mrs. Kath Lacy, while kneeling at the altar rail, removed the wafer from her mouth and "treade the same breade under her fote." The bread distributed at communion was just that, Lacy's provocation announced—bread—and nothing more. To underscore the point, the Reformers replaced the high altar of the medieval Church with the communion table, moving it forward in the sanctuary and removing the railings that separated the priest from the laity. No longer would the priest perform the liturgical acts of consecrating the host and then elevating it for all to see, the dramatic highlight of the mass. The ringing of a bell and swinging of the incense as the host was elevated, which enhanced the sensory impact of the Roman ritual, were eliminated, too, by the Reformers. (Though Eamon Duffy reminds us that the communion table could arouse the senses as well, especially when draped with colorful cloth stitched together from confiscated chasubles, canopies, or altar hangings.) The stripped-down, Protestant version of the sacrament reduced what had been a moment of supernatural transcendence into an ordinary meal. The point was to commemorate Christ's last supper with his apostles before his death, not to reenact his incarnation and sacrifice on the cross.[31]

The "stripping of the altars" that Duffy and other historians see as the paradigmatic move of the Reformation thus entailed stripping the eucharist itself of its numinous and sensory power. This was a devastating loss of power for the priest, as well. Catholics warned that the reformed notion of communion would elevate the laity to the same plane as the clergy: if, they demanded, "it is defended that the substance remains unchanged, what esteem can the

---

31. Milton imagined the path of the host through the body's digestive tract, where, after being "driven through all the stomach's filthy channels," it "shoots it out—one shudders even to mention it—into the latrine" (quoted in Maggie Kilgour, *From Communion to Cannibalism: An Anatomy of Metaphors of Incorporation* [Princeton, N.J., 1990], 84). See also Piero Camporesi, "The Consecrated Host: A Wondrous Excess," in Michel Feher, Ramona Naddaff, and Nadia Tazi, eds., *Fragments for a History of the Human Body*, part 1 (New York, 1989). "Treade the same breade": quoted in Alexandra Walsham, *Church Papists: Catholicism, Conformity, and Confessional Polemic in Early Modern England* (Woodbridge, U.K., 1993), 90. Communion table: Eamon Duffy, *Saints, Sacrilege, and Sedition: Religion and Conflict in the Tudor Reformations* (London, 2012), 124. Matthew Milner explores the complex ways in which Reformed piety was "sensed" in Milner, *The Senses and the English Reformation* (Farnham, U.K., 2011).

Minister hope from the administration of it? . . . A little more peevish sub-tlety would bring this Sacram't too within the power of the Laity." Catholics and Protestants alike understood the struggle over the eucharist as a contest of power, in other words: the power wielded by priests and the power wielded by the consecrated wafer itself. The two were inseparable.[32]

The reformed communion ritual never entirely lost its aura of supernatural power. The annals of Anglo-American churches are filled with stories of pa-rishioners hesitant to come to communion out of fear they would be damned and of clergy trying to persuade them that the sacrament itself did not have the power to either damn or save. Those who "ate and drank unworthily," as the saying went, put their eternal souls at risk if they took communion while in a state of sin. Implicit in this reluctance to communicate was an unstated attachment to the discredited sacrament of penance, which in the traditional mass was a prerequisite for receiving the eucharist. The reformed sacramental regime had done away with penance, and this left potential communicants in a state of heightened spiritual anxiety as they approached the communion table. In rural North Carolina, the SPG minister cited his parishioners' re-sistance to taking communion as something "that makes me weary of living here." When he announced his intention to distribute communion on Eas-ter, one said to him, "Now Mr. Taylor is going to damn his Parishioners, I suppose he said this, because he thought, that they that would receive were very unfit for it, and would Eat and Drink unworthily and so eat and Drink Damnation to themselves." Taylor dismissed their fears as yet more proof that "the People here generally, and almost all of them are very ignorant, and very irreligious," a not-uncommon view among the university-educated Anglican clergy.[33]

The contest between the pre- and post-Reformed vision of the eucharist initially played out in English parishes over the question of what kind of

32. Eamon Duffy, *The Stripping of the Altars: Traditional Religion in England, c. 1400–c. 1580* (New Haven, Conn., 1992); "Notes on the Catholic Church in Europe, ca. 1575–1775," Milton House Archives, box 3, folder 58, MPA.

33. Mr. Taylor to the Secretary, Apr. 23, 1719, in Saunders, ed., *Colonial Records of North Carolina*, II, 331. Edward L. Bond notes that Anglican eucharistic doctrine "steered a middle path between Catholic transubstantiation and Zwinglian memorialism," retaining the notion of Christ's real presence in the sacrament (Bond, *Damned Souls in a Tobacco Colony: Religion in Seventeenth-Century Virginia* [Macon, Ga., 2000], 122). For a good dis-cussion of lay fears of the eucharist's power to damn, see Erik R. Seeman, *Pious Persuasions: Laity and Clergy in Eighteenth-Century New England* (Baltimore, 1999).

bread should be used in the ceremony. The 1559 Act of Uniformity had specified that "to take away the superstition which any person hath or might have
in the bread and wine," the communion bread should be "such as is usual to
be eaten at the table with other meats, but the best and purest wheat bread
that conveniently may be gotten." Priests and the laity apparently interpreted
this act in different ways, as the Church of England continued to use wafers
in its communion services while some of its parishioners demanded ordinary
bread. One priest who tried to celebrate in the customary way faced a revolt:
several members of his congregation rejected the wafers "because the bread
was not common." By the 1580s, the Church had decided that wafers were too
popish and prohibited their use during the mass, provoking another round of
wafer wars. This time, whole congregations rebelled against the ban on wafers
and refused to accept bread: "In the Berkshire parish of Hartford there was
a communion standoff at Easter 1584." The stubborn attachment of men and
women to *both* bread and wafers in the Elizabethan era is probably as good a
measure as any of the incomplete nature of the English Reformation and the
hybrid quality of lay faith.[34]

These early skirmishes over bread versus wafers had subsided by 1600, but
they were a harbinger of conflicts to come. The sacrament of communion
generated so much unease and friction in post-Reformation Anglo-American
parishes because it was so *visible:* the anonymity of the congregation dissolved
as each person stepped forward to receive the bread directly from the hands
of the minister. The communion table revealed the parish and its internal
fault lines to itself, moreover, as those in the pews watched the parade of
communicants to the table. The choreography of the ritual required those at
the back—the unimportant, the poor, and the unfree—to wait their turn.
Some Protestant churches drew a line around the circle of those entitled
to commune, limiting the sacrament to full members in good standing, but
whatever the rules of participation, only a subset of the congregation would
typically partake on any given Sunday. So communion was both a ritual of
inclusion and exclusion.

For recusants, there was no hiding in the pews at the time of communion,
no taking refuge in the silent recital of Latin prayers or hidden fumbling
of rosary beads. (Which isn't to say that recusants didn't try to sham their
sacramental duty: Elizabeth Coulson was discovered "hiding her Protestant

34. Christopher Haigh, "'A Matter of Much Contention in the Realm': Parish Con-
troversies over Communion Bread in Post-Reformation England," *History*, LXXXVIII
(2003), 393–404 (quotations on 394, 396, 401).

communion bread, claiming that 'a pain in her side and a cough' were preventing her from swallowing it.") Whatever tricks of mental reservation or dissimulation church papists had perfected in order to outwardly conform could not shield them from the direct gaze of the priest and their fellow parishioners. Pretending that one was "out of charity" with a neighbor and hence unfit to communicate might work once or twice, as would planning a trip around Easter to avoid the annual obligation in one's home parish. But the pressure to be seen at communion was inescapable. Even the Catholic Church recognized this. Catholic authorities warned those tempted to conform ("secrete Catholics") against using various "subtil and secret meanes" to evade detection, such as "seeming to receave although he do not," "giving his name to the vicar as having receaved," or equivocating by answering "No forsooth, meaning in his *visible* quantitie" when asked, "Is the bodye of Christe in the blessed Sacrament?"[35]

Among the Counter-Reformation religious societies, the Jesuits stand out for their insistence on frequent communion. Most traditional Christians took communion only once a year before the Reformation; it was more important to see, than to eat, the eucharist at mass to receive the full soteriological benefits. Lisa McClain notes, "It was not uncommon for laypersons to go from altar to altar and from church to church to witness many elevations on the same day, to see Christ over and over again." This kind of promiscuous lay piety was exactly what the Council of Trent tried to suppress in the Counter-Reformation, and the focus of eucharistic devotion shifted from partaking of the actual sacrament to "spiritual reception," one of the mental exercises developed for recusants living in Protestant lands. The Jesuits, however, held firm to the necessity of frequent face-to-face communion in their overseas missions. And since Jesuits provided most of the missionaries on the ground in the English colonies, their views dominate our scholarly assessment of lay participation in the sacrament of the eucharist.[36]

35. Natalia Muchnik, *"Conversos* versus Recusants: Shaping the Markers of Difference (1570–1680)," in Yosef Kaplan, ed., *Religious Changes and Cultural Transformations in the Early Modern Western Sephardic Communities* (Leiden, 2019), 43–70 (quotation on 43); Gregorie Martin, *A Treatise of Schisme: Shewing, That Al Catholikes Ought in Any Wise to Abstaine Altogether from Heretical Conventicles* (London, 1578), chap. 1, par. 18 (emphasis added).

36. Tricia T. Pyne, "The Maryland Catholic Community, 1690–1775: A Study in Culture, Religion, and Church" (Ph.D. diss., Catholic University of America, 1995), 90–97; Lisa McClain, *Lest We Be Damned: Practical Innovation and Lived Experience among Catholics in Protestant England, 1559–1642* (New York, 2004), 118.

We know from surviving sermons that frequent reception was a common theme of colonial Jesuit homilies, some of which went so far as to encourage daily communion. As Louis Roels preached, "How many are there who slight Jesus, by receiving him only once a year, whom they ought to receive *daily*"—or, he qualified, "at least be worthy to receive him" every day. Daily communion meant daily immersion in what Jesuits called the experience of "metanoia," or radical conversion from one spiritual state to another. Roels explained that "the effects of the other sacraments are more limited; for Baptism blots out original sin, Confirmation strengthens us to profess our holy faith, Holy Orders qualifies us to exercise the sacred functions, Extreme Unction fortifies us against death and the devil, but the Blessed Sacrament diffuses its virtues through the whole man." But most Jesuits seem to have adopted the middle position represented by Augustine Jenkins: "It were to be wished that all Christians would dispose themselves weekly for this holy table. However, since this is rather to be wished, than hoped for, at least no business ought to hinder anyone from communicating at least once a month."[37]

Daily, let alone monthly, communion was, of course, beyond the reach of even the most dedicated colonial lay Catholics. Only those living in the Jesuit manors had regular access to the eucharist; the reality for most colonial Catholics was that, beyond the Maryland mission, they could hope to communicate at best once or twice a year, when an itinerant priest visited. Reports from the mission field give a mixed picture of lay sacramental participation. Antoine Biet boasted that four hundred "had taken Holy Communion at Easter" in St. George parish, Barbados, during the mid-seventeenth century. Yet by the mid-eighteenth century, John Carroll was complaining about those who "have continued year after year to seclude themselves" from communion. "When, on one side, I view the number who call themselves children of the Church; and on the other, the list, the very short list of those, who during this Easter time have offered themselves to partake of Christ's sacred body and blood, I am confounded, and disheartened and terrified." His fellow Jesuit George Hunter was less pessimistic. Hunter reported to Richard Challoner, the vicar apostolic for the London District, that about half of the sixteen thousand Catholics living in Maryland in 1765 were taking communion, though it's not clear whether he was referring to the yearly Easter obligation or more regular participation. The gap in these assessments reflects, in

<hr />

37. Joseph C. Linck, *Fully Instructed and Vehemently Influenced: Catholic Preaching in Anglo-Colonial America* (Philadelphia, 2002), x (metanoia), 122, 124–125 ("holy table").

part, the difference between serving as an itinerant missionary on the islands, where lay Catholics deprived of any access to the sacraments showed up in droves when a priest arrived, and serving in the Maryland mission, where a network of private chapels provided a semblance of regular congregational life to the area's recusants by the eighteenth century. Maryland priests such as Carroll could afford the luxury of complaining about poor attendance at communion.[38]

Itinerancy posed special challenges to sacramental practice. We have already seen how itinerant priests modified the altar vessels used in the mass to fit into portable saddlebags, even at the cost of tarnishing their liturgical luster. The eucharist placed additional demands, and risks, on traveling missionaries because of the need to protect the wafers from spoil or desecration. An anecdote that comes to us from seventeenth-century England gives a glimpse of these hazards. William Weston, fresh from his imprisonment at Wisbech Castle, reported ruefully that "[it] used sometimes to happen that in Catholic houses there were no altar breads for celebrating Mass." As a "precaution," Weston packed an abundant supply of "altar-breads" to carry with him on his itinerant travels. "With the constant jogging of the horse, however, they shook their way out and gradually, first three or four, then a large number dropped out and lay scattered on the public road for the space of nearly half a mile." Weston was forced to retrace his steps to retrieve this "trail of unconsecrated communion wafers." One can only imagine that colonial missionaries, traveling much greater distances over primitive roads and paths, faced even greater trials in safeguarding the wafers stowed in their saddlebags. But the main challenge for colonial priests was the scarcity, not the abundance, of wafers and wine. Priests who fled to Virginia from their sanctuary in Maryland during the Civil Wars of the 1650s complained that "there is not a supply of wine, which is sufficient to perform the sacred mysteries of the altar."[39] Supply routes from the English mission abroad and the colonies were unreliable

38. Larry Gragg, "The Pious and the Profane: The Religious Life of Early Barbados Planters," *Historian*, LXII (2000), 264–283 (quotation on 276–277); Linck, *Fully Instructed and Vehemently Influenced*, 73, 123.

39. McClain, *Lest We Be Damned*, 121; Annual Letter of 1655 and 1656, in Clayton Colman Hall, ed., *Narratives of Early Maryland, 1633–1684* (New York, 1910), 142. Shona Helen Johnston has emphasized the difficulty in supplying missionary priests with "vital ritual tools, such as holy water, holy oil, and Eucharistic tablets"; see Johnston, "Papists in a Protestant World: The Catholic Anglo-Atlantic in the Seventeenth Century" (Ph.D. diss., Georgetown University, 2011), 112–113.

and frequently disrupted by war, privateering, and storms. The Maryland Jesuits had an iron press (now in the museum at St. Francis Xavier shrine in Old Bohemia) to make wafers; elsewhere, missionaries had to make do with whatever improvised means were at hand to manufacture the "altar-bread." In these circumstances, it's likely that the wafers served at Catholic masses resembled the ordinary bread of Protestant communion in the colonies.[40]

We can reconstruct one particular colonial mass—or, rather, a series of masses celebrated over a period of weeks—from an unusual set of documents. The depositions gathered by the governor of Barbados in 1689 to prove the perfidy and treason of two Catholic gentlemen include specific accounts of who attended mass, how many, when and where, and what was said and done at these clandestine services. The officiating priest was a French Jesuit brought over from Martinique by Sir Thomas Montgomery and Willoughby Chamberlain to serve the largely Irish population of the island, and the masses were held in the homes of Montgomery and Chamberlain, with the two men assisting the priest in his sacerdotal duties. Only one other person, an Irish planter named Mr. Gall, was observed assisting at mass, a function clearly reserved for the most prominent layman present. Chamberlain was said to have boasted that he had "five hundred people or more" gathered to hear mass at his house; another time, he "expected two hundred at the mass." The two planters dispatched their Irish servants to "goe to several plantaçons to give notice to all persons that were of the Roman Catholique perswasion that there was Mass to be said at the House of Mr. Chamberlain and that all persons should receive good entertainm't that came there."[41]

The details about what transpired at these gatherings are sketchy, surely because of fears of legal repercussions but also because sacramental habits had atrophied by the 1680s on the island. One witness admitted that he had to "direct" Montgomery "how to perform that duty" of officiating at the eucharist, "Sir Thomas having not bin very expert thereat." One of the lengthier descriptions comes from Thomas Hogan, who explained that, soon after his

---

40. A set of iron bread cutters listed in the inventory of a Maryland recusant household may be an indication that the laity took over the task of making communion wafers outside the Jesuit manors; see Beatriz Betancourt Hardy, "Women and the Catholic Church in Maryland, 1689–1776," *Maryland Historical Magazine*, XCIV (1999), 400.

41. Deposition of Edward Bishop, Esq., in "Papers Relating to Montgomerie and Chamberlayne" Jan. 27, 1689, CO 28/37, no. 7 xlvi ("five hundred"); Deposition of Thomas White, ibid., no. 7 xlix ("goe to several plantaçons"); Deposition of Mr. John Rowe, ibid., no. 7 li ("two hundred").

arrival at Chamberlain's house, he was invited to "walk into a room that he believes is called the Hall where was the Jesuit (soe called)." There, "the door was Shut and the Jesuit (soe called) produced a paper and called Mr. Chamberlayne to the Altar (wch was there erected)." The priest then "lay his upon a Book (wch the dept believes was the Bible) but the contents of the said paper does not know It being as he thinks in Latin." Chamberlain then proceeded to "officiate as Clerk to the said Jesuit in the celebration that very day." The mysterious "paper" was, Hogan believed, Chamberlain's sworn recantation of Protestantism, an odd addition to the Roman mass, if indeed that's what it was. But this anomalous detail aside, Hogan's account includes the essential items of a private mass: a dedicated room in a gentry house, an altar, the Bible, and Latin.[42]

James Pennoyer, a servant of Montgomery's, was anxious to distance himself from the unseemly goings-on in his master's household and provided another version of the same mass. He testified that "he saw the Reputed Jesuit several times Read a certain Devotion (or what you please to call it) which he believed was called Mass and yet hee saw his said Master at the said Mass but knows not the form they use in itt being not of their principle." Pennoyer insisted he had never attended mass himself but only glanced in the room where it was being performed as he passed by the open door. From his restricted vantage point, he recalled that he "once . . . saw a Plate in his said Masters hand in Mass time but what was on it or how he made use of it he cannot tell for he went from the Door where the Mass was." To this composite portrait of a Catholic mass, we can add John Rowe's testimony that he was instructed to "doe and kneel . . . as they did" by the priest and his assistant. (Rowe, too, was a servant in the Montgomery household.)[43]

The overall picture, then, is of a large gathering of recusants, the majority of whom were Irish servants, being led through the steps of a mass by a French priest in the home of their wealthy English patron. This is probably not too far off the mark as a description of a "typical" colonial mass, apart from the size of the congregation. Like their Anglican counterparts, Catholic gentry preferred to receive communion at home in their private chapels, where they could maintain some control over the event. Even on the French islands in the Lesser Antilles, where churches were abundant, private masses

42. Examination of Thomas Brown, ibid., no. 7 xix; Deposition of Thomas Hogan, ibid., no. 7 xxxvii.

43. Deposition of Mr. John Rowe, ibid., no. 7 li; Deposition of James Pennoyer, ibid., no. 7 lii.

were preferred by the planter class. The Capuchin priest who ministered to the faithful on Martinique and St. Christopher reported saying mass "at the home of Mr. Cornette," much to the priest's displeasure. The desire for "les chapelles Domestiques" over the parish church was a perennial sore spot for Catholic missionaries wherever they served in plantation colonies. In the privacy of their own homes, much of the majesty and mystery of the sacrament was lost; John Gother complained of English recusants who came to communion at home "in such a disrespectful undress" that the sacrament was reduced to "nothing less than stepping out of Bed to the Altar."[44]

So far, the recollections of what took place in Montgomery's and Chamberlain's houses could have described either an Anglican or Catholic service. But the words of Dominick Rice transcend these liturgical elements to provide a glimpse into the sacramental heart of the mass. When asked by Elizabeth Smith "where he had been," Rice "made answer that hee had been att Gods house and in the presents [presence] of God and that he had seen Gods face." *Seeing* God—not just hearing his word preached—was a uniquely Catholic way of describing the experience of viewing the elevated host and consuming Christ's body at communion.[45]

The masses held on Barbados in 1688 were inescapably political as well as sacramental events. We know about them only because the colony's governor, in the wake of the regime change from James II to William and Mary, feared a general uprising of disaffected Irish Catholics aided by the French. For Colonel Stede, the religious crime of performing and attending a Catholic mass was inextricable from the political crime of sedition. The geopolitics of empire explain why we know so much about these masses; the micropolitics of class and race are equally on display in the mise-en-scène of a covert gathering of Irish servants invited to the home of a wealthy planter for "entertainment," there to be "instructed" in the gestures of deference and submission (kneeling, bowing) by their masters, who knew much less about Catholic rituals than

44. V. C., "Journal des missionnaires d'amerique de 1680 à 1738," Martinique, M69, Beinecke Lesser Antilles Collection, Hamilton College, New York, entries for 1714 and 1716, https://litsdigital.hamilton.edu/do/4c57bb2f-adf7-40c5-a935-e69b03e69219; John Bossy, *The English Catholic Community, 1570–1850* (New York, 1976), 128.

45. Deposition of Mary Richardson, in "Papers Relating to Montgomerie and Chamberlayne," CO 28/37, no. 7 lxii, TNA. In Peter Marshall's words, the elevation of the host was "a moment of direct visual contact with the most sacred of imaginable things"; see Marshall, *Heretics and Believers: A History of the English Reformation* (New Haven, Conn., 2017), 10.

they did. The same men who welcomed them into their homes would urge the Barbadian Council, several years later, to limit the number of Irish servants imported into the colony and impose harsh restrictions on their ability to move about freely in the wake of another panic about rebellious Irish and Africans joining together to attack the white settlers.

Did Irish and African Catholics sit together in these masses? There are no African names or "Negroes" identified on the list of participants compiled by the governor, but we know that several people enslaved by Montgomery were present at some of the seditious table talk reported in the depositions. The only evidence of African involvement in the masses comes from the minutes of the Barbados Council, which ordered three Africans who had been "in the time of the Jesuits . . . often seen at Mass" to be "sold or transported." So it is reasonable to assume that some enslaved Africans were present at the private masses held in Montgomery's home, as servants if not as full participants. If we know a little about how African Catholics viewed the sacrament of baptism, we know next to nothing about what they thought of communion. One possible point of phenomenological connection between the sacrament and traditional African cultic practice is the West African custom of drinking alcohol mixed with blood and dirt. Jason T. Sharples notes that consuming blood served multiple political and theological ends in West Africa and cites, as an example of transatlantic syncretism, the Afro-Caribbean practice of identifying criminals by "swearing oaths that involved drinking mixtures of rum, blood, and grave dirt." The notion that wine could be turned into blood by ritual power might have struck a familiar chord with captives from this region of Africa.[46]

---

46. Deposition of Charles Collins, Esq., in "Papers Relating to Montgomerie and Chamberlayne," CO 28/37, no. 7 xli, TNA. Collins recounted a dinner party at Montgomery's in which the "Company" reproved one guest for voicing fears of a combined Irish-African uprising since "several Negroes" were "in the room attending on their Masters at dinner." Barbados Council quoted in Shaw, *Everyday Life in the Early English Caribbean*, 123. Tricia T. Pyne suggests that Black and white Catholics were separated at the masses performed in the Jesuit missions, with the enslaved relegated to the back or along the sides of the chapel; see Pyne, "Roman Catholicism in the English North American Colonies, 1634–1776," in Stephen J. Stein, ed., *The Cambridge History of Religions in America*, I, *Pre-Columbian Times to 1790* (Cambridge, 2012), 425–426. See also John LaFarge, "The Survival of the Catholic Faith in Southern Maryland," *Catholic Historical Review*, XXI (1935), 14. "Swearing oaths": Jason T. Sharples, "Discovering Slave Conspiracies: New Fears of Rebellion and Old Paradigms of Plotting in Seventeenth-Century Barbados," *American Historical Review*, CXX (2015), 811–843 (quotation on 830).

On a less abstract level, the intimacy of communion—the physical close-ness of the communicants at the altar, the touching of lips by the priest as he placed the wafer on the tongue—would have placed Black and white Cath-olics on the same physical and spiritual level for a moment in time. Every sacrament brought the priest and laity together in physical proximity, but in the case of baptism, marriage, and last rites, the larger sacramental circle was limited to kith and kin. Only communion brought the entire commu-nity together in an enclosed space—a space, moreover, that was especially intimate in the case of private masses held in the home. Slaveholders could dictate the social arrangement of the other sacraments in which the enslaved participated, but not the eucharist. Given the lengths to which slaveholders went to erect emotional and psychological barriers between themselves and their bondspeople, the prospect of communing together must have been dis-turbing.[47] Even without the presence of Africans, the act of taking commu-nion required wealthy planters like Montgomery and Chamberlain to kneel before the priest, to place themselves in a posture of submission that might have been galling for men accustomed to wielding almost total power in their own households. Communion, in other words, violated all the carefully con-structed protocols of race and class that sustained the plantation economy. For that reason, it might have been a moment of empowerment or a moment of profound unease for enslaved Africans. (Or both.) It is not surprising that we have no firsthand accounts of Black and white Catholics sharing communion in colonial North America.

We are on firmer historical ground in assessing Indigenous understand-ings of communion, given the richness of ethnographic accounts written by English and French missionaries about Native converts and their ritual practices—distorted as they may be by Christian bias. For missionaries and converts alike, the eucharist was a feast, and feasting had deep cultural and ritual meaning in both societies. As a "truly Christian Neophyte" told Gabriel Lalemant of the St. Joseph de Sillery mission, "When I hear the bell ring which calls me to holy Mass, my heart leaps for joy; it seems to me that I am called to some great feast." But feasting was also an occasion for unspeakable violence and barbarism in certain contexts. The sacrament of communion, with its cannibalistic overtones, recalled Indigenous traditions of ritually kill-ing and consuming the flesh and heart of one's enemy. Jesuits described the

47. Anglican slaveholders shared this discomfort over interracial communion with their Catholic counterparts; one "young Gent" told Francis Le Jau that "he is resolved never to come to the Holy Table while slaves are Recd there" (Klingberg, ed., *Carolina Chronicle*, 102).

ritual torture and eating of human flesh by some victorious Indian communities as a "feast"—a barbaric and perverse meal, but one that nonetheless shared common features with their own sacramental feasts. The communal nature of the feast, its ceremonial dimension, its use of sacred vessels made of precious metal (copper kettles, in the case of the Native ritual) in which the dead body was given new metaphoric and spiritual life, all marked Native feasting as a savage form of communion. These cultural affinities did not go unnoticed and provoked ambiguous responses. Pierre Roubaud recalled with horror the "feast" he was forced to attend following the slaughter at Fort William Henry in 1757, when the Native allies of the French put hundreds of fleeing English to the sword. "I perceived . . . these inhuman creatures eating, with a famished avidity, this human flesh; I saw them taking large spoonfuls of this detestable broth, without being able to satiate themselves." Roubaud was upbraided for refusing "a piece of this English roast" by a young warrior who said to him, *"Thou have French taste; me Savage, this meat good for me."* Beneath their outrage, however, Jesuits such as Roubaud were uncomfortably aware that Protestants would have considered their squeamishness rank hypocrisy. The theological wars of the sixteenth and seventeenth centuries had cemented the association between the eucharist and cannibalism, and in voicing their disgust at Native "feasts" of human flesh, Catholic missionaries were trying to distance themselves from their own sacramental cannibalism. Native converts, for their part, understood the torture and death of Christ on the cross within the warrior tradition of a heroic death and the consuming of Christ's body and blood in the eucharist as the culminating act in this ritual complex. The Catholic eucharist was more legible within Indigenous cultural systems than the disembodied Protestant communion, one reason (among many) for the greater success Catholic missionaries enjoyed in Native communities.[48]

"Feasting" did not only take place during the sacrament of communion. A rigorous seasonal calendar of feast and fast days structured the daily lives

48. Thwaites, ed., *Jesuit Relations*, XXX, *Hurons, Lower Canada, 1646–1647*, 155–157, LXX, *All Missions, 1747–1764*, 125–127. On the affinity between communion and cannibalism in early modern religious debates, see Susan Juster, *Sacred Violence in Early America* (Philadelphia, 2016), 32–42. For a discussion of the sacramental vessels used in both Christian and Native communion ceremonies, see Carla Cevasco, "'This Is My Body': Communion and Cannibalism in Colonial New England and New France," *New England Quarterly*, LXXXIX (2016), 556–586. See Jane T. Merritt, "Dreaming of the Savior's Blood: Moravians and the Indian Great Awakening in Pennsylvania," *WMQ*, 3d Ser., LIV (1997), 723–746; Merritt, *At the Crossroads: Indians and Empires on a Mid-Atlantic Frontier, 1700–1763* (Williamsburg, Va., and Chapel Hill, N.C., 2003).

of Catholics on both sides of the Atlantic. Fully half the calendar year was devoted to special days of feasting, fasting, or abstinence: 65 days of fasting (including the 40 days of Lent); 104 days of abstinence (every Friday and Saturday outside of Lent); and 36 feast days, or holy days of obligation. Both fasting and abstinence required Catholics to refrain from eating all flesh and "white meats" (the dairy products made from animals); in addition, while fasting, they were to limit themselves to one full meal a day. On holy days, they were to attend mass, if possible, where they would receive the eucharist (i.e., feast). To observe colonial Catholics fasting or abstaining, we would have to peer into their households at mealtimes, a near impossibility given the scarcity of personal documents for the southern and island colonies especially. We know Church leaders cautioned English recusants that fasting weekly might make them too conspicuous to their neighbors; William Stanney counseled "houshoulders" to "use some restraints" in their dietary choices and "insteede of strict fasting, to redeeme [fast days] with almes deedes or prayer," trading one devotional act for another. Southern colonial householders presumably faced less scrutiny over their food habits, scattered as they were in isolated plantations across the landscape. As slaveholders consolidated their social and political power in the eighteenth century, the dining room became a space for the conspicuous display of fashion and abundance, which surely diluted the religious meaning of the meals consumed in recusant gentry households.[49]

In some cases, we know more about the feasting habits of the enslaved than we do about their masters, since the ritual calendar observed by both Anglicans and Catholics (though the Anglican calendar included far fewer days of feasting and fasting) created rare moments of freedom from work and want for their laborers. One historian has determined that in the early eighteenth century, Chesapeake slaveholders provided nine holidays for their laborers (three days each at Christmas, Easter, and Whitsuntide). Slaves, too, "feasted" on these holy days along with their masters and mistresses on the more prosperous plantations. For enslaved Catholics, the perverseness of being offered plentiful meat on the days of the year when it was expressly forbidden by their faith must have rankled indeed. There are even suggestions that, in certain zones of the Catholic Atlantic, the enslaved observed fast days, as well. One seventeenth-century visitor observed that in the French

49. Pyne, "Ritual and Practice," *U.S. Catholic Historian*, XXVI, no. 2 (Spring 2008), 31–33; William Stanney, *A Treatise of Penance* (London, 1617), 259. McClain notes that this kind of sacramental trading "recurs frequently in the pastoral literature of this period" (*Lest We Be Damned*, 50).

Caribbean "there are some Negroes who punctually observe abstinence all the time of Lent, and all the other Fasting-days appointed by the Church, without any remission of their ordinary and continual labour." As implausible as it may seem given the constant threat of malnutrition that hung over even the most prosperous plantations, observing the ritual calendar was one way enslaved Catholics could practice their faith in an environment of severe sacramental scarcity.[50]

Feast and fast days appear in the colonial archive in another way: as a means of marking time. The public records of Maryland are filled with references to various saints' days and "red-letter" days (holy days listed in red ink on liturgical calendars) as marking public occasions or obligations. The inventorying of probated estates, for example, was to be completed by "the ffeast of St. Michael the Archaengell," or the "ffeast of All Saints next." The governor called the General Assembly into session on August 29, 1641, "the morrow after the Feast of Saint Simon and Jude." These calendar references disappear by the end of the seventeenth century, a sign of the increasing marginalization of the colony's Catholics after the Glorious Revolution.[51]

Holy days of obligation provoked far more commentary—and resistance— in the colonies. The issue was labor, not food. Catholics were supposed to refrain from "servile labor" on Sundays and on holy days of obligation, a burdensome requirement for all heads of household and an intolerable one for slaveholders. Even in England, most working men and women could not observe the prohibition on labor on holy days; as in so many other aspects of early modern life, the freedom to *not* work was reserved to the propertied alone. The Jesuits who served English America initially insisted that servants and slaves were not exempt from the ban on "servile labor," but even they had recognized the futility of persuading Catholic slaveholders to honor the ban by the early eighteenth century. In 1722, the Jesuits requested a waiver from the labor ban during the tobacco season (May through September) from

50. Lorena S. Walsh, "Slave Life, Slave Society, and Tobacco Production in the Tidewater Chesapeake, 1620–1820," in Ira Berlin and Philip D. Morgan, eds., *Cultivation and Culture: Labor and the Shaping of Slave Life in the Americas* (Charlottesville, Va., 1993), 177. Curran maintains that the fifteen days of abstention from labor that the church mandated were a "special attraction" for enslaved Catholics (*Papist Devils*, 157). For a discussion of the custom of giving slaves "time off" from work and extra rations of food on holy days, see Nicholas M. Beasley, "Ritual Time in British Plantation Colonies, 1650–1780," *Church History*, LXXVI (2007), 541–568. "Punctually": Charles de Rochefort, *The History of the Caribby-Islands, viz. Barbados, St. Christophers, St. Vincents, Martinico, Dominico, Barbouthos, Monserrat, Mevis, Antego, etc. . . . In Two Books* (London, 1666), book 2, 201.

51. *Archives of Maryland*, I, 71–72, 113.

the vicar apostolic of London for "all hands belonging to or working in the Crop," with the exception of the four most prominent feast days: Ascension Day, Whitmonday, Corpus Christi, and Assumption Day. The "obligation of hearing Mass on all Holy days remains in full force," they clarified, and advised "Masters and Mistresses" to "procure all their Servants and Slaves" for "some spiritual reading in their familys" if they could not attend mass. The vicar apostolic was sympathetic and granted their request; two years later, he further exempted laboring "hands" from fasting and abstaining during the tobacco season as well. Tobacco came first in Maryland.[52]

From the household to the fields, the sacraments of feasting and fasting forced colonial Catholics to confront the challenges of interracial fellowship on an ongoing basis. White and Black Catholics did not have the same access to the sacrament of communion, did not share the same obligations to fast on certain days and to avoid labor on others. When they did partake together in these rituals, they did so largely within the households of wealthy planters, governed as they were by strict protocols of racial separation.

Matrimonial Politics

Whereas the ritual calendar of early modern Catholicism was saturated with occasions to feast and fast, the sacrament of marriage was (theoretically) a once-in-a-lifetime event. Stubbornly high death rates and the constant arrival of new, unseasoned migrants to the colonies meant that many Catholics married more than once in the Americas, but—unlike their Protestant counterparts—they believed that marriages could not (should not) be dissolved except by death. When the Reformers demoted marriage from a religious sacrament to a civil contract, they opened the door to the prospect of marital dissolution, though in practice divorce remained exceedingly rare in England and its American colonies.

For centuries, Europe's Christians had understood a marriage to be valid if both parties consented and had consummated the relationship, even if their parents or guardians objected and no priest was present. At its core,

---

52. The Vatican steadily chipped away at the number of holy days of obligation, reducing them to thirty-four in 1642 and again to twelve in 1777, in response to lay resistance (Bossy, *English Catholic Community*, 119–120). "Procure all their Servants and Slaves": Regulations re. Holy Days, 1722, box 2, folder 9, MPA. For the vicar apostolic's decisions, see Old Records, 1724–1815, box 3, folder 8, ibid. Hardy notes that by the end of the colonial period, the number of fast days observed in Maryland had fallen by one-third, to sixty-three ("Papists in a Protestant Age," 184).

a marriage was a promise by two consenting adults to be sexually exclusive, raise children together, and form a productive household. This was as true of Anglo-American Protestants as it was of Catholics. Blessed by a minister or priest and ratified by the larger community of family and friends present to bear witness, marriage was nonetheless a union made by two individuals. The Reformation did not fundamentally change this understanding, although the politicization of the sacraments that was the inevitable outcome of confessionalism led Protestant and Catholic authorities alike to exert greater ecclesiastical control over marriage. Despite the best efforts of Protestant and Catholic clerics alike to bring marriages into the church, marriage in early modern Anglo-America remained essentially a civic as much as a religious event. Or, to put it another way, marriage is a domesticated sacrament, governed as much by the rules and agendas of the profane world as by canon law.[53]

We would thus expect colonial marriages to reflect the unsettled social condition of the periphery, and this is in fact the case. Colonial records are filled with laments about disorderly marriages: irregular or fraudulent, bigamous, polygamous, incestuous, marred by high rates of abuse and desertion. Colonial men and women apparently married on a whim and separated at will, left spouses behind when they immigrated or moved to a different settlement and took new ones, cohabited with their nieces or stepchildren or stole a brother's wife. They tricked ministers into marrying them without proper license or publication of the banns, lied about which parish they belonged to in order to find the most permissive minister, lied about their age, their previous marital status, their economic prospects. And those who were determined to skirt the law or custom found rogue ministers aplenty to abet them in their marital schemes.[54] Unlicensed ministers made a living by performing irregular marriages, placing the children of such unions in peril of bastardy. "One that pretended himself to be a Clergy man" had "marryed all that came to him" over the course of twenty-four years on the island of Barbados, forcing

---

53. Shannon McSheffrey, *Marriage, Sex, and Civic Culture in Late Medieval London* (Philadelphia, 2006); Mary S. Hartman, *The Household and the Making of History: A Subversive View of the Western Past* (Cambridge, 2004).

54. Some examples taken from the colonial records: Robert Holt and Christian Bonnefield were accused of bigamy when they married in 1658, since both had spouses still living (*Archives of Maryland*, XLI, 228–230); George Layfield contracted a "pretend Marriage" when he married his niece in 1697 (ibid., XXIII, 391); Governor William Gooch complained to Bishop Gibson in 1730 of the raft of "incestuous Copulations" taking place in Virginia (Gooch to Gibson, July 23, 1730, Fulham Papers, XII, fols. 156–157); Rev. Wilkerson

the governor to "passe a bill for the confirmation of those marriages to prevent Suites of Law" in 1690. "Vagabond couples" thwarted by the Anglican ministers of Virginia fled into the Carolinas "after their unlawfull attempts to consummate marriages are frustrated in this colony," complained one SPG missionary, "and there accomplish their most unwarrantable practices, Such as polygamy, Incest, Adultery, etc." The unholy combination of "pretended" clerics and "vagabond" settlers made a mockery of church marriages in the eyes of many colonial leaders.[55]

Into this environment of marital chaos and uncertainty stepped colonial ministers. Protestant and Catholic clergy alike struggled to adjudicate what constituted a valid marriage amid a population of people who were often strangers to one another, with no deep ties of family or community to anchor competing claims. One of the earliest incidences of marital confusion comes from Maryland, where the absence of Protestant ministers in the early decades of the colony's existence led Giles Tomkinson to take matters into his own hands. When accused by the constable of living with a woman who was not his lawful wife, Tomkinson asserted "in open Court" that "his marriage was as good as possibly it Coold bee maed by the Protestants hee beeing one" because no Protestant minister had been available to perform the ceremony. Moreover, as lay Christians had done for centuries, Tomkinson insisted that a minister was not necessary; as long as a couple "publish them selves Man and wife till death them doe part . . . for the worlds Satisfaction," the union was valid. A more scandalous incident from the same colony featured a mock ceremony by one Thomas Seamor (not "a Little disturbed in Drink"), who sat Mary Cole and Joseph Edlow down on stools in his small cabin, joined their hands together, recited the "Common prayer Book" service, and bade them "goe to bed together." A visitor to Jamaica in 1687 noted that "the rude and common sort of people seldom marie acording to the ceremony of the church, but are soe full of faith as to take one another's words, and soe live together,

---

charged one of his parishioners with an "incestuous marriage" and another with cohabiting with her "father-in-law" (Rev. Christ Wilkerson to the bishop of London, May 26, 1718, in William Stevens Perry, ed., *Historical Collections Relating to the American Colonial Church*, IV, *Maryland* [Hartford, Conn., 1878], 107); and one minister accused another in Bridgetown, Barbados, of "marrying . . . clandestinely" in his parish without permission (quoted in Beasley, "Domestic Rituals," *Anglican and Episcopal History*, LXXVI [2007], 342).

55. Letter from Gov. Richard Dutton to Mr. Secretary Jenkins, Barbados, May 30, 1690, CO 29/3, fols. 67–68, TNA; "Memorial of Alexander Forbes, Presented to the General Assembly," May 9, 1723, Fulham Papers, XI, fols. 305–308.

and begett children, and if they fall out or disaagree, they part friendly by consent."[56]

More than the problem of self-marriage, however (which, after all, was not unique to the colonies), colonial ministers were troubled by the widespread incidence of marriage by partners of differing faiths. The religious mixing found in so many colonial communities led inexorably to the phenomenon of marriages that crossed confessional lines. No other issue generated so much ministerial angst. The Anglican missionary on Antigua worried in the 1740s that the "increase of Papists in these Islands" threatened to destroy Protestant families from within through the instrument of marriage. "I have been as watchful as possible to prevent their making any proselytes among us," he reported to Bishop Gibson on the heels of several disconcerting cases in the sugar colony where local Catholics "married Protestants and seduced them afterwards." Mixed marriages were also not new; they had vexed church and state leaders in post-Reformation Europe ever since marriage had been desacralized and brought under secular control. Catholic authorities, in particular, denounced mixed marriages in their territories as "detestable unions" and a form of sacrilege. Marrying someone of a rival faith not only turned "the other" into a beloved spouse; it exposed the children born of that union to both faiths, bringing the viper of heresy into the very bosom of the family. Conversion and mixed marriages were "the two greatest taboos" in early modern religious life, Benjamin Kaplan notes, "for it was through mixed marriage that a great deal of the movement between faiths occurred." Nonetheless, as Kaplan points out, no confession questioned the legitimacy or "binding character" of mixed marriages between Christians, no matter how abominable they found the practice.[57]

Rather than forbid interconfessional marriages altogether, post-Reformation communities developed a system of customary rules governing the hot-button issue of how to raise the children of mixed households. Catholic authorities were quite clear on the question: all the children of mixed marriages should be raised as Catholics, and they insisted that Protestant spouses agree to do so before allowing them to marry in the church. Despite the unanimity of opinion from local priests up to the Vatican, however, it quickly

56. *Archives of Maryland*, Nov. 14, 1665, LIII, 599; ibid., 1657, X, 549–551; David Buisseret, ed., *Jamaica in 1687: The Taylor Manuscript at the National Library of Jamaica* (Kingston, Jamaica, 2008), 240.

57. Francis Byam to Bishop Gibson, Antigua, June 16, 1744, Fulham Papers, XIX, fols. 275–276; Benjamin J. Kaplan, *Divided by Faith: Religious Conflict and the Practice of Toleration in Early Modern Europe* (Cambridge, Mass., 2007), 267–268, 277, 278.

became the pattern that daughters followed the faith of their mother while sons were brought up in the religion of their father. As one Anglican minister in the predominantly Catholic county of St. Mary's, Maryland, complained, "My Parish abounds with Papists. . . . Many families amongst us are but half Protestant; the husband of one and the wife of the other persuasion. The women who are Papists and intermarry with Protestant husbands make it a part of their contract that all their daughters shall be brought up in the romish faith." The wife of the governor of Nova Scotia, the daughter of French Catholics, brought to her marriage a contract by which she promised to "breed her daughters to her perswasion." Such a gendered division of spiritual labor was commonplace in recusant households, as we have seen. Protestant authorities were not blind to the subversive implications of this arrangement, which leveraged the reproductive power of women for the recusant community. By raising Catholic daughters who would go on to raise Catholic daughters of their own, women became the engine of expansion for England's beleaguered Catholic minority.[58]

Interfaith marriage proved as difficult to police in the colonies as it did in the metropole. In colonies such as Antigua with large populations of Irish Catholics, periodic attempts by the legislature to pass acts "to prevent intermarriage of Protestants and Roman Catholics" were thwarted by the governor's council, who feared the disapproval of the Board of Trade. In fact, when John Wilson, "a Spaniard," petitioned the Barbados Council to be allowed to keep his estate despite being married "to an Englishwoman," the council agreed, in direct violation of English law forbidding Catholics from owning property in the colonies. Irish and Spanish spouses certainly troubled the Church establishment more than English Catholic ones, but, as did their counterparts in the British Isles, colonial authorities connived at interfaith marriages (which were almost always interethnic, as well) when it suited their larger geopolitical goals to do so.[59]

58. Arthur Holt to Rev. Samuel Smith, All Faiths, St. Mary's County, May 21, 1734, Fulham Papers, III, fols. 174–175; Richard Watts to Bishop Gibson, Annapolis Royal [Nova Scotia], Apr. 24, 1729, ibid., I, fols. 77–78. This pattern, of girls being raised Catholic in mixed marriages while boys were raised as Protestants, was "the most common practice in early modern Europe," Kaplan concludes (*Divided by Faith*, 288).

59. See the back-and-forth between the assembly and council in the 1690s over the proposed Act to Prevent Intermarriage of Protestants and Roman Catholics (Minutes of Council and Assembly of Antigua, September 1698, CO 155/2, fols. 279–283, and Sept. 21, 1699, CO 155/2, fols. 321–323, TNA). "A Spaniard": Minutes of the Council of Barbados, I, 1654–1656, from the original in Barbados, PRO 31/17/43, Feb. 5, 1655/6, 126, TNA.

In the proprietary colony of Maryland, on the other hand, the authorities did not hesitate to deploy the law to ensure orthodox households, even to the point of the forcible seizure of children, especially during the fraught decades of the late seventeenth and early eighteenth century, when control of the colony was up for grabs. Successive Catholic and Protestant regimes used the law to weaponize the family in the ongoing battle over which religion should prevail in the colony. One of the grievances of the Protestant majority, who enacted their own version of England's Glorious Revolution in 1689, was Catholic magistrates' disregard for the law stipulating that orphans should be placed with guardians of the same religion as the child's deceased parents. Under the Calverts, the rebels charged, there had been cases too "endless" to enumerate of children being "committed to the tutlage of papists, and brought up in the Romish Superstition." Even adults were not safe: "Wee could instance in a young woman that has been lately forced by order of Council from her husband committed to the custody of a papist, and brought up in his religion." After the colony was royalized following the ousting of the Catholic proprietor in the early eighteenth century, the assembly retaliated by passing a law stipulating, "Where any Person being a Protestant that shall die and leave a widow and Children and such Widow shall Intermarry with any person of the Romish Communion or be herself of that opinion and profession[,] it shall and may be lawful for his Majestys Governor . . . to remove such Child or Children out of the Custody of such parents and place them where they may be Securely Educated in the protestant Religion." Under this law, Peter Wild petitioned that his nephew John Wild be removed from his Catholic guardians, Daniel and Mary Delahuntee, and placed in his custody to avoid John's "being perverted to popery by them." The council agreed and ordered John to be removed from the Delahuntees' household.[60]

Charges of children being kidnapped from their homes by rival religious factions were a recurrent feature of Maryland's sacramental politics, dating

60. "The Declaration of the Reason and Motive for the Pres't Appearing in Arms of His Maj'tys Protestant Subjects in the Province of Maryland," July 25, 1689, *Archives of Maryland*, VIII, 103; "Petition of Philip Lee Esq. to Governor Calvert," July 5, 1728, ibid., XXV, 496; Council Meeting, Feb. 22, 1722/3, ibid., XXV, 403. The 1715 Act for the Administration of Justice in Testamentary Affairs included a provision that allowed the council to remove the children of deceased Protestants from the custody of their mother if she was a Catholic or remarried a Catholic (ibid., XXX, 334). Hardy points out that this measure was designed in part to discourage recusant landowners from falsely claiming to be Protestant in order to hold office in the colony, since doing so put their children at risk of being raised Protestant after their death ("Papists in a Protestant Age," 136–137).

back to the earliest years of the colony's existence. Scarcely a decade after the *Ark* and *Dove* made landfall on the shores of the Chesapeake, a Virginia woman, Mary Ford, accused Lord Baltimore's agent Thomas Cornwallis of raiding Protestant households over the border to steal children for their new venture. Cornwallis, she charged, "stole from Mrs ffoord here in towne two Childeren the one a boy about 3. or 4. yeares ould, the other a daughter about 5. or 6. yeares of age, . . . carrying them away into Maryland and seduceing them to po'py." Such stories were part of the polemical lore of antipopery, of course, but they spoke to the very real fear that the Protestant household was under siege by the combined forces of a feudal Catholic lord and recusant women. The kind of power that could invade the sanctity of a man's home and steal away his children was the very essence of popery: seductive, operating in the interstices of intimate relationships.[61]

Sometimes the altar itself became a battleground in the war between Protestants and Catholics in Maryland. Gathering testimony in the 1750s about the "illegal Methods" used by "Popish Priests" to "withdraw our People from the Communion of the Church of England," the Maryland Assembly's Committee of Grievances uncovered several incidents of priests verbally and even physically attacking prospective Protestant brides and grooms who refused to convert or promise to raise their children in the Roman Church. James Warrick related a story told to him by his Catholic wife of a mixed marriage being disrupted by the presiding Jesuit, who would not proceed with the final vows until the Protestant groom would "swear, on a Book which he kissed, that he should renounce all Religion but the Popish Religion, and that he should bring up all his Children in that Persuation." In Charles County, another priest, upon discovering that a young couple were of different faiths ("the Man a Papist, the Woman a Protestant"), reportedly "turned them both violently out of the Chapel, in the Presence of the Congregation." Clearly embellished for partisan effect, these stories of dramatic confrontations at the altar were parables of the social and political disorder mixed marriages introduced into the polity.[62]

If this discussion has focused more on the politics of marriage than on the sacrament itself, it is because we know very little about how colonial men and women of any faith actually married one another. The persistent lack of clergymen in every colony meant that a variety of other officials were often

---

61. "The Humble Peticon of Mary Foorde in the Behalf of the Protestant Inhabitants in Virginia and Maryland," Apr. 25, 1646, *Archives of Maryland*, III, 169, 171.

62. Committee of Grievances, October/November 1753, ibid., L, 199, 204.

pressed into service to perform improvised ceremonies. In the fisheries of Newfoundland, it was the naval chaplains and "Masters of Vessels" who were most often called upon to marry and christen the local inhabitants on board their ships. In the Jerseys, it was the justices of the peace who assumed the power to marry in the absence of regular clergy, despite the fact that many of them were "very mean Fellows, Butchers and of low lifed Trades." The result was predictable: "We have very irregular and unlawful Marriages amongst us." The long-suffering SPG missionary Francis Le Jau of Goose Creek Parish, South Carolina, complained to no avail about the "Lay teachers who are mightily multiplyed here of late" who "marry People with Insolence at my very Doors after their own way." Civil ceremonies performed by justices of the peace were apparently the norm in the Carolinas, even in the backcountry, where the chaplain who accompanied the commissioners sent to survey the boundary line between Virginia and North Carolina "cou'd perswade nobody to be marry'd because every Country Justice can do that Jobb for them." What these "irregular" ceremonies looked like is lost to view. We do know that radical dissenters such as the Puritans and the Quakers disdained most of the material trappings of the Anglican rite, viewing "marriage ring[s] as heathenish" and preferring a civil service performed by a magistrate to a church service performed by a minister. But these groups aside, most Anglo-American Protestants preferred to be married by a minister. And too often, none could be found in North America.[63]

Even where ministers were available, lay Christians both Protestant and Catholic evinced the same preference for private ceremonies performed at home that we saw in the case of baptism. In the sugar islands, the "great majority" of weddings took place in homes rather than in parish churches. One British naval officer observed in the 1710s that among the "particular Customs" of Barbadian planters was that marriages were "always solemnized in their houses (never in the Churches)." A 1734 act acknowledged, "It has been customary and usual here to marry in Private-houses, and not in the Churches" and levied a £25 fine on any householder who allowed a clandestine wedding to take place "in his or her House, or in any Backside, Yard, Garden,

63. Joseph Gorham, Lieutenant-Governor of Placentia [Newfoundland], to Bishop Terrick, Nov. 12, 1771, Fulham Papers, I; Robert Jenney to Bishop Sherlock, Philadelphia, May 23, 1751, ibid., VII, Pennsylvania 1680–1762, fols. 314–315; Le Jau to SPG Secretary, July 4, 1714, in Klingberg, ed., *Carolina Chronicle*, 143; William Byrd, *Histories of the Dividing Line betwixt Virginia and North Carolina* (New York, 1967), 89. Another naval chaplain, Mr. Carey, performed "clandestine Marriages" in Port Royal, Jamaica, in the 1730s; see

or other place." Outside the sacralized interior of the church, these gentry weddings became more social than religious events. The Anglican commissary in Maryland tried to "restrain" his clergy from "marrying at private houses for several inconven[ience]s, but especially because some Clergymen have been complained of for being drunk at such times and places." As Nicholas Beasley points out, ministers who officiated in a "Charles Town drawing room or in a Barbadian great house" were "guest[s] in another's space," employees of the rich planters upon whose largesse they relied. Only those clergy who were willing to forego the fees they customarily collected when performing a church wedding—a small minority—could avoid being replaced by civil officials or, worse, reduced to the lowly status of house servants.[64]

It was one thing for an Anglican wedding to take place in a home; it was another thing for a Catholic wedding (a sacrament) to be held in a "great house." English priests had long become accustomed to residing as honored guests in recusant gentry households, but in the colonies, their status was far more precarious. Rather than dictating the ritual life of recusant communities, colonial priests found themselves being dictated to. The priests who ministered in the French islands chafed at what one called the "new and ridiculous honors" they had to bestow on the plantocracy, including treating them "in the manner of a lord" when officiating at mass. On Martinique, Father de Vire struggled to abolish "several poor customs that existed in the parishes" on the islands, including that of "bless[ing] marriages with and without the mass" in the homes of planters. Issuing strict orders that all marriages should be properly performed in a church, de Vire found himself ignored by the laity and priests alike on the island. "This did not prevent some religious from

---

William May to Bishop Gibson, Kingston, May 30, 1737, Fulham Papers, XVII, fols. 272–273. "Heathenish": quoted in Henry Wilder Foote, ed., *Annals of King's Chapel from the Puritan Age in New England to the Present Day*, 2 vols. (Boston, 1900), I, 18–19.

64. Beasley, "Domestic Rituals," *Anglican and Episcopal History*, LXXVI (2007), 330–332; "T. Walduck's Letters from Barbados, 1710," *Journal of the Barbados Museum and Historical Society*, XV (1947), 43–44; An Act for Preventing Clandestine Marriages, in Richard Hall, ed., *Acts, Passed in the Island of Barbados, from 1643, to 1762, Inclusive* (London, 1764), 300; Rev. Christopher Wilkinson to the bishop of London, Chester River in Queen Ann's County, Maryland, May 26, 1718, in Perry, ed., *Historical Collections Relating to the American Colonial Church*, IV, 109. The Reverend John Thomas of New York wrote to the SPG that he had reluctantly agreed to perform the marriage service "Gratis" to outbid the justices of the peace, who had siphoned off the business from the local clergy, and "in Order to bring Marriages to the Church." See John Thomas to Secretary, Hampstead, LI, Apr. 22, 1707, SPG Letters "A" Series, III, no. 67.

overstepping the prohibition on performing marriage ceremonies in private homes," he fumed. "They did so on the pretext that they had not been left a copy of these interdictions"—a "pitiful" excuse.[65]

A perennial bone of contention between planters and Catholic missionaries was the insistence of the latter that enslaved Africans who were baptized be allowed to marry in the church. Even more than baptism, the sacrament of marriage conferred upon the enslaved civil rights that masters found intolerable. According to the Church, the sacrament of marriage could not be dissolved for any reason—including the greed of slaveholders looking to maximize profits by separating husbands from wives, parents from children, at the auction block. Where they could, the Jesuits who served English America performed church marriages for the enslaved in their parishes. Two Black couples were married on May 23, 1767, in St. Inigoes Manor church in Maryland: "James and Rebecca, Negroe," and "Ignatius and Theresia, Negroes." (The names of the latter pair suggest they might have been baptized in the Spanish islands before being sold to the Maryland mission.) Altogether, over a ten-year period between 1767–1776, 159 marriages were celebrated at St. Inigoes, one-third of which were for enslaved Catholics.[66]

Beyond their own manors, however, the Maryland Jesuits had little sway over colonial slaveholders who refused to allow their bondsmen and -women

---

65. "Journal des missionaires d'amerique de 1680 à 1738" (entries for 1688 and 1725). As late as 1810, home marriages were still the rule for Catholic couples; the U.S. bishops demurred in "making immediately a general rule for the celebration of marriages in the Church," since "it was thought premature now to publish an ordinance to that effect" (J[ohn Carroll, archbishop of Baltimore, et al.], "Ecclesiastical Discipline," Baltimore, Nov. 15, 1810, transcr. and publ. in *American Catholic Historical Researches*, XI [1894], 32).

66. Baptismal and Marriage Records for St. Indigos, 1767–1769, box 5, folder 10, MPA; James Walton's Diary, box 4, fol. 2 [photocopy], ibid. Pyne notes that the proportion of enslaved couples in the marriage register corresponds to the baptismal figures for the same period. Of the fifty-three slave marriages, close to one-third of the couples were listed as having the same slaveholder, suggesting that "the couples were either members of the same household or that an arrangement had been made prior to the marriage to bring the partner into the household" ("Ritual and Practice," *U.S. Catholic Historian*, XXVI, no. 2 [Spring 2008], 39). Helen A. Kilburn's analysis of the 1681 Maryland Act concerning Negroes points out that, uniquely among colonial legislation outlawing interracial unions, the Maryland Act penalized any "preist" or "Minister" who performed such marriages, suggesting that the Jesuits' willingness to marry enslaved couples in the church was widely known—and resented (Kilburn, "Catholics in the Colonies: Nation, Religion, and Race in Seventeenth-Century Maryland" [Ph.D. diss., University of Manchester, 2018], 216). The 1681 act can be found in *Archives of Maryland*, VII, 203–205.

to marry in the church. Some white recusants did provide Catholic weddings for their slaves; one such comes from an eighteenth-century Maryland court case recounting the 1681 marriage of "Irish Nell" and "Negro Charles" on the plantation of Major William Boarman. From a distance of some seventy years, eyewitnesses or their descendants recalled that Nell was defiant in the face of efforts by the local gentry (even Lord Baltimore himself, according to several people) to dissuade her from marrying "a Negro"; they warned her that "she would put a mark by that upon her Children and bring them into Slavery." Within their own community, Nell and Charles found more support for their union—an elderly woman recalled that "she heard several people wish them much joy" and that Nell "behaved as a Bride." For the remainder of their long and fruitful marriage, "Negro Charles and Irish Nell were always deemed as man and wife, and did acknowledge themselves as such." Nell's and Charles's own religious beliefs were unrecorded, though it is likely both had been baptized, either in their homelands (Ireland for Nell, Africa for Charles) or in North America.[67]

Elsewhere in English America, where there were no priests except fugitive ones of foreign extraction, the situation for enslaved men and women who wished to marry in the church was dire. Those who had been baptized and instructed in the faith by French or Spanish missionaries before being sold to English planters or seized in the many wars of conquest fought in the Caribbean at least had enough familiarity with the Roman rites to improvise their own religious ceremonies. One couple with a typically peripatetic Caribbean spiritual itinerary—baptized in French St. Christopher, seized by the English in 1690 when they conquered the island, then sold to the English governor of Antigua—finally escaped to Guadeloupe. There, they told the superior general of the Jesuit mission to the French West Indies how they had managed to secretly practice their faith while in captivity to the English. Being "moved by the fear of God and having no priest," the pair "got married in the presence of their Catholic friends, performing the ceremonies that they remembered having seen in [Catholic] weddings." Their five children were then "baptized according to Catholic customs." As the enslaved population in the Caribbean exploded in the eighteenth century, slave marriages exhibited the same blend of African and Christian elements that marked other aspects of plantation

67. "Depositions from *Butler v. Boarman*," fols. 240 ("wish them much joy"), 241 ("she would put a mark"), 243 ("deemed as man and wife"), https://msa.maryland.gov/megafile /msa/speccol/sc5400/sc5496/000500/000534/html/00534sources.html. Charles was described as a "saltwater Negro" by William Simpson, suggesting his African origins (fol. 242).

culture. On Guadeloupe, marriages followed the custom of individual African "nations," performed with traditional dance and music. It is likely that slave marriages in the English Lesser Antilles incorporated traditional African customs as well, though we have no record of it.[68]

On the mainland, outside of the Maryland mission, we have very few references to slave marriages by either Protestant or Catholic clerics. By all accounts, Anglican planters universally denied their bondsmen and -women the right to marry. One anonymous petition to the bishop of London lamented that in "this Land of Verjennia . . . wee are kept out of the Church and matrimony is denied to us. and to be plain they doe look no more upon us then if we were dogs." The result, the Reverend John Sharpe deplored, was that "their marriages are performed by mutual consent without the blessing of the Church" in a jumble of "Heathenish" and Christian customs. Christian marriages among the enslaved were notoriously difficult to enforce, in Sharpe's view, due to stubborn attachment to the African practice of polygamy and the practical impediments of life under slavery. "Some are kept off [barred from church marriage] because of their polygamy contracted before baptism where none or neither of the wives will accept a divorce. Others (the husband and wife seldom happening to belong to one family) have one of the married parties sold at some hundred miles distance where they can never hope to meet again and have not continence to persevere single. Some agree to break by mutual consent their negro marriages as I may call it and marry a Christian spouse. In these cases it is difficult how to proceed without giving scandal or matter of temptation." Such hand-wringing was the common response of ministers faced with the task of bringing Christian marriage to a system of labor exploitation that severed human relationships on a daily basis.[69]

68. Peabody, "'A Dangerous Zeal,'" *French Historical Studies*, XXV (2002), 86 (quotation on 54).

69. Anonymous petition to Bishop Gibson, July 4, 1723, Fulham Papers, XVII, fol. 167–168. On occasion, Anglicans did permit the enslaved to marry in the church; Edward Reading reported to the SPG that he had "baptiz'd a Negro Man and his wife, and have since publickly married them in the Church." Reading is the exception to the rule, however. See Reading to Henry Maule, Jamaica, Feb. 15, 1723, ibid., fols. 159–160. "Some are kept off": "Rev. John Sharpe's Proposals, Etc. March 1713," *Collections of the New-York Historical Society for the Year 1880*, XIII (New York, 1881), 339–363 (quotations on 355). The SPG missionary John Bartow complained in 1725 that the enslaved in his circuit "marry after their heathen way and divorce and take others as often as they please"; see Bartow, Nov. 5, 1725, SPG Letters "A" Series, 19/184.

Given the mixing of men and women from different regions of Africa and from different Caribbean islands in the early English colonies, it is likely that more enslaved Africans experienced "mixed marriages" uniting people of two different faith traditions than did white settlers. Thinking of slave marriages in the context of the confessional debates over mixed marriages—how should the children be raised? Who would take the lead in the spiritual instruction of the household, including servants?—is problematic, since by law and custom, most enslaved parents had no say in how their children were raised and did not constitute separate households. But the reality remains that, among colonial Catholics, enslaved Africans experienced mixed marriages to a far greater degree than white recusants. How they navigated the emotional and spiritual challenges of loving someone of a different faith is one of the lost stories of colonial Catholicism.

Marriage thus remained the most elusive sacrament for enslaved Africans in English America, whether they resided on the Jesuit manors or in the households of wealthy Catholic or Anglican planters. Pockets of sacramental conformity certainly existed, lending some stability to enslaved families who faced the constant threat of separation whenever there was a death or financial crisis in the master's household. Those Africans who were owned directly by the Jesuit farms ("Priest slaves") had the most sacramental protection and married in the church at the same rate as their white counterparts. What those marriages meant, however, is less clear, and the Jesuits did not hesitate to break up families by sale when they faced their own financial crisis after the order was dissolved in the 1770s.

Of the three sacraments considered in this chapter, baptism entailed the lowest level of commitment on the part of slaveholders to a shared ritual community. Once they had erected legal and customary barriers to the association between baptism and freedom, they could extend the sacrament to their bondspeople without straining the protocols of racial exclusion that governed white-Black interactions. A baptized slave required little more of a planter than an unbaptized slave beyond the right to a Christian first name and attendance at mass whenever a priest happened by. Communion and marriage troubled those protocols on a deeper level. The feast of the eucharist brought whites and Blacks together in a physically intimate setting, on a semiregular basis, to confront the mystery of transubstantiation. These moments of transcendence were few and far between for most colonial Catholics, however, who had neither regular access to the sacrament of the mass nor the desire to commune side by side with the Africans and Natives in their midst.

Marriage was, in contrast, a singular event for Catholics. But it conferred a permanent change in status that cut to the heart of the slaveholders' power: the right to make and unmake families. Ethically as well as legally, marriage was (in theory, at least) a sacramental bond that all members of the Catholic community were bound to respect. It's an open question whether we should be more impressed that some colonial Catholics did respect the marriage bond between enslaved men and women or that so many did not.

Conclusion

The rituals of life considered together in this chapter were intended by the Catholic Church to give life to individuals and communities alike. Baptism initiated the newborn child or new convert into the faith, but it was also a participatory ritual for the entire congregation who stood witness to the event. Marriage created a new family out of two individuals, who were then enjoined to "be fruitful and multiply." From marriages came new households and new children, the building blocks of any community of faith. Communion was, as its very name suggests, the most communal of all the Catholic sacraments: a daily, weekly, or monthly sharing of the body and blood of Christ that knit the congregation into one body. Beyond these discrete sacraments lay a host of more quotidian activities that continued the life-giving power of the rituals beyond the walls of the church: the bestowing of names that recalled beloved saints or family members, the selection of godparents to serve as fictive kin to the baptized child, the prayers and penances that prepared the communicant to receive the eucharist, the donning of best clothes to honor God in his house, the preparing of certain foods and the abstaining from others in the seasonal cycle of feasts and fasts, the posting of banns three times in the church to announce an upcoming marriage, the exchange of rings that were visible tokens of the couple's union, the intimacies of the marriage bed and the communal rituals of childbirth. Collectively, these acts small and large made up the substance of lived religion for Anglo-American Catholics.

Rituals of life could—and often did—take place in the home as well as in the church. The Church and its priests fought the domestication of the sacraments even as they recognized the necessity of moving some rituals from the church to the home in an environment where priests were scarce and penal laws unforgiving. Lay Catholics both in England and abroad had no such qualms, and time and again expressed their preference for baptisms and marriages to take place at home. That private religious rituals rarely make an appearance in public documents has made the early English colonies (outside of Puritan New England) appear a sacramental wasteland to observers then and now. The lament was universal: too few churches, too few clergy, and too few laws to govern the unruly multitudes who insisted on baptizing and marrying in their own time and in their own way. Despite the tumult of high mortality rates, disordered households, and the violence of plantation slavery, however, colonial Catholics fell in love, married, christened their children, feasted and fasted, hosted mass for their families and neighbors on occasion, all within the confines of the household.

That simple fact highlights a crucial point of convergence between Protestant and Catholic ritual practice in the North American colonies. However much the Tridentine Church wanted to enclose lay piety within the walls of the church, colonial Catholics—like their Protestant neighbors—preferred to perform the sacraments of faith at home. This was a challenge on a global scale for the early modern Catholic Church wherever its missionaries ran up against local customs and frontier conditions, but it was a burden shared in the Americas by the more liturgical Protestant denominations (such as the Anglicans) as well. The domestication of Christian ritual had far-reaching consequences for both faith communities: it undercut the power of the ministry by reducing clerics to the status of supplicants in colonial households, it enhanced the spiritual authority of women as guardians of custom while exposing fault lines of wealth and privilege within the larger colonial community, and it exposed rituals intended to unify the mystical body of Christ to the corrosive effects of racial slavery.

For Catholics, however, domesticated space could never fully be holy space. The shift to receiving the sacraments at home meant an inevitable loss of connection to the universal church; that was the price of colonial adaptation. Only in a consecrated church, under the ministration of a priest, could the full salvific power of the sacraments—most crucially, the eucharist—be realized. Colonial recusants, especially those who were fortunate enough to maintain their own households, did their best to transform ordinary space into sacred space by opening their homes to itinerant priests, setting aside dedicated rooms and furnishings for religious services, investing in precious liturgical vessels, and inviting their poorer neighbors to participate in the sacrifice of the mass. Weddings and baptisms were celebrated in parlors, using everyday objects like tables and basins in place of altars and fonts. The line between the sacred and the profane was thus especially porous in colonial recusant communities. Whether this was experienced as a spiritual loss or as an opportunity to develop a more lay-centered piety is an open question. We know that the American Catholic Church that emerged after the political and legal revolutions of the late eighteenth century broke the back of the establishment was unusually attentive to lay concerns. The roots of lay Catholic empowerment lie in the colonial household.[70]

When colonial Catholics came to the end of their lives, they died and were often buried within the environs of those same households. Perhaps at no other moment in the ritual life of a Catholic was the presence of a priest more necessary and desired, for only a priest could hear one's final confession, administer last rites, and pray for one's soul. How colonial Catholics navigated the final sacramental frontier of death is the topic of the next chapter.

70. Leslie Woodcock Tentler, *American Catholics: A History* (New Haven, Conn., 2020); Farrelly, *Papist Patriots*.

CHAPTER FIVE

"They Make a Great Adoe at Their Burials"

Rituals of Death

O N OCTOBER 26, 1623, an upper floor of the French ambassador's residence in Blackfriars, London, collapsed. Some two hundred to three hundred English Catholics had gathered to hear the Jesuit Robert Drury preach, overstraining the old wooden structure. As the building pancaked, dozens of worshippers were crushed to death, "buried and brused between the rubbish and the timber." The final death toll would reach nearly one hundred—"a wofull spectacle" to the crowds who gathered to view the wreckage the next day.[1] It did not escape notice that, in the "new stile" calendar Britain had yet to adopt, October 26 was November 5, a day of infamy in Jacobean England. The gruesome demise of so many Catholics in the final years of James I's reign sparked horror, grief, and (among Protestants) righteous delight. Amid the public fascination with the event as a sign of God's judgment in the ongoing confessional battles of Stuart England, one simple question stood out: What happened to the bodies? England's recusant community was accustomed to dealing with death on an individual or family scale, finding ways to circumvent or flout the prohibition on burying excommunicates in the nation's Anglican churchyards when a loved one died. Now they had to find a way to inter some one hundred Catholic corpses in the heart of the capital. It was a daunting task for a community that normally operated in the shadows.

---

1. *Something Written by Occasion of That Fatall and Memorable Accident in the Blacke-Friers on Sonday, Being the 26 of October 1623* (London, 1623), 25. This pamphlet claimed there were two hundred people in attendance, where another claimed three hundred; see W. C., *The Fatall Vesper; or, A True and Punctuall Relation of That Lamentable and Fearefull Accident, Hapning on Sunday in the Afternoone Being the 26. of October Last, by the Fall of a Roome in the Black-Friers . . .* (London, 1623). Alexandra Walsham provides a superb reading of the textual and visual representations of this event in the London press in "'The Fatall Vesper': Providentialism and Anti-Popery in Late Jacobean London," *Past and Present*, no. 144 (August 1994), 36–87.

An untold number of bodies vanished overnight from the wreckage, presumably rescued by family members for private burial. Some of the wealthier victims were claimed by their relatives and (we presume, again) buried in parishes using the Anglican rites, the typical fate of church papists and crypto-Catholics. Many more—somewhere between thirty and sixty, depending on which source one credits—were hastily buried in two mass graves dug by the French ambassador's staff on the grounds before they could be subject to desecration from the Protestant "throng" urged on by the bishop of London, who directed that the dead (as excommunicates) be stripped and "buried on the refuse pile." A "blacke Crosse of wood, about foure foot high" was erected over the "great pit" that served as a common grave for forty-plus bodies, though the cross was removed the next day to avoid any "scandall" from "the people that then, and after, came to that house" to gawk and jeer. A smaller pit was then dug in the ambassador's "Garden," where perhaps another fifteen bodies were interred. Although there are lists of the presumed dead, we don't know for sure who was buried in the ambassador's grounds, who received a Catholic burial in a secret location, or who was buried in an Anglican churchyard. It was the "meaner sort" who were most likely interred on the grounds, "without mass or matins," while "great persons" were "stolen away by their friends." At the end of the day, we can account for only about two-thirds of the bodies, leaving us forever in the dark about the postmortem fate of some two dozen recusants.[2]

The Blackfriars calamity offers a snapshot of the various ways England's Catholics buried their dead in the penal age. Death was the final front in England's confessional wars, the site where belief, law, prejudice, custom, and memory clashed over recusant bodies. Of all the rituals of life and death that Protestants and Catholics participated in, none generated more soteriological angst or public confrontations than funerals. The Reformation had so thoroughly assaulted the theological foundations and the sacramental complex surrounding death that no aspect of the process of dying was unaffected—the initial laying out and preparation of the body in the home, the ringing of bells to announce the death and summon the faithful to the graveyard, the

2. Lisa McClain, *Lest We Be Damned: Practical Innovation and Lived Experience among Catholics in Protestant England, 1559–1642* (New York, 2004), 174 ("refuse pile"); Thomas Goad, *The Dolefull Even-Song; or, A True, Particular and Impartiall Narration of That Fearefull and Sudden Calamity, Which Befell the Preacher Mr. Drury a Jesuite, and the Greater Part of His Auditory, by the Downefall of the Floore at an Assembly in the Black-Friers* . . . (London, 1623).

FIGURE 15. *No Plot No Powder.* 1623. Satirical print depicting the collapse of the Catholic chapel in the home of the French ambassador, Blackfriars, London. Published by Thomas Jenner (London, 1623). Courtesy of the British Museum

procession of the coffin through the streets, the ceremonial interring of the corpse either in the church itself or in the cemetery, the customs of mourning that followed burial, and the seasonal commemorations of the date of death by the larger community. At each step along the way, the Reformers dismantled old customs and created a ritual vacuum in which antagonisms flourished.

After a brief overview of these Reformation-era disputes over how and where to bury the dead, we turn to the "mortuary politics" of England and its North American colonies. Death was a far more disordered affair in the colonies, at least during the early decades of English settlement, which meant that the opportunities for confessional improvisation were greater as well. For too many men and women who died far from home, whether home was originally East Anglia, Ireland, or the Kongo, a decent burial with rites they would have recognized as orthodox within their native faith traditions was beyond their grasp.[3]

Reforming Death and Dying

In the late medieval world, burial was not a discrete sacrament but rather a composite of several sacramental acts. Traditional Christians expected a priest to visit the sick, anoint them with holy oil (the sacrament of extreme unction), hear confession and administer the eucharist (two more sacraments), and pray with the family for a peaceful passing. The moment of death would then be announced by the pealing of church bells, which rang on and off until the final handful of dirt was thrown on the coffin. (Given the high mortality rates, bell ringing was an omnipresent feature of village life.) The corpse would be washed and wrapped in a shroud, which typically featured a cross either embroidered in the cloth or placed on the body. Other ritual objects might be enclosed within the shroud, a rosary or a pilgrim badge, perhaps. Along the route to the burial ground, the procession stopped at every public cross to circle the cross, kneel, and pray. Burial was always in consecrated ground—the cemetery for most people and under the floor of the church for the highborn (the closer to the altar, the better). The funeral would be followed by a wake, a gathering of the family and friends to feast, drink, share stories, and mourn. Only then did the real work of salvation begin: the procuring and performing of prayers for the dead to guide the soul through purgatory to heaven. Whenever they could afford it, England's medieval Christians paid the local priest to pray for their dead loved ones. These bequests could range from a shilling or two to enormous gifts of gold intended to purchase hundreds of years of prayer. The wealthiest built chantries, chapels staffed with resident priests whose sole purpose was to recite prayers for the dead.[4]

3. The phrase "mortuary politics" comes from Vincent Brown's path-breaking work on death and deathways in colonial Jamaica, *The Reaper's Garden: Death and Power in the World of Atlantic Slavery* (Cambridge, Mass., 2008).

4. For a good discussion of the sacramental complex of death before and after the Reformation, see Peter Marshall, *Beliefs and the Dead in Reformation England* (New York, 2002).

To undo such a complex and multilayered process was the work of generations of Reformers. They tackled it with zeal. As early as 1551, Bishop John Hooper issued a set of injunctions that attacked the mortuary culture of traditional Christianity. He banned "knells or forthfares" and prohibited crosses of any kind (wax or wood) to be buried with the body. A decade later, Bishop James Pilkington of Durham enumerated the many "superstition[s] . . . wherein the papists infinitely offend": "masses, diriges, trentals, singing, ringing, holy water, hallowed places, years', days', and month-minds, crosses, pardon-letters to be buried with them, mourners, *de profundis,* by every lad that could say it, dealing of money solemnly for the dead, watching of the corpse at home, bell and banner, with many more than I can reckon." By the 1600s, little seems to have changed, although Catholics had become more inventive in adapting their burial rituals to skirt the law: a 1607 checklist of popish superstitions included "superfluous ringing, superstitious burning of candles over the cor[p]se in the day time, after it bee light. Or praying for the dead at crosses or places where crosses have beene, in the way to the church, or any other superstitious use of crosses with towells, palmes, met-wands, or other memories of idolatry at burialls." Now Catholics used everyday objects like towels and staffs (metewands) instead of consecrated sacramentals to form crosses on top of the corpse and stopped at places where there were only ghost memories of the wayside crosses that had once dominated the spiritual topography of England. Again, we see the rich sensory environment of Catholic rituals, in which bells and candles in particular figure prominently as spiritual conduits.[5]

In stark contrast, the Reformed burial ritual was an austere affair. It was no longer necessary for a priest to visit a dying person, though a minister might offer comfort to her and her family. No religious objects of any kind were to be buried with the corpse, either tucked in the shroud or placed in the ground, and the procession to the graveyard made no detours along the way. Bells were rung only three times (the "threefold peal"): one short peal at the time of death, one before the burial, and one after. There was a strong association between bells and prayers for the dead, which explains in part

5. Marshall, *Beliefs and the Dead,* 97, 135; "An Exposition upon Nehemiah," in Rev. James Scholefield, ed., *The Works of James Pilkington, B.D.* (New York, 1968), 318. The 1607 injunctions were issued repeatedly in the first third of the seventeenth century, revealing a strong current of lay resistance to the Reformed burial ritual and a special attachment to the presence of the cross.

why Reformers were so determined to curb them. The burial itself was short, even perfunctory by medieval standards, in keeping with the Reformed notion of deritualization. A funeral sermon might accompany the burial if the family wished to pay for it, though none was required. Excessive mourning—especially the Irish custom of keening—was discouraged, as was excessive feasting and carousing at the wake. Most important, there were to be no prayers for the dead: since purgatory itself had been eliminated by the Reformers, there was no longer any need for the prayers of the living to shorten one's time in spiritual limbo. The dead were dead, and the living had no soteriological connection to them.[6]

Like most early moderns, Anglo-Americans were accustomed to treating certain dead bodies as pollutants that needed to be ritually destroyed—suicides were buried at a public crossroad with a stake through their hearts, for example, and traitors were disemboweled and quartered after (and sometimes before) death. Soldiers who died in the continent's many religious wars were often denied "decent Rites of Burial," as was the case in France, where the bodies of English soldiers were "thrown into a Hole like a Dog," according to one newspaper report.[7] But the extension of these rites of desecration to fellow *English* Christians was a new thing in the Reformation era. Sixteen Protestants who died in jail during Mary's reign were reputedly denied "Christian burial" and buried "in Dung-hils" instead. In an act of retributive justice, the authorities suggested throwing recusant Anne Foster's body on a "dung heap" (dung is a common motif in the polemical literature) after she died in prison in 1587; the archbishop of York instead decreed that her corpse be "laid openly on the bridge in the common street for all the world to gaze and wonder at" like a common criminal.[8]

---

6. This is a simplified account of the Reformation of the dead; as Erik Seeman points out in his important revision of the standard narrative, the link between the living and the dead was severed in theory but not always in practice in Anglo-American Protestant communities (Seeman, *Speaking with the Dead in Early America* [Philadelphia, 2019]).

7. *Flying-Post: or, The Post-Master* (London), Aug. 28–30, 1712; another account of the sacrilegious burial of English soldiers who were "deem'd Hereticks" by the French appeared in the *American Weekly Mercury* (Philadelphia), Aug. 5, 1724, [2]. Those who deserted from the English army were sometimes treated in a similar manner, out of fear that churches would "be Polluted with their Carcases," as the *Observator* (London), May 1, 1703, put it.

8. *Weekly Journal, or, British Gazetteer* (London), Feb. 16, 1717; Peter Marshall, "Confessionalisation and Community in the Burial of English Catholics, c. 1570–1700," in Nadine Lewycky and Adam Morton, eds., *Getting Along? Religious Identities and Confessional Relations in Early Modern England—Essays in Honour of Professor W. J. Sheils* (New York, 2016), 57–75 (quotations on 65–66). Foster's husband, John, was the city's coroner, and he was able to strike a bargain to "bury her where he would, without any other solemnity than to put

Amid these more spectacular displays of rage against the heretical corpses in their midst, many English parishes went about the business of burying their dead—Protestant and Catholic—with little fanfare or overt conflict in the sixteenth and seventeenth centuries. Not until 1606 were England's recusants routinely considered "excommunicates" and hence undeserving of Christian burial; before then, only those who failed to turn up when summoned to the ecclesiastical courts were deemed excommunicates. Following the passage of this parliamentary act, Archbishop Bancroft acknowledged the Church's "slacknes hitherto" in allowing Catholics access to parish graveyards and ordered ministers to "bury neither in the church nor the churchyard . . . any popeish recusants, that dye excommunicated," but enforcement of his injunctions was, in the words of one historian, "limp" at best. Throughout the seventeenth century, the record reveals as much collusion as conflict between recusants and parish ministers. Whereas it took a company of "armed papists" to forcibly inter Alice Wellington in the churchyard at Allens Moore in 1605, Dorothy Lawson's corpse was escorted to the door of All Saints' Church in Newcastle by the town's Protestant "magistrates and aldermen" before being "deliver'd . . . to the Catholicks only" for burial. Clearly, many factors went into deciding the fate of a Catholic corpse: status, wealth, gender, region, and (most important) the attitude of the parish minister and the local community.[9]

When recusants faced a hostile minister or congregation, they resorted to a number of tactics to bury their dead in consecrated ground. Secret nocturnal burials were commonplace in certain areas of the country; the parish records of Hathersage in Derbyshire recorded thirteen nighttime burials of recusants in a span of two years (1629–1631). Because such burials were illegal, it's rare to find open endorsement of the practice in parish records. More common are such after-the-fact acknowledgments as "James Pattinson (being excom'd) was secretly buryed by some" or "the body of Ellen wife of Richd Ensor, a popeling" was "cast into the ground." Some degree of connivance was surely required to pull off these clandestine burials, which involved, at a minimum, candles, a procession of sorts, and a priest. More surreptitiously,

---

her in the grave." The enterprising John placed his wife's body in the grave of the martyred earl of Northumberland, fulfilling her desire to be buried in Catholic ground, if not with Catholic rites; see Lisa McClain, *Lest We Be Damned: Practical Innovation and Lived Experience among Catholics in Protestant England, 1559–1642* (New York, 2004), 273–274.

9. Marshall, "Confessionalisation and Community," in Lewycky and Morton, eds., *Getting Along?* 63, 66. The 1606 Act of Parliament deemed all those convicted of recusancy to be "reputed to all intents and purposes disabled, as a person lawfully and duly excommunicated" (quoted ibid., 58–59).

some recusant families managed to smuggle a bit of consecrated dirt from the local parish churchyard into the coffin of their loved one, even when they were barred access to the churchyard itself. One archbishop claimed in 1606 that it was "a secret practice of the Papists" to place a layer of earth, blessed by a priest, between the sheets wrapped around the corpse "and so bury them they care not where, for they say they are thus buried in consecrated earth."[10]

Women played a starring role in many of these battles as the executors of their deceased husbands' wishes and guardians of collective memory. A striking number of the graveyard clashes in Britain and North America involved women—as mourners, protestors, or corpses. Katherine Ingleby of North Yorkshire was buried surreptitiously "at sunset" in 1600 by nine women. In Dublin, an English minister who tried to intervene in a recusant burial was attacked by the women present and thrown into the open grave, where they threatened to "bury him, until he promised not to trouble them further." A riot broke out in 1623 at the funeral of a Protestant daughter of an Irish Catholic peer, orchestrated almost entirely by women determined to reclaim the apostate for the recusant community. Four "weomen being the Captainesses," accompanied by "about foure score other weomen," assaulted the minister at the door of the church, "rent his surplis, toare out a leafe of the Communion booke, and with blowes did offer him such violence that the better disposed people were inforced to reskue him."[11]

Women were the custodians of the dead in the early modern world: they washed the bodies, wrapped them in shrouds, and led the community in mourning rituals. The sense of special ownership that recusant women felt over the disposition of their dead comes through clearly in these accounts and is part of a broader post-Reformation pattern of female sacramental activism. The *Boston Gazette* reprinted an account of a graveyard confrontation in Germany between Catholics and Protestants that occurred when a "Calvinist" tried to bury his child "at the common Burying-Place, by Women, according to the Custom there, without Singing, or Ringing the Bells." The

10. Ibid., 60–61, 70.

11. For a discussion of women's role in English graveyard confrontations, see Marshall, *Beliefs and the Dead*, 139. Katherine Ingleby: John Bossy, *The English Catholic Community, 1570–1850* (New York, 1976), 141. "Bury him": Clodagh Tait, *Death, Burial, and Commemoration in Ireland, 1550–1650* (London, 2002), 55–56. Peter Lake and Michael Questier narrate the story of one recusant female rebel in *The Trials of Margaret Clitherow: Persecution, Martyrdom, and the Politics of Sanctity in Elizabethan England* (London, 2011). On the role of female recusants in resisting the Church establishment more generally, see Roland Connelly, *Women of the Catholic Resistance: In England, 1540–1680* (Durham, U.K., 1997).

local Capuchins intervened and "obliged the Women to go away without burying the Child," then gathered a "Mob" by ringing the bells "to call the People together" to block the door of the church. The bereaved parents "were obliged to deposit the Child's Body in a Cellar" until the authorities sorted out the matter. By the seventeenth century, recusant women were accustomed to safeguarding the family's Catholicism in the face of punitive fines for Non-conformity, but these episodes also speak to early modern women's role as the guardians of custom as well as creed.[12]

Women played such a prominent role in Catholic funeral rituals because the site of burial for most recusants was private land. Burials, too, became domestic sacramental affairs for England's Catholics, especially those living in the north, where seigneurial Catholicism flourished. Steep recusancy fines and exclusion from parish life led one poor man to prefer a final resting place in a field near his home to the churchyard; "I have now a house from which I cannot be driven." Some recusant communities were able to establish private cemeteries of their own on manorial lands, such as "Harkirke" (or the New Churchyard) created by a Catholic landowner in Lancashire in 1611. William Blundell recalled, "The churches in all parts denied them [recusants] burial; some were laid in the fields, some in gardens, and others in highways as it chanced. One of these, as I have heard it credibly reported, being interred in a common lane, was pulled out by the hogs and used accordingly." In order "to prevent the like for the future," Blundell's grandfather enclosed part of his estate "for the decent burial of such poor catholics as were otherwise likely to want it." Between 1611 and 1686, "above one hundred lay catholics and a dozen or fourteen priests" were buried in Harkirke, according to Blundell. The existence of the Catholic burial ground was an open secret in the diocese. Gentry women presided over these private burials as they did over the baptisms and marriages taking place within their domains.[13]

All corpses needed to find a final resting place, preferably in hallowed ground. That was the hard truth with which England's sparring religious communities had to reckon in the centuries following the break with Rome. In the words of Christopher Haigh, "Everyone wanted Christian burial—and

12. *Boston Gazette*, Nov. 21–28, 1726, [2].

13. "I have now a house": Marshall, "Confessionalisation and Community," in Lewycky and Morton, eds., *Getting Along?* 70; Margaret Blundell, ed., *Cavalier: Letters of William Blundell to His Friends, 1620–1689* (London, 1933), 246, quoted in David Cressy, *Birth, Marriage, and Death: Ritual, Religion, and the Life-Cycle in Tudor and Stuart England* (New York, 1997), 465–466.

the Church of England had the graveyards." As the victims of the Blackfriars tragedy learned, for many Catholics that meant an unceremonious burial in yards, ditches, and gardens as the final act of their earthly journey. Colonial Catholics living (and dying) beyond the reach of the Jesuit manors in Maryland faced a similar fate, in their case compounded by the alienation of dying in a strange land far from home. How colonial Christians, Protestants and Catholics alike, navigated the sacramental perils of death and dying in English America is the subject of the remainder of this chapter.[14]

Dying in English America: Grave Matters

The chronic shortage of clergy and churches throughout much of English America in the seventeenth and early eighteenth centuries created unprecedented challenges when it came to death and dying. Death was as omnipresent as clergy were scarce in every colony outside New England. Phantasmic visions of death saturate the earliest chronicles of the first English settlements in North America. The Pilgrims who arrived on the coast of Massachusetts in 1620 found a macabre scene of abandoned Indian villages littered with dead bodies rotting where they fell, victims of the smallpox epidemic of 1616–1618 that wiped out nearly the entire Native population. The thousands of "bones and skulls . . . lying above the ground" resembled nothing so much as a "new found Golgatha." An English soldier would use the same image to describe newly conquered Jamaica in the 1650s, when there were "soe many funerals, and graves all the towne over that it is a very Golgotha." Every new colony had its own "starving time," when food was scarce and relations with the native inhabitants precarious, though Virginia's season of misery would become infamous for reported incidents of English cannibalism.[15] The staggering mortality rates of the early years, in which as many as 80 or 90 percent of new immigrants died within a few years of their arrival in the Americas, did slowly recede as the seventeenth century gave way to the eighteenth, but

14. Christopher Haigh, *The Plain Man's Pathways to Heaven: Kinds of Christianity in Post-Reformation England, 1570–1640* (New York, 2007), 6.

15. William Bradford, *History of Plymouth Plantation* (New York, 1890), 38–39 ("bones and skulls"); Thomas Morton, *New English Canaan; or, New Canaan, Containing an Abstract of New England* (n.p., 1632), 18–19 ("Golgatha"); C. H. Firth, ed., *The Narrative of General Venables: With an Appendix of Papers Relating to the Expedition to the West Indies and the Conquest of Jamaica, 1654–1655* (London, 1900), 142 ("soe many funerals"); Kathleen Donegan, *Seasons of Misery: Catastrophe and Colonial Settlement in Early America* (Philadelphia, 2014).

epidemics and near-constant warfare of both the imperial and the racial kind kept the killing machine going. Just when white mortality began to stabilize, the influx of thousands of enslaved Africans—debilitated by the brutalism of the Middle Passage, which itself killed 10 to 25 percent of captives—caused death rates to soar once again in certain regions. It is a commonplace of early modern societies that death stalked the living, but death strode through English America with a swagger. And every death prompted a spiritual reckoning. This was true whether the gods one worshipped were white or Black.[16]

We might expect that the universal experience of untimely death would dampen the skirmishes over funerary rites that rent so many English parishes after the Reformation, but in fact the same quarrels and tussles occurred in the North American colonies. Anglicans and Puritans faced off in New England over where and how to bury their dead, while Dutch Reformed and Lutherans battled over the fate of corpses in the middle colonies. The island colonies, with their motley ethnic and denominational makeup, saw their fair share of graveyard confrontations. And everyone complained about the extortionate fees charged by ministers for burials. Where recusants fit in this larger story of mortuary politics is difficult to discern. In most places, their numbers were too small to embolden the kind of collective challenge to the Anglican monopoly of churchyards that occurred in northern England. The retarded nature of sacramental practice in large swaths of the North American backcountry means, too, that funerals were often hasty and ramshackle affairs for many colonials, Catholic and Protestant. The creation of formal burial grounds (churchyards) usually lagged behind the creation of churches, so Christians of all stripes had to make do with informal burials even after parishes were established.

The archaeological record shows that the earliest burials in the first permanent English settlement in North America—Jamestown, Virginia—were rushed affairs, even though a rudimentary church had been erected within

---

The classic account of Virginia's "starving time" is Edmund S. Morgan, *American Slavery, American Freedom: The Ordeal of Colonial Virginia* (New York, 1975). For a more recent analysis of the charge of cannibalism, see Rachel B. Herrmann, "The 'Tragicall Historie': Cannibalism and Abundance in Colonial Jamestown," *WMQ*, 3d Ser., LXVIII (2011), 47–74.

16. The study of colonial deathways is thriving in the academy. To cite just a few examples, see Erik R. Seeman, *Death in the New World: Cross-Cultural Encounters, 1492–1800* (Philadelphia, 2010); Brown, *Reaper's Garden;* Nancy Isenberg and Andrew Burstein, eds., *Mortal Remains: Death in Early America* (Philadelphia, 2003).

two months of landfall. Graves were shallow and haphazardly arranged, bodies interred in their clothes rather than in proper shrouds (one even had a pipe and a spoon still in his pockets). An old wooden packing crate served as the makeshift coffin for one of the few corpses lucky enough to have one at all. The Virginia House of Burgesses tried repeatedly through the 1620s and 1630s to legislate proper burial in a churchyard, defined as "a place empaled in, sequestered only to the buryal of the dead." The authorities' desire to maintain proper English customs was thwarted, however, by the obscene mortality rates of the early years, in which people dropped like flies and were buried as quickly as possible. Very few had the comfort of a priest—Protestant or Catholic—as they lay dying; "Many dep[ar]te the World in their owne dung for want of help in their sicknes," one observer lamented in 1623. The Virginia Assembly tried to fix this, too, mandating that "When any person is dangerouslie sicke in any parrish, the mynister haveing knowledge thereof shall resort unto him or her to instruct and comfort them in their distresse." They were fighting a losing battle against religious indifference and the geography of dispersal, however, and by the 1630s, the vestrymen of one parish in Accomack had agreed that those living "remote" from the parish could bury their dead on "the land of william Blower where william Berriman liveth," after notifying the minister and providing "convenient meanes for his coming ther to bury the dead." Private burials had thus become the norm within a single generation of settlement in Virginia—a pattern that would be repeated throughout English America.[17]

As with private baptisms and weddings, home burials imposed an extra financial burden on colonial households, which exacerbated the tensions over funerary rites. Anglican ministers routinely charged more for private burials than for those performed in the churchyard; a schedule of fees from South Carolina specifies "Burials in the Churchyard 9 s.—in Plantations 15 s." Strictly speaking, the Anglican clergy were not supposed to charge any fee for Christian burial. But fees had long since become customary (to the point

17. William M. Kelso, *Jamestown, the Buried Truth* (Charlottesville, Va., 2006), 163–166; William Waller Hening, ed., *The Statutes at Large; Being a Collection of All the Laws of Virginia, from the First Session of the Legislature, in the Year 1619* . . . (New York, 1823), I, 122–123, 157–158; Susan Myra Kingsbury, ed., *Records of the Virginia Company of London*, IV (Washington, D.C., 1935), 23; Susie M. Ames, ed., *County Court Records of Accomack-Northampton, Virginia, 1632–1640* (Washington, D.C., 1954), 54. The law was reenacted multiple times, in 1632 (ibid., 161, 185) and in 1640 (227). See Seeman's discussion of the legal effort to reform burial practices in colonial Virginia in *Death in the New World*, 97–98.

of excess, many thought) both in England and in the colonies, and disputes over burial fees were endemic. "Catholic or protestant, puritan or conformist, the clergy of the sixteenth and seventeenth century were notorious for their exaction of fees," David Cressy concludes in his survey of English ritual life. In the colonies, the vestry of Kent Island, Virginia, wrote to complain to the bishop of London that their rector only bothered to perform funerals if there was a fee for a sermon attached: "As to burying the dead, if there is to be a funeral sermon in the case, he seldom fails coming, but if the deceased be poor so that [there is] no sermon, it is altogether vanity to expect him." Farther to the south, when a series of deadly epidemics hit Charleston in the summer of 1711, the SPG commissary Gideon Johnston did his duty but grumbled about the paltry compensation he received for his labors. "Nver was there a more sickly or fatall season than this for the small Pox, Pestilential ffeavers, Pleurisies, and fflex's have destroyed great numbers here of all Sorts, both Whites, Blacks, and Indians," he wrote. "Three Funeralls of a day, and som times four are now very usual; and all that I gett by these is a few rotten Glov's and an abundance of trouble day and night." Johnston's frustration was typical of colonial ministers—they both relied on and resented the fees that supplemented their meager stipends. The line between fair compensation and extortion was difficult to draw, even for the established church, and this was doubly so in the colonies, where clerical salaries were always a bone of contention.[18]

The ever-more-lavish funeral festivities that Anglo-Americans of all ranks and confessions indulged in over the course of the seventeenth and eighteenth centuries stoked tensions. At a minimum, a "decent" burial involved feeding the mourners and providing them with tokens of commemoration. The will of John Lloyd of Maryland directed that he be "decently buried in the Ordinary burying place of St Maries Chappell yard" and provided for those who "shall carry my Corps to Church each of them a black mourning Ribbon and a payre of gloves." Samuel Sewall of Boston was an inveterate funeral-goer and noted in his journal every burial he attended and what he received. In January 1698, he calculated that over the previous two years he had "been a [Pall] Bearer" at thirty funerals, for which he had received a

18. "Further Notes Attributed to Charles Martyn," Apr. 11, 1762, Fulham Papers, X, fols. 153–154; Cressy, *Birth, Marriage, and Death*, 456–457; vestry of Kent Island to bishop of London, July 1726, complaints against Rev. Thomas Phillips, in William S. Perry, ed., *Historical Collections Relating to the American Colonial Church*, 5 vols. (Hartford, Conn., 1870–1878), IV, 257; Frank J. Klingberg, ed., *Carolina Chronicle: The Papers of Commissary Gideon Johnston, 1707–1716* (Berkeley, Calif., 1946), 99.

variety of funerary items—"Scarf, Gloves, Ring." But these minimal expectations were often exceeded. Sewall's fellow Bostonian Benjamin Colman provided 144 pairs of gloves for his daughter's funeral in 1735, a relatively modest number in an era when a wealthy family might distribute a thousand or more gloves to mourners. The poor as well as the rich wanted to bury their dead in style. When the widow of an "ordinary planter" died in Maryland in 1662, the executor of her estate was outraged at the invoice presented by James Lee for funeral expenses, which included "three barrells of beer" and "36 yards of black Ribining at 12 lb per yard" plus two pounds of gunpowder for a "rediculous" display of ceremonial shooting such "as thay doe at a young souldiers death or other Commanders in warre." The very ordinary Ursula Lenton did not deserve such honors, in the eyes of some of her neighbors. Although orthodox Puritans like Sewall were the most vocal critics of the commercialization of death, complaints about the high cost of funerals to mourners crop up throughout Anglo-America. This was more than a financial concern; the creeping ritualization of Protestant life threatened to reintroduce an untoward materialism into the Reformed churches. By the late seventeenth century, gloves and rings had replaced crucifixes and rosaries as the material accompaniments of death, to the dismay of theological hardliners.[19]

Sewall's assiduous record-keeping of funerals (those he attended *and* those he avoided) also provides a window into the growing tensions between Puritans and Anglicans over proper burial rites, a harbinger of the graveyard politics that were the inevitable consequence of religious coexistence. On August 5, 1686, he recorded that "Wm Harrison, the Bodies-maker [bodice-maker], is buried, which is the first that I know of buried with the Common-Prayer Book in Boston." Three months later came the burials of "One Robison Esqr." and "Jno Griffin," the second and third to use the Anglican rite. The

---

19. *Archives of Maryland*, June 26, 1658, XLI, 116; *Diary of Samuel Sewall, 1674–1729*, I (Boston, 1878), 469–470. By the late seventeenth century, Cressy observes, "The English were said to be famous for cheap weddings and lavish funerals" (*Birth, Marriage, and Death*, 453). Benjamin Colman: Steven C. Bullock and Sheila McIntyre, "The Handsome Tokens of a Funeral: Glove-Giving and the Large Funeral in Eighteenth-Century New England," *WMQ*, 3d Ser., LXIX (2012), 305–346, esp. 305. Lee's funeral expenses: "Petition of James Lee re. the Charges He Incurred in Burying Ursula Lenton," Mar. 4, 1661/62, *Archives of Maryland*, LIII, 194, 209. The administrator of the Lenton estate refused to pay and was sued by Lee. On the material accompaniments to Anglican burials, see Lauren F. Winner, *A Cheerful and Comfortable Faith: Anglican Religious Practice in the Elite Households of Eighteenth-Century Virginia* (New Haven, Conn., 2010), chap. 5, "'To Comfort the Living': The Household Choreography of Death and Mourning."

Anglican "Office for Burial is a Lying, very bad office," he groused, since it "makes no difference between the precious and the vile." The burial of the royal governor's wife in February 1688 with full pomp and ceremony, including bell ringing and "unwonted illumination," incensed Sewall with its popish overtones. As had been (and still was) the case in England, the more sensory elements of the burial service—the "Flashing Tapers," torches, and bells that accompanied Lady Arabella's corpse through the streets of Boston—were often the focal point of sectarian ire.[20]

The animosity between the Congregationalists and Anglicans, who shared the Third Church meetinghouse in these years, spilled over into open confrontation. At the funeral of Edward Lilley, an "indecent conflict" broke out between the minister and the deacon over the Lilley family's wishes for a Nonconformist service. Deacon Frairy was arrested for "forbidding Ratliff [the rector of King's Chapel] to read Comon Prayer at the grave of old Lilly" after the family "had requested the parson to forbear." A few months later, the Puritan faction was better prepared and had "men enough ready in the streets" to ensure that the funeral of Major Howard take place as his wife directed rather than "in the buriing place" of the Church of England. Howard's corpse was accompanied to the North Church and interred in the churchyard there, demonstrating to the outraged Anglicans that the Puritans intended to "take upon them to dispose of the dead as well as they do of the Living." Rev. Gordon, one of the first SPG missionaries to breach the Puritan stronghold of Long Island, was buried "partly by fair means partly by force . . . in a Dissenting Meeting House" after he succumbed to disease only days after his arrival. These colonial versions of the graveyard battles of seventeenth-century England involved Puritans and Anglicans rather than Catholics, but the root of Nonconformist resistance to the established church was the same: a community's desire to bury their dead according to their own rites. More than a half century after the battles of the 1680s, Anglicans and Congregationalists were still accusing one another of interfering in burials.[21]

20. *Diary of Samuel Sewall,* I, 146, 156–157, 235. Sewall's response to Lady Arabella's funeral is quoted in Henry Wilder Foote, ed., *Annals of King's Chapel from the Puritan Age of New England to the Present Day,* 2 vols., I (Boston, 1900), 75, 189.

21. Foote, ed., *Annals of King's Chapel,* I, 75, 189; Rev. Joshua Moody to Increase Mather, Jan. 8, 1688, in Massachusetts Historical Society, *Collections,* 4th Ser., VIII (Boston, 1868), 370–371; Edward Randolph to bishop of London, Oct. 26, 1689, CO 5/855, no. 42, TNA; "Col. Lewis Morris of East Jersey to Mr. Arch Deacon Beveridge," East Jersey, Sept. 3, 1702, SPG Letters "A" Series, 1702–1737, I, no. 65, *British Online Archives,* https://britishonlinearchives .com. A writer to the *Boston Gazette, or Weekly Advertiser,* Apr. 17, 1753, [1], complained that

More stories of graveyard politics come from the mid-Atlantic colonies, where, in the eighteenth century, rival factions of German Lutherans competed for the souls (and bodies) of the Palatinates who had settled in the province. Henry Muhlenberg, the orthodox missionary, recorded one such dispute in 1747 when the sons of a Pietist "wanted to have their father buried in the Herrnhuter cemetery. The Herrnhuter preacher refused to bury him, so they asked Mr. Kurtz to deliver a funeral sermon in the Herrnhuter church." After some back-and-forth between the two ministers, the man was finally buried in the churchyard of the Pietist congregation but without its pastor; the interloper, Mr. Kurtz, "had to deliver his address standing in the snow beside the grave." In another church, the two factions used the dead body of a widow as a weapon. The local Pietists ("tosspots and loafers," according to Muhlenberg) took advantage of Muhlenberg's temporary absence from town to quickly dig a grave, so that when the embattled minister arrived the following day, "I found that the woman had been buried and that the congregation was divided." The congregation in Raritan-in-the-Hills was so deeply split over the proper way to inter their dead that the archaeological record reveals two distinct patterns of burial in the cemetery: a "corporate pattern" favored by the orthodox and a "familial or individual" pattern used by the Pietists. Some 250 years later, the bitter divisions that rent these communities are still visible in the land.[22]

On the sugar islands, graveyard confrontations were as likely to be about class as about creed. One story comes from Edward Long's 1774 *History of Jamaica*, which tried to paint a balanced portrait of the virtues and vices of the island's Anglican clergy but had to concede that most were "better qualified to be retailers of salt-fish, or boatswains to privateers, than ministers of the Gospel." Long recounted one particularly nasty altercation between some "brother tars" and a minister over the latter's hasty burial of three sailors. The minister "thought to make quick work" of the burial by reading only one

---

the Congregationalist ministers in town routinely "intrude[d]" upon Anglican burials by "tak[ing] it upon themselves to accompany the funeral procession" without invitation and urged his fellow Anglicans to erect a "Hedge" between the two denominations to deter future intrusions.

22. Theodore G. Tappert and John W. Doberstein, trans., *The Journals of Henry Melchior Muhlenberg*, I (Philadelphia, 1942), 97, 172; John W. Lawrence, Paul W. Schopp, and Robert J. Lore, "'They Even Threaten the Sick That They Will Not Be Buried in the Churchyard': Salvage Archaeology of the Raritan-in-the-Hills Cemetery, Somerset County, New Jersey," *Historical Archaeology*, XLIII (2009), 93–114 (quotations on 112).

service over the three bodies, but the seamen "insisted upon three several readings, in honour of their comrades." The rector refused, and "the dispute came to blows," with the minister, the clerk, and the entire congregation "engaged pell-mell" in the fracas. Order was restored only when the rector "hurl[ed] two or three of the combatants headlong into the very grave that had been prepared for their inanimate friends." This was indeed, as the participants understood, an affair of "honour." All early modern burials were at heart, as Benjamin Kaplan has noted, rituals of honor—designed to separate the law-abiding from the criminal, the true believer from the heretic, the worthy from the unworthy. The ceremony performed was supposed to be appropriate to the social status of the deceased person.[23]

To bury a corpse with dishonor, with not enough or with too much pomp and ceremony, was a political as well as religious affront. Protestants and Catholics both understood this. When a member of the English delegation sent to Montreal died suddenly while inquiring into the fate of several captives taken in the region's ongoing wars, his corpse was treated as a malefactor's. Nathaniel Wheelwright described the "shameful" treatment of the Protestant dead at the Ursuline convent: "As is the Custom (to their shame be it spoken) if a Protestant dies among them, the Judge as soon as he is informed is obliged to demand the Body and . . . order it to be carried without the City and buried, as though the person had been a thief or a murderer." Aided by a sympathetic Quebecois, Wheelwright was able to arrange a clandestine burial for his colleague—"he was kind enough to give it a place in his Garden, where he was secretly and decently buried."[24]

The right to a "decent" burial was a universally understood code of honor in the early modern Atlantic world. Even in times of war, when moral codes could be suspended by belligerent nations, the proper disposition of the enemy dead was one of the rules of "just war" theory. To desecrate corpses or refuse to allow one's enemy to bury their own dead was a mark of savagery. No wars were more "savage" in this respect than the North American Indian wars of the seventeenth century, in which atrocity tales of bodies

23. Edward Long, *The History of Jamaica: Reflections on Its Situation, Settlements, Inhabitants, Climate, Products, Commerce, Laws, and Government*, 3 vols. (1774; rpt. Montreal, 2002), II, 238–239; Benjamin J. Kaplan, *Divided by Faith: Religious Conflict and the Practice of Toleration in Early Modern Europe* (Cambridge, Mass., 2007), 93.

24. Ann M. Little, "Cloistered Bodies: Convents in the Anglo-American Imagination in the British Conquest of Canada," *Eighteenth-Century Studies*, XXXIX (2006), 187–200 (quotations on 197).

scalped, burned, hacked apart, and denied burial circulated in rumor and print. During King Philip's War (1675–1677), English casualties were widely reported to "lye naked, wallowing in their blood" on the battlefield, unretrieved and unburied. This was the inevitable result of the disrespect for Native graves and corpses that the English had displayed for half a century by that point; indeed, mortuary politics played a key role in the conquest of the Americas as Indian graves were targeted for looting and destruction from the very beginning. In one of the first recorded acts of grave desecration in North America, Captain John Martin and his Jamestown crew "Beate the Salvages outt of the Island burned their howses ransaked their Temples, Tooke down the Corpes of their deade kings from of[f] their Toambs, and Caryed away their pearles Copp[er] and braceletts wherewth they doe decore their kings funeralles." This was a calculated affront to Native spiritual traditions as well as an act of colonial greed. The desecration of Indian graves was a precursor to the dismemberment of Indian bodies. A group of armed Narragansetts met with Roger Williams of Providence in 1655 to "demaund Satisfaction for the robbing of Pesiccush his Sisters grave and mangling of her flesh," a form of colonial violence that became a signature of European-Indian warfare in the seventeenth century.[25]

Honor rarely intruded into the mortuary politics of the plantation colonies, where brute force prevailed and Africans were deemed human chattel. But even slaveholders recognized that the withholding of Christian burial could be an effective instrument of discipline over the enslaved. Sometimes this meant outright refusal to bury Africans who had been baptized into one or another of the Christian sects. In the West Indies, where the Moravians had significant success in converting the enslaved, a recently baptized man was refused burial by his owner, who ordered that his body "be left to rot in the hut" as a punishment for converting to this Pietist sect. Two missionaries were able to "secretly" retrieve his body and give it "proper burial." Other times, this meant stripping the burial rite of its ceremonial and liturgical elements for enslaved Africans. New York's assembly passed a law in 1737 forbidding the

---

25. Jill Lepore, *The Name of War: King Philip's War and the Origins of American Identity* (New York, 1999), 79; Christopher Heaney, "A Peru of Their Own: English Grave-Opening and Indian Sovereignty in Early America," *WMQ*, 3d Ser., LXXIII (2016), 609–646; George Percy, "A Trewe Relacyon of the P[ro]ceedings and Ocurrentes of Momente W[hi]ch Have Hapned in Virginia . . ." (1625); Roger Williams to John Winthrop, Jr., ca. Feb. 15, 1654/55, in Glenn W. LaFantasie, ed., *The Correspondence of Roger Williams*, II, *1654–1682* (Providence, R.I., 1988), 425.

use of Anglican liturgical items in the burial of slaves—"no Pawl [will] be allowed or admitted at the Funeral of any Slave; and if any Slave shall hereafter presume to hold up a Pawl, or be a Pawl-bearer at the Funeral of any Slave, such Slave shall be publickly Whipped at the Publick Whipping Post." In either case, the message was clear: enslaved Africans had no honor in death as in life, no claim on the communal promise of a "decent" exit.[26]

Some graveyard politics involved the commemoration of the long dead rather than the burial of the newly deceased. Religious minorities on both sides of the Atlantic had deep memories of the desecrations their forbears had suffered for the faith. The Quakers of Massachusetts, who saw four of their own go the gallows in the 1650s and 1660s, tried several times to create a memorial on the site of their execution. Sewall reported in his diary for June 1685 that several Quakers had approached the governor to "ask leave to enclose the Ground the Hanged Quakers are buried in under or near the Gallows, with Pales." Since the execution site was Boston Commons, the town's council "unanimously" rejected the proposal. It was "very inconvenient," they declared, for "persons so dead and buried in the place to have any Monument." Undeterred, the Quakers went ahead and enclosed "a few Feet of Ground . . . with Boards," as Sewall reported two months later. A visiting Quaker in search of the site "where several of our Friends had suffered Death for the Truth" found the bedraggled memorial a few years later: "a kind of Pit near the Gallows, and full of Water, but two Posts at each End, which had been set there by means of . . . a reputable Friend." In New York, the bodies of Jacob Leisler and Jacob Milborne, the ringleaders of the Protestant faction that seized control of the colony in 1689 following the ouster of James II, were exhumed from their unconsecrated grave at the foot of the gallows seven years after their execution and reburied in the Dutch Reformed church over the vigorous opposition of the local pastor. According to contemporary accounts, the ritual disinterment of these Protestant "martyrs" occurred at midnight, accompanied by the "sound of trumpet and drumms." After lying in state for "some weeks," the (headless) bodies were buried inside the church on

26. Johann Jakob Bossard, ed., *Oldendorp's History of the Mission of the Evangelical Brethren on the Caribbean Islands of St. Thomas, St. Croix, and St. John* (Ann Arbor, Mich., 1987), 472; "A Law for Regulating the Burial of Slaves," *New-York Weekly Journal,* Mar. 13, 1737. The Moravians were one of the few Christian denominations to bury Black and white congregants together in their cemeteries, which they called "God's Acre"; see Jon F. Sensbach, "Race and the Early Moravian Church: A Comparative Perspective," *Transactions of the Moravian Historical Society,* XXXI (2000), 1–10.

October 20, 1698, and their "arms and hatchments of honor" hung on the walls. Not everyone was pleased—the anti-Leislerians (among whom were surely those recusants who had survived Leisler's papist purge) denounced the ceremony as the work of "the scum" of the colony.[27]

So far I've been exploring the terrain of colonial graveyard politics without much regard for the religious identity of those involved. The takeaway is that rituals of death were often flashpoints in the local, confessional, and racial politics in which Anglo-Americans of all persuasions were enmeshed after the Reformation. Certain themes recur on both sides of the Atlantic: the importance of bells, candles, trumpets, and drums in providing the sensory backdrop to theological arguments, the role of women as agitators, the codes of honor that dictated how and where the dead should be interred. Funerals were public affairs, then as now, and even burials that took place on private property left visible markers—sacramental scars—that could not be entirely concealed or disguised.

In North America, however, the chaotic conditions of the early settlement years, when ecclesiastical institutions were weak or absent and death omnipresent, leveled the sacramental playing field and left all denominations scrambling to find decent ways to bury their dead. Ritualized defilements of Native and African corpses reprised the "rage against the dead" that marked the Reformation in Europe; in so doing, they blurred the traditional lines between honorable and dishonorable burials by replacing creed with race as the axis of difference. Colonial Catholics had no churchyards of their own outside the Jesuit manors in Maryland and thus were forced to acquiesce to Anglican burials or find ways and places to inter their loved ones outside the ecclesiastical structure. In such an environment, the distinction between a Protestant and a Catholic burial—or an Anglican, Puritan, or Quaker one—threatened to collapse altogether.

Death and Colonial Catholicism

For recusants, burial in consecrated ground was the final ritual hurdle of a life lived on the ecclesiastical margins. Whether one succeeded depended on who one was and where one lived. This was as true in the colonies as it was in

27. *Diary of Samuel Sewall*, I, 82–83, 91; *A Journal of the Life of Thomas Story: Containing, an Account of His Remarkable Convincement of, and Embracing the Principles of Truth, as Held by the People Called Quakers* . . . (Newcastle upon Tyne, 1747), 195–196; Randall Balmer, "Traitors and Papists: The Religious Dimensions of Leisler's Rebellion," *New York History*, LXX (1989), 341–372 (quotations on 367–368).

England. As a group, colonial Catholics are in an analogous position to the vanished bodies of the Blackfriars tragedy—we know where and how some were buried, but most have simply disappeared from view.

We can begin to trace the trail of Catholic corpses by following the missionary priests on their journeys through the colonies. As we have seen, priests were an intermittent presence in North America outside Maryland, and their arrival in a community sparked a rush to receive the sacraments. Colonial Catholics were especially eager for a priest when ill or dying. The Jesuits were the only clerical game in town in early Maryland, and they visited both Catholics and Protestants on their deathbeds, a practice that fed Protestant fears of forced conversions. Cautionary tales of people being pressured to convert— in both directions—on their deathbeds were a staple of the controversialist literature of post-Reformation England. Such tales flowed out of northern England and Ireland (the hearth cultures of many of the servants and exiles who were transported to the colonies), where the hold of the established church was more tenuous in the face of substantial Catholic populations and the clergy more determined to protect their flocks from deathbed machinations. The early-seventeenth-century chronicler Fynes Moryson reported on religious customs during his travels, including the plight of Protestant converts in Ireland: "upon their dead bedds and in the hower of death," they were assailed by their Catholic kin, who "denyed them releefe or rest, keeping meate and all thinges they desyred from them, and the wemen and Children continually pinching them and disquieting them when they would take rest, that they might thereby force them to turne Papist agayne." In England, a "very excellent lady," Elizabeth Skilling, made it her personal mission to visit "numerous Protestants in their last moments" and "gained over many of them" to the Roman Church. Here again, we see women asserting their role as guardians of the faith in early modern Catholicism.[28]

In this polemical context, the encounters of Jesuit missionaries and colonial Marylanders on their deathbeds could never be entirely innocent. A missionary visited the home of a dying man in 1638 and "absolved him from his sins and anointed him with the sacred oil," scandalizing his neighbors, who had no suspicion of his Catholicism. Another missionary hurried to give the sacrament of extreme unction to a "zealous disciple of the Protestant religion" suffering from snakebite but was turned away by the master of the

28. Graham Kew, "The Irish Sections of Fynes Moryson's Unpublished Itinerary," *Analecta Hibernica*, no. 37 (1998), 1–137 (quotation on 92); Henry Foley, *Records of the English Province of the Society of Jesus: Historic Facts Illustrative of the Labours and Sufferings of Its Members in the Sixteenth and Seventeenth Centuries*, III (London, 1878), 422–423.

household, who, "divining his intention, tried to thwart his pious efforts" by posting a guard at the man's door. The determined priest kept watch outside the bedroom, and "at midnight, when he supposed the guard would be especially overcome by sleep, he contrived, without disturbing him, to pass in to the sick man; and at his own desire, received him into the Church." Were these men secret papists or fearful Protestants coerced into converting by conniving Jesuits? To dispel such doubts in another case, the Jesuits insisted that "a very bright light has often been seen at night around [the man's] tomb, even by Protestants."[29]

For all the anxiety (hysteria?) over scheming Jesuits stalking the sick and dying, the reality is that most Catholics in Maryland probably died without a priest present. And so most died without receiving last rites. To guard against this, John Jarboe requested that his friend John Jordan send for "Mr. Foster to give him the last Sacraments" should "God Allmighty . . . take him before he could make his will in writing." Richard Moy bequeathed two thousand pounds of tobacco to the Jesuit Henry Carew "for his Love to me in the time of my Sickness." But the distances were simply too great from the Jesuit chapels to the scattered farms that comprised the distinctive settlement pattern of the Chesapeake. There were no towns or villages to speak of outside St. Mary's in the seventeenth century, and St. Mary's itself was largely an administrative complex with few actual residents. The average circuit of a Jesuit attached to one of the Society's manors covered many hundreds of miles, miles of rivers and uncleared land and few roads. The suddenness with which death could strike, from an outbreak of disease to a fall from a horse, left the seriously ill and injured to the spiritual ministrations of their family (if they were lucky enough to have one). Beatriz Hardy's analysis of Maryland wills suggests it was not until the eighteenth century that recusants left bequests to (in the words of one) "the Preist that is Assisting to me at my Death" rather than to the Society or the priest whom they expected to preside over their burials. But whereas the laity could perform a plausible semblance of a baptism in cases of extremity, they could not anoint the sick, hear confessions, administer the eucharist, or pray for the souls of the dead. Their role was limited to providing physical comfort and prayers for an easy death. Those Catholics (Irish, German, French) who did not speak English were even more

29. "From the Annual Letter of 1638," in Clayton Colman Hall, *Original Narratives of Early Maryland, 1633–1684* (New York, 1910), 121; Andrew White, *Relatio itineris in Marylandiam . . . Narrative of a Voyage to Maryland*, ed. E. A. Dalrymple (1634; rpt. Baltimore, 1874), 56–57, 59–60.

isolated, since all the Jesuits sent to serve in the Maryland mission were English. The loss of last rites was one of the most traumatic sacramental losses that colonial recusants faced; we know the desperate lengths to which English Catholics went to secure a priest when a loved one was dying, even at the risk of exposure to episcopal courts. The parable of Lord Stourton, who outwardly conformed to the established religion but kept two priests in attendance at his house at all times so as not to be caught unprepared at the hour of his death, was well known in Jesuit circles; Stourton suffered a fatal accident when both priests were absent, and he died in great "grief at being deprived of the rites of the Catholic Church when he most wished to receive them."[30]

If they died unanointed, most Maryland Catholics were at least interred in sacred ground during the seventeenth century. The cemetery at the great brick chapel in St. Mary's City served as the community's main burial ground for nearly sixty years. The closing of the chapel by government order in 1704, however, also meant the closing of the cemetery; there are no tombstones or other markers left to tell us who was buried there and when they died. All that remains is a grassy field. Thanks to the efforts of the archaeological team at Historic St. Mary's City, dozens of individual graves have now been located in the cemetery, and the placement of burial shafts under the floor of the church has been mapped. Two findings from the archaeological explorations are particularly striking: the paucity of sacramental objects such as rosaries or crucifixes found in the cemetery and the uniquely Catholic placement of the hands (crossed over the chest) evident in many of the skeletons. These were "Catholic internments [sic]," despite the absence of the kinds of ritual objects one might find in an English recusant graveyard. Crossed hands were one way to signal religious affiliation in an environment where material tokens of faith were scarce and fragile (as we saw in Chapter 3).[31]

30. Testimony of John Jordan, 1675, *Maryland Prerogative Court Wills*, II, *1635–1704, Archives of Maryland,* 67; Codicil to Will of Richard Moy, December 1675, ibid., 372; Beatriz Betancourt Hardy, "Papists in a Protestant Age: The Catholic Gentry and Community in Colonial Maryland, 1689–1776" (Ph.D. diss., University of Maryland, College Park, 1993), 351; Foley, *Records of the English Province,* 444.

31. Timothy B. Riordan, "'Carry Me to Yon Kirk Yard': An Investigation of Changing Burial Practices in the Seventeenth-Century Cemetery at St. Mary's City, Maryland," *Historical Archaeology,* XLIII (2009), 81–92 (quotation on 90). The findings from Historic St. Mary's City belie Jon Butler's claim that seventeenth-century Maryland was a "liturgical wasteland" due to "Catholic paralysis," most evident in the failure to provide sanctified burials. See Butler, *Awash in a Sea of Faith: Christianizing the American People* (Cambridge, Mass., 1990), 51–53.

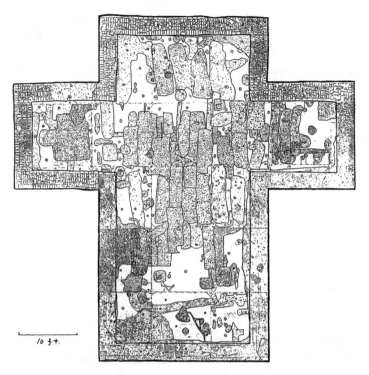

FIGURE 16. Diagram of burial shafts in the "great brick chapel." Ca. 1667.
Courtesy Historic St. Mary's City

After the great brick chapel was dismantled, the Jesuits moved their operations onto the Society's manors and into the private chapels of wealthy
recusant families. These home chapels were slow to incorporate separate
burial grounds, however, so most well-to-do Catholics were buried on their
plantations (as Protestants had been throughout the seventeenth century in
Maryland). Henry Spinke hoped for the restoration of the Jesuit chapels but
made a contingent plan in his 1719 will, providing 1,000 pounds of tobacco
toward the building of a church "if Ever their Be liberty to Rebuild St. Ignatius Chappell," and "if no Liberty," then he pledged "200 lbs tob. toward
pailing a grave yard for our own family." In a manner analogous to the reuse
of consecrated bricks from the great brick chapel to build satellite churches,
recusants carried handfuls of consecrated soil from the Jesuit cemeteries back
home to place in private graves. The material chain of transmission affirmed
the power of objects as spiritual conduits but also represented a pragmatic

adaptation to colonial conditions. With no bishop available to consecrate a chapel or cemetery, indeed, with no priest at hand to perform the sacraments in consecrated spaces, colonial Catholics had to find creative ways to sustain the chain of holiness linking the periphery to the universal church.[32]

In time, cemeteries were established at all the Jesuit chapels, albeit segregated into Black and white sections. We are fortunate to have a surviving register of the burials performed by one Jesuit in eighteenth-century Maryland. Father Joseph Mosley performed 340 burials over the span of thirty-five years, starting in the 1760s. From his perch at St. Joseph's, Mosley recorded the gender, age, and race of each body he interred, whether he delivered a funeral sermon, and sometimes the location of the grave. Daniel McDaniel was buried "at Mr. Tuite's in the orchard," whereas Anthony Dunlevy was laid to rest in "our grave yard" at St. Joseph's. One man was apparently buried "on the road" and another in the "forest." The patterns confirm what we have learned about the rhythm of sacramental life among colonial recusants: that most Catholics preferred to receive the sacraments in the privacy of their own homes rather than in the public space of a church. Of the 170 burials for which a location was recorded, a majority (96) took place on the plantation of the deceased rather than in the Jesuit chapel (74). Before the 1770s, home burial was almost universal, occurring in 55 out of 57 cases. Only in the later decades of the century did burials at church become more popular. This is a remarkable finding in the one colony where recusants had relatively easy access to priests and chapels. Mosley's brief notes reveal that some private graveyards housed generations of Maryland recusants by the mid-eighteenth century; on August 17, 1767, Lucy Seth was buried at "the old burying place" on her family's plantation.[33]

---

32. John Little (1666) requested "to be Interred on the top of the hill before the door of my Dwelling house and near my Grave it is my Will to have Planted one apple tree and one Plum Tree"; Sampson Cooper wished "to have Christian and Decent burial in the Land of Col John Saybrook Esq. in his burying place" in 1659. Little and Cooper were both Protestants. See *Maryland Prerogative Court Wills*, I, 216, 266. "If Ever their Be liberty": ibid., Jan. 6, 1718/19, XV, 66–70 (quotations on 69–70). The custom of transporting consecrated soil continued into the early nineteenth century; Father John Grassi recounted how some Catholics living in rural areas rode hundreds of miles at Easter to hear mass and baptize their adult children, "carrying back a handful of consecrated earth to cast upon the graves of their dead" ("The Catholic Religion in the United States in 1818," *American Catholic Historical Researches*, VIII [1891], 98–111 [quotation on 108]).

33. Baptisms and Funerals, St. Joseph's, Talbot County, Maryland, box 31, folder 1, MPA.

These private burials were select affairs, limited to the social peers of the family and sometimes to fellow recusants. Anthony Neale's 1723 will stipulated that he be buried in the family plot "without Great Funerall doing only my Children and nearest Relations to be invited and such others as may be proper to pray for my soul." His son Raphael made a similar request, asking that only those who "will pray for my soul" attend his funeral. Other recusants were more ecumenical—most of the ten mourning rings that James Paul Heath ordered to be distributed to his friends at his funeral went to Protestants, in recognition of the mixed social world he inhabited during his lifetime. The desire for a domestic burial did not mean that Maryland's wealthier recusants disdained the intercessory services of the Jesuits at the time of their death, as the numerous bequests for "prayers for my soul" in their wills attest. Charles Maynard left "Francis Fitzherbert Esq." four hundred pounds of tobacco "humbly desireing the prayers of the Holy Catholick Church and in testimony that I dye a Roman Catholick." John Turner outdid Maynard, bequeathing Fitzherbert four hundred pounds of tobacco *a year* for "Prayers in the Holy Obla[tion]" over the next six years and "further requesting him that he say for those next five years yearly one Mass of requiem for my Soul." James Langworth's will made provision for "three hundred and fifty pounds a year for the three first Ensuing years after my Death in testimony that I dyed a Roman Catholick and Desire the Prayers of the Holy Church." Tobacco was the universal currency in the Chesapeake colonies; John Shirtcliffe gave "one [hogshead] of Tobb." to his priest "for his good Prayers," as did William Evans, who asked "to be remembered at the holy Altar."[34]

It may be significant that one of the two churchyard burials recorded in Mosley's register before 1770 was that of an enslaved African man. When burials at church began to rise steeply in the 1780s, enslaved Africans were interred in the churchyard at a greater rate than whites. This speaks as much to the reluctance of white recusants to be buried alongside their slaves in private graveyards as it does to the Jesuits' commitment to sacramental racial equality. In the absence of burial records for the seventeenth century, before the legal and social codes of slavery were so entrenched in the Chesapeake, we don't know the racial geography of the cemetery attached to the great brick chapel. The laity called the shots in English America, as we have seen before, and the emergence of segregated burial grounds for white and Black Catholics on the Jesuit manors was a concession to the prevailing racial economy.

---

34. Hardy, "Papists in a Protestant Age," 211–212; *Maryland Prerogative Court Wills*, I, 134 (Langworth), 167 (Turner), 174 (Shirtcliffe), 310 (Maynard), 332 (Evans).

Those enslaved Catholics who served Protestant masters lacked even this accommodation. On the plantation of Thomas Reader, whose overseer was "a professed Roman Catholic," the death of one of his "Negroes"—a man named Richard—exposed the extent of proselytizing on the plantation. When Richard "thought he would die," he surprised his master by requesting a "Priest" rather than "a Clergyman of the Church of England." Reader was dismayed to find that several of his "Negroes" were "perverted and turn'd Roman Catholics, unknown to him, notwithstanding he has brought the most of them up, from Children, in the Protestant Religion" and refused the request. In this one encounter, we can glimpse the uneasy coexistence of Catholic and Protestant, white and Black, in colonial Maryland, where masters and slaves might be of different faiths and where priests and planters sparred over the bodies and souls of the enslaved.[35]

In Philadelphia, the only other British colonial settlement that boasted a formal Catholic church, the small cemetery attached to St. Joseph's filled quickly during the 1730s. By midcentury, more than 200 deaths had been recorded in the parish, far more than the graveyard could hold. Those who could afford it made provisions to be buried privately; the will of Dr. Browne instructed his heirs to inter his body "in as private a manner as Possible" in "a Burying Place, or Grave yard" erected in the garden "for the use of my Family and Kinsfolks as may Die in the Neighborhood." The capacious graveyard was to be encircled by a "lime and Stone Wall of common thickness and six feet High." But most recusants were buried in the public square at Sixth and Walnut Streets, sharing the lot with the city's paupers; the northwest corner of the square was Potter's Field, and the southeast section was reserved for Catholics. The lack of burial space became acute in the 1750s with the arrival of more than 400 Acadians, victims of the crown's policy of ethnic cleansing that expelled more than 7,000 French Catholics from Nova Scotia, many of whom arrived in desperate straits and succumbed to disease soon after. The church sought to purchase a plot of land in 1758 for a new cemetery; the subscription list contains the names of 84 recusants who donated altogether £328, a not-inconsiderable sum. It's safe to assume that most of the city's enslaved African and Irish Catholic corpses continued to be relegated to the pauper's lot.[36]

35. *Archives of Maryland*, October / November 1753, L, 202–203.

36. Joseph L. J. Kirlin, *Catholicity in Philadelphia: From the Earlier Missionaries down to the Present Time* (Philadelphia, 1909), 65 (Browne's will), 87–88; *Pennsylvania Gazette* (Philadelphia), Apr. 13, 1758.

The plantation colonies presented recusants with a range of burial options, from interment in the Anglican church (the preferred option for Anglo-Irish Catholics of means) to home yard burials for enslaved Africans. Based on their wills, many West Indian Irish planters who had escaped the poverty and stigma of indenture by simply surviving chose to identify as Anglicans in their later years. Nicholas Rice, who hailed from Limerick, requested to be "decently buryed in the Chancell of the Church of St Phillips" on Barbados. Nicholas added a further bequest, however, that suggests his continued attachment to the Catholicism of his youth; he left "The Roman Catholique Clergy of the Citty of Lymericke where I was borne one hundred and twenty pounds sterling." His nephew George remembered the Catholic poor both in Ireland and Barbados in his will, leaving fifty pounds to the former and "fourteen Pounds ster[ling]" to the "poor Irish people" of St. Philip's. He might also have tried to posthumously ensure his daughter Katherine's marriage to a recusant by instructing her to wed "one of the name of Rice being of birth and education suitable and not within the sins of consanguinitie"; as Jenny Shaw points out, Irish Catholics were notoriously prone to marrying within the forbidden degrees of consanguinity—a fate George wished to avoid for his child. Shaw's analysis of more than one hundred Irish wills filed in Barbados between 1650 and 1715 shows a distinct pattern of appointing wives as executors, as Catholic men were accustomed to doing in Ireland, and leaving the burial arrangements in their hands. Patrick Collins of St. Michael's Parish (1681), for example, designated his wife as executrix and requested "to be decently intered as it shall seem most meet to my executrix." Cornelius Bryan, who had arrived in Barbados as a servant and once suffered twenty-one lashes for a profane outburst, commended "his soule to God and my body to the earth to be decently buried in my garden." His wife, Margaret, was entrusted to see to the details.[37]

Most of the Irish on the sugar islands, of course, were too poor to make wills. They had little, if anything, to bequeath, and they lacked the literacy to write a will or the means to hire others to write one on their behalf. For the most part, they lived and died anonymously. Scholars have tended to assume their Catholicism died along with their dreams of an independent life in the colonies. But there is compelling evidence to the contrary. "One Anderson"

37. Jenny Shaw, *Everyday Life in the Early English Caribbean: Irish, Africans, and the Construction of Difference* (Athens, Ga., 2013), 115–117, 127. Whereas almost half of the wills left by Irish men named their wives as executors, only about one-quarter of those made by English men did so.

openly "carryed a Cross before his wife's body when she was Caryed to her burial" on Montserrat, a breach of the tacit connivance of the island's Protestant ministers toward the majority Catholic Irish in their congregations. Anderson's gesture of defiance brought trouble to Governor Roger Osborne, who faced a series of charges in the 1650s for being too cozy with the recusants on the island. The Irish-born Osborne was accused of allowing "Publique Masse, marrying by a Masst Preist, and at funerals the crosse to be carried before the dead Corpse." Were there others who managed to procure or craft a crucifix (as Anderson did, carving his cross out of wood) to announce to the community that, in death if not always in life, they and their kin were true Catholics?[38]

Where was Anderson's wife buried? The funeral procession might have forced its way or been invited into the local parish churchyard. Most likely, she was buried privately by her friends and family. In the absence of Catholic churches, the homes of the wealthy served as private meeting places for the local recusant community on the islands as they did on the mainland. The substantial home of the Hamilton family fulfilled that role in Montserrat, which, despite its majority Catholic population, did not have a formal chapel until the nineteenth century. Leading planters might have set aside a portion of their estates for a community burial ground as Dr. Browne did in Philadelphia, but poor and rich did not mingle in the same way on the islands. Poor "Sectaries" on the nearby island of Barbados (Quakers and Catholics) buried their dead "in fields and hedges" rather than in the churchyard or the plantation cemetery, according to the governor.[39]

Although the Irish tended to avoid the parish when it came time to marrying and burying, the poorest among them didn't always have a say about their final resting place. The truly dispossessed were often consigned to the nether regions of the churchyard. A 1678 burial register from St. Michael's Church on Barbados is a roll call of the disinherited: "Margaret, a

---

38. Samuel Waad to Lord Protector, Dec. 6, 1654, CO 1/12, no. 31 ii ("Publique Masse"), no. 31 iii ("carryed a Crosse," "Wooden Cross"), TNA; see also Donald Harman Akenson, *If the Irish Ran the World: Montserrat, 1630–1730* (Montreal, 1997).

39. Akenson, *If the Irish Ran the World*, 123; "Answer to the Several Heads of Inquiry Made in This Island Given to Sr Rich. Dutton by Order of the Lords of Trade and Plantations," Barbados, June 11, 1691, CO 29/3, fols. 80–81, TNA. George Fox was bothered by this casual interment and directed the Quakers on Barbados to find "Convenient buryeing places for frends for in many places they burey there owne in theire gardens"; see Norman Pennye, ed., *Journal of George Fox*, 2 vols. (Cambridge, 1911), II, 195.

distracted woman"; "Humility Hubs, from the Almshouse"; "John Williams, from the Prison"; "An Irishwoman"; "a child of Daniel and Margaret Suillivant"; "Hagar a Christian Negro"; "Dearman Sullivant, out of prison"; "a poor woman"; "Mary Morris a Christian Negro." Those who belonged to no one were buried in the churchyard alongside the bodies of church papists not wealthy enough to buy their way into the chancel itself. The geography of death on the sugar islands thus divided the landscape into discrete zones of social belonging: the wealthy Protestant and Anglo-Irish church papists inside the church, the destitute and middling planters in the churchyard (presumably in different sectors), elite recusants and their servants and slaves on the plantations. Life in the tropics presented a challenge to this pattern: the authorities on Montserrat found it necessary to impose a one thousand pound fine on anyone interring a body inside the church since "it has been found by Experience, that the burying of Bodies in a Church, or very near it, in this hot Climate, has been very nauseous to the People assembled together at Divine Service."[40]

Burial outside the church meant one thing for wealthy white planters who chose to reside on their plantations after death rather than rub shoulders with the common folk in the Anglican cemeteries; it meant something quite different for servants and slaves. What was a choice for the former was the product of circumstance, custom, and prejudice for the latter. Ironically, the enslaved probably had more freedom than servants to bury their dead as they wished, given the need for dissimulation that hampered open expressions of Irish Catholicism and the indifference of white planters to the religious lives of their slaves. The enslaved received more care and attention from their masters at their deaths, at least according to John Taylor: "When their English servants are sick, their [sic] is not half that car[e] taken of 'em as over their Negros, and when dead noe more ceremony at their funurale than if they were to berey a dogg." The archaeological evidence lends support to Taylor's observation: the body of an adult male servant uncovered on the grounds of the Drummond

40. Baptismal and Burial Registers, Barbados Parishes, 1678, CO 1 / 44, nos. 47 iii–xxiv, St. Michael's, no. 47 iv, TNA; Akenson, *If the Irish Ran the World*, 124 n. 30. Whereas the tropical climate of the islands exacerbated the problem, the elimination of incense from the Reformed rite made church burials a malodorous affair everywhere in Protestant lands. Cressy notes, "A distinctive smell in early modern churches must have been the odour of human decomposition, not always masked by the scent of floral garlands and incense that the reformers were seeking to abolish" (*Birth, Marriage, and Death*, 463).

plantation in Virginia was buried in his coat without a coffin, "in isolation among the refuse heaps."[41]

The hasty burial of servants allowed planters to avoid public scrutiny of the way they treated their servants while alive. Governor Atkins of Barbados complained that "they must not bury any Christian Servant till so many free-holders of the Neighbourhood have viewed the Corpse under a considerable penalty of ten thousand of sugar by a Law of the Co[u]ntry that it may be discovered whether by some Ill usages of his Master he came by a violent death"—a "custom . . . they will not easily forsake." The Burgesses in Virginia showed more sympathy to the plight of abused servants, legislating in 1661 that "Whereas the private burial of servants and others gives occasion of much scandal against divers persons and sometimes not undeservedly of being guilty of their deaths, be it enacted that there be in every parish three or more places set apart for places of public burial, and before the corpse be buried there, three or four neighbors be called who may view the corpse." Living so far from one another, and from parish churches, in a society where the plantocracy wielded enormous (and unchecked) power over their households, white servants lived and died in an atmosphere of fear and suspicion. Few of them, Protestant or Catholic, had the comfort of Christian burial.[42]

"Howling and Dancing": Death in African and Native America

The presence of two "Christian Negroes" in the 1678 St. Michael's burial register is an anomaly. The simple fact is that most Africans were unbaptized in the English Atlantic, so forbidden from burial in consecrated ground. "The

41. David Buisseret, ed., *Jamaica in 1687: The Taylor Manuscript at the National Library of Jamaica* (Kingston, Jamaica, 2008), 276. Many of these "English servants" were, of course, Irish. "In isolation": Arthur C. Aufderheide et al., "Lead in Bone III. Prediction of Social Correlates from Skeletal Lead Content in Four Colonial American Populations (Catoctin Furnace, College Landing, Governor's Land, and Irene Mound)," *American Journal of Physical Anthropology*, LXVI (1985), 353–361 (quotation on 357). The Drummond plantation had separate burial grounds for family and servants in the seventeenth century; among the latter were numbered three enslaved Africans and six white servants, two of whom were Irish, according to a 1677 inventory.

42. Governor Jonathan Atkins to Lords of Trade and Plantations, Barbados, Mar. 26, 1680, CO 1/44, no. 45, TNA; June Purcell Guild, ed., *Black Laws of Virginia: A Summary of the Legislative Acts of Virginia concerning Negroes from Earliest Times to the Present* (New York, 1969), 40.

historical data are very strong that the great majority of slaves were buried in unmarked plantation cemeteries that were scattered throughout the island," the foremost archaeologist of Barbados asserts. This would be as true of the enslaved who had been baptized previously by Spanish or French missionaries or by the Jesuits during their forty-year interlude on the island. Their final resting place unknown and unmarked, the graves of most enslaved Africans in the English colonies have remained largely unexcavated by archaeologists. Much of our knowledge of the burial customs of African and Native peoples thus rests on the commentary of white Christians—neighbors, SPG missionaries, and colonial officials—who painted a portrait of African and Indigenous funerals as disorderly, raucous, and excessive: in a word, barbaric.[43]

White settlers who showed remarkably little curiosity about the religious beliefs or practices of the enslaved while they were alive were fascinated by their burial habits. In contrast to white servants, most Africans were buried by their own communities and not by their masters, and they were afforded considerable latitude (at least on the larger plantations in the Lowcountry and the Caribbean) to conduct their funerals according to their own customs and rituals. "The Negroes . . . bury one another in the ground of the plantation where they die, and not without ceremonies of their own," a white Barbadian noted in 1676. Even in colonial New York City, where most enslaved Africans lived in close quarters with white and Native members of the household, the Anglican minister complained in 1713 that the enslaved were "buried in the Common by those of their country and complexion without the office [Anglican liturgy], on the contrary the Heathenish rites are performed at the grave by their countrymen." The strong attachment of the enslaved to African burial rites was an impediment to their conversion, according to the SPG missionaries who served in the plantation colonies. "I myself offer'd to baptize a sensible well-inclin'd Negro," wrote John Venn of Jamaica, "but he declin'd it, saying that after that he must go to no more Dances, nor have any of their antic Ceremonies about his Grave, of which these poor ignorant Creatures are fond of to a surprizing degree." Venn recognized that barbaric treatment of the bodies of slaves who had rebelled or committed suicide (burning alive or posthumously) was a calculated affront to traditional African beliefs and practices: "To deprive them of their funeral Rites, by burning their dead

43. Jerome S. Handler, "A Prone Burial from a Plantation Slave Cemetery in Barbados, West Indies: Possible Evidence for an African-Type Witch or Other Negatively Viewed Person," *Historical Archaeology*, XXX (1996), 79–86 (quotation on 76).

Bodies, seems to Negroes a greater Punishment than Death itself. This is done to Self-murders."[44]

Whereas home burial among white Christians was an assertion of gentry exclusiveness, burial in the slave quarters was a communal act that harkened back to West African traditions. "House-yard" burials, or the custom of burying one's kith and kin within the domestic compound, were common in West Africa and made their way to the New World. In the English Caribbean, the enslaved reportedly buried their dead "at the back of their huts and sometimes under their beds." A late-eighteenth-century account comes to us from Governor Parry of Barbados: "Negroes are superstitiously attached to the burial places of their ancestors and friends. They are generally as near as can be to the houses in which they live. It is frequent to inter a relative under the bed-place on which they sleep, an unwholesome and dangerous practice which they would think it the utmost tyranny to alter." The deep attachment of the enslaved to place that so many observers noted, both in the era of Atlantic slavery and after its abolition, speaks to the living presence of the dead in the slave quarters—not to nostalgia for plantation life, as so many slaveholders wished to believe.[45]

English planters and ministers often saw only an undifferentiated barbarism in the songs, dances, and feasts that accompanied slave funerals, but in fact the funerary rites of the enslaved in the Lowcountry and the islands resembled those of the Kongo and combined elements of Catholic and African practices. Commentators then and now noted the striking similarities

44. Atkins quoted in Jerome S. Handler, Frederick W. Lange, and Robert V. Rordan, *Plantation Slavery in Barbados: An Archaeological and Historical Investigation* (Cambridge, Mass., 1978), 173; Rev. John Sharpe, "'Proposals for Erecting a School, Library, and Chapel at New York,' 1712–13," in *Collections of the New-York Historical Society for the Year 1880*, XIII (New York, 1881), 339–363 (quotation on 355); John Venn to Bishop Sherlock, Jamaica, June 15, 1751, Fulham Papers, XVIII, fols. 45–52. On the desecration and dismemberment of slave corpses as a punitive measure, see Douglas R. Egerton, "A Peculiar Mark of Infamy: Dismemberment, Burial, and Rebelliousness in Slave Societies," in Isenberg and Burstein, eds., *Mortal Remains*, 149–160.

45. Extract of a letter from Governor Parry to the Right Honourable Lord Sydney, Aug. 18, 1788, House of Commons Papers, *Parliamentary Papers, 1789*, XXVI, 13–24, esp. 17, quoted in Handler et al., *Plantation Slavery in Barbados*, 174; see also Douglas V. Armstrong and Mark L. Fleischman, "House-Yard Burials of Enslaved Laborers in Eighteenth-Century Jamaica," *International Journal of Historical Archaeology*, VII (2003), 33–65 (quotations on 40).

in grave decoration: the presence of conch shells, pebbles, ceramics, flowers, household items, and tools that were last used by the deceased on top of the grave.[46] These ritual objects were a species of *nkisi*—material objects animated by spirit—as was the burial site. As Jason Young explains, in the Kongo mortuary complex, "Mourners regularly placed the last used implements of the dead atop the grave in order to excite the burial mound, to invest the soil with something of the spark of life and the power of the deceased." A late-seventeenth-century burial site in West Africa was decorated with a porcelain cup and a musical instrument, whereas a grave in Jamaica from the same era displayed a pipe and a fire kit to accompany the soul in its journey to the otherworld. The concept of *minkisi* (the plural form of *nkisi*) was a powerful node of connection between Catholic and African spiritual traditions; in time, the Catholic Church itself became a kind of nkisi. In both traditions, the dead were not only revered but maintained a lively communication with the living through these ritual objects. The minister of St. Lucy's on Barbados explained how the enslaved were "very tenaciously addicted to the Rites, Ceremonies, and Superstitions of their own Countries," especially in burying the dead. "If . . . in digging a Grave, they find a Stone which they cannot easily get out, they immediately conclude, that the Deceased is unwilling to be buried there; therefore they dig elsewhere, until they find a Place more propitious to the supposed Inclination of the Dead." Graveyard dirt, in particular, was believed to hold a special relationship to the spirits of the dead. Its occult qualities were respected by Africans on both sides of the Atlantic. In the West Indies, enslaved ritual practitioners worked "black magic through soil from a grave," leaving a coin on top of the grave in payment—a "common" practice, according to folklorists.[47]

---

46. Folklorists were the first to make the connection between African and Kongo burial practices, albeit through the lens of an uncompromising ethnocentrism. In the 1890s, two articles described the "savage" and "childlike" adornment of "Negro" graves in South Carolina, which closely resembled those found in the Kongo; see H. Carrington Bolton, "Decoration of Graves of Negroes in South Carolina," *Journal of American Folklore*, IV (1891), 214; Ernest Ingersoll, "Decoration of Negro Graves," ibid., V (1892), 68–69. From these unpromising beginnings developed a sophisticated analysis of cultural syncretism and hybridization in African and Christian burial practices, the most influential example of which is Robert Farris Thompson, *Flash of the Spirit: African and Afro-American Art and Philosophy* (New York, 1983).

47. Jason R. Young, *Rituals of Resistance: African Atlantic Religion in Kongo and the Low-country South in the Era of Slavery* (Baton Rouge, 2007), 148–149, 162–164; Griffith Hughes, *The Natural History of Barbados . . .* (London, 1750), 15 n. 9; Elsie Clews Parsons, *Folk-Lore of the Sea Islands, South Carolina* (New York, 1923), 212.

African mortuary practices shared many ritual elements with Irish customs, in particular, including music and dance, grave goods to help the soul on its journey to the afterlife, and periodic pilgrimages to the gravesite by women to mark stages of mourning. A rare description of a slave funeral from 1687 Jamaica would have struck a familiar chord with those English Protestants who deplored the barbaric Irish customs of keening and carousing at funerals. "When those slaves die they make a great adoe at their burials, for haveing caryed them to the grave in a verey mournfull manner, all both men and women which accompany the corpse sing and howle in a sorrowfull manner in their own language." The SPG missionary on Barbados was similarly appalled by the noise and tumult of slave funerals and "heartily wished" that the local planters would restrain their slaves from "howling and dancing about the graves of the Dead." Anglo-American observers noted the congruences between African and Gaelic funeral rites, usually as a prelude to dismissing both as "superstition." Edward Long provided one of the most detailed descriptions we have of African ritual and culture when he visited Barbados in the 1770s and he was struck by the similarities he observed between "Negroe" and Scots/Irish burials. "The Negroe funeral calls to mind the *late-wake* of the highlands in Scotland. . . . The evening after the death of any person, the relations and friends of the deceased meet at the house, attended by bag-pipe and fiddle. The nearest of kin, be it wife, son, or daughter, opens a melancholy ball, dancing and greeting (i.e. crying violently) at the same time." The rites of the "antient Irish" also resembled those of the enslaved Africans on the island, particularly the "custom of using earnest reproaches and expostulations with the corpse, for quitting this world, where he (or she) enjoyed so many good things, so kind a husband, such fine fine children, etc." There is, he concluded, a "striking conformity between this antient rite and that in use among the Negroes."[48]

Loud cries and excessive emotion also linked Catholic and Native burial traditions. In Massachusetts, William Wood and John Josselyn were struck by the sheer noise of the Indian burials they witnessed. "To behold and heare their throbbing sobs and deepe-fetcht sighes, their griefe-wrung hands, and teare-bedewed cheeks, their dolefull cries, would draw tears from Adamantine eyes," Wood commented in 1634. The cries of Native mourners

48. Buisseret, ed., *Jamaica in 1687*, 272; Arthur Holt to Bishop Gibson, Christ Church, Barbados, Mar. 7, 1728/9, Fulham Papers, XV, fols. 266–267; Long, *History of Jamaica*, II, 422. See Shaw on the "confluence of Gaelic and African practices" in Barbadian funerals (*Everyday Life in the Early English Caribbean*, 108).

reminded Wood and his fellow New Englander Josselyn of the "howlings" of the Gaelic Irish. After the "glut of their griefe" had passed, Wood continued, the mourners gave way to "Irish-like howlings." Josselyn likewise wrote that "their mournings are somewhat like the howlings of the Irish," though in the burial he observed the keening happened not graveside "but in the Wigwam where the party dyed, blaming the Devil for his hard heartedness, and concluding with rude prayers to him to afflict them no further." Thomas Morton was far less orthodox in his piety than his Puritan compatriots, but he, too, observed ritual congruences between Indian ossuaries and Irish burial huts. "The Natives of New England are accustomed to build [the dead] houses," he noted, "much like the wild Irish."[49]

It is not accidental that these shared ritual elements in African and Native deathways—the choreographed movement, the loud expressions of grief, the invocation of supernatural spirits (demonic or divine), the intimacy between the living and the dead—were precisely those aspects of the Catholic funeral complex that most offended Protestant ears and eyes. But if the affinities between African and Catholic spiritual traditions lurked at the margins of slaveholders' determination to keep their slaves and their servants apart, the parallels between Indigenous and Catholic ritual practice were front and center of English colonial apologetics for their own meager missionary efforts. The success of the Jesuits in New France and the Capuchins, Franciscans, and other missionary orders in New Spain in converting thousands of Native men and women to Catholicism was a constant source of frustration for the English in North America. Anglican ministers in the southern colonies complained that Catholic influence had penetrated into the very words the Indians spoke—"their Language is inricht with abundance of Spanish words, pticularly those ptaining to Religion"—putting the Anglicans at a severe disadvantage from the beginning. In the context of the demographic devastation wrought by colonial conquest, the Catholic missionary enterprise of necessity turned on its success in reforming Indian deathways and bringing them into congruence with Christian notions of death and the afterlife. The task was made easier by the commonalities linking the Native and Catholic mortuary complex: belief in the numinous power of bones, the importance of proper rituals to ensure the smooth transition to the afterlife for the deceased, notions of the transmigration of souls to an imagined "home" (Africa, heaven,

49. William Wood, *New Englands Prospect: A True, Lively and Experimental Description of That Part of America, Commonly Called New England . . .* (London, 1634), 93; John Josselyn, *An Account of Two Voyages to New-England,* 2d ed., MHS, *Colls.,* 3d Ser., III (1675; rpt. Cambridge, Mass., 1833), 300; Morton, *New English Canaan,* 24.

purgatory) from which the souls of the departed maintained an ongoing connection with the living. Among some Algonquian peoples (the Mi'kmaq of Gaspésie, for example), precontact burial grounds even bore a superficial resemblance to Christian graveyards. "The burial-places of these people are readily recognised by the Crosses which they place over their tombs; and their cemeteries, distinguished by this sign of salvation, appear more like those of Christians than of Indians."[50]

Because so many Native converts were brought to Christianity in the first place by watching their loved ones die in the terrible epidemics the missionaries brought with them, baptism and burial were inextricably linked in Native communities. Men and women were often baptized and given last rites at the same time in Catholic mission towns; in fact, for the first few decades of the missionary enterprise, the Jesuits in New France refused to baptize anyone who was not in imminent danger of dying, cementing the connection between Christianity and death in the minds of the Native inhabitants. A gravely ill "Savage" was brought to the Jesuits' hospital in St. Joseph de Sillery in 1647 and "spoken to concerning baptism." He recoiled at first, insisting that "he did not yet wish to die,—imagining that that Sacrament of life would cause his death," and accused the nuns of "wish[ing] to hurry him to his death" by their entreaties. But, in a commonplace trope of missionary accounts, his heart was changed "in a moment" and "that headstrong man [became] gentle" and submitted to baptism. The *Jesuit Relations* abound in such stories of miraculous deathbed conversions among the Native peoples of New France. Their English brethren in Maryland had tales of their own to tell; one early report from the Maryland mission described how the Jesuits "hastened to visit" a Piscataway man convicted of murder "in the hopes of making him an Xian [Christian] before his execution." The man "earnestly" asked to be baptized, and the Jesuits complied.[51]

This Piscataway convert did not abandon traditional deathways after his baptism, however. As he was led to his execution, he requested to "sing before

50. Robert Stevens to the Society, Goose Creek, S.C., ca. 1705, SPG Letters "A" Series, 1702–1737, II, no. 156; Father Chrestien Le Clercq, *New Relation of Gaspesia: With the Customs and Religions of the Gaspesian Indians*, ed. William F. Ganong, Publications of the Champlain Society, V (Toronto, 1910), 151. On the centrality of rituals of death to French conversion strategies in the New World, see Seeman, *Death in the New World*, chap. 4, "Holy Bones and Beautiful Deaths in New France," 106–142.

51. Emma Anderson provides an incisive reading of the connections between baptism and burial in Native-European religious encounters in "Blood, Fire, and 'Baptism': Three Perspectives on the Death of Jean Brébeuf, Seventeenth-Century Jesuit Martyr," in Joel W. Martin and Mark A. Nicholas, eds., *Native Americans, Christianity, and the*

he was put to death" in line with Native custom. The missionaries instructed him instead "to repeat with devotion the Sacred Name of his Saviour, and the holy Name of the Virgin Mother." The Jesuits were convinced he "died with those blessed names on his lips," a self-serving embellishment at best. This tension between Christian conversion and Native burial customs is a leitmotif in the literature of religious encounter in the Americas. In New France, Henry Membertou, a neophyte convert who had "confessed and received extreme unction," told Father Pierre Biard that "he wished to be buried with his fathers and ancestors" in the traditional burial ground rather than in the mission cemetery. The offended Jesuit told him that this would be an act of "contempt" toward his Christian faith and refused. His fellow missionary Charles Biencourt de Saint-Just, however, promised Membertou that "they would have the burial place blessed" so he could be interred there. Biard refused to budge and insisted he would "have to disinter the Pagans who were buried there" before the Native site could be consecrated. This "good Savage" conceded, according to Biard, and "said that he wanted to be buried in the common burying ground of the Christians"—and "died a very good Christian." But by all accounts, Biard's intransigence was unusual. Most Jesuits accommodated Native burial customs so long as the primary liturgical elements of the Roman rite were respected. The use of grave goods, in particular, remained commonplace throughout Indian cemeteries in the Jesuit missions despite the missionaries' disdain for them as superstitious holdovers. "If these poor ignorant people were refused the privilege of placing in the graves of their dead their few belongings, to go with them to the other life," Paul Le Jeune explained, "they say, they would also refuse to allow us to approach their sick." Pragmatism often won out over doctrinal orthodoxy in the missionary fields of North America, contributing to the blurring of confessional boundaries between Protestant and Catholic ritual that we have been tracing throughout these chapters.[52]

Reshaping of the American Religious Landscape (Chapel Hill, N.C., 2010), 125–158. "Spoken to concerning baptism": Reuben Gold Thwaites, ed., *The Jesuit Relations and Allied Documents: Travels and Explorations of the Jesuit Missionaries in New France, 1610–1791 . . .* (Cleveland, 1896–1901), XXXI, 159. On early Jesuit practices with regard to baptism in New France, see Kenneth M. Morrison, "Baptism and Alliance: The Symbolic Mediations of Religious Syncretism," *Ethnohistory*, XXXVII (1990), 416–437.

52. Province Notes on the Mission of Maryland, 1633–1874, box 3, folder 7, pp. 31–32, MPA; "Biard's Relation," 1616, in Thwaites, ed., *Jesuit Relations*, III, 203–205; "Le Jeune's Relation, 1635," ibid., VIII, 269. On the presence of Native grave goods in both Jesuit and Protestant missionary cemeteries, see Morrison, "Baptism and Alliance," *Ethnohistory*,

We can find tangible evidence of the hybridization of Native and Christian burials throughout the mission towns in the archaeological record. The twenty-one Indigenous graves excavated in the cemetery of the Wendat-Huron mission of Sainte-Marie, for example, exhibit a mix of Catholic and Native elements, including rosary beads and traditional grave goods such as pipe stems. One burial stands out as an exemplar of the material commingling of religious cultures in colonial America. In grave 19, the archaeological team found two skeletons buried in a single coffin. The larger was that of an adult man buried in a flexed position, with his knees drawn up, surrounded by both Christian and Native objects—blue, red, and white rosary beads embedded in his ribs, a pewter pipe etched with fleurs-de-lis, and a small copper vessel pierced with a hole in the bottom (to allow his spirit to escape). In the same coffin was a traditional Huron-Wendat burial bundle of smaller, disarticulated bones, which appear to belong to the man's non-Christian wife. The presence of the bundle within the man's coffin suggests that he had arranged for his wife's bones to be removed from the communal burial scaffold after his death so the two could be reunited in their journey to the afterworld.[53]

Conclusion

We thus end where we started: with a common grave. Across multiple dimensions of being and belonging, the inhabitants of North America found themselves buried side by side when they died, with or without their consent. The phenomenon of religious commingling across the racial divide in early America is a familiar story by now, given what we know about the adaptive and accretive nature of the major African and Indigenous spiritual traditions and the willingness of Catholic missionaries, especially, to incorporate Native gods and ritual customs into their sacramental programs of conversion.

How far this pattern of spiritual hybridization extended to the ritual practices of white settlers is less clear. The usual assumption is that the direction

---

XXXVII (1990), 421; Stephen W. Silliman, "Change and Continuity, Practice and Memory: Native American Persistence in Colonial New England," *American Antiquity*, LXXIV (2009), 211–230; James Axtell, "Last Rites: The Acculturation of Native Funerals in Colonial North America," in Axtell, *The European and the Indian: Essays in the Ethnohistory of Colonial North America* (New York, 1981), 110–128.

53. Wilfrid Jury and Elsie McLeod Jury, *Sainte-Marie among the Hurons* (Toronto, 1954), 93. On the use of copper kettles as burial vessels to liberate the spirit among the Hurons, see Carla Cevasco, "This Is My Body: Communion and Cannibalism in Colonial New England and New France," *New England Quarterly*, LXXXIX (2016), 556–586, esp. 582.

of cultural change ran one way only, from European to Native and African American. By and large, the evidence presented in this chapter and the previous one on the sacramental habits of colonial Catholics supports this view. Anglo-Irish Catholics continued to practice the Roman rituals whenever they could, even if they modified them to fit an environment of liturgical scarcity, and continued to regard Native and African rituals as barbaric and pagan even when practiced by individuals who had been baptized into the same church. English Protestants might have seen Indigenous and African funeral rituals as variants of the common genus of Catholic mourning ("howling")— Anglo-Irish recusants (at least those who left written records) did not. The latter's refusal to acknowledge any affinity between Roman Catholic ritual and the home traditions of the enslaved does not mean those affinities did not exist, however, nor even that they were invisible to white Catholics. I imagine there was a spectrum of recognition across English America, with Jesuit missionaries and wealthy recusants at one end and the nameless Irish exiles and servants who constituted the majority of Catholics at the other end. If we had greater access to the thoughts and attitudes of the Irish who lived and worked alongside enslaved Africans in the plantation colonies, we might see a more fluid cultural exchange in which European and African ritual complexes meshed from both directions.[54]

The evidence for cross-fertilization among Catholic and Protestant ritual cultures is more discernable in the sources. In certain respects, colonial Catholicism was Protestantized, whereas in other respects, Reformed Christians began to act more like Catholics. Catholics grew accustomed to using ordinary bread in their communion services, for instance, rather than stamped wafers. Protestants, in turn, started to baptize and marry in the kinds of private ceremonies that recusants had long resorted to by necessity. Most Catholics died at home without the intercessory help of a priest—which means they died like Protestants. Some Catholics buried their dead in Anglican churchyards using the Reformed rite, whereas some Protestants asked (paid) the parish priest to bring the burial service to them on their plantations. Material commemorative items, derided by rigid Reformers as popish trash, began to appear at Protestant funerals throughout Anglo-America in the seventeenth century. Christianity experienced its own forms of creolization in North America.

54. Catholicism in the Caribbean was, one survey concludes, "a mixture of European folk Catholicism, indigenous beliefs, and African religion" (Ennis B. Edmonds and Michelle A. Gonzalez, *Caribbean Religious History: An Introduction* [New York, 2010], 45).

The unsettled nature of colonial religion in the early years created the conditions for such creolization to take place. But the commingling of the Protestant and Catholic dead did not end with the growing Anglicization of the political and material landscape of English America in the eighteenth century. During the Revolutionary War, the Anglican minister Samuel Cooper abetted the Catholic burial of a French man (killed in a street brawl) in Boston's venerable King's Chapel—a "shocking mingling of sacred space" according to one historian, though perhaps not so shocking given what we now know about the heterogeneity of colonial burial grounds. Burial in consecrated ground was the universal aspiration of colonial Christians, Protestant and Catholic, and the landscape itself bears mute testimony to the inescapable coexistence of rival religious traditions in North America.[55]

55. Katherine Carté, *Religion and the American Revolution: An Imperial History* (Williamsburg, Va., and Chapel Hill, N.C., 2021), 254 (quotation); see also Charles W. Akers, *The Divine Politician: Samuel Cooper and the American Revolution in Boston* (Boston, Mass., 1982), 264–267, 278–281. On Anglicization, see T. H. Breen, "An Empire of Goods: The Anglicization of Colonial America, 1690–1776," *Journal of British Studies*, XXV (1986), 467–499. The essays collected in Ignacio Gallup-Diaz, Andrew Shankman, and David J. Silverman, eds., *Anglicizing America: Empire, Revolution, Republic* (Philadelphia, 2015) provide an updated examination of the Anglicization paradigm.

Conclusion

ATHOLICISM WAS a fugitive faith in English America. It thrived on the margins and in the recesses of colonial settler communities, occasionally emerging from its places of hiding to encounter the light of bureaucratic and archival exposure. Tracking this multilingual, multiethnic community over more than a century and an entire continent has been an exercise in bricolage, collecting partial and scattered fragments of textual and material evidence in the hope of finding larger patterns or at least coherence.

But coherence proved elusive in the mixed confessional world of English America. When I began this project, my aim was fairly straightforward: to find as many Catholics as I could in the early English colonies and learn how they lived their faith as a proscribed community. I expected the project would be centered in Maryland, the one colony with a Catholic proprietor and a policy of religious toleration (at least until the 1690s), with some attention to the northern and southern border regions, where English North America butted up against French and Spanish territories. My previous work studying varieties of Protestantism in the early modern British Atlantic, from New England Baptists to Revolutionary-era prophets, had predisposed me to expect clear lines of demarcation between Protestant and Catholic identities and practices: Catholicism, after all, was the negative other against which English Protestants defined themselves and marked the boundaries of legitimate belief and behavior. However much actual colonial Catholics might have deviated from orthodox devotional practices or theological commitments, their Protestants neighbors knew who and what they were. Or at least they wrote as if they did, regularly churning out printed denunciations of "papists" that recycled time-worn stereotypes of Catholics as deceitful, seductive, and—most damning of all—disloyal. Steeped in the polemical literature of "antipopery," colonial Protestants seemed to encounter Catholics primarily in their fevered imaginations. The few Catholics who managed to evade restrictions on their emigration to the colonies imposed by Protestant joint-stock companies, proprietors, and the crown were (outside of Maryland) too small in number and too dispersed to warrant much attention from colonial officials or modern scholars. Or so I thought.

What I found instead was a far more complex and interesting story of religious indeterminacy. The evidence for the existence and activities of colonial Catholics abounded in contradiction: they were everywhere and nowhere, they clung to their traditional ways or they disappeared into the mass of conforming Anglicans as other dissenting groups (Huguenots, most notably) had done in the tolerant air of the Americas.[1] They rebelled—alone or in combination with their French, Spanish, and Native allies at pivotal moments of political crisis—or they went out of their way to prove themselves loyal subjects of the British crown by mustering against foreign invasions. They "howled" like the Gaelic Irish and pagan Africans during funerals in the sugar islands, supped with their fellow planters at genteel Chesapeake home weddings, labored side by side with the Protestant poor in the fisheries of New England, became governors of the royal colonies of New York (Thomas Dongan) and the Leeward Islands (William Stapleton). Most perplexing of all, they did not inhabit a stable religious identity during their time in the colonies, moving between Protestant and Catholic personas depending on circumstances—sometimes with ease, sometimes with great anguish of heart.

Once I abandoned my original presumptions about the firmness of the Protestant/Catholic divide in post-Reformation Anglo-America, however, what appeared to be a problem became an opportunity for a more nuanced examination of identity, belonging, and coexistence. The central dilemma of *A Common Grave* became how to study a community whose very identity threatened to dissolve under scrutiny. Colonial Catholics confounded Protestant settlers and authorities because they embodied the incomplete nature of the Reformation itself. However much English Catholics might have wished to remain orthodox followers of the Church of Rome, their precarious legal and political position left them little choice but to adapt, to make compromises that stranded them in liturgical limbo. The domestication of Catholic ritual life was the most far-reaching transformation of the Reformation era for those living in Protestant lands. With no or very limited access to priests and hence to the sacraments, Catholics in England and its overseas possessions lived

1. Huguenots have been the paradigmatic "vanishing faith" in colonial North America; see Jon Butler's classic study, *The Huguenots in America: A Refugee People in New World Society* (Cambridge, Mass., 1983). Owen Stanwood's more recent exploration of the global Huguenot diaspora qualifies but does not overturn this view (*The Global Refuge: Huguenots in an Age of Empire* [New York, 2019]).

a religious life that outwardly differed little from that of their Protestant neighbors. Nowhere is this more apparent than in the shared preference of colonial Christians for celebrating the important sacramental milestones of life at home: Anglicans and Catholics alike baptized their children, got married, and were buried in their homes and on their plantations.[2] At the same time, many English Christians who adopted the Reformed way of worship did so with mixed feelings, holding on to certain traditional ideas and rituals even as they conformed to the Anglican establishment. Sitting side by side in the same pew in a local parish church might be a Catholic who attended to avoid the punitive fines for recusancy and a Protestant who prayed to the Virgin Mary in times of peril. Both might be well known to one another, but not to the authorities who enforced the penal laws or to the historian who follows the paper trial left by the ecclesiastical courts. Judged only by the standard metric of attendance at the parish church, both the "church papist" and the half-reformed Protestant would count as Anglicans for the purposes of religious classification.

It is impossible to write a story of early modern religion in Anglo-America without falling into the convention of calling some people Protestants and some Catholics. I have done so throughout this book, even when the evidence points to a more contingent or hybridized understanding of faith. That is because these categories did matter, and they had the force of law behind them. Without question, there were people of fierce conviction on both sides who can unreservedly be labeled Catholics and Protestants. For true believers, there was no middle ground of faith, no equivocation or dissimulation. That so much of the history of colonial religion has been written from their perspective is no accident: the archives are full of the reports of missionaries, Protestant and Catholic alike, and the spiritual diaries of "hot Protestants," such as the Puritans, Baptists, and Quakers, who gloried in their persecution at the hands of the state church. The lives and beliefs of people of moderate faith—David Hall's "horse-shed Christians," Alexandra Walsham's "church papists," worldly Quakers who abandoned the austerity of their forbears to embrace Atlantic-style capitalism—are less documented, but we can venture some generalizations: most would have considered themselves Protestant or Catholic in the broad sense, if not in all particulars, and most made a

---

2. The fullest exploration of "household religion" among colonial Anglicans is Lauren F. Winner, *A Cheerful and Comfortable Faith: Anglican Religious Practice in the Elite Households of Eighteenth-Century Virginia* (New Haven, Conn., 2010).

good-faith effort to participate in the organized religious life of their communities.[3] They would probably be offended at my efforts to locate traces of forbidden or suppressed ritual practices, whether of pre-Reformed, Indigenous, or African origin, in their religious observances. To acknowledge the unstable and porous quality of religious identity in the early modern world is not to deny that categories long established in law, polemic, and custom continued to resonate deeply in people's personal and public lives.

This still leaves a sprawling population of men and women of indifferent, indeterminate, or mixed faith unaccounted for in our histories of colonial religion. I have tried to include people from every position on the spectrum of belief: the Jesuit itinerants and the gentrywomen who hosted them; the second- and third-generation recusants who lived miles from any church and rarely received the sacraments; the ambitious courtiers and government officials who switched religious allegiance with every new monarch in England; the poor white farmers in Maryland who resented the wealth of the Jesuit manors even while they were dependent on their sacramental largesse; the Irish servants who labored in the shops and plantations of the English colonies; and the enslaved Wabanaki, Mayaca, Angolans, and Kongolese whose Catholicism was not acknowledged by their masters or by modern scholars. Trying to assign percentages of "Catholicity" to these subgroups would be a fool's errand. (As would attempting to assess the quotient of true Protestantism in the beliefs and behaviors of colonial Anglicans and the various dissenting sects that proliferated in the colonies.) Rather than apportion authenticity among discrete groups of Catholics and Protestants, my aim has been to explore the areas of overlap between these broad confessional categories.

These overlaps are most visible in the realm of ritual and material culture. We have known for some time that the Reformers did not entirely eschew ritual when they broke from Rome, despite their logocentrism, and that vestiges of traditional sacramental practice endured in the more conservative Protestant denominations. The Anglican Church, in particular, retained many of the liturgical elements of traditional Christianity—godparentage, "the sign

3. On "horse-shed" Christians, see David D. Hall, *Worlds of Wonder, Days of Judgment: Popular Religious Belief in Early New England* (Cambridge, Mass., 1989), 15–17; on "church papists," see Alexandra Walsham, *Church Papists: Catholicism, Conformity, and Confessional Polemic in Early Modern England* (Woodbridge, U.K., 1993); on the taming of Quakerism in the eighteenth century, see Jack D. Marietta, *The Reformation of American Quakerism, 1748–1783* (Philadelphia, 1984); and Christopher Leslie Brown, *Moral Capital: Foundations of British Abolitionism* (Williamsburg, Va., and Chapel Hill, N.C., 2006).

of the cross" in baptism, saints' names as toponyms for parish churches, the churching of women after childbirth, the "threefold" peal announcing a death in the community. The material "tokens" of Catholicism were not fully destroyed, either, despite the vigor of the iconoclastic campaigns that periodically ravaged England and the Low Countries. Personal devotional objects were most likely to survive the iconoclasts' hammers, though portable liturgical objects (baptismal fonts, altar crucifixes) hidden away in times of danger could also resurface. The archaeological and documentary record of the early English colonies has uncovered a few of these religious objects, sometimes in surprising places. These objects, too, often lived religiously indeterminate or hybrid lives. A baptismal font created in West Africa for Catholics in New France ends up in Protestant New England as a trophy of war. A manual on the Roman mass is shelved next to the Anglican Thirty-Nine Articles of Religion in the personal library of a man whose religious identity seesawed between Protestant and Catholic during his time in the colonies. A silver reliquary is buried in a coffin under the floor of the parish church in Virginia while "gaudy" statues adorn the altar of a repurposed Catholic-turned-Anglican church in Jamaica. These are but fragments of the elusive material world of English Catholicism.

The fragmentary nature of material religion in the colonies is, in fact, the common denominator here. Objects in pieces (beads instead of rosaries) or out of place (a reliquary in an Anglican church) constitute the material record of Catholicism in English America. This is partly a function of the ravages of time and climate that have destroyed so much of the material culture of the early colonies. But it is also a consequence of the process of colonization itself. The patchwork of beads, miniaturized crucifixes, and broken medals discovered by archaeologists in colonial sites where recusants lived and worshipped is a mirror of the sporadic nature of sacramental practice itself in these communities, where priests were scarce and churches even scarcer. The very *incompleteness* of Catholic devotional life in the colonies stands out as its defining characteristic.

The biggest drawback of the pointillist approach I've adopted in *A Common Grave* is the flattening of any sense of change over space and time. An English Catholic in 1630s Maryland lived under very different constraints than his coreligionist a century later, after the colony's proprietor had converted to Anglicanism and the penal laws against Catholics were in full force. An Irish or African Catholic in Barbados during the 1650s might have been as impoverished and unfree as an Irish Catholic convict in 1650s Boston, but the geopolitical climate of the two colonies allowed the former to occasionally worship with other Catholics in the homes of recusant planters, whereas the latter had no opportunity to receive the sacraments. Local context was everything in shaping the parameters of lived experience for colonial recusants. Denominational and antiquarian historians have given us rich local studies of what it meant to be a Catholic in the microcommunities that dotted the English Atlantic in the seventeenth and early eighteenth centuries. A quick scan of the footnotes will reveal my debt to these local studies. My focus here, however, has been on the collective experience of white, Black, and Indigenous Catholics as they navigated a colonial environment marked by new kinds of liberty (fewer laws and coercive institutions) and new forms of violence (chattel slavery, Indigenous and imperial wars).

Stepping back from the broad canvas view to consider change over time, two intertwined trends stand out. First, the skewed sex ratio and slow emergence of stable settler families in the colonial South (including the sugar islands) provided the precondition for a domesticated Catholicism to take hold in Maryland, the Carolinas, and the Lesser Antilles. Without domestic spaces in which to perform the rituals of faith, and without women to preside over these spaces and host itinerant priests, most recusants had no hope of receiving the eucharist, observing the ritual calendar of fasts and feasts, having their children's marriages blessed by a priest, or burying their dead at home using the Roman rite. Only after the brutal mortality rate and skewed sex ratios of the early decades began to subside were colonial households able to sink deep roots, let alone create multigenerational communities of believers. The enslaved who labored in these settler families, some of whom had already been baptized in their homeland or in the Spanish and French Caribbean, experienced this growth in domestic Catholicism as a double-edged sword: although they were able to participate in the sacramental life of the household to a much greater extent than the enslaved in Protestant communities, the deepening of slavery as an institution left them at the mercy of market forces that could and did destroy their own families. Enslaved Africans and Natives felt keenly the paradox of an emerging seigneurial Catholicism that brought them access to the sacraments on the one hand and threatened to exile them from the sacramental community on the other with every change of ownership or financial downturn.

The demographic shift that enabled domestic Catholicism to emerge coincided with another major trend: the strengthening of the Anglican establishment after 1660 in the English colonies, even in New England and Pennsylvania, the strongholds of dissent. The growth of establishment meant not only more churches and more ministers but also more laws and more scrutiny of Nonconforming behavior. The creation of the SPG was a pivotal moment for the history of colonial religion and its documentation in the archival record. Starting in 1701, Anglican missionaries spread out across the colonial countryside, bringing the Book of Common Prayer and its ritual complex to settler communities that had suffered from (or enjoyed, depending on one's perspective) alarming levels of liturgical truancy. They baptized thousands of men and women who had grown to adulthood without ever encountering a font and forced cohabiting couples to marry in the church. They sniffed out heretical and lax practices and imposed a uniform system of ritual accounting on parishes, requiring yearly reports of every baptism, marriage, and funeral performed (and the fees collected for these services). There were still large stretches of the North American backcountry where religious indifference and institutional neglect reigned, but along the Atlantic coast and on the islands, parish life began to assume a more regular and settled aspect. Bells now called men and women to service and pealed the end of life when they died—even in Puritan Boston.

Colonial recusants were thus pulled in two competing directions by the demographic and institutional changes of the late seventeenth and early eighteenth centuries: toward a flourishing of sacramental life within their own homes and toward greater sacramental exposure and danger in their public lives. The precise balance of these two pressures depended on where and when they lived and whether they had sympathetic or hostile neighbors. A virulent antipapist such as Edwyn Stede could make life hell for Barbadian Catholics while an indulgent governor such as Roger Osborne turned a blind eye to Gaelic funeral processions on Montserrat. The Catholic governor of New York, Thomas Dongan, brought his own priests with him in the 1680s but did nothing to ease the restrictions on public worship for his fellow Catholics in the colony; his Anglican counterpart, Sir Nathaniel Johnson, showed extraordinary leniency toward the Catholic inhabitants of the Leeward Islands during the same period. These are just a few examples of the contradictions and inconsistencies that abound in the political history of Catholicism in English America, complicating generalizations across time and space.[4]

The push-pull between the private and the public aspects of faith was a constant in the lives of colonial Catholics, who—like their coreligionists at

---

4. Johnson reported that "soon after my arrival" he was "petitioned by the Roman Catholicks of the severall Islands within my Government, for the free exercise of their worship and Religion which was forthwith granted" (Sir Nathaniel Johnson to Committee, Nevis, Mar. 3, 1687/8, CO 1/64, no. 28, TNA).

home—were particularly vulnerable to the winds of political change. With the ascension of every Tudor and Stuart monarch, the political calculus of opportunity and risk shifted for recusants. A period of uncertainty followed each new coronation: would James I's Protestant upbringing triumph over the Catholicism of his martyred mother? Would the Catholic wives of Charles I and Charles II persuade their husbands to relax the penal laws and allow recusants to once again worship openly? Could England accept a Catholic monarch in the person of James II if he promised to uphold the established church? Would the coup that brought William and Mary to the throne extinguish the embers of Catholicism in the three kingdoms? Each regime change in England created ripples of confusion and fear in the colonies as recusants anxiously awaited news that was often obsolete by the time it reached North America. False rumors thrived in this environment: when word of the "Popish Plot" of 1678 reached Maryland, Protestant settlers crafted their own false narrative of such a plot by accusing the province's Catholics of conspiring with the local Indians to massacre all the Protestants. The matrix of expectation, dread, and hope that surrounded Catholics in the English Atlantic between the founding of the first colonial settlements and the outbreak of the Seven Years' War is difficult to capture in a single narrative.[5]

There was no "typical" Catholic, no standard way to worship or to form a community of faith, in Anglo-America. What, then, can we learn by pulling colonial Catholics into a common frame of analysis? Several patterns emerge when we stand back and look at the whole. The centrality of women is one. We can speak with some confidence about the experiences of white women, but there are hints that enslaved African and Native women also played a central role in sustaining the faith in settler communities. As they had in England, white women served the recusant community in two critical ways—as the guardians of ritual and commemorative practices and as palpable reminders of the vicissitudes of faith in a post-Reformed world. Their role in maintaining the recusant households and private chapels that sustained Catholicism after the faith was driven underground is well documented. Less visible is the degree to which women were emblems of the porous and unstable nature

5. Carla Gardina Pestana, *Protestant Empire: Religion and the Making of the British Atlantic World* (Philadelphia, 2009), 139–140. The rumored plot led to the arrest of Captain Josias Fendall for treason in 1681; Izbell Bright testified in July 1681 that she had heard "Captn ffendall say . . . that he beleived in his Conscience the Papists and Indians joined together to destroy the Protestants" (*Archives of Maryland*, XV, 390).

of Catholicism itself. The religious choices of seventeenth- and eighteenth-century women, like those of all Catholics, were constrained by their circumstances and subject to external domestic and political pressures. Women, like Catholics more generally, were prone to adjust their religious identities when their domestic conditions changed, when they moved in and out of service or captivity, or when they were widowed, sold, or redeemed. Their alliance with the priests and missionaries who celebrated mass in their homes destabilized the boundary separating public and private and threatened to subvert the integrity of the household—as Catholicism did within the broader body politic. Because women were legal dependents, their religious decisions (to attend mass or not, to baptize their children using the Anglican or the Roman rite) fell into a gray zone of personal liability. Recusant households exploited this legal ambiguity by shielding their more subversive activities behind women's skirts, an apt metaphor (in Protestant eyes) for the disorders of papistry. In all these ways, women stood in discursively for Catholics writ large.[6]

White colonial recusant women experienced this double existence as the purveyors and symbols of Catholicism to a heightened degree given their demographic scarcity (outside New England) for much of the seventeenth century. Although the colonial era was not the "golden age" historians of women once imagined it to be, it is nonetheless true that wives and widows (white ones, at least) in English America enjoyed certain freedoms—to choose their own spouses, to keep possession of their property during and after marriage, to remarry at will, to leave substantial legacies for their daughters—because they were in such short supply. Catholic men were even more likely than Protestants to put household decisions in the hands of their wives by making them coheirs with their sons and executors of their wills. Protestant husbands ceded spiritual oversight of their children to their Catholic wives in mixed families. The handful of references we have to Catholic slaveholders manumitting their bondspeople suggest that women might have been the driving force behind this (admittedly rare) display of spiritual fellowship across the color line. When sacramental clashes occurred over the proper way to bury the dead across or within confessional lines, women were on the front lines. Protestant polemicists exploited this association of popery with female power and often put a female face to their depictions of Catholic treachery: a "Complaint from

6. Frances E. Dolan, *Whores of Babylon: Catholicism, Gender, and Seventeenth-Century Print Culture* (Ithaca, N.Y., 1999).

Heaven" accusing the proprietary party in Maryland of assorted crimes in 1676 laid the blame at the feet of the governor's wife.[7]

Gender also structured opportunities and risks for enslaved or captive Catholics and for the communities that housed them. Indian captivity brought Catholicism into Protestant English households primarily through women. Settler women were more likely than men to be taken captive during the Indian wars of the late seventeenth and early eighteenth centuries and more likely to convert to the religion of their Native or French captors (Esther Wheelwright and Eunice Williams being the most famous examples). Even those who resisted the pressures to convert had rare firsthand knowledge of Catholicism; as Laura Chmielewski notes, they "attended masses, knew convents, met Catholic priests, viewed environments suffused with Catholic visual culture, witnessed miracles that Catholics claimed were wrought by the relics of saints, and refused or accepted communion with the Roman Catholic Church through sacramental participation."[8] The taint of betrayal that clung to these girls and women once they had returned to their homes was the stench of Catholicism. Redeemed captives became living reminders of the power of Catholicism to invade hearts and households. Just as the sacramental loot that New England troops carried home from their skirmishes with the soldiers of New France was a tangible emblem of the uncomfortable proximity of Protestantism to Catholicism on the frontier, so too were redeemed women with their memories of incense and miracles.

Where do enslaved women fit into the gendered story of colonial Catholicism? We know that in Iberian and French territories, Catholicism in the enslaved African community often presented a feminine face. Through baptism, godparentage, and female sodalities, enslaved women forged ritual and imagined links between the religion of the enslavers and the African spiritual traditions they had been raised in or remembered (which, for some, were one and the same). In places like New Orleans and other colonial enclaves of Black Catholicism, African women were the first to seek baptism

7. "Complaint from Heaven with a Huy and Crye and a Petition out of Virginia and Maryland," 1676, *Archives of Maryland*, V, 134.

8. Laura Chmielewski, *The Spice of Popery: Converging Christianities on an Early American Frontier* (Notre Dame, Ind., 2012), 78. On Indian captivity more generally, see Alden T. Vaughan and Daniel K. Richter, "Crossing the Cultural Divide: Indians and New Englanders, 1605–1763," *Proceedings of the American Antiquarian Society*, XC (1980), 53–62; on Wheelwright and Williams, see Ann M. Little, *The Many Captivities of Esther Wheelwright* (New Haven, Conn., 2016); John Demos, *The Unredeemed Captive: A Family Story from Early America* (New York, 1994).

in the Roman Church, and they, in turn, catechized their daughters, sponsored infants as godmothers, and formed all-female devotional societies. In the words of Emily Clark and Virginia Meacham Gould, they "contributed the vital current of blood motherhood" that anchored the colonial church in the African-descended community.[9] Indigenous African religious traditions had provided women with their own domains in which to exercise spiritual power as members of secret societies and as oracles, healers, and priests; in the Americas, enslaved women found Catholicism a more hospitable culture than Protestantism for these female-centered practices.[10] As Spanish and French territories became absorbed into the English empire (Jamaica in 1655; Minorca and Nova Scotia in 1713; Florida, Quebec, and most of the Spanish and French Caribbean in 1763), enslaved Catholics were absorbed into English Protestant households.[11] With almost no firsthand accounts of enslavement written by women before the nineteenth century, we are not privy to the effects this injection of an African-inflected female spirituality might have had on white settler communities. But we can imagine that enslaved Catholic women in English America also sought to keep faith alive by instructing their daughters, observing the ritual calendar whenever possible, praying to the saints for protection, and honoring the dead.

A related thread running through accounts of colonial Catholicism is the importance of the sensory. The sensorium of Catholic ritual was acknowledged (and celebrated or denounced) by observers across the confessional spectrum. Protestant polemicists loved to mock the sensory aspects of the

9. Emily Clark and Virginia Meacham Gould, "The Feminine Face of Afro-Catholicism in New Orleans, 1727–1852," *WMQ*, 3d Ser., LIX (2002), 409–448 (quotation on 446). As they argue, the intergenerational transmission of Catholicism to enslaved Africans was "a matrilineal process" (446).

10. Henryk Zimoň, "The Role of Women in African Traditional Religions," *Acta Ethnographica Hungarica*, LI (2006), 43–60; Barbara Bush, *Slave Women in Caribbean Society, 1650–1838* (Bloomington, Ind., 1990); Hilary McD. Beckles, *Natural Rebels: A Social History of Enslaved Black Women in Barbados* (New Brunswick, N.J., 1989); J. Lorand Matory, *Black Atlantic Religion: Tradition, Transnationalism, and Matriarchy in the Afro-Brazilian Candomblé* (Princeton, N.J., 2005); Jon Sensbach, "Prophets and Helpers: African American Women and the Rise of Black Christianity in the Age of the Slave Trade," in Daniella Kostroun and Lisa Vollendorf, eds., *Women, Religion, and the Atlantic World (1600–1800)* (Toronto, 2009), 115–135.

11. Jessica L. Harland-Jacobs, "Multi-Confessional Governance: Incorporating Catholics in the British Empire, 1713–1783," in Robert A. Olwell and James M. Vaughan, eds., *Envisioning Empire: The New British World from 1763 to 1773* (New York, 2020), 83–108.

Catholic rite—the clouds of incense, incessant bell ringing, chanting, and unholy relish of the "body and blood" of Christ that constituted the Roman mass. Sensory excess, intellectual vacuity, and political corruption went hand in hand, in their view. Colonial recusants, for their part, continued to seek out sensory communion with the divine through the sacraments. Catholics on Barbados talked about having "seen the face of God" at mass. Enslaved Africans, Indigenous converts, and Irish servants celebrated funerals with song and dance. The need for discretion inevitably curtailed the more exuberant forms of devotion that marked continental Catholicism, but the longing for such tactile and redolent spiritual encounters comes through in the records. That so much of the sacramental wrangling of the colonial era centered on the sensory dimension of the rituals—should bells be rung three times, once, or not at all when someone died? Should there be singing, loud wailing (keening), or gluttonous feasting at funerals? Should infants be anointed with oil, dipped in the font, or merely sprinkled with water at a christening?—is a consequence of the importance Protestants and Catholics alike placed on sensation as the portal to the supernatural (divine and demonic).[12]

There was, of course, a close and abiding association between the sensory and the female in the early modern world. According to the prevailing humoral theories of the day, the porousness of women's bodies left them open to external forces and sensations that overwhelmed their weak brains and led them into all sorts of folly, from witchcraft to sexual deviance to religious heresy. Women were famously ruled by their hearts and not their heads and thus were especially vulnerable to blandishments of the devil—and to the sensory allures of Catholicism. A feminized faith was almost by definition a sensual faith. So Catholicism in English America was doubly marked as "other" by the centrality of women as religious actors and by the sensuality of its rituals.[13]

One final theme connects the stories recounted in this book. Throughout,

12. Matthew Milner, *The Senses and the English Reformation* (Farnham, U.K., 2011); Jacob M. Baum, *Reformation of the Senses: The Paradox of Religious Belief and Practice in Germany* (Urbana, Ill., 2019); David Howes, "Introduction: 'To Summon All the Senses,'" in Howes, ed., *The Varieties of Sensory Experience: A Sourcebook in the Anthropology of the Senses* (Toronto, 1991), 3–21; Edward Muir, *Ritual in Early Modern Europe* (New York, 1997); C. M. Woolgar, *The Senses in Medieval England* (New Haven, Conn., 2006). Steve Pincus provides a good overview of the place of the sensory in the polemical battles of Stuart England; see Pincus, *1688: The First Modern Revolution* (New Haven, Conn., 2009).

13. Histories of colonial American religion have been slow to explore the sensory dimensions of faith, though that is changing. This, too, is a symptom of the Protestant bias

I've resorted to conditional or provisional language to describe what colonial Catholics were thinking, seeing, or doing. The further the story moved away from the lives of white English recusants, the greater the degree of speculation in my account. The need to venture behind documentary evidence to imagined reconstructions is a familiar challenge for medieval and early modern historians, especially those who want to understand the inner thoughts and feelings of the illiterate, the unremarked, and the incongruent. But in *A Common Grave*, the imaginative is more than a methodological tool for uncovering the lives of marginal peoples living a clandestine faith on the edges of empire. Anglo-American Catholicism itself was an act of imagination, a speculative faith. In important respects, it sustained itself through a purposeful set of mental exercises designed to circumvent the strictures on public worship imposed on the community after the Reformation. Catholics on both sides of the Atlantic imagined themselves receiving communion, performed mental pilgrimages in the privacy of their own homes and gardens, recited the Roman liturgy in their heads while sitting in the pews of the local parish church.

Memory—reflexive and cultivated—was the key to survival in a hostile environment. Anglo-American Catholics drew on a well of personal and collective remembrances to perform the rituals of faith as their parents and grandparents had. They invested the very land under their feet and the sites that once had been or were rumored to have been chapels with spiritual power. Catholics in Maryland constructed long chains of memory connecting every brick and nail used to build the first Jesuit chapels in the province to the material reservoir of English recusancy. In Philadelphia, the city's Catholic residents genuflected when they passed the corner of Front and Walnut Streets because they recalled that mass had once been celebrated in a private home on the site. Of course, communities of memory were circumscribed by ethnicity, race, status, and gender, and non-English Catholics had their own memories of sacred places and practices to draw upon to establish new spiritual lives in

---

that continues to dominate the field. For one exception, see Leigh Eric Schmidt, *Hearing Things: Religion, Illusion, and the American Enlightenment* (Cambridge, Mass., 2000). For general studies of the senses in early American history, see Richard Cullen Rath, *How Early America Sounded* (Ithaca, N.Y., 2003); Peter Charles Hoffer, *Sensory Worlds in Early America* (Baltimore, 2003). For good overviews of the field of sensory history, see Martin Jay, "In the Realm of the Senses: An Introduction," *American Historical Review*, CXVI (2011), 307–315; Mark M. Smith, "Producing Sense, Consuming Sense, Making Sense: Perils and Prospects for Sensory History," *Journal of Social History*, XL (2007), 841–858.

North America. Whether these memories recalled real or fictive events, they served the essential function of tying a dispersed and displaced community together.

The archival traces of these mental acts of faith are faint indeed. They surface occasionally in missionary reports, planters' records, firsthand memoirs (of which we have no more than a handful from the colonial era), and antiquarian histories written at a considerable remove. Modern scholars are fortunate that Anglo-American Catholics had (and have) a very strong sense of tradition and went to great lengths to preserve the words and deeds of their antecedent communities. Recusant Studies is a sturdy subfield in the history of post-Reformation Britain, thanks in no small part to the documentary efforts of the Catholic Record Society, which since 1904 has produced nearly one hundred volumes on the English recusant community.[14] The missionary orders themselves—primarily the Jesuits—were prolific chroniclers of their own efforts, allowing us to eavesdrop on conversations between missionaries and their Indigenous converts and watch a colonial church take shape from the ground up. The historian of post-Reformed Catholicism is awash in sources, in other words. But this generative sense of tradition among English recusants and their historians conceals as much as it reveals, leaving the two most numerous groups of colonial Catholics (Irish and African) out of the picture and privileging a narrative of heroic survival over the messier story of ambivalence and compromise.

Working within and against this tradition has led me down geographic, archival, and methodological byways I did not anticipate: to the sugar plantations of the West Indies and the fisheries of the North Atlantic, to archaeological field reports of burial pits, to imagined scenarios of covert burials and interracial communion services. Colonial Catholics, it turns out, shared more in common with their Protestant neighbors and rivals than the historical literature would suggest. They can be found in every colony, in every social and economic stratum and racial category. Their religious orientation ran the full gamut from indifference to conformity to fervor. Outwardly, many attended their local parish church regularly, or as infrequently as the law required, whereas some (a few? a sizable minority?) preferred to worship at home with or without the services of an itinerant priest. Catholic slaveholders extracted the productive and reproductive labor of their enslaved workers—even those

14. See the website of the Catholic Record Society for a complete list of publications, including documentary volumes, academic journals, and monographs: https://www.crs .org.uk/.

who shared their faith—and sold them when times were tough, just as Protestant slaveholders did. The Irish, African, and Native servants and slaves who worked in recusant households might have enjoyed access to the sacraments of baptism, communion, and marriage, but they were rarely buried side by side with their Catholic masters. Many colonial Christians of whatever variety did not inhabit a stable *public* religious identity over their lifetimes, switching religious codes with the winds of political and economic fortune, whatever their personal convictions. Distinguishing the conforming Catholic from the Protestant is less revealing than exploring the shared terrain of ambiguity, adaptation, and flux that marks both as colonial creations.

INDEX

Page numbers in italics refer to illustrations.

152; marriage in, 221; funerals in, 244, 250, 269; graves in, 268

James I (king of England), 6, 80, 126, 235, 284

James II (king of England), 6, 36, 42–43, 99, 105–107, 110, 158, 213, 253, 284

James and Rebecca (Black couple married in St. Inigoes), 228

Jamestown Colony, 1–2, 37, 130, 164–167, 245–246, 252

Japan, 9

Jarboe, Bennett, 197

Jarboe, Charles, 197

Jarboe, Jean, 197

Jarboe, John, 256

Jarboe, Joshua, 197

Jarboe, Rachel, 203

Jarboe, Richard, 203

Jesuits (Society of Jesus): and the counter-Reformation, 9–10; and colonial sources, 16, 82, 290; itinerant, 21; and Douai College, 25; and St. Omer's College, 25, 107; and Catholic population in Americas, 29–31, 36, 51, 72–73; and unfree labor, 44; brothers of, 47, 84; and Maryland's settlement, 47–50; ministry of, to Natives, 66, 90, 133–134, 270–272; and ministry to Africans, 68–71, 266; "priest slaves" of, 69, 231; and supposed gentleness of slavery practices, 69–70; in disguises, 81–88, 102, 107–108, 111; and trade and commerce, 86–87; and mixed households, 107; and Quakers, 113; *Jesuite in Masquerade* (1681), 115; and devotion, 116; and racialization, 117; and crosses, 130–134; and liturgical culture, 139–143; and consecration, 144; and iconoclasm, 149–151; and rosaries, 156–159; iconography of, 163; and relics, 165, 168; execution of, 167; and baptisms, 193–199, 203; and communion, 208–216; and holidays, 218; and marriage, 225–231; and death rituals, 255–257, 270–274; *Jesuit Relations*, 271. *See also* Loyola,

Ignatius (St. Ignatius); Manors/plantations, Jesuit

Jews: and European racial constructs, 2–3, 7–8, 76–77, 80, 117; in Western Hemisphere, 2–3; Sephardic, 7; crypto-, 77; and religious passing, 80

Jogues, Isaac, 30, 102

Johnson, Henry, 34

Johnson, Nathaniel, 105, 283

Johnston, Gideon, 33, 89, 247

Jones, Henry, 34

Jones, Hugh, 112

Jordan, Hugh, 43

Jordan, John, 256

Josselyn, John, 269–270

Joyner, Robert, 50

Judith (enslaved laborer for the Smith family), 203

Kettle, John, 83

King Philip's War (1675–1677), 252

Kinship, 9, 188, 191, 202, 215, 232, 255, 261, 263, 269

Kneeling, 13, 115, 141, 148, 183, 187, 205, 212–215, 238

Kongo/Kongolese, 8, 61, 65–66, 135–136, *137*, 198, 238, 267–268, 280

Lacy, Kath, 205

Laity: innovation led by, 9, 11; and sources, 24–25; and slavery, 44, 69; and priests, 50–51, 82, 86, 173, 194; and wills, 51; and religious hybridity, 78–79, 100–117, 121, 207; and religious passing, 80; and religious structures, 92, 116; and religious identity, 101–103, 106; and mass, 116–117, 178; and material culture, 126, 128, 146–148, 153–156, 158, 160, 167, 171, 173; Anglican, 153, 183; Mary as protector of, 156; and religious practice, 171, 185, 232–234; and baptism, 189, 193, 198, 201, 203; and indulgences, 194; and communion, 204–211, 215; and marriage, 221, 226–227; and burial, 243, 260; and last rites, 256